New Canadian Readings

QUEBEC SINCE 1945

SELECTED READINGS

Edited by
Michael D. Behiels

Copp Clark Pitman Ltd.
A Longman Company
Toronto

ISBN 0-7730-4615-1

Editing: Barbara Tessman
Design and Cover Illustration: Kathy Cloutier
Typesetting: Compeer Typographical Services Limited
Printing and Binding: Webcom Ltd.

Canadian Cataloguing in Publication Data

Main entry under title:
Quebec since 1945: selected readings

(New Canadian readings)
Bibliography: p.
ISBN 0-7730-4615-1

1. Quebec (Province) — History — 1936–1960.*
2. Quebec (Province) — History — 1960–   . 3. Quebec
(Province) — History — Autonomy and independence
movements. I. Behiels, Michael D. (Michael Derek),
1946–   . II. Series.

FC2925.Q43 1987   971.4'04   C86-094764-5
F1053.2.Q43 1987

Copp Clark Pitman Ltd.
495 Wellington Street West
Toronto, Ontario
M5V 1E9

Associated Companies:
  Longman Group Ltd., London
  Longman Inc., New York
  Longman Cheshire Pty., Melbourne
  Longman Paul Pty., Auckland

Printed and bound in Canada.

FOREWORD

New Canadian Readings is an on-going series of inexpensive books intended to bring some of the best recent work by this country's scholars to the attention of students of Canada. Each volume consists of ten or more articles or book sections, carefully selected to present a fully-formed thesis about some critical aspect of Canadian development. Where useful, public documents or even private letters and statistical materials may be used as well to convey a different and fresh perspective.

The authors of the readings selected for inclusion in this volume (and all the others in the series) are all first-rank scholars, those who are doing the hard research that is rapidly changing our understanding of this country. Quite deliberately, the references for each selection have been retained, thus making additional research as easy as possible.

Like the authors of the individual articles, the editors of each volume are also scholars of note, completely up-to-date in their areas of specialization and, as the introductions demonstrate, fully aware of the changing nature of the debates within their professions and genres of research. The list of additional readings provided by the editor of each volume will steer readers to materials that could not be included because of space limitations.

This series will continue into the foreseeable future, and the General Editor is pleased to invite suggestions for additional topics.

J.L. Granatstein
General Editor

LIST OF ABBREVIATIONS

AFL   American Federation of Labour
ALN   Action Libérale Nationale
API   Association professionnelle des Industrielles
CCL   Canadian Congress of Labour [CCT]
CCT   Congrès canadien du travail [CCL]
CECM   Commission des écoles catholiques de Montréal
CEQ   Corporation des enseignants du Québec; *later* Centrale des enseignants du Quebec
CFTC   Confédération française des travailleurs chrétiens
CIC   Corporation des instituteurs et institutrices catholiques
CIO   Congress of Industrial Organizations
CLC   Canadian Labour Congress [CTC]
CMTC   Congrès des metiers et du travail du Canada [TLCC]
CSD   Centrale des syndicats démocratiques
CSN   Confédération des syndicats nationaux
CTC   Congrès du travail du Canada [CLC]
CTCC   Confédération des travailleurs catholiques du Canada
FAS   Fédération des affaires sociales
FLQ   Front de libération du Québec
FNS   Fédération nationale des services
FPTQ   Fédération provinciale de travail du Québec; *or* Fédération provinciale des travailleurs du Québec
FQF   Front du Québec français
FRAP   Front d'action politique
FTQ   Fédération des travailleurs et travailleuses du Québec [QFL]
FUIQ   Fédération des unions industrielles du Québec
IQOP   Institute québécois de l'opinion publique
MSA   Mouvement Souveraineté-Association
PLQ   Parti libéral du Québec
PNP   Parti national populaire
PQ   Parti québécois
PSQ   Parti socialiste du Québec
QFL   Quebec Federation of Labour [FTQ]
RC   Ralliement des Créditistes
RIN   Rassemblement pour l'indépendance nationale
RN   Ralliement national
SFPQ   Syndicats des fonctionnaires provinciaux du Québec
SLPA   Socialist Labour Party of America
SPEQ   Syndicats des professeurs de l'État du Québec
TLCC   Trades and Labour Congress of Canada [CMTC]
UN   Union Nationale
WPA   Workers' Party of America

CONTENTS

INTRODUCTION

Since the early 1960s there has been an incessant preoccupation with trying to find satisfactory answers to the question, "What does Quebec want?" That the question even had to be asked was a frank admission that the persistence, well into the twentieth century, of Canada's two solitudes had contributed to each culture's abysmal ignorance of the other. During and after the Second World War the institutional, geographic, cultural, and occupational barriers that had kept Quebec's two societies segregated since the Conquest came under increasing scrutiny. Some of these barriers began to break down under the pressures exerted by a new round of urbanization and industrialization accompanied, this time, by the emergence of new ideologies and a revolution of mentalities. The process was greatly accelerated by postwar prosperity and the proliferation of the electronic media, especially television.

An increasingly vocal and influential minority of middle-class French Canadians became concerned with the absence of a Francophone bourgeoisie that had at its disposal a dynamic, interventionist state. They were convinced that the economic inferiority of French Canadians, individually and collectively, posed the most serious threat to the continued survival of their nation since Lord Durham's Report. Neo-nationalist historians at the Université de Montréal blamed this crisis on the Conquest of 1760 and concluded that only greater political autonomy, perhaps independence, would enable the French-Canadian nation to survive. By the 1950s, Quebec society was swept up in a struggle between those groups desperately trying to preserve a traditional Catholic social order based on a rapidly eroding agricultural way of life, and those who favoured a new, yet undefined, social order based on a secular, consumer-oriented industrial economy run by a powerful nation-state. This challenge of building a modern, dynamic French-Canadian society consumed an inordinate amount of energy for increasing numbers of French Canadians for four decades. Given the nature of the Canadian federal system, it was, in retrospect, inevitable that this internal modernization process would have serious ramifications for the rest of Canadian society. Quebec's demands for political equality placed severe strains on the federal system. The political crisis reached a climax during the 1980 referendum. Quebeckers voted to remain in Canada and Prime Minister Trudeau responded by initiating the difficult process of constitutional renewal, which culminated in the patriation of the British North America Act, an amendment formula, and the Charter of Rights. Quebec's unrelenting nationalist aspirations had forced Ottawa to act, but the nationalists reaped none of the rewards they so dearly anticipated.

Since the late 1950s, a wide variety of journalists, a few participants, and considerable numbers of social scientists, including a handful of historians, have addressed various facets of the "quiet" and "not-so-quiet" revolutions that transformed, in very fundamental ways, the mentality, or ethos, of a majority of French Canadians and the social and political institutions that serve them. It is high time that a selection of this literature reach a wider audience so as to create the basis for an informed debate about the precise nature and significance of postwar developments in Quebec. The material has been organized under seven topics. An annotated bibliography of pertinent literature on each topic is provided in the Further Reading section. Other topics, no doubt, are just as valid, but the selected ones focus on the central themes of the period under review. A wide variety of authors provide a full spectrum of interpretations. The divergent assessments provoke and enlighten the reader but also leave many unanswered questions. Ideally, these questions will serve as a catalyst for further inquiry into and analysis of these and related topics.

I wish to thank Barbara Tessman for her inspired editing. As always, Linda, Marc, and Justin have been patient and supportive. This collection is dedicated to them. The fact that several of the articles appear for the first time in English is a tribute to the growing number of fine translators.

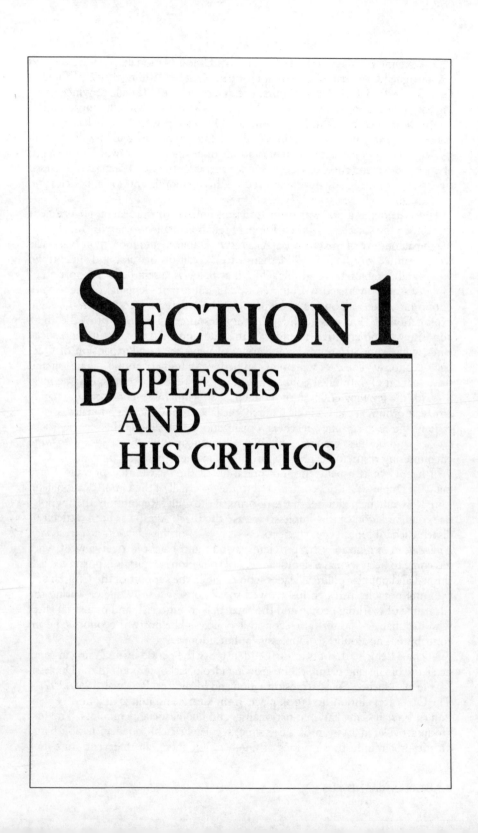

SECTION 1

DUPLESSIS AND HIS CRITICS

The regime of Maurice Duplessis and his Union Nationale party has always intrigued Canadians, both in and outside Quebec. Riding a tide of French-Canadian nationalism, Duplessis first became premier of "la belle province" during the politically turbulent 1930s. He soon lost favour with the more radical nationalists when he refused to nationalize Quebec's private hydro-electric companies. His party was defeated in October 1939 because he had lost all credibility with the nationalist movement, and his opposition to the war had brought about the direct intervention of the federal Liberal Party. The defeat gave Duplessis time to regain his failing health and rethink his economic and social policies and political strategy.

The wartime and postwar reconstruction policies of the federal government threatened the social fabric of traditional French-Canadian society by undermining the autonomy of the province. As a result, Duplessis and the Union Nationale were returned to office in 1944 thanks to a coalition of rural and small-town voters and notables, the Catholic Church at all levels, a significant proportion of Quebec's non-organized working class, and important elements of the Anglophone and American business community who wanted to get on with the rapid exploitation of Quebec's abundant natural resources. Duplessis proved to be a very shrewd and effective defender of the traditional social structure and social elites, while supporting in a wide variety of ways the rapid expansion of Quebec's economy. The ever widening gap between rapid economic expansion and the retention of outmoded political and social institutions accounts, in large measure, for the growing criticism of the Duplessis regime by several vocal and highly articulate groups in the Catholic Church, the labour movement, nationalist organizations, the municipalities, teachers' organizations, and among the science, social science, and business graduates of Quebec's Francophone universities who were encountering restricted career opportunities in their own province.

In history, it is usually the interpretation of the victors that prevails. Since many of Duplessis' critics contributed to the downfall of the Union Nationale in June 1960 and helped usher in the reforms of the Quiet Revolution, their wholesale condemnation of the Duplessis era as "the Black Ages" has been difficult to dispel. Richard Jones begins the process of revision in his *Duplessis and the Union Nationale Administration* by providing a solid and balanced overview of what has come to been seen as a significant era of transition. Duplessis is portrayed as a shrewd and popular political leader who retained the support of the Church and the rural notables through his avowed social conservatism while capturing the allegiance of working people and the financial, commercial, and industrial elites with his unabated laissez-faire economic policies. The postwar economic boom contributed, no doubt, to Duplessis' political longevity.

Michael Behiels attempts to further demystify the period by analysing in some detail the origins and nature of the growing ideological opposition to the Duplessis regime in "Quebec: Social Transformation and Ideological Renewal, 1940–1976." The Quiet Revolution first took place in the hearts and minds of a new generation of French-Canadian neo-nationalists and liberal social democrats. The first group articulated a vision of a dynamic, secular French-Canadian nation based on the urban/industrial realities of Quebec. For them, an interventionist state rather than the Church was henceforth to be the dominant institution in the defence and development of a revitalized French-Canadian nationality. Liberals and social democrats in the *Cité libre* movement also advocated the democratization and secularization of Quebec society but rejected nationalism because they believed it was fundamentally incompatible with liberal and democratic values.

DUPLESSIS AND THE UNION NATIONALE ADMINISTRATION†

RICHARD JONES

Maurice Le Noblet Duplessis, Prime Minister of Quebec from 1936 to 1939 and again from 1944 until his death in 1959, was indeed a colourful figure. Although physically unremarkable, he did possess an elongated nasal appendage that delighted cartoonists. He dressed conservatively, and usually immaculately, except for a well-worn hat that he said brought him "closer to the people." Intelligent and quick-witted, he was not at all an intellectual; indeed he would often boast of having both feet on the ground. His private life was rather austere, at least after his return to power in 1944, and he had few hobbies apart from listening to music and going to baseball games. He was, in essence, a politician and, as a bachelor, he liked to say he was married to his province.

And yet few Canadian politicians since Confederation have been as controversial as Duplessis. Admired by his friends, denounced by his enemies, he dominated the Quebec political scene for a quarter of a century. After his death, others attempted to build a new and more modern Quebec, liberated from what they perceived as the yoke of Duplessism, and numerous commentators, sharing the aspirations of Jean Lesage's new Liberal government after 1960, painted a sombre portrait of the Union Nationale years under Duplessis. History's judgments, though, are never final and other observers of the period, after 1970, have sought to study Duplessis with great impartiality and even some sympathy.

The student of Duplessis is immediately faced with varying and even contradictory interpretations of the man. Even though he suffered daily humiliation in the Legislative Assembly at the premier's hands, Georges-Émile Lapalme, leader of the Liberal opposition from 1950 to 1958, did not hide his admiration for this politician who "sensed the vibrations of the population as though he had applied a stethoscope." Father Georges-Henri Lévesque, former Dean of the

†(Ottawa: Canadian Historical Association, booklet no. 35, 1983).

Faculty of Social Sciences at Laval University and a bitter critic of the Union Nationale government, noted that Duplessis possessed "truly exceptional ability, an extraordinary lucidity," but that at the same time he was "a very small-minded politician, since nearly all his political decisions, nearly all his deeds, were petty." Duplessis' biographers also disagree in their judgments of the man and the regime. For the journalist Leslie Roberts, "the Chief" — as he titled his book — was motivated first and foremost by a "lust for power"; once in control, he acted "as brazenly as any Latin-American dictator." The historian-priest, Lionel Groulx, professed in his *Mémoires* never to have had any illusions about Duplessis. Pierre Laporte, then a reporter for the newspaper *Le Devoir*, described Duplessis as generous, but "unbelievably mean toward those he disliked"; he was a "colourful, captivating" parliamentarian, "but had no respect for democratic principles." Conversely, Robert Rumilly, another historian, unceasingly praises the Union Nationale leader for his "profound love of his province and people" and his unfailing "instinct for Quebec's national interests." Assuredly, if all were looking at the same individual, all were not seeing the same man.

There can certainly be no doubt that Duplessis' success at the polls, except for the disaster of 1939, was remarkable. But as soon as historians attempt a thorough study of the regime, they encounter serious problems of interpretation. Was Duplessis really a corrupt dictator whose only thought was the fate of his party and his own place at its head? Or should he rather be seen as the leader of his people, expressing their ambitions, personifying their will, defending their interests? Should it be concluded, as some suggest, that he "retarded" Quebec's evolution, that he impeded progress towards a "modern society"? Or did he not, on the contrary, appreciate that French Canada constituted a distinct culture that had to be defended against the unflagging assaults of enemies who wanted to destroy it? In any case, Duplessis the person had multiple facets and, depending on which ones have been deemed important by historians and other authors who have studied him, the portrait of the man and of the regime varies greatly.

The Rise to Power

The fact that Maurice Duplessis entered provincial politics as a Conservative, a member of a party exiled to Quebec's political wilderness since 1897 and showing few signs of revival, can be largely explained by family tradition. Had his father, Nérée, not been a Conservative member of the Legislature from 1886 to 1900? It should also be remembered, in order to understand his future relations with the Roman Catholic Church, that Duplessis' birthplace of Trois-Rivières was the seat of the diocese of Msgr. Louis-François Laflèche and thus a bastion of ultramontanism and conservatism.

Duplessis was the type of politician, attentive to the needs and preoccupations of his constituents, who would become the backbone of the Union Nationale after 1944. From the time of his first election campaign, that of 1923 which resulted in his only defeat, Duplessis sought to develop a close relationship with voters, and he responded to any local event that could be classed as noteworthy — births, baptisms, marriages, deaths, awards, and so on — by sending appropriate congratulations or condolences. Such attention was possible in rural areas and in small towns where there were relatively few voters — Trois-Rivières had about 5,000 electors in 1927 and the average district in the province contained only 6,700. But thirty years later, when the average number of electors per district had climbed to 26,000 and when regional and provincial issues were to some extent replacing questions of purely local interest, this type of personal relationship was, except in underpopulated rural districts, much more difficult to practise. Such a change was to deal a heavy blow to the Union Nationale.

When Duplessis was elected as the member for Trois-Rivières for the first time in 1927, he joined a tiny Conservative caucus of nine MLAs in a Legislature dominated by seventy-five Liberals comfortably installed in power. Worse, under Arthur Sauvé's leadership, the Conservative opposition was declining in strength (the party had elected nineteen candidates in 1923) and was being ravaged by internal strife. Camillien Houde, then mayor of Montreal, replaced Sauvé in 1929, but he lost his own seat in the 1931 election, although the Conservatives did succeed in increasing their proportion by the vote of nearly eight percent. Houde's own leadership increasingly came under fire and he finally resigned in September 1932; Duplessis was chosen by the caucus as parliamentary Leader of the Opposition.

In his new capacity, Duplessis manifested some preoccupation for economic nationalism and he attacked the financial interests which he asserted were closely linked to the Liberal party. Duplessis also called for a provincial agricultural credit plan and proclaimed the philosophy that he would respect as premier: in a speech given in the Legislature at the beginning of 1933, he invited the government to "look at the evidence and recognize, through its legislation and its deeds, that the province of Quebec has always been and will always be essentially agricultural." And yet, according to the 1931 census, sixty-five percent of the province's citizens lived in towns and cities!

At the leadership convention held at Sherbrooke in October 1933, Duplessis easily defeated (by 332 to 214 votes) Onésime Gagnon, a Conservative MP who favoured closer links with the federal wing of the party and "the supreme leader, R.B. Bennett." Is one to see in this victory the beginnings of the autonomism that Duplessis would champion later when he would boast of having established a provincial party free of all ties with any federal organization? Duplessis surely sensed Bennett's growing unpopularity, but he himself proposed a resolution of support for the federal leader, although it was phrased in words that were less than glowing. If Duplessis triumphed at Sherbrooke, he did so mainly because his organization was superior to his rival's, and not because of any nationalistic positions he espoused.

During the Depression, many groups within Quebec set about proposing solutions that, while avoiding socialism, would correct the worst abuses of the capitalist system. Under the aegis of the Jesuit-directed École sociale populaire, a group of well-known Catholic laymen including Albert Rioux of the Catholic farmers' union, Wilfrid Guérin of the credit unions, and Alfred Charpentier of the Catholic labour unions, drew up in 1933 the "Programme de restauration sociale." This document provoked considerable interest amongst certain Liberals, like Paul Gouin, son of a former Quebec premier, Lomer Gouin. In 1934, these dissidents formed a new political party, Action Libérale Nationale, and attracted reform-minded nationalists like Philippe Hamel, Ernest Grégoire, and René Chaloult. Their program, inspired by the principles of the "Programme de restauration sociale," promised a vigorous war against the trusts, especially the electricity trust; a cleaning-up of elections; the creation of a ministry of commerce; and the institution of certain labour reforms, although, it is true, unions themselves were not mentioned. Nevertheless, the very first article of the program dwelt on agricultural reforms, the authors affirming their belief that "the task of economic restoration is principally a task of rural restoration, based on family-type agriculture and cooperatives."

The Quebec premier and Liberal party leader, Louis-Alexandre Taschereau, then at the height of his power and used to a two-party system that he could manage, evidently did not relish the establishment of a third party on the eve of the 1935 elections; Maurice Duplessis, leader of the Conservative Party, was scarcely more enthusiastic. What change would a divided opposition have of upsetting a regime so solidly ensconced in power? It was no surprise then that Duplessis, who roundly denounced Taschereau for favouring foreigners, neglecting the farmers, and undermining traditions and religion also attacked Gouin whom he considered an upstart, and promised that a Conservative candidate would run in every district. For their part, the ALN leaders were suspicious of Duplessis whom they judged to be opportunistic and equivocating, especially in regard to the policy he would apply to the electricity trust, condemned with such vigour by Philippe Hamel. Yet the circumstances were to lead, inevitably, to a marriage of reason between the two opposition groups, a step that neither Gouin nor Duplessis would actively promote.

It seems clear, in retrospect, that the rank and file of both parties pushed their leaders towards an alliance. In spite of the impressive oratorical resources of the ALN and of the parliamentary expertise of the Conservatives, both groups lacked the funds to wage an effective campaign against Taschereau. Finally, a stormy meeting between the main spokesmen for each party, in Duplessis' absence, resulted in an agreement concerning the distribution of electoral districts between Conservatives and ALN candidates as well as the leadership of the new coalition. The agreement specified that, in the next election, from twenty-five to thirty ridings would be reserved for the Conservatives and some sixty would go to the ALN, and that after victory Maurice Duplessis would become premier while Paul Gouin would name the majority of the cabinet. In spite of the ALN's apparent advantage in the number of districts where its members would run, many candidates of the party were actually Conservatives who believed their chances would be improved under the ALN banner. On 7 November 1935, then, Duplessis and Gouin publicly proclaimed the formation of the "Union Nationale Duplessis-Gouin" in order to present a "united front against the enemy of the people of the province of Quebec: the Taschereau regime." Its official program was that of the ALN. In the elections held on 25 November, the Liberal government was seriously shaken: forty-eight Liberals were elected compared to forty-two members of the Opposition. Of these latter, sixteen were officially Conservative while twenty-six were members of the ALN.

The events of the following months confirmed Duplessis as sole leader of the Union Nationale. His adversaries have always held that the Conservative leader manoeuvred to undermine Paul Gouin's position within the Union Nationale so that, once Duplessis became premier, he would be able to eliminate the other reform-minded spokesmen of the ALN and, finally, discard the most radical aspects of the program, particularly the struggle against economic dictatorship. Nevertheless, most observers portray Gouin as an intellectual who lacked leadership qualities and was incapable of dealing with politics on a day-to-day basis. Moreover, it is true that Duplessis attempted to reinforce his position with the members of the ALN. In this regard, the party's parliamentary secretary later confirmed: "In the minds of our members, in the facts also, it was evident that the only man capable of leading them was Maurice Duplessis." This leadership was to be demonstrated convincingly at the time of the celebrated hearings of the Public Accounts Committee.

Perhaps it really was just a "tempest in a teapot," as the jurist Jean-Charles Bonenfant would later affirm; perhaps the so-called scandals of the Taschereau administration were but peccadillos. Still, the committee's hearings, personally conducted by Maurice Duplessis, provoked immense public interest and discredited the Taschereau regime. Maybe it was not really important that a minister, Irénée Vautrin, donned trousers paid for out of the public purse before setting out on hikes in the woods, but the cry of "Vautrin's pants" would resound across Quebec during the next election campaign and would contribute to sweeping away the old regime. Opposition members realized that these attacks were taking their toll and Duplessis' star accordingly rose. It was also evident that Duplessis sought a rupture with Gouin, a break that finally occurred in June 1936. Shortly afterwards, at a meeting of the caucus convened by Duplessis in Sherbrooke, thirty-five of the forty-two opposition members gave him their support. Duplessis had undeniably become the leader of the Union Nationale.

Events moved quickly in that summer of 1936. Taschereau handed in his resignation as premier on 11 June and was replaced by Adélard Godbout. Elections were scheduled for 17 August. The Union Nationale program, as outlined by Maurice Duplessis at the opening of the campaign, maintained its reformist cast. Without going into detail, Duplessis promised to rid the province of the "odious and exploiting trusts"; several of his candidates, led by Hamel and Grégoire, went further and gave priority to this issue. Duplessis also pledged to establish a provincial farm credit system in order to "save agriculture" and stem the flight from the farms to the cities. In addition he promised a number of political reforms that he would never implement, such as a requirement for parties to furnish a list of their contributors, a law on honest elections, and public tenders for contracts awarded by the state. Duplessis also devoted a significant part of his campaign to denouncing the abuses of the Taschereau-Godbout administration and there is no doubt that this issue had an enormous impact on the outcome of the vote. After a bitter struggle, the Union Nationale overwhelmed the Liberals, taking seventy-six seats to the Liberals' fourteen; Adélard Godbout himself, the Liberal leader and premier, went down to defeat. The Liberals' popular vote declined from 50.2 percent in 1935 to 41.8 percent whereas the Union Nationale increased its proportion from 48.7 percent to 57.5 percent. This was indeed a dramatic upset, and there could be no uncertainty that Duplessis and the Union Nationale had won a strong mandate.

Duplessis' First Term, 1936–1939

When one compares the Union Nationale's first brief term with its long incumbency after 1944, it is perhaps tempting to see two very different regimes, even two very different premiers. The first mandate did end in an electoral hecatomb whereas, after 1944, Duplessis succeeded in consolidating his hold on party and government to such an extent that he was able to win four consecutive elections and, had he lived, there is every reason to believe that he would have won a fifth in 1960. Even allowing that the Union Nationale lacked organization and experience during the years 1936–39 and that a depressed economy worked against it, the resemblances between the two administrations appear quite as striking as the contrasts.

Duplessis rapidly transformed the Union Nationale into a conservative party, undoubtedly with the support of most of his caucus and his organizers who were no more convinced than he was that the government should play a more active role in the economy and society. In truth, what counted was to gain power, and to hold it. But several well-known reformers, like Hamel, Chaloult, Grégoire, and Oscar Drouin, who favoured unflinching pursuit of nationalist economic policies, quickly broke with Duplessis over his apparent refusal to implement his program. Their attacks on this "most deceitful of all politicians" — as Hamel described Duplessis — were bitter. Indeed, in 1937 they created a new party, the National Party. There is certainly no question that Duplessis indefinitely put off the campaign against the trusts just as he did most of the political reforms he had promised. Chaloult affirmed that Duplessis told him a few weeks after the victory: "A program is good before the elections and the elections are over now." But perhaps it is also true, as Msgr. Georges Gauthier, Archbishop of Montreal, opined, that "the population is more interested in the price of milk than in the price of electricity." And even then Duplessis did succeed in negotiating certain reductions in electricity rates in urban areas.

Relations between government and labour deteriorated rapidly. The Legislature adopted Bills 19 and 20, which exempted public works executed on behalf of the government from the purview of the Fair Wages Act, prohibited the closed shop, and authorized the state to modify collective agreements unilaterally. Then, in August 1937, ten thousand textile mill workers, members of the Confédération des travailleurs catholiques du Canada (CTCC), went on strike with the support of the clergy. The government appeared to side with the employers, and William Tremblay, labour minister, was described as "the assassin of the working class." Actually, it was not surprising that the unions already found Duplessis quite unaccommodating. Although he promised to defend the worker, the Union Nationale leader had never attempted to court the unions. Things would change little after 1944.

Still, Duplessis did not just stir up opposition during his first term. Other measures taken by the Union Nationale government won him support, especially from the farmers who, once the storm of 1939 had passed, remained staunchly loyal to him. On numerous occasions, Duplessis expounded his fundamentally conservative and ruralist philosophy: "Agriculture is an element of economic stability and social order. We must maintain and protect our rural base." And he gave tangible expression to such statements by establishing a system of agricultural credit and taking other steps to assist agriculture.

Duplessis' conservatism also took the form of an unrelenting battle against the supposed communist threat in Quebec. In these years of economic crisis and of epic combats in Europe between the left and the right — civil war broke out in Spain in 1936 — the Catholic clergy increasingly worried over subversive activity in the province. Cardinal J.-M.-Rodrigue Villeneuve declared that communism had become "a reality. The fire is lit among us and it is urgent to extinguish it since there is little time left." In October 1936, fifteen thousand faithful, amongst them the cardinal, the mayor of Quebec City, and the new premier of the province, launched a crusade against communism at a rally held at the Quebec City coliseum. Then, when the infamous "Padlock Law" was adopted in March 1937, the clergy greeted it enthusiastically and insisted that it be applied rigorously. This campaign would continue throughout Duplessis' second administration.

Thus, instead of attempting to portray a Duplessis quite different from the one who would take power again in 1944, it would perhaps be more accurate to see a party leader preparing the foundations on which he would base his power after his return to office. Nevertheless, it seems evident that, in the course of the years 1936–39, Duplessis did neglect the Union Nationale's organization, with the result that the party was ill-prepared for battle when the premier suddenly called an election in the autumn of 1939. Quebec's public finances were in a sorry state and Ottawa now controlled provincial borrowings. Duplessis intended to campaign on the theme of provincial autonomy, especially fiscal autonomy, and he denounced what he called the federal plan for "assimilation and centralization." Indeed, the election was fought on a nationalistic issue, but that issue was not provincial autonomy. Military conscription was the theme, and the bogey of 1917 returned to haunt the politicians. The Quebec members of the federal cabinet, with Ernest Lapointe in the lead, maintained that Duplessis' reelection would signify a vote of non-confidence in them and that they would have to resign. And if they left the cabinet, who would stop an Anglophone government from having recourse to conscription once again? Adélard Godbout, provincial Liberal leader, himself promised to resign if a single French Canadian was mobilized against his will by a Liberal administration. Later, Duplessis' supporters would condemn this blackmail and insist that Quebec had voted out of fear. Nonetheless, a majority of voters judged that Quebec's federal ministers constituted a better guarantee than Duplessis against the possibility of conscription for service overseas. The results of the election were catastrophic for the Union Nationale, which elected only fifteen members to the Liberals' seventy. Moreover, the Union Nationale's popular vote fell precipitously from 57.5 percent in 1936 to 39.2 percent in 1939.

The Union Nationale in Opposition, 1939–1944

Some observers believe that Duplessis' decision to declare a surprise election in 1939 constituted the "one occasion when he misjudged his own people."

Afterwards, though, Duplessis appeared fortunate in having been defeated since he was able, as Leader of the Opposition, to watch from the sidelines while his dire prophecies on conscription and provincial autonomy were fulfilled. Indeed, in order to pursue the war effort, the federal government set about centralizing public finances as well as increasing its activities in the economic and social spheres. But even though Duplessis' predictions did come true, one must not conclude that he hoped for defeat in 1939; on the contrary, he seems to have found that setback very bitter.

On the morrow of its debacle, the Union Nationale, like other movements that had grown out of the Depression and disappointed their adherents, seemed destined to oblivion. Duplessis appeared to be no more than a fleeting star in the political heavens — a historical has-been — and a group of conservatives was already seeking to dislodge him from the party leadership. A triumphant English Canada proclaimed that Quebec had voted for national unity and for the war effort. Then, in 1940, the Rowell-Sirois Commission on Dominion-Provincial Relations published its report, one of whose recommendations was that the provinces abandon all direct taxes to Ottawa in return for federal grants and the payment of existing debts. Duplessis had challenged the commission's very mandate when it was created in 1937; he now declared that the report constituted "the apotheosis of the dictatorship of money over the ruins of autonomy, guardian of our most cherished traditions and of our most sacred rights." At a press conference, he reaffirmed Quebec's claim to all revenues accorded by the British North America Act of 1867. Godbout, however, had little choice: in 1942 he would be forced to conclude an agreement on the "rental" of provincial taxes to Ottawa.

In Western Europe, only England still held firm against the Nazi aggressor. In Canada, more and more Anglophones felt their country was not doing its share. Faced with rising pro-conscriptionist sentiment within his own party, W.L.M. King, the Canadian prime minister, decided to hold a referendum in which electors would be asked to release the government from its earlier anti-conscriptionist pledges. In Quebec, the Ligue pour la défense du Canada campaigned for the "no" and, in fact, the "no" triumphed easily in the province in the plebiscite of April 1942. By contrast, the rest of Canada voted overwhelmingly "yes." Out of the league evolved the Bloc populaire, an anti-conscriptionist, anti-imperialist, autonomist, and reformist party with federal and provincial wings, the latter led by André Laurendeau. Once again, as in 1935, the opposition was split and Duplessis risked being surpassed by another party more nationalistic than his own. He might well accuse the Bloc of dividing anti-Liberal political forces and thus helping Godbout keep power; this time there would be no anti-government coalition and three separate parties would participate in the provincial elections of 8 August 1944. During the campaign, the Liberals could point to several important though controversial pieces of legislation adopted during their term of office. They had given women the right to vote, made education compulsory for children aged six to fourteen, passed laws on civil service reform and on labour relations, and nationalized two private electricity companies, Beauharnois and Montreal Light, Heat and Power, "the two cancerous children of forty-four years of Liberal regime," as Duplessis mocked. The Union Nationale leader accused

Godbout of trying to "electrocute the population" in order to hide the real issue of the election: the shameful weakness of the provincial Liberal government in the face of the centralizers from Ottawa. Abandoned by the federal Liberals, the provincial party attempted to convince voters that "to beat Godbout would be to beat King, and to beat King would be to play into the hands of those who wanted conscription." Yet this issue no longer had the same relevance it had in 1939.

The Liberal and Union Nationale parties waged a close race in 1944 with the Bloc playing the role of nuisance whose presence probably favoured the Union Nationale, particularly in certain rural counties outside of Montreal and in the Eastern Townships. The Liberals did win the largest share of the popular vote, 39.5 percent, but because of the way in which it was distributed — the party piled up huge majorities in certain English-speaking districts of Montreal — they elected only thirty-seven candidates. The Union Nationale, with 35.8 percent of the vote, carried forty-eight seats. Already the efforts of the 1936–39 years were paying dividends and the party won a majority of the numerous sparsely-populated rural ridings. Maurice Duplessis was again premier of Quebec.

The Foundations of Power

By the war's end, Quebec was no longer what it had been ten years before. The Depression was now only a bad memory and the province was again the scene of rapid industrialization. Stimulated by war needs, the metal and chemical industries, among others, underwent prodigious growth; in an unusual occurrence, the value of manufacturing production increased at a faster rate in Quebec than in neighbouring Ontario. Nevertheless, Ontario still had a greater share of high-paying heavy industry while Quebec was well-represented in sectors like textiles, dependent on an abundant labour force and paying relatively low wages. Wartime industrial development also stimulated the growth of unions whose membership in Quebec doubled, rising from 105,000 in 1939 to 209,000 in 1946. The CTCC, however, reputed by employers to be less militant, saw its growth slow — its share of unionized workers in the province dropped from 37 percent in 1936 to only 24.2 percent in 1946 — while the international unions made rapid progress.

During the decade ending in 1941, the province's population increased by 16 percent to a total of 3.3 million; for the years 1941–51, the growth rate accelerated to nearly 22 percent. Although the Depression temporarily halted the tide of rural migration, the industrial growth of the 1940s signalled new population losses for the countryside so that, by 1951, more than 67 percent of Quebeckers inhabited the towns and cities. The agricultural vocation, the traditional attachment of French Canadians to labour in the fields, was becoming little more than a myth: 25.2 percent of the population derived a living from agriculture in 1941 while by 1951 this figure had dropped to barely 19.5 percent. Between 1938 and 1947, agricultural production averaged only 12.4 percent of the net value of goods produced in Quebec. Moreover, many so-called farmers worked off the farm for up to six months a year. Decidedly, the Quebec of Maria Chapdelaine no longer existed.

In the face of such change, it appears paradoxical to maintain that Duplessis' strength resided in the defence of conservative virtues, such as ruralism, religion, the safeguarding of traditions, and economic laissez-faire, to which large sectors of Quebec society, and certainly the elite, were still attached. The Union Nationale continued to assist farmers, defend the traditional role of the Catholic Church in Quebec and particularly its presence in social and educational institutions, and combat "heretics" — like communists, socialists, and Jehovah's Witnesses. It endeavoured to repulse the federal government's centralizing assaults in areas like revenue-sharing and legislative competency, all in the name of preserving a distinct society. And it favoured social peace in order to attract private investment, create jobs, and assure the province's economic prosperity. In addition, the party effectively used patronage in order to ensure the dependence and indebtedness of at least part of the electorate. The keystone in this structure was Maurice Duplessis himself.

In the agricultural sector, the farm credit system set up during the Union Nationale's first term was continued: between 1937 and 1955, some fifty thousand farmers profited from the plan. Then, in 1945, Duplessis himself introduced a bill establishing a Rural Electrification Bureau to help co-operatives bring electricity to rural areas. Whereas only 20 percent of rural properties had access to electricity in 1944, some 90 percent benefited from the service in 1955.

The support that these undertakings, and others concerning colonization and land improvement, generated in the countryside was disproportionately magnified by constituency boundaries which were increasingly outmoded, as well as unjust for urban dwellers, because they accorded enormous political weight to small rural ridings. For example, in 1956, the ten largest electoral districts in the province contained an average of 70,000 electors each: collectively they sent to the Legislature six Liberals, out of a total of twenty Liberals who won seats in that year's election, as well as four members of the Union Nationale. At the other end, the ten smallest ridings, with an average of only 8,500 voters, elected nine Union Nationale candidates. This disequilibrium explains in part the Union Nationale's stranglehold on the Legislative Assembly, with eighty-two out of ninety-two MLAs in 1948, sixty-eight out of ninety-two in 1952, and seventy-two out of ninety-three in 1956. It should be remembered, however, that, in each of these three elections, the governing party obtained, though barely, an absolute majority of the popular vote. Is it necessary to affirm that the Union Nationale's support did not come only from rural Quebec, and that even working-class constituencies usually gave a majority of their votes to Duplessis? Indeed, the Union Nationale's anti-labour policies appear not to have hurt it at election time, possibly because the unions still aroused suspicion among the working class, or because the party redeemed itself in other ways, or simply because there was no alternative. In fact, the only districts where the Union Nationale always did poorly were in the English-speaking areas on the western end of the Island of Montreal.

Most observers of the Duplessis period have underlined the high degree of co-operation between the government and the province's Catholic clergy. Certainly, after the tension of the Taschereau era, Church-state relations appeared generally harmonious; indeed, certain bishops seem to have believed that a return to power of the Liberals would unleash a wave of secularization. However, in the latter years of the Duplessis regime, relations between certain members of the clergy and the Union Nationale government deteriorated, although both authorities continued to appreciate the advantages of close collaboration. On the one hand, faced with growing financial needs and in the absence of statutory subsidies for social institutions and schools, the clergy was constantly forced to solicit special grants. In return, manifestations of gratitude were *de rigueur*. In the dioceses established in newly developed regions, appeals for funds were more pressing as well as more frequent, and expression of thanks so effusive, that certain bishops, among them Msgr. J.A. Desmarais, Bishop of Amos, actually seemed to behave as though they were agents of the Union Nationale. And the clergy endorsed Duplessis' campaigns against the communists and the Jehovah's Witnesses. Although this repression was vigorously condemned outside the province, Catholics within Quebec generally approved. On the other hand, Duplessis, who had become a model of fiscal orthodoxy after the severe financial problems he had encountered between 1936 and 1939, could not but recognize that institutions run by the clergy saved the public treasury huge sums of money in salaries. All in all, Duplessis and the majority of the clergy, above and beyond their special interests, spoke the same language and shared a common vision of society.

The Liberal opposition, and later the new Liberal government that succeeded the Union Nationale in June 1960, often criticized Duplessis for his negative defence of provincial autonomy and blamed him for refusing federal initiatives and thus costing Quebec's taxpayers millions of dollars in lost grants. And yet the context of the 1940s and 1950s was very different from the early 1960s. In the wake of a disastrous Depression and of a World War that appeared to necessitate the mobilization of the country's resources, the federal government tried, with considerable success, to centralize fiscal and even legislative powers in Canada. After the war, for social, economic, and political reasons, the King and St. Laurent governments continued in the same vein by setting up several new social programs, by concluding tax-rental agreements with all provinces but Quebec, and by instituting a system of grants to Canadian universities. Duplessis defended the traditional autonomist position and told federal centralizers: "You shall not crucify the province of Quebec, even on a cross of gold."

In the area of federal-provincial relations for the years 1944–59, two questions stand out in particular: the federal grants to the universities, established in October 1951, and the debate over the provincial income tax instituted by Duplessis in 1954. In the case of the university grants, Duplessis asserted that the project constituted a "dangerous usurpation of power by the federal government, in a sector of activity exclusively reserved to the provinces" and, except for the first year, he refused to accept the subsidies in spite of the growing needs of the province's university system. Nationalist groups supported him, and even Pierre Elliott Trudeau, habitually a critic of the regime, condemned the federal plan which, he said, did not respect the principle of a clear attribution of responsibility in a federal system. In the second case, the Union Nationale government decided to establish a provincial income tax equal to fifteen percent of the federal tax and claimed full deductibility in order to avoid double-taxing Quebeckers. Nationalists rallied to Duplessis, and Gérard Filion, usually not a friend of the government, approved in *Le Devoir*: "Quebec is again on the offensive." Ottawa refused the principle of deductibility, but finally agreed to reduce its own personal income tax by a ten percent. It is obviously impossible to judge the electoral benefits that Duplessis was able to reap from his autonomist campaigns just as it would be difficult to demonstrate that Duplessis' position on the question cost the Union Nationale votes. Still nationalist groups did support the cause of autonomy, whose standard-bearer was Duplessis, and they castigated the Liberals for not giving sufficient guarantees on the issue.

In economic matters, however, nationalist values assuredly had little impact upon the regime's policies. In fact, critics denounced the flagrant contradiction between the poltical nationalism that Duplessis practised so zealously and the enormous concessions he granted in order to attract foreign investors. Vast tracts of Crown lands, especially in Northern Quebec, were ceded to American corporations, royalties were fixed at levels decried by the Liberals as scandalously generous for the companies, and numerous tax concessions were accorded. In addition, the province's financial health made it possible to keep taxes relatively low. As far as labour was concerned, the government sought, through its laws and their application, to favour "social peace." The controls it imposed explain in part why between 1945 and 1959 Quebec had an average of only thirty-five strikes a year with a loss of 335,000 work days, compared to Ontario's average yearly losses of 700,000 work days. Thanks to a climate of economic prosperity, in Quebec as well as internationally, development capital flowed into the primary and secondary sectors.

The question of Quebec's economic development in this period has aroused considerable debate. There is no doubt that the province's economy did grow rapidly and it is possible to use all manner of statistics to make a convincing demonstration. But it seems that the gap that existed in 1939 between Quebec and Ontario, in regard to the economic performance of the two provinces, persisted in Ontario's favour throughout the 1940s and 1950s. Moreover, it should be noted that, although the number of jobs increased in all sectors, the increase was more important in the tertiary sector, particularly transportation, commerce, and services, than in the resource and manufacturing sectors. But in spite of certain structural weaknesses, the rapid economic development of the period reinforced the position of the governing party and contributed to attenuating the effects of anti-government criticism. In marked contrast with the tension that characterized relations between government and the unions, ties with business remained cordial.

Maurice Duplessis' conservatism surely pleased large and influential fractions of the Quebec population. But one should not minimize the role of political organization and patronage in securing votes for the Union Nationale. From 1944, Joseph-D. Bégin, minister of colonization, supervised the party machine, while Gérard Martineau, named to the Legislative Council, occupied the position of party treasurer after 1946. Those who "donated" to the party treasury were, in the main, the businesses and commercial establishments of the province. The government would grant contracts for roadworks, without tenders, to party contributors. Patronage became an instrument of blackmail, even of intimidation, a veritable octopus whose tentacles extended to all areas of provincial administration.

In the words of Jean Lesage, Liberal leader after 1958, "everyone got something, even the voter who, on the eve of the election, received a load of gravel to spread on the mud in the entry to his farm." And the manna could disappear if the voters preferred the opposition candidate. Duplessis himself stated at a political rally in Verchères in 1952: "I warned you in 1948 not to vote for the Liberal candidate. You didn't listen to me. Unfortunately your county did not receive the grants, the subsidies that would have made it happier. I hope that the lesson will suffice." Alas! The voters' obstinacy lasted through one more election and it was only in 1956 that the Union Nationale candidate would be elected. As the years went by, traditional politics, where patronage on an individual as well as on a collective level played no small role, would be criticized by an ever more vocal minority of voters. Nonetheless, it seems apparent that patronage as practised by the Union Nationale contributed to obtaining the support of those whom it benefited.

Duplessism Challenged

The electoral support accorded to the Union Nationale remained remarkably stable between 1948 and 1956. Even in the 1960 election, after the deaths of both Duplessis and his successor, Paul Sauvé, and at a time when the third Union Nationale leader in less than a year, Antonio Barrette, was facing bitter dissension within the party, the Union Nationale lost only five percent of the popular vote. At the same time, the Liberals, with a dynamic new leader, vaunted their "équipe du tonnerre" and proposed a program of reform symbolized by their slogan: "It's time for a change!" There is no doubt that Duplessis' critics became more numerous and more vocal in the last years of the regime, but their impact on the electoral base of the Union Nationale seems to have been relatively slight. Perhaps the strong opposition to which Duplessis was constantly subjected by intellectuals explains a tendency, for commentators close to this milieu, to exaggerate the significance of such anti-Duplessis groups.

When he wished to boast of the power he wielded, Duplessis would often declare that "the bishops eat out of my hand." In spite of much evidence of close co-operation between the Church and the Union Nationale government, as already discussed, there were discordant notes. The clergy's attitude at the time of the famous Asbestos strike of 1949 — the bishops went so far as to order that collections be taken up for the strikers' families — certainly displeased Duplessis. When Msgr. Joseph Charbonneau, Archbishop of Montreal and a fervent defender of the workers, resigned a few months later, some saw Duplessis' vengeful hand at work; later research would seem to show that other reasons explain the archbishop's departure. Msgr. Charbonneau's successor, Msgr. Paul-Émile Léger, maintained proper relations with the government, but was not in the habit of coming to Quebec City to beg for funds. Other priests, acting individually, also criticized Duplessis. In particular, there were the cases of Father Georges-Henri Lévesque of Laval University, and Fathers Gérard Dion and Louis O'Neill, authors of a text that appeared in August 1956 denouncing political corruption in Quebec.

But it was in the unions that the regime's most steadfast opponents were to be found, even though certain labour organizations, like the Fédération provinciale du Travail du Québec (FPTQ), sought to collaborate with the government in return for favours. In 1949, Duplessis attempted to place drastic curbs on the unions through his Bill 5, which prohibited the closed shop and specified the conditions under which the right to strike could be exercised. The proposed legislation also went so far as to stipulate that any union permitting "communists" to occupy posts in its organization or on its executive would lose the certificate it held from the Board of Labour Relations and thus its right to negotiate with the employer. The unions fought the Legislature bitterly and the Church also condemned the bill; although Duplessis withdrew it, he did eventually succeed in passing many of its components in piecemeal fashion, notably through Bills 19 and 20 that the Legislature adopted in 1954, both retroactive to 1944. The CTCC, which had become much more militant after the asbestos strike and a series of other bitter confrontations in 1952 in which police were frequently used against strikers, joined with the Fédération des Unions industrielles du Québec to combat the legislation. The FPTQ and the FUIQ united in 1957 to form the Fédération du Travail du Quebec, which would conduct the interminable strike staged that same year at Murdochville.

The Duplessis regime was also under attack by a growing minority of intellectuals. Amongst the opponents stood out the Montreal daily, *Le Devoir*; the small review, *Cité libre*, guided by Pierre Elliott Trudeau and Gérard Pelletier; the magazine, *Relations*, published by the Jesuits; and, in the universities, Laval's Faculty of Social Sciences. Of course, these critics constantly censured the Union Nationale's electoral corruption, the abuses of the patronage system, and the scandals, like the natural gas scandal of 1958, in which the administration was involved. But they went further since, in their eyes, the Quebec of the 1950s lagged seriously behind the other Canadian provinces, particularly in regard to the role that the state should play in a modern society. These intellectuals denounced the social conservatism inherent in the doctrine of provincial autonomy as defended by Duplessis. They were not anticlerical, but they did believe that the state should be more concerned with education and social welfare, then largely under the control of the Catholic clergy. Regarding education in particular, curricula had to be revised, teacher training improved, and rates of school attendance increased. *Cité libre* even took the rather revolutionary step of asserting that a department of education should be established. In the economic sector, *Le Devoir* maintained that the government should stop allying itself with the employers in oppressing workers and that it should impose much more drastic conditions on foreign investors whose profits from the exploitation of the province's natural resources were judged to be excessive. But in order to accomplish these reforms, the Quebec state would need an expanded civil service based on competence rather than allegiance to the party in power. Nonetheless, the opposition was divided, and many of the Union Nationale's critics felt ill at ease with Lapalme's Liberals whom they viewed as still too much under the control of the old guard. Only a new leader with a revised program could bring these diverse elements together into an anti-Duplessis front. In effect, that is precisely what occurred with the arrival of Jean Lesage in 1958.

Maurice Duplessis died suddenly on 7 September 1959. Brandishing his slogan "Henceforth," the new leader and premier, Paul Sauvé, gave the impression that Duplessism was no more but, before he could make his mark on the province, death struck him down too in early January 1960. The Union Nationale caucus finally designated Antonio Barrette as his successor, but Barrette was not accepted by certain elements of the party machine. On 22 June 1960, the Union Nationale was defeated, though barely, by Lesage's Liberals and Quebec embarked upon the period later termed the "Quiet Revolution." The new government took control of most institutions in the spheres of education, health, and welfare; it adopted a new labour code; it favoured a certain economic nationalism; it pursued an aggressive autonomist policy in relations with Ottawa; and it fought to curb patronage and eliminate political corruption.

In this atmosphere of enthusiasm and energetic action, the Liberals and their sympathizers were inclined to judge the Duplessis years harshly as a period of obscurity akin to the Dark Ages. Their arrival in power, they felt, heralded a sort of rebirth, a thaw, the beginning of a new era. The Duplessis regime may well have endured for too long, the Union Nationale leader's traditionalist policies may well have been anachronistic when compared with the relatively modern society that, in many respects, the Quebec of the 1950s had already become. It is also possible that the Liberals and their reform-minded team, entrusted with power in 1960, had little choice but to act with haste on all levels in order to move Quebec forward. However, the supporters of the new government did not enjoy the benefits of hindsight necessary to analyse the old regime with a certain impartiality. In addition, they could scarcely anticipate the weaknesses of the reforms that they were in the process of implementing.

Duplessis and his regime will continue to fascinate observers of Quebec society and research will be pursued as new sources of information become available and new monographs are written. Freed to a large extent of the partisan constraints so present during these last years, they will undoubtedly be able to shed new light on this complex period of Quebec's history.

QUEBEC: SOCIAL TRANSFORMATION AND IDEOLOGICAL RENEWAL, 1940–1976†

MICHAEL D. BEHIELS

Despite the steady migration of rural French Canadians to the towns and cities of Quebec, New England, and Ontario since the 1870s, the myth of French Canada being an agrarian society remained prevalent until World War II. Many outside observers retained the outmoded impression of a pleasantly quaint and stable community steeped in the values of Catholicism and a rural life cycle that had remained, in their essentials, unchanged for over two centuries. Few could foresee the fundamental changes this society would experience as a result of a new round of industrialization and urbanization initiated by the war and prolonged by postwar economic expansion. The emergence of the social welfare state in Ottawa, coupled with the creation of a consumer-oriented society, was to have profound social, economic, ideological, and political implications for all classes of the French-Canadian society, in particular the established clerical and secular elites.

Just what were the major socio-economic changes experienced by the Francophone society of Quebec in the three decades following the outbreak of the war in 1939? These changes will be examined along with the critical responses of a growing number of individuals, groups, and associations. In the first stage, these individuals and groups articulated a critique of the prevalent ideology of conservative, clerical nationalism. They then proceeded to propose alternate ideologies based on welfare-state liberalism, social democracy, and eventually, democratic socialism. The Francophone intelligentsia was to become increasingly divided on the question of whether or not their respective liberal, social democratic, or socialist visions of society should be structured according to neo-nationalist imperatives, that is, oriented primarily toward the development of a dynamic and powerful Québécois nation-state. The neo-nationalists were divided over

†From Michael S. Cross and Gregory Kealey, eds., *Modern Canada 1930s–1980s* (Toronto: McClelland and Stewart, 1984), 144–76.

whether or not the achievement of their nationalist-imbued objectives could be attained within a renewed Canadian federal system or via the acquisition of full political independence.

Demographic, Economic, and Social Transformation

Since 1940, Quebec has experienced social change on an unprecedented scale. In the mid-1950s this upheaval prompted the director of *Le Devoir*, Gérard Filion, to remark that the province of Quebec was undergoing a degree of socio-economic change unparallelled in any other Western industrialized country.[1] A great deal of the pressure for change was prompted by a considerable increase in Quebec's population. Most of the growth was due to natural increase but this was supplemented by the influx of immigrants in the postwar years. Furthermore, immigration to the United States had remained difficult for most Quebeckers, thereby forcing them to seek employment at home or in other parts of Canada. As a result of this pattern, Quebec witnessed a 22 percent increase in its population in the 1940s, a 30 percent increase in the 1950s, and another 15 percent in the 1960s. In 1971 over 6 million people lived in "la belle province" compared with 3.3 million three decades earlier.[2]

The renewal of industrial and urban expansion brought about a precipitous decline of agriculture both as an economic activity and as a way of life for what remained of the rural society. Widespread rural depopulation, caused by a sharp decline in agricultural commodity prices, became one of the dominant features of postwar Quebec. Not only were one out of every two sons leaving the ancestral home as in the past, but entire families were abandoning farming in pursuit of employment in the factories in and around metropolitan Montreal or in the towns associated with such resource industries as mining and pulp and paper. Within a generation, the number of French Canadians on farms declined from 1.1 million to 285,000, that is, from 41 percent of the Francophone community in 1941 to 6 percent in 1971. The number of French Canadians living in urban centres rose from 1.5 million in 1941 to over 3.7 million or 78 percent of the Francophone population by 1971. Metropolitan Montreal, with 40 percent of Quebec's population by 1961, dominated the economic and cultural life of the province. Montreal became the new home for two-thirds of those French Canadians leaving their farms as well as for virtually all the postwar immigrants. Because Montreal's Anglo-Scottish financial, commercial, and industrial elite dominated the Canadian and Quebec economies, the language of work and, to a degree, social intercourse inevitably was English. It was just as predictable perhaps that Montreal, the point of contact between Francophone and Anglophone communities, would emerge as the centre of contemporary French-Canadian neo-nationalism in the 1950s.[3]

Quebec was able to absorb the vast majority of its native-born sons and daughters as well as thousands of immigrants largely because of the rapid growth in the provincial economy. Between 1946 and 1956 the gross provincial product grew by 45 percent in constant dollars. The traditional manufacturing sectors, such as food, textiles, clothing, tobacco, rubber, leather, and wood, all increased their production. But the newly created or expanded high-technology and capital-intensive industries, such as non-ferrous metals, non-metallic minerals, iron, transportation, electrical appliances, and chemical and petrochemical products, experienced the strongest growth in production and employment. Quebec entered the 1950s with a bullish and diversified economy.[4] The vibrant domestic and American demand for Quebec's mineral resources and forest products and relatively cheap hydro-electricity spurred the rapid development of these resources. The spin-offs for the industrial and service sectors were tremendous.

One of the most significant social aspects of the expansion and diversification of Quebec's economy has been the dramatic shift in employment from the primary sector to the tertiary or service sector. The dramatic decline of agriculture and the ever-increasing mechanization of the resource sector explain the drop in proportion of employment in the primary sector from 32.4 percent in 1941 to 7.5 percent in 1971. Employment in the manufacturing sector grew only slightly in this period, but the proportion of Quebeckers employed in the service sector — utilities, transportation, public services, commerce, and professions — rose from 41 percent to 62.9 percent of the labour force.

This shift to jobs in some cases requiring a higher degree of education, and therefore providing higher economic remuneration, has not been as extensive for French Canadians as for Quebec's other ethnic groups. While French Canadians are now slightly overrepresented in manufacturing jobs and have made significant gains in the clerical and sales category, in 1971 they remained significantly underrepresented in managerial and administrative positions.[5] Because the growth in prosperity has not been distributed very evenly, with managerial, administrative, and highly skilled unionized employees reaping the highest rewards, French Canadians as a collectivity were found by the Royal Commission on Bilingualism and Biculturalism to rank near the bottom of the income scale in 1961.[6] This situation has improved to some extent during the past two decades.[7] Nevertheless, the growing awareness of the cultural division of labour during the 1950s and 1960s prevented a clear understanding of the increasing rigidity of the class structure in contemporary Quebec. More importantly, this ethnic cleavage contributed to the re-emergence of strong neo-nationalist sentiments among well-educated, middle-class French Canadians whose aspirations for upward mobility were being thwarted.

Perhaps the most significant ideological and political development emanating from this rapid process of socio-economic change was the emergence of an expanded and diversified middle class in French Canada. The traditional French-Canadian professional petty bourgeoisie of doctors, lawyers, notaries, journalists, clerics, and small entrepreneurial businessmen was expanded to incorporate social scientists, scientists, engineers, technicians, and private and public managers and administrators. This was due in large measure to the partial modernization of French Canada's educational institutions.[8]

Deeply concerned with the serious problems facing the French-Canadian *petite et moyenne* bourgeoisies in competing with the Anglo-Canadian and American financiers and industrialists, the Liberal government of Lomer Gouin created in 1907 the Écoles des hautes études commerciales in Montreal as well as encouraged the expansion of several commercial academies at the secondary level. Nearly half of the Francophone economic elite by the 1940s had been educated in these or similar institutions in order to maintain and hopefully extend their role in the development of the Quebec economy. Concerns with overcrowding and serious competition from other ethnic groups prompted the Francophone professional petty bourgeoisie to advocate the creation of faculties of science at Laval and the Université de Montréal in the 1920s.[9] Similar concerns, coupled with the emergence of a liberal interpretation of Catholic social doctrine and social action, led to the creation of faculties of social science at both Francophone universities in the 1930s and 1940s.[10] Hampered by the unwillingness and, often, the inability of classical college graduates to pursue careers in these new faculties, as well as by the non-existence of a Francophone public secondary system providing its successful graduates with automatic access to university faculties, the growth of the new faculties of pure and applied sciences was slow and the social sciences even slower.

This situation changed dramatically during and after World War II. By the academic year 1952–53, the number of Laval and Montreal students enrolled in the faculties of science and commerce was almost on par with those enrolled in medicine, law, and dentistry. Furthermore, nearly 40 percent of these students did not have a classical college degree but had been recruited from the *écoles primaire supérieur* or the commercial academies.[11] As a result of this expansion, considerable numbers of graduates from these non-traditional faculties were on the job market by the 1950s. Most of them faced two difficult choices. French-Canadian scientists, engineers, and business managers had to seek employment primarily in the private sector, which was largely dominated by Anglo-Canadian and American companies. These French Canadians found the competition with Anglophones particularly tough, and when they were hired it was usually "in sales, public relations, and personnel work rather than in production and general administration."[12] French-Canadian social scientists, administrators, and educators sought employment in the health, social welfare, and educational institutions, but this meant they had to work under the direction of religious personnel since the Catholic church owned and operated the vast majority of these institutions. Indeed, this process of co-opting members of French Canada's new middle class strengthened momentarily the position of the traditional political and clerical elites.[13]

With the arrival in 1960 of the Liberal Party led by Jean Lesage and the beginning of the process of political modernization, this new middle class became the most vociferous advocate of the ideology of neo-nationalism. It would effectively use a rejuvenated and modernized Quebec state to wrestle control from the Catholic church over all health, social welfare, and educational institutes, as well as to begin to challenge the Anglophone elite's control over Quebec's economy.[14]

Ideological Renewal

Quebec's "quiet revolution" originated during the Depression, gained momentum in the 1940s and 1950s, and eventually found political expression in the 1960s and 1970s. In retrospect, it was primarily an ideological revolution. It was initiated by a renewed and reinvigorated Francophone intelligentsia intent on instituting a social revolution that would install it as the dominant ruling class in contemporary Quebec. Prior to 1940, ideological pluralism existed in Quebec, but the Francophone intelligentsia was committed pretty exclusively to the ideology of traditional French-Canadian nationalism. With the exception of a small handful of outspoken individuals, such as the journalist Jean-Charles Harvey and Senator T.D. Bouchard, economic and social liberalism did not find favour with French Canada's clerical or professional petty-bourgeois elites. Liberalism found a forum only in the ranks of international unions, the commercial and industrial *petite et moyenne* bourgeoisies, and the Quebec Liberal Party of Premier Alexandre Taschereau.[15]

During the 1940s and 1950s the Francophone intelligentsia became quite diversified, thereby ending its long-standing monolithic outlook. This occurred in the face of a Catholic church intent on preserving the only rural and Catholic nationality in North America as well as in the climate of the socially regressive political regime of Maurice Duplessis. His Union Nationale administration, while co-operating with the traditional clerical and petty bourgeois elites, encouraged the rapid exploitation of Quebec's natural resources by American capital for American needs. Neither Duplessis nor his clerical and secular supporters showed much insight into or sympathy for the problems of the burgeoning proletariat created by the economic boom.

Cité libre Liberalism

Since the late 1930s, the Francophone Catholic labour movement of Quebec, faced with the threat of being undermined by the American industrial unions, became increasingly militant and aggressive in its demands and collective bargaining tactics. This process culminated in the famous 1949 Asbestos strike. In the aftermath of this turbulent strike during which over 5,000 French-Canadian workers courageously defied an anti-labour coalition of the Duplessis government and American mining interests, a young, dynamic group of Francophone liberals, social democrats, and democratic socialists came together in June 1950 to found a new periodical entitled appropriately *Cité libre* or "open society." Co-edited by Pierre Elliott Trudeau and Gérard Pelletier, *Cité libre* served as a focal point for labour advisers and militants, such as Charles Lussier, Réginald Boisvert, and Pierre Vadeboncoeur, and such literary critics and journalists as Maurice Blain, Guy Cormier, and Jean Le Moyne, as well as a number of social scientists, namely Marcel Rioux, Fernand Dumont, Jean-Charles Falardeau, and Léon Dion. *Citélibristes*, as they came to be called, undertook a wide-ranging, in-depth analysis of Quebec's socio-economic and political institutions and of the ideology of traditional French-Canadian nationalism they saw being used by the established clerical and professional petty-bourgeois intelligentsia to retain its control over the Francophone society. *Citélibristes* were ardent French Canadians and practising Catholics who wanted to modernize and democratize Quebec's Francophone and Catholic institutions at all levels and in all areas of activity.

The first prominent institution to be challenged by *Cité libre* was the Catholic church in Quebec. Many of *Cité libre*'s members had participated actively in the anti-nationalist and social-oriented Catholic action movements established in Quebec during the 1930s. Most members had also absorbed the "liberating" and inspiring personalist philosophy of France's left-wing Catholicism as articulated by Jacques Maritain, author of *Humanism intégrale*, and Emmanuel Mounier, editor of *Esprit*.[16]

As a result of these influences and their own experience with growing up in Catholic institutions, *Citélibristes* called for three reforms. First, the church had to democratize its internal operations by allowing lay participation in its councils. This step would help rid it of its excessive authoritarianism, dogmatism, and social conservatism.[17] Second, there had to be a separation of church and state. The administrative clericalism that stemmed from the church's control over health, social welfare, and educational institutions threatened to compromise severely the church's spiritual mission. Only a complete separation of church and state in these areas would enable the French-Canadian society to modernize and expand these essential services without jeopardizing the Catholic church's autonomy and its spiritual role.[18] This reform would also undermine the more insidious form of social clericalism whereby church officials and priests used the power and the influence they garnered in the spiritual realm to impose their views on social and political issues. The church, *Citélibristes* contended, had no right to determine the nature and extent of social and political debate in Quebec society. French Canada was no longer a "sacralized" society. It had become a secular society in which the relationships between human begins were considered just as important as those between an individual and the Creator. For democracy and pluralism to flourish in Quebec, French Canadians had to realize that they, not some distant providential power, were responsible for the development of the temporal City.[19] Third, the Catholic church in Quebec had to end its long-standing practice of censuring public debate on important secular issues, such as education and political morality. It also had to end its historic intolerance of other religious groups and allow French Canadians freedom of choice. Freedom of thought and expression coupled with an acceptance of religious pluralism were essential if the French-Canadian society were to become genuinely open, pluralistic, and democratic.[20]

The second major impediment to the political and social modernization of Quebec was the prevalence of the ideology of traditional French-Canadian nationalism. "What had nationalism and the nationalists given Quebec?" was the rhetorical question posed by Trudeau in his celebrated introduction to a monograph on the asbestos strike. By the 1950s French Canadians faced an anti-social, anti-democratic, anti-labour, and excessively pro-capitalist regime. Premier Maurice Duplessis spoke the rhetoric of traditional French-Canadian nationalism and never failed to denounce the federal government for its "centralist" social welfare policies. Yet in the same breath Duplessis would deny the need to reform Quebec's anachronistic health, social welfare, and educational institutions on the grounds that they were uniquely French and Catholic. He would then go on to extol the virtues of selling off Quebec's national resources at ridiculously low prices without thinking that this policy might well be against the best interest of French Canadians.[21]

Trudeau and several of his colleagues, Blain, Vadeboncoeur, Dumont, and Rioux, advanced the thesis that an ever-growing credibility gap had developed between the realities of modern French Canada and the dominant clerical and petty-bourgeois vision of nationalism that had prevailed since the mid-nineteenth century. Traditional French-Canadian nationalists had, out of their desire to create a distinct society, construed an ideal society that was totally unprogressive, anti-modern, and destructive of the individual. In a postwar Quebec deeply transformed by successive waves of industrialization and urbanization, this vision of a homogeneous rural society no longer corresponded to the new realities.[22]

Citélibristes, led by Trudeau, argued effectively that traditional French-Canadian nationalism had prevented French-Canadian intellectuals from drawing on new developments in the modern social sciences and had led to a reactionary interpretation of the social thought of the Catholic church. The pervasiveness of this nationalism on the political level had made it impossible to implement solutions to socio-economic problems proven successful for the Protestant and "materialistic" Anglo-Saxons. The traditional nationalists' equation of state intervention with communism and socialism had made the implementation of a meaningful provincial autonomy impossible and impeded the growth of a democratic concept of authority and the role of the state. The solutions proposed by nationalists since the early part of the century, such as return to the land, small buisnesses, co-operatives, Catholic labour unions, and Christian corporatism, were all, in Trudeau's estimation, conservative and even reactionary programs intended to impede the necessary secularization and democratization of French Canada's values and institutions. Unfortunately, many of French Canada's most important institutions — the Société Saint-Jean Baptiste, the École sociale populaire, the classical colleges, the universities, the church, and the Catholic unions — had been imbued so thoroughly with traditional French-Canadian nationalism that it was virtually impossible for them to make the transition to the modern secular world.[23]

Since nationalism had served the French-Canadian society so poorly, *Cité libre* proposed that only a widespread and genuine commitment to the ideology of liberal democracy would bring about the urgently required regeneration and modernization of French Canada. *Citélibristes* were convinced that the persistence of an authoritarian, conformist, and patronage-ridden political regime led by Duplessis was largely because French Canadians were anti-democratic. Out of historical necessity and a devotion to national survival, French Canadians had learned early on to use democracy rather than adhere to it as political philosophy to be fought for and cherished in its own right.[24] Hence the rallying cry for *Citélibristes* became "democracy first."

They set out, after the notorious dirty-tricks provincial election of 1956, to create a political movement, called *le Rassemblement*, to help establish genuine parliamentary democracy in Quebec.[25] In doing so, *Citélibristes* were opting for a society that placed its priority on the defence and development of individual rights and freedoms via liberal democratic institutions. *Cité libre* called for the creation of a ministry of education as soon as possible, for the creation of a modern educational system would allow the full and effective realization of every individual's potential. The ministry should undertake the building of a Franco-phone public secondary system administered by new regional school boards. This system would replace the elitist church-controlled classical college system and the truncated *école primaire supérieur* system, thereby providing all Franco-phones with equal access to all levels of post-secondary education.[26] *Citélibristes* also supported the eventual secularization of Quebec's Catholic universities and colleges and strongly opposed the church's plans to allow the Jesuit order to build a new university in Montreal.[27]

The revenues for necessary reforms could be obtained, according to *Cité libre*, from a more rational development of Quebec's vast natural resources. The modern neo-liberal state had a clear responsibility to intevene in the economy to ensure high employment, orderly and planned development, and a reasonable return for the treasury from the exploitation of publicly owned resources.[28] The wholesale sell-out of iron ore deposits in Ungava for one cent per ton was considered a violation of the public's right to equitable resource rents and detrimental to the overall development of Quebec's economy. Natural resources had to be processed within the province to increase the quantity and quality of jobs in the manufacturing sector. A more productive and diversified economy would enhance the revenues accruing to the treasury, making more funds available for social programs and education reforms.[29]

Finally, *Cité libre*'s perception of federalism and federal-provincial relations was determined by its strong advocacy of liberal and social democratic policies and practices. *Cité libre* vigorously opposed not the social objectives but the fiscal and monetary goals of the "new federalism" that emerged in the federal bureaucracy during and after the war. Following Trudeau's assessments of postwar economic developments in Ottawa, *Cité libre* rejected Maurice Lamontagne's plea that French Canada accept the imperatives of the modern world and participate in a lucid integration of Quebec into the new federalism.[30]

As a result of this line of thinking, Trudeau on behalf of *Cité libre* objected strongly to the federal government's decision in 1951 to grant subsidies to Canadian universities as recommended in the Massey Commission Report. Trudeau maintained that federal grants to universities violated the spirit and the law of the constitution. Agreeing with neo-nationalists at *Le Devoir*, he was adamant in his belief that the federal government should not use its general taxing powers to encroach on provincial responsibilities. It was up to Quebec voters to pressure their provincial government to provide a better financial deal for postsecondary education because this area was a provincial, not a federal, responsibility. It was only logical, given this conception of federalism, that Trudeau and his colleagues supported the imposition of a provincial income tax by the Duplessis government in 1954. Most of the revenue was slated for education and the legislation was a perfect example of the government responding to public pressure.[31]

The provincial income tax created quite a row with Prime Minister St. Laurent and the federal bureaucrats. Following several months of verbal bombast, Ottawa consented, albeit reluctantly, to share in a minor way the personal income tax field. While *Citélibristes* rejected the nationalists' claim that the provinces had an exclusive or priority right in the area of direct taxation, they supported their proposal that Quebec taxpayers be allowed to deduct, to a certain level, provincial income tax from their federal taxes. In short, there should be a sharing of the taxing resource base to serve both levels of government in proportion to their respective constitutional responsibilities. Among Ottawa's responsibilities Trudeau included financial equalization between the have and have-not provinces, economic stabilization, and full employment programs. Canada, *Citélibristes* firmly believed, could have strong autonomous provinces financing their own responsibilities as well as a strong federal government capable of directing and regulating a rapidly expanding industrial and technological society.[32] *Citélibristes* did not believe that constitutional changes pertaining to the division of powers between both levels of government were necessary or advisable. French Canadians had all the provincial powers they required to build an open, democratic, and pluralistic society under their control. Given this perspective, it was only natural that *Cité libre* would characterize the re-emergence of separatism in the early 1960s as the new treason of the intellectuals and would denounce the separatists as political counter-revolutionaries.[33]

The Birth of Neo-nationalism

Indeed, the neo-nationalism formulated by a small contingent of French Canada's intelligentsia during the 1940s and 1950s could easily be given a separatist orientation by disgruntled and ambitious members of French Canada's rapidly expanding new middle class. In fact, neo-nationalist historians at the Université de Montréal — Michel Brunet, Maurice Séguin, and Guy Frégault — were developing a secular nationalist interpretation of Quebec's past that weighed heavily in favour of political independence as the only viable guarantee of the survival of the French-Canadian nationality in North America. In the 1950s most neo-nationalists were not yet willing to accept this interpretation. Yet in 1952, to his rhetorical question, "Is there a crisis of Nationalism?" André Laurendeau responded with a categorical yes. In the wake of the demise of the Bloc populaire canadien in 1947, the creation of Ottawa's welfare state, and the growing identification of nationalism with the regressive policies and practices of the Duplessis administration, nationalists had become terribly confused. In fact, as Laurendeau was quickly discovering, much to his chagrin, many were indifferent and some were hostile to nationalism.[34]

French Canadians generally, but in particular the rural professional petty-bourgeoisie and the clerical leaders, rejected an abrupt departure from past practice. Consequently the Union Nationale, with its vigorous defence of the rural way of life, of the strong presence of the Catholic church in education, health, and welfare, and of the constitutional prerogatives of the province against an ever-encroaching Ottawa bureaucracy, was able to regain and retain power with relative ease for a decade and a half following its defeat of the Liberal and Bloc parties in the 1944 election.[35]

If French-Canadian nationalism, argued André Laurendeau and Gérard Filion, were to become once again an effective ideological force in contemporary Quebec, capable of influencing the direction of government policies and programs, it would have to be reformulated to reflect the needs and aspirations of an urban/industrial society. The neo-nationalist leaders, Filion and Laurendeau, were well placed to undertake this task. In April 1947 Filion had become director of *Le Devoir*, French Canada's most influential nationalist daily. He then hired Laurendeau as editor-in-chief. This was an inspired move because Laurendeau had impeccable nationalist credentials and, despite his liberal-reformist leanings, was generally acceptable to the more traditional nationalists. In 1948 Laurendeau was also reappointed for a second five-year term as director of French Canada's leading nationalist periodical, *l'Action nationale*. During the 1950s *Le Devoir*'s editorial staff included Paul Sauriol, Pierre Vigeant, Pierre Laporte, and Jean-Marc Léger. *Le Devoir* quickly became the centre of the debate about the future of the Francophone society and its role in Canada.

At the very heart of the political and ideology crisis facing French-Canadian nationalism was its inability to win over the hearts and minds of French Canada's dominant social class, the urban working class.[36] There were a number of divergent reasons for this: the homogenizing nature of the industrialization process; the lack of an urban French-Canadian culture and institutions; the foreign domination of Quebec's economy.[37] But the most important reason, according to neo-nationalists, was that the traditional nationalists had simply lost touch with the people by failing to elaborate a realistic and meaningful doctrine and program of action. A group of Université de Montréal students, who had created the Équipe de recherches sociales in 1947 to inculcate a social conscience in their fellow students, contended that the traditional nationalist elite of petty-bourgeois professionals and clerics was more concerned with defending its own particular class interests than with advancing the collective interest of the French-Canadian nation.[38] Somewhat surprisingly, the students found immediate support for their interpretation from abbé Gérard Dion and Joseph Pelchat of the Department of Industrial Relations at Laval, as well as from Claude Ryan, an organizer in the Catholic action movement, and Jean-Paul Robillard, a former Bloc militant. André Laurendeau gave the interpretation qualified support while encouraging the group to pursue its activities.[39]

The solution to the crisis was not, as the *Citélibristes* proposed, to abandon nationalism but rather to reorient and redefine it to meet the needs of contemporary Quebec. French-Canadian neo-nationalists accepted the fact that their society was no longer rural and agricultural but urban and industrial. The challenge confronting the French-Canadian people was to assimilate the new urban/industrial order and turn it to the advantage of a revitalized French-Canadian nation.[40] Neo-nationalists set out with considerable determination to break the identification of nationalism with anti-social, anti-labour, xenophobic, and petty-bourgeois values and interests. Nationalism, for them, was to become an ideology of socio-economic reforms, an ideology that would help undermine the dehumanizing and depersonalizing aspects of the urban/industrial social order. With the revitalization of such institutions as the family and the community, and the acquisition of greater autonomy for the individual, perhaps nationalism might well become a valued ideology among French Canada's working-class majority.[41]

The neo-nationalists' concern with the integration of the French-Canadian working class into the nationalist mainstream was reinforced by a growing awareness that the social, political, and economic interests of the French-Canadian middle class, old and new, were in serious jeopardy. This predicament was the natural outgrowth of the ever-increasing economic inferiority of French Canadians as individuals and as a collectivity. This issue was at the very centre of the neo-nationalists' concerns throughout the 1950s. It contributed directly to their decision to look toward the Quebec state as the key to the creation of a modern, secular society under the leadership of a new Francophone middle class.

Neo-nationalists observed the postwar economic boom with considerable trepidation. While Duplessis' laissez-faire economic policies and strong encouragement of foreign investment certainly created plenty of jobs and profit in the resource sector of the economy, they also accelerated the economic inferiority of French Canada's financial, commercial, and industrial *petite et moyenne* bourgeoisies. It was painfully apparent that French Canada lacked a financial and industrial *haute* bourgeoisie to compete with Montreal's Anglo-Canadian and American capitalists who dominated the most crucial sectors of Quebec's economy.[42] French Canadians, who constituted 30 percent of Canada's population, could lay claim to only 8 percent of the country's wealth. In Quebec, where they formed 80 percent of the population, they could lay claim to merely 25 percent of the wealth. Little wonder that only 5 percent (400) of the 8,000 company directorships listed in the 1954 *Directory of Directors* were French Canadians and only a small proportion of these held sizable stock portfolios.[43]

In general, neo-nationalists accepted the standard explanations for the absence of a French-Canadian bourgeoisie. While it remained true that French-Canadian family-based businesses feared the risks of going to the open market for expansion funds, it was no longer true that French Canada lacked internal capital resources. The real challenge was how to marshal those resources in an effective and efficient manner to enable the emergence of a Francophone *haute* bourgeoisie.[44] Laurendeau, Filion, Léger, and Laporte all had been convinced for some time that the Francophone majority's only effective method of achieving control over the provincial economy was to create a dynamic, interventionist, and secular nation-state. Consequently, they were very receptive to a reinterpretation of French Canada's past proffered by the Université de Montréal's neo-nationalist historians. Michel Brunet, Guy Frégault, and Maurice Séguin were contending that the Conquest of 1760 was the single most important event explaining the absence of a modern secular bourgeoisie in French Canada.[45] In short, their political explanation for French Canada's position of economic subservience encouraged other neo-nationalists to believe that a political solution was an important element in the attempt to redress an untenable situation.

Extensive governing intervention, it was believed, was needed in the planning and development of the economy. To become economic masters in their own house, French Canadians must start by regaining control over their vast natural resources — hydro-electricity, pulp and paper, and mining. If private companies refused to allow French Canadians to become the majority stockholders and managers of the resource corporations or to provide the citizens of Quebec an equitable share of the economic rents of their resources, the Quebec state had no alternative but to nationalize the companies.[46] Neo-nationalists were particularly incensed at the Duplessis government's decision in 1946 to grant the Iron Ore Company, a consortium of several American steel companies, the right to develop the iron ore deposits in northern Quebec for a fixed annual royalty of

$100,000. This amounted to little more than one cent per ton of ore! Certainly jobs were created, but the public's share was meagre indeed. They might also have added that Francophones were conspicuous by their absence in the upper echelons of the corporation. Duplessis' resource policy appeared particularly galling when he proclaimed time and time again that his government lacked the revenue to improve educational and social services. It was also imperative, argued neo-nationalists, for the government to create, as soon as possible, a state-controlled steel corporation to mine and process Quebec's iron ore.[47]

After initially resisting the call for increased provincial activity in the social welfare and health fields for fear of alienating the church, neo-nationalists by the late 1950s supported organized labour's pleas for provincial medicare and hospitalization programs. Neo-nationalists perceived the reform of Quebec's anachronistic and uncoordinated education institutions as the central element in their drive to create a modern, secular, French-Canadian nation-state.[48] Indeed, the pressures for educational reform were quite widespread by the 1950s, a fact that was clearly demonstrated by the 140 briefs on education presented to the Tremblay Commission on Quebec's constitutional problems (1953–55). Over fifty organizations also participated in a highly publicized provincial conference on educational reform in June 1958 to deal with such urgent problems as the low participation rate of Francophones at the secondary and postsecondary levels, the abysmal lack of funding at all levels, the persistence of undemocratic structures and procedures, poorly qualified and underpaid teachers, and finally, the total lack of co-ordination between the various levels.[49]

Neo-nationalists, led by the work of Arthur Tremblay, a Laval education specialist and the moving force behind the 1958 conference, supported raising the compulsory age of attendance from fourteen to sixteen to ensure that French Canadians were better prepared to face the demands of the work world and to pursue, if qualified, further education at the postsecondary level.[50] Neo-nationalists also wanted school boards and the Conseil de l'Instruction publique to become fully secularized and democratized — all lay members were to be elected by universal suffrage.[51] They also came to realize that French-Canada's private secondary and postsecondary system of classical colleges was totally inadequate to serve the needs of a modern society. Unlike the *Citélibristes* who wanted to scrap the system in its entirety, the neo-nationalists wanted to make the classical Latin-science curriculum available to all qualified students through a network of secular, state-supported regional high schools. This would democratize access to secondary education and provide the universities with well-prepared recruits for the science and social science faculties and the professional schools. Only in this manner could French Canada provide itself with a modern, secular middle class capable of managing the apparatus of an interventionist state, and thereby gain control over Quebec's foreign-dominated economy.[52]

Much of the reform at the primary and secondary levels was dependent on the modernization of Quebec's three French-language universities run by the church. Well-funded, dynamic, secular Francophone universities were seen by neo-nationalists as a *sine qua non* for the flourishing of an autonomous Québécois nationality.[53] Neo-nationalists in the late 1950s still remained cautious about demanding the reinstatement of a ministry of education for fear of arousing the wrath of the church, thereby endangering the growing consensus for reform at the other levels. Laurendeau recommended in 1960 that the newly elected Liberal government of Jean Lesage establish a Royal Commission to investigate all aspects of education and prepare the groundwork for long overdue reforms.[54] Lesage agreed and created the Parent Commission, named after its neo-nationalist chairman, Monsignor Alphonse-Marie Parent, former rector of Laval. With Filion and Arthur Tremblay appointed to the Commission, neo-nationalists were in an excellent position to influence the direction of education reform in contemporary Quebec.

Inevitably, the neo-nationalists' campaign for a dynamic, interventionist nation-state was to have serious implications for their perception of Quebec's role within the Canadian federal system. Their initial reaction was to demand that Ottawa respect the provincial and cultural compacts nationalists argued were inherent in the British North America Act of 1867. In due course they came to feel that fundamental constitutional revisions to entrench the equality of the French-Canadian nation and to accommodate the urgent requirements of the "new" Quebec were imperative.

This shift was consolidated by two full-scale battles between Ottawa and Quebec over taxing powers and education. The first struggle entailed the Duplessis government's rejection of the tax-rental scheme Premier Godbout had signed in 1942, and which expired in 1947. While Duplessis refused to sign a new agreement, his government also refused to take any decisive action to counter this fiscal centralization. The neo-nationalists campaigned aggressively for the province to exercise its taxing powers by imposing a personal income tax. This action would produce one of two effects. The federal government might conceivably allow Quebec citizens to deduct their provincial tax from their federal tax or Ottawa could choose to reduce its personal tax level by an amount equivalent to the provincial tax. If Ottawa refused to budge, Quebec's politicians could effectively blame it for imposing double taxation.

Thanks to the co-ordinated efforts of the neo-nationalists, the Chambre de Commerce de la Province de Québec, and the Chambre de Commerce de Montréal, the Tremblay Commission was able to persuade a very reluctant Duplessis to implement a provincial income tax in 1954. When the federal government agreed after several months of turmoil to share in a very small way the personal income tax field, the neo-nationalists were elated.[55] As subsequent events demonstrated, Ottawa's decision marked the effective demise of the tax-rental system and the beginning of a new era of fiscal sharing. While Duplessis refused to press his hard-won advantage, the neo-nationalists, having seen their strategy of aggressive provincial autonomy reinforced by success, expressed the view that this was merely the beginning. Just think, they wondered out loud, what the province could accomplish if its political leaders subscribed wholeheartedly to a policy of state-building!

The second issue to arouse the ire of nationalists, old and new, was the federal government's decision to provide direct grants to universities as recommended by the Report of the Royal Commission on National Development in the Arts, Letters, and Science (1951). The scheme was a direct challenge to the neo-nationalists' campaign to develop a dynamic Quebec state because it involved the federal government in an area of provincial jurisdiction. That area, education, was considered sacred to the survival and development of a distinct French-Canadian nationality. No national minority could allow central government bureaucrats and politicians, who mostly represented the values and aspirations of Canada's English-speaking majority, to control its educational institutions. In the words of the Ligue d'Action Nationale and Michel Brunet, Quebec City, not Ottawa, was the capital of the French-Canadian nation.[56] The Duplessis government accepted the federal grants for 1951–52, but the vociferous reaction of all nationalists forced it to reject all future subsidy proposals of the federal government. Neo-nationalists kept pressuring the Duplessis administration to put its money where its mouth was and start providing the necessary financial support to Quebec's hard-pressed universities, especially the Francophone universities, which were facing rapidly increasing enrolments and enduring antiquated and totally inadequate facilities. They proposed that Ottawa, as an alternative, provide Quebec with a larger slice of direct taxes, personal or corporate, or increase the province's equalization grant by two million dollars. Pressure could then be put on Duplessis to spend this money on postsecondary education.[57] In fact, after several years of wrangling and continued poverty for Quebec's Francophone universities, the first proposal was precisely the solution that Ottawa and Quebec adopted after lengthy negotiations between Premiers Paul Sauvé and Jean Lesage and the Diefenbaker government.

The significance of these federal-provincial disputes was that they prompted neo-nationalists to consider seriously the need to revise the constitution. Two constitutional options emerged. The Ligue d'Action Nationale in its brief to the Tremblay Commission, authored by Jean-Marc Léger, proposed the creation of a highly decentralized confederal system in which the provinces had expanded prerogatives, including all residual powers, while the central government retained only limited and specific economic, military, and political responsibilities. Maximum decentralization was imperative if the French-Canadian nation, which had its homeland in Quebec, was going to survive and achieve equality with the English-Canadian nation.[58] The second option was proposed by the Société Saint-Jean-Baptiste de Montréal in its brief, authored by Michel Brunet, to the Tremblay Commission. Since it appeared that English Canadians considered Ottawa to be their national government, it was not likely that they would support a highly decentralized system. If the French-Canadian nation, in its view, was to survive and achieve equality, it required its own highly autonomous nation-state. That state could be none other than Quebec. A revised constitution had to recognize the "special role" of Quebec by granting it greater taxing powers than other Canadian provinces as well as complete control over all social security, health, education, and cultural responsibilities. In short, Quebec required a constitutionally entrenched "special status."[59] The Tremblay Report sanctioned both of these proposals while suggesting a couple of practical methods of moving toward greater fiscal decentralized and provincial control over all social programs. To facilitate intergovernmental relations, the commissioners proposed the creation of a Federal-Provincial Relations Secretariat and a Permanent Council of the Provinces.[60]

Laurendeau and Filion strongly favoured the special-status option, and *Le Devoir* would become, in the 1960s, one of the most strident voices for a renewed constitution entrenching this special status. The emergence of a bureaucratic middle class intent on establishing its control over the urban/industrial French-Canadian society had focussed considerable attention on the powers and prerogatives of the Quebec state. It was only a matter of time before some members of this new middle class would begin to question the serious constraints of federalism and North American monopoly capitalism.

Parti pris: Quest for a Socialist and Independent Quebec

The Quiet Revolution of the 1960s symbolized more than a political changing of the guard from the conservative, rural notables of the Union Nationale to the progressive, urban technocrats of the Liberal team of Jean Lesage. For many young French Canadians it marked the end of the *ancien régime* and the beginning of a cultural and ideological revolution whereby a new intelligentsia, with the support of a progressive middle class, would bring about a wholesale social revolution. Just as the *Cité libre* and neo-nationalist movements had developed, in part, as response to the policies and practices of the Duplessis regime, the various movements for an independent and socialist Quebec were, to a large degree, a response to the perceived shortcomings of liberal neo-nationalism and its proponents, the Liberal Party. The Rassemblement pour l'indépendance nationale (RIN), created in September 1960 as a political movement, became a centre-left political party in March 1963 under the leadership of Pierre Bourgault. While right-wing separatist groups also flourished — the Alliance Laurentienne (1957), the Parti Républicain du Québec (1962), and the Ralliement Nationale (1964) — it was the combination of secessionist nationalism and socialism that provided the most innovative and politically challenging ideological development of the 1960s.

In 1963–64 three periodicals, *Parti pris*, *Socialisme*, and *Révolution québécoise*, appeared on the scene to articulate and disseminate the ideology of socialist nationalism. *Parti pris* proved to be the most dynamic and influential of the three because of the composition of its editorial team and its strong neo-nationalist orientation. The five founders of *Parti pris*, Pierre Maheu, Jean-Marc Piotte, Paul Chamberland, André Brochu, and André Major, were all in their early twenties. All except Major, the poet, were university-educated and were heavily influenced by the socialist-nationalist theories pertaining to the decolonization movement of the Third-World countries, such as Frantz Fanon's *Les damnés de la terre* (1961), Albert Memmi's *Portrait du Colonisé* (1957), and Jacques Bergue's work on Arab countries.[61]

Parti pris militants and ideologues set themselves the challenge of creating an independent, secular, and socialist Quebec.[62] The tremendous difficulties of reconciling the "class" imperatives of their socialism with the "nationalist" imperatives of their commitment to independence for the Québécois nation plagued *Parti pris* throughout the entire five-year period of its existence. *Parti pris* members were caught in a dilemma not entirely of their own making. A genuine working-class consciousness did not, as of the mid-1960s, exist among the vast majority of French-Canadians workers, as was clearly demonstrated by the lack of political success of the Parti socialiste du Québec or the Quebec wing of the

New Democratic Party. Quebec's labour leaders were simply unable or unwilling to ensure that unionists would vote for a working-class party devoted to a socialist and independent Quebec. Socialism had been anathema to the French-Canadian society for several generations. Nationalism, on the other hand, had been part of the ideological and political landscape since the early nineteenth century. In the 1960s and 1970s, neo-nationalism dominated the political, cultural, and social environment even to the point of becoming, perhaps for the first time, a genuine mass, as opposed to a middle-class, ideology. This historical development helps to explain, in part, why nationalism prevailed so easily over socialism in the *Parti pris* elaboration of its ideas and its strategy of political action.[63]

The commitment to political independence for Quebec was paramount. Relying on the revisionist work of the neo-nationalist historians at the Université de Montréal, *Parti pris* members argued that the Québécois nation had become, since the Conquest of 1760, a colonized nation, first by Great Britain and then by English Canada. This imperialism had debilitating and destructive effects on the French-Canadian people such as creating a deep sense of inferiority and alienation.[64] Only complete political independence would destroy the persistent colonial subordination of the French-Canadian nation by the English-Canadian nation.[65] It was imperative, given the Marxist view of society elaborated by *Parti pris*, that the national revolution not be controlled and monopolized by the neo-bourgeoisie to create a powerful national bourgeoisie that would merely perpetuate the exploitation of the working class under new political structures. French-Canadian workers could achieve complete decolonization of themselves and their society only if the political revolution was followed by an economic and social revolution.[66]

The *Parti pris* assessment of the nature and extent of the social reforms required in Quebec was based on a neo-nationalist rather than a socialist interpretation of the crisis facing their society. Following the theory of several Quebec sociologists, *Parti pris* viewed the French-Canadian society essentially as a proletarian nation — an ethnic class — because the exploited and dominated French-Canadian working class constituted the vast majority of the French-Canadian nation.[67] The French-Canadian bourgeoisie, old and new, was weak and ineffectual and, largely, beholden to the dominant Anglophone community for its minor political, social, and economic privileges. Given this reality, it was only natural that French-Canadian workers, in attempting to come to grips with their sense of alienation and inferiority, did so in ethnic rather than class terms.[68] The struggle for the survival of the French-Canadian national culture — essentially a working-class culture — entailed, according to the *Parti pris* manifesto of 1965–66, an overthrow of the Anglo-Canadian and American colonial and capitalist dominations, which had brought a foreign "mass culture" to Quebec.[69] In an independent Quebec, the working class could secularize all institutions and end the negative effects of an authoritarian Catholicism on the family and the individual. It could also ensure that education at all levels served the needs of the working people rather than the interest of the bourgeoisies. Finally, the working class could create the institutions needed to develop a genuine and humanistic Québécois culture, one allowing for the achievement of an individual's full potential within the framework of the nation.[70]

The *Parti pris* assessments of industrial capitalism and the role of the state were also influenced by its neo-nationalist outlook rather than by a genuine socialist analysis. Quebec had a neo-capitalist industrialized economy that exploited and alienated workers, but this had not created a class reaction. Instead, it had fostered a sense of greater ethnic cleavage, especially among ambitious middle-class professionals, managers, industrialists, and businesspeople because the development of the provinces's natural resources and a large part of the manufacturing sector were controlled by foreigners. Quebec's economy was underdeveloped because it relied on the export of primary products and the importation of manufactured goods, thus ensuring that the standard of living was considerably lower for French Canadians than for Canadians in general.[71] Finally, the existing system of neo-capitalism fostered a petty-bourgeois business unionism that concentrated on economic gains while refusing to develop a working-class consciousness and a working-class party. Hence, the unions were not in position to lead either the national or the social revolutions.[72] The Quebec state, argued *Parti pris*, was controlled by a ruling class comprising a foreign bourgeoisie and a subservient French-Canadian neo-bourgeoisie. The increased role of the Quebec state in the 1960s, such as the nationalization of hydro-electricity and the modernization of the education system, served primarily the interests of the foreign bourgeoisie by creating better-educated workers. The process also enhanced the political power of, and job opportunities for, the French-Canadian neo-bourgeoisie, which controlled the state apparatus.[73]

Parti pris, nevertheless, rejected the logic of its fairly crude Marxian analysis of Quebec society. Instead, its neo-nationalism brought it to argue that its priority was to achieve independence because, with the use of the modern state being established in Quebec by the bureaucratic middle class, it would be possible to create a new society. Chamberland contended that the French-Canadian petty bourgeoisie lacked internal cohesion. This would enable the working class to gain control eventually of the state and use it as a tool for its own liberation.[74] This meant, of course, that *Parti pris* would, for what it argued were tactical and strategic reasons, support all reformist elements of the new petty bourgeoisie that supported the cause of independence. The acquisition of an independent, democratic, and bourgeois state was a great gain because it allowed the working class to conquer "selon le mot de Marx, *le terrain de la lutte*."[75]

By the summer of 1965 it appeared that the thrust had gone out of the Quiet Revolution as the conservative forces within the Liberal government were gaining the upper hand. It also appeared to some members of the *Parti pris* that organzied labour was finally becoming militant and even showing signs of political action. They formed the Mouvement de Libération populaire, developed a "minimum" program that would appeal to the working class, and joined forces in March 1966 with the Parti Socialiste du Québec (PSQ) to contest unsuccessfully a handful of seats in the 1966 provincial election. The PSQ was lukewarm at best on the issue of independence and the projected ties with organized labour never materialized.[76] *Parti pris* quickly abandoned its support for the PSQ. Piotte, in the fall of 1966, called for a return to the former strategy of revolution by stages, that is, a tactical support for the progressive wing of the French-Canadian petty bourgeoisie.[77] Other members, including Gabriel Gagnon, Luc Racine, and Gilles

Bourque, disagreed strongly with this strategy. Any attempt to consolidate the power of the French-Canadian petty bourgeoisie would, they maintained, be suicidal for all socialist groups and would undermine any chance of building a genuine socialist labour party.[78]

The "independence first" faction, led by Piotte, retained the upper hand in this ideological dispute. Since the Liberal Party was out of office, and its progressive wing had abandoned it, *Parti pris* decided to support the RIN, a petty-bourgeois party devoted to an independent, socialist Quebec.[79] In the fall of 1968, the RIN was swallowed up in the vortex of the newly created Parti Québécois, and this reopened the ideological crisis within the *Parti pris*. The socialist faction led by Bourque and Racine rejected the concept of sovereignty-association because it denied both the socialist and nationalist revolutions and they decided to quit *Parti pris* in the summer of 1968.[80] The neo-nationalist faction defended the strategy of "independence first" and joined forces with the emerging Parti Québécois. *Parti pris* disappeared from the scene, a victim of the ideological struggle between left-wing neo-nationalists who gave their priority to independence and the ardent socialists who wanted to achieve their revolution through a working-class party founded on a militant organized labour movement.

The Impact of Ideological Renewal

By the mid-1960s, the ideological landscape of Quebec was certainly a lot more pluralistic and complex than had been the case some thirty years earlier. This was largely a reflection of the expansion and diversification of the Francophone middle class. Each sector of this new middle class — public- and private-sector middle managers and administrators, unionized professionals and semi-professionals, and organized labour leaders — developed its own particular ideological outlook to attain control over the levers of power represented by the recently expanded state. The three groups represented the neo-liberal, the social-democratic, and the socialist wings of the new middle class. Nevertheless, these three groups overlapped considerably depending on what issues were being debated.

The ideological evolution of the Catholic labour movement demonstrates well the impact of changing socio-economic and political structures. Thanks to *Cité libre*, welfare-state liberalism found a small but vocal intelligentsia willing and able to articulate and disseminate a societal model based on neo-liberal assumptions and tenets. Under the influence of liberal social Catholicism and encouraged by *Cité libre* activists, the Catholic labour movement abandoned its long-standing commitment to social corporatism and campaigned for the establishment of industrial democracy in Quebec through a system of co-management, profit-sharing, and co-ownership of industry. The emphasis was placed on the democratization and humanization of the workplace as a prelude to the democratization and humanization of contemporary society.[81] This step was particularly important because it encouraged the Catholic labour movement, led by Gérard Picard and Jean Marchand, to come to terms with the welfare state and, by 1958, to support the creation of national hospitalization and medicare systems administered concurrently by Ottawa and the provinces.[82]

The Catholic labour movement's commitment to neo-liberalism was also symbolized by the gradual secularization of its outlook and its operations during the 1940s and 1950s. This process culminated by 1960 in the adoption of a new set of principles and a new name, Confédération des syndicats nationaux (CSN). During the first half of the 1960s, the CSN actively supported the Liberal administration's reforms of the social service systems, the provincial bureaucracy, the political institutions and process, and the labour code, as well as its attempts to gain control over the Quebec economy through government planning, regional economic development, and direct intervention, such as nationalization of the private hydro-electric companies after the 1962 election.[83]

While the Lesage government was no doubt motivated by its commitment to the creation of a liberal democratic society, the most pervasive and influential ideological force behind the Quiet Revolution proved to be neo-nationalism because the various sectors of the new middle class quickly perceived that if the modernization of Quebec society was accomplished by the state under the aegis of nationalist goals and aspirations, it was imperative to gain firm control over the levers of power. Only then would the new middle class, or at least one segment of it, emerge as the dominant social class, displacing the traditional Francophone petty bourgeoisie, the church, and, it might be hoped, the Anglo-Canadian and American bourgeoisies who controlled the economy. Neo-nationalism was a perfect ideology to appeal to the masses for the political support essential in a system of parliamentary democracy. Moreover, the emergence of a powerful new class (and the internal struggle between its various elements) was camouflaged by the rhetoric of collective rights and aspirations.

By the mid-1960s, disenchantment set in over the limitations of the Quiet Revolution. The three groups of the new middle class parted ways. The public-sector managers and administrators, the unionized professionals whose power was based on knowledge, and the private-sector petty bourgeoisie and emerging Francophone bourgeoisie clashed over the issue of political sovereignty for Quebec as well as over the question of the kind of society that should be created in Quebec — a neo-capitalist welfare state or a decentralized social-democratic society with a high degree of public ownership of important sectors of the economy. After the Liberal defeat in 1966, René Lévesque led a small radical wing out of the party and created the Mouvement Souveraineté-Association, which several months later became the Parti Québécois. The Parti Québécois articulated the national and social vision of the middle-class technocrats, bureaucrats, and professionals — the men of knowledge, such as Deputy Minister of Education Arthur Tremblay, Deputy Minister of Intergovernmental Relations Claude Morin, and economist Jacques Parizeau. These state managers and professionals formed part of a bureaucracy that expanded dramatically in the 1960s, from 2,103 professionals in 1964 to 4,646 in 1971. The vast majority were committed to using the powers of a politically independent Quebec state to create a modern Québécois society controlled increasingly by them.[84]

After considerable wrangling, the Quebec Liberal Party of Jean Lesage, who was replaced by Robert Bourassa in 1970, rejected both the special-status and sovereignty-association options and argued for a strong Quebec within a renewed federal system. The various Anglophone and Francophone private-sector bour-geoisies that supported the Liberal Party wanted no further economic expansion of the Quebec state. Bourassa agreed and put the emphasis on encouraging the private sector to create urgently needed jobs for the fastest growing labour force in the western world. Increasingly under pressure from neo-nationalists in all quarters, Bourassa introduced language legislation, known as Bill 22, that made French the official language of the province, limited the choice of schooling of new Quebeckers, and encouraged the use of French in the work world. These measures, it was felt, would help stem the integration of immigrants into the Anglophone community and would in time open the English-dominated sectors of the economy to newly educated Francophones. Bourassa, encouraged by his party's landslide victory in 1973, pursued these policies until his government was defeated by the Parti Québécois on 15 November 1976.[85]

Organized labour also became increasingly disenchanted with what it consid-ered to be the petty-bourgeois limitations of the Quiet Revolution. The recently expanded public and para-public unions, most of them affiliated with the CSN, found the bourgeois-dominated governments, be they Union Nationale or Liberal, to be extremely hard-nosed, even provocative, in negotiations. After 1968, organ-ized labour found itself confronting what some others have called the coercive or disciplinary state.[86] Of course, the emergence of a socialist-imbued, neo-nationalist intelligentsia, albeit fractious and immature, helped to create an ideological and psychological climate conducive to the radicalization of the labour movement.

Both Quebec centrals, the CSN and the FTQ (Fédération des travailleurs du Québec), responded to these circumstances by adopting a neo-Marxist interpre-tation of the working class's continued exploitation and subordination. The CSN, in its 1971 pamphlet *Ne comptons que sur nos propres moyens*, denounced the powerful American economic elite—supported by its Anglo- and French-Canadian compradors—that controlled the federal and provincial governments. The CSN and its fiery president, Marcel Pépin, called upon the workers to carry out a program of co-ordinated direct action to overthrow the existing neo-capitalist system and establish a democratic socialist society in Quebec. The FTQ, not wanting to be left behind in the struggle for new members, and under the leader-ship of the dynamic Louis Laberge, followed the road to democratic socialism after 1965. In its 1971 pamphlet *L'État, rouage de notre exploitation*, the FTQ denounced the bourgeois liberal states, federal and provincial, for serving primarily the interests of American economic imperialists and of the English- and French-speaking bourgeoisies. The bourgeois liberal state confiscated public capital and transformed it into private capital, thus reinforcing all forms of exploitive capitalism. In 1971 Laberge called for a Common Front (*Un seul front*) of all progressive forces to liberate Quebec society from the bondage of neo-capitalism and the bourgeois liberal state and to create a democratic socialist society.[87]

The CSN and the FTQ leaders organized a general strike of over 200,000 public and para-public workers in the spring of 1972. The Common Front cam-paigned for an expansion of the collective bargaining parameters — the right to negotiate at a central table the amount of the government budget to be devoted to salaries. In particular, the Common Front wanted a minimum wage of $100 per week for all public employees. The Bourassa government stonewalled the labour leaders with delays, court injunctions, and finally, Bill 19, which forced all public-sector employees back to work. The leaders, Pépin, Laberge, and Yvan Charbonneau (then president of the Centrale des Enseignants du Québec), advocated civil disobedience of the Bill—for which they were later charged and jailed—but the Common Front disintegrated as the majority of strikers returned to work. While the CSN lost some members over the strike, the general outcome was the further radicalization of labour's ideological outlook and a toughening of its resolve to gain greater powers.[88]

Public-sector bargaining became the central focus of conflict between competing elements of the new Francophone middle class. By the mid-1970s, organized labour leaders and militants felt that perhaps public-sector negotiations might become more successful if the incumbent Liberal government of Bourassa was replaced by the Parti Québécois. While the CSN refused to endorse officially the PQ, the FTQ decided to support the party, despite the fact that the PQ was not a working-class but rather a petty-bourgeois party. Laberge proposed to radicalize the PQ from within. In reality, the force of neo-nationalism and a common class interest were slowly eroding organized labour's distrust of the bourgeois state. An internal class conflict, reflected in divergent ideological perspectives, was being overshadowed by an ethnic conflict as reflected in the struggle over language and the role of the Québécois nation within the Canadian federal system.

Conclusion

The relationship between social transformation and ideological renewal was, in the case of Quebec, quite direct. *Cité libre*'s liberalism, *Le Devoir*'s and *l'Action nationale*'s neo-nationalism, and *Parti pris*' socialist neo-nationalism articulated the aspirations of various wings of the new Francophone middle class. In time, Quebec's political parties came to represent some of these divergent ideologies. But the re-emergence of an ethnic conflict between this new middle class and the Anglophone economic elite that controlled Quebec's economy fuelled the fires of neo-nationalism and camouflaged the internal struggle over which sector of this middle class was going to control the power levers of the newly expanded state. The Lesage Liberal Party made a valiant attempt to bring liberals and neo-nationalists together, but the latter gained the upper hand, forcing such *Citélibristes* as Pierre Trudeau and Gérard Pelletier to turn to the national Liberal Party to fight separatism and restore democracy to Quebec. After the Liberal defeat in 1966, those neo-nationalists favouring political independence for Quebec followed René Lévesque out of the party and helped found the Parti Québécois, a party committed to political independence and the creation of a social-democratic society in Quebec under the aegis of a Francophone bureaucratic and technocratic middle class that controlled the state. Even CSN and FTQ labour leaders and militants, committed ostensibly to socialism, eventually supported the "petty-bourgeois" Parti Québécois and helped it defeat the Liberal Party of Bourassa.

The question that some authors have been asking is, "Were the real needs of the people being served by this process of political modernization, symbolized by the Quiet Revolution, which has been underway in Quebec since the defeat of the Union Nationale in 1960?''[89] The answer to the question is at best a qualified yes for some and a categorical no for others. Most commentators remain cautiously optimistic. A dynamic, creative, and increasingly autonomous Quebec will survive and prosper, argues one social critic, if the various elements of the new middle class recognize and set aside their self-serving ways and a new pragmatic collective ethic comes to prevail.[90] Others feel that neo-nationalism, as demonstrated by the defeat of the sovereignty-association option in the 1980 referendum, is on the wane while liberalism and individualism are once again back in vogue throughout much of Quebec society, including the new middle class.[91] While no one can predict the final outcome of what has been a very complex process of social change, ideological renewal, and incessant struggle for political hegemony, it is always helpful to try to understand a little better the historical process of change and continuity.

Notes

1. Gérard Filion, "Un avertissement sévère," *Le Devoir*, 9 janvier 1954.

2. *Annuaire du Québec, 1974*, 226, tableau 3.

3. Kenneth McRoberts and Dale Posgate, *Quebec: Social Change and Political Crisis* (Toronto, 1980), 52, table 7.

4. Jean Hamelin and Jean-Paul Montminy, "La mutation de la société québécoise, 1939–1976. Temps, ruptures, continuités" in Fernand Dumont et al., *Idéologies au Canada français 1940–1976* (Quebec, 1981), I: 34–5.

5. McRoberts and Posgate, *Quebec*, 40–3.

6. *Report of the Royal Commission on Bilingualism and Biculturalism* (Ottawa, 1969), IIIB: 23.

7. F. Vaillancourt, "La situation démographique et socio-économique des francophones du Québec: une revue," *Canadian Public Policy* 5 (Autumn 1979): 542–52.

8. Hubert Guindon, "Social Unrest, Social Class and Quebec's Bureaucratic Revolution," *Queen's Quarterly* 71 (1964), 153.

9. Pierre Dandurand and Marcel Fournier, "Développement de l'enseignement supérieur, classes sociales et luttes nationale au Québec," *Sociologie et société* 12 (avril 1980): 103–7.

10. Michael Behiels, "Le père Georges-Henri Lévesque et l'établissement des sciences sociales à Laval, 1938–1955," *Revue de l'Université d'Ottawa/University of Ottawa Quarterly* 52 (juillet–septembre 1982): 355–76.

11. Arthur Tremblay, *Les Collèges et les écoles publiques. Conflict ou coordination?* (Quebec, 1954), 11–12, 15–18.

12. Jacques Brazeau, "Quebec's Emerging Middle Class" in *French-Canadian Society*, edited by Marcel Rioux and Yves Martin (Toronto, 1964), 322.

13. Hubert Guindon, "The Social Evolution of Quebec Reconsidered" in *French-Canadian Society*, 157–8.

14. Jacques Brazeau, "Les nouvelles classes moyennes," *Recherches sociographiques* 7 (janvier–août 1966), 157.

15. Yves Roby, *Les Québécois et les investissements américains (1918–1929)* (Quebec, 1976), 207–20.

16. Gérard Pelletier, "Trois paroles d'Emmanuel Mounier," *Cité libre* 3 (mai 1951): 45–6.

17. Jean LeMoyne, "L'atmosphère religieuse au Canada français," *Cité libre* 12 (mai 1955): 1–12; Maurice Blain, "Sur la liberté de l'esprit," *Esprit* 20 (août–septembre 1952): 243–4.

18. Gérard Pelletier, "Crise d'autorité ou crise de liberté," *Cité libre* 5 (juin–juillet 1952): 6–7.

19. Jean LeMoyne, "Jeunesse de l'homme," *Cité libre* 2 (février 1951): 10–12; Pierre Vadeboncoeur, "Réflexions sur la foi," ibid., 12 (mai 1955), 21.

20. Vadeboncoeur, "Réflexions sur la foi," 3–4; Pierre Elliott Trudeau, "Matériaux pour servir à une enquête sur la cléricalisme I," *Cité libre* 7 (mai 1953): 31–2.

21. Pierre Elliott Trudeau, "La province de Québec au moment de la grève," in *La grève de l'amiante* (Montreal, 1979), 19–37.

22. Pierre Vadeboncoeur, "L'irréalisme de notre culture," *Cité libre* 4 (décembre 1951): 20–1; M. Rioux, "Idéologie et crise de conscience du Canada français," ibid., 14 (décembre 1955): 3–14.

23. Trudeau, "La province de Québec," 14–37, 88.

24. This theme was developed primarily by Trudeau with the full support of his colleagues: "Réflexions sur la politique au Canada français," *Cité libre* 6 (décembre 1952): 53–7; "Some Obstacles to Democracy in Quebec," *Canadian Journal of Economics and Political Science* 24 (August 1958), reprinted in *Federalism and the French Canadians*, 103–23.

25. Trudeau, "Un manifest démocratique," *Cité libre* 22 (octobre 1958), 2–29.

26. Léon Lortie et al., in *L'éducation* (Rapport de la troisième conférence annuelle de l'Institut canadien des affairs publique, 1956).

27. Ibid.; Gérard Pelletier, "Visite aux supérieurs I–III," *Le Devoir*, 11–12 janvier 1949; Roger Rolland, "La lettre contre l'esprit. Un témoignage sur l'enseignement secondaire, I–III," ibid., 13, 20, 27 septembre 1952; M. Rioux, "Remarques sur l'éducation et la culture canadienne-française," *Cité libre* 8 (novembre 1953): 40–2.

28. P. Charbonneau, "Défense et illustration de la gauche," *Cité libre* 18 (1958): 37–9.

29. Pierre Elliott Trudeau, "*Le Devoir* doit il préparer ses lectures au socialisme?" *Le Devoir*, 2 fevrier 1955; "Les Canadiens français rateront (encore une fois) le tournant . . .," ibid., 29 janvier 1960.

30. Maurice Lamontagne, *Le fédéralisme canadien: évolution et problèmes* (Quebec, 1954).

31. Pierre Elliott Trudeau, "De libro, tributo et quibusdam aliis," *Cité libre* (octobre 1954), reprinted in *Federalism and the French Canadians*, 63–78.

32. Trudeau, "Federal Grants to Universities," *Cité libre* (février 1957), reprinted in *Federalism and the French Canadians*, 79–102.

33. Trudeau, "La nouvelle trahison des clercs," *Cité libre* 46 (avril 1962): 3–16; "Les separatists: des contre-révolutionnaires," ibid., 67 (mai 1964): 2–6.

34. André Laurendeau, "Y a-t-il une crise du nationalisme? I," *Action Nationale* (cited hereafter as *AN*) 40 (décembre 1952), 208.

35. Richard Jones, *Duplessis and the Union Nationale Administration* (Ottawa, 1983), 12–17, and reprinted in this volume.

36. André Laurendeau, "Le quatrième état dans la nation," *AN* 30 (octobre 1947): 83–8.

37. Laurendeau, "Conclusions très provisoires," *AN* 31 (juin 1948): 414–16; "Y a-t-il une crise du nationalisme? I," 215–17.

38. Jean-Marc Léger, d'Iberville Fortier, Pierre Lefebvre, and Camille Laurin, "L'ennemi dans nos murs," *AN* 31 (fevrier 1948), 107.

39. G. Dion and J. Pelchat, "Repenser le nationalisme," *AN* 31 (juin 1948): 408–11; C. Ryan, "Le sens du national dans les milieux populaires," *AN* 31 (mars 1948): 171–3; J.-P. Robillard, "Pour un nationalisme social," *AN* 31 (avril 1948): 286–8; Laurendeau, "Conclusions très provisoires," 413–24.

40. Jean-Marc Léger, "Le Canada français à la recherche de son avenir," *Esprit* 20 (septembre 1952), 261.

41. Léger, "Urgence d'une doctrine nationale," *AN* 46 (octobre 1956): 137–8.

42. Gérard Filion, "Une double tentation," *Le Devoir*, 12 mai 1954.

43. Jean-Marc Léger, *Notre situation économique: progrès ou stagnation* (Montreal, 1957), 1–21. Studies for the Royal Commission on Bilingualism and Biculturalism based on the 1961 census data confirmed the economic inferiority of French Canadians as individuals as well as the desperate plight of the Francophone private sector (*Report*, IIIB: 11–60).

44. Roland Parenteau, "Quelques raisons de la faiblesse économique de la nation canadienne-française," *AN* 45 (décembre 1955): 320–5; Laporte, "L'enjeu: notre survivance ou notre disparition," *Le Devoir*, 23 août 1957.

45. Cf. Dale Miquelon, ed., *Society and Conquest: The Debate on the Bourgeoisie and Social Change in French Canada, 1700–1850* (Toronto, 1977).

46. Gérard Filion, "La reprise de nos richesses naturelles," *Le Devoir*, 25 novembre 1953; Paul Sauriol, "Entre la servitude économique et la nationalisation," ibid., 20 octobre 1958.

47. Pierre Laporte, "Une province que se contente des miettes I–VIII," *Le Devoir*, 24–25, 27–30 janvier, 1, 3 février 1958.

48. Paul Sauriol, "*Le Devoir* et la libération de notre groupe," *Le Devoir*, 29 janvier 1960; André Laurendeau, "A l'heure des réformes," ibid., 15 mars 1958.

49. Cf. Jean-Louis Roy, *La marche des Québécois: le temps des ruptures (1945–1960)* (Montreal, 1976), 245–308.

50. Arthur Tremblay, "La conjoncture actuelle de l'éducation," in *L'éducation au Québec face au problèmes contemporains* (Saint-Hyacinthe, 1958), 39–40.

51. Gérard Filion, "Crise scolaire," *Le Devoir*, 26 novembre 1955; "Il ne faut pas faire des éveques des boucs émissaires," ibid., 9 novembre 1960.

52. Filion, "Il faut des techniciens, on nous donne des plaideurs," *Le Devoir*, 1 juin 1955; André Laurendeau, "Le cours classique à l'école publique," ibid., 25 avril 1955.

53. Laurendeau, "Premier but: l'université," *Le Devoir*, 10 juin 1955; "Où va le Canada français? XIII," ibid., 21 mai 1959.

54. Laurendeau, "Pour une enquête royale sur l'éducation," *Le Devoir*, 15 novembre 1960.

55. Gérard Filion, "Le fédéralisme canadien I–IV," *Le Devoir*, 21–24 juillet 1954; "Un accord, non une capitulation," ibid., 29 février 1956.

56. Ligue d'Action Nationale, "Conditions d'un État Français dans la Confédération canadienne. Mémoire à la Commission royale d'enquête sur les relations fédérales-provinciales," *AN* 43 (mars–avril 1954): 312–16.

57. Gérard Filion, "L'aide fédérale à l'enseignement III," *Le Devoir*, 1 avril 1952; "Le devoir du Québec envers ses universités," ibid., 27 octobre 1956; "L'aide fédérale aux universités," ibid., 13 octobre 1956.

58. Ligue d'Action Nationale, "Conditions d'un État Français," 328–44.

59. Société Saint-Jean Baptiste de Montréal, *Canada français et union canadienne* (Montreal, 1954), 54–125.

60. *Tremblay Report*, III, Book 2, 227–8, 233–7, 255–72, 294–5.

61. Pierrette Bouchard-Saint-Amant, "L'idéologie de la revue *Parti pris*: le nationalisme socialiste," in *Idéologies au Canada français 1940–1976*, I: 315–17; Roch Denis, *Lutte des classes et question nationale au Québec 1948–1968* (Montreal, 1979), 359–62.

62. "Présentation," *Parti pris* 1 (octobre 1963): 2–3.

63. Bouchard-Saint-Amant, "L'idéologie de la revue *Parti pris*," 317–19. The author argues that the *Parti pris* demise can be explained by the review's inability to develop a rigorous theory of the relationship between social classes and the nation. Nationalism and socialism, in her view, can only be reconciled if they are both authentic products of the working class.

64. Paul Chamberland, "De la domination à la liberté," *Parti pris* 1 (juin–août 1964): 64–81; Pierre Maheau, "L'oedipe colonial," ibid., 20.

65. Chamberland, "Aliénation culturelle et révolution nationale," *Parti pris* 1 (novembre 1963): 15–16.

66. "Manifeste 65–66," *Parti pris* 3 (septembre 1965): 7–41; "Jean Lesage et l'État béquille," ibid., 2 (février 1965), 4; Chamberland, "Aliénation culturelle," 16.

67. Jacques Dofny and Marcel Rioux, "Les classes sociales au Canada français," *Revue française de sociologie* 3 (juillet–septembre 1962): 290–300; Guy Rocher, "Les recherches sur les occupations et la stratification," *Recherches sociographiques* 3 (1962): 183–4.

68. Jean-Marc Piotte, "Sens et limites du néo-nationalisme," *Parti pris* 4 (septembre–octobre 1966), 29; Pierre Maheau, "Québec politique," ibid., 5 (avril 1968), 11.

69. "Manifeste 65–66," 17.

70. Pierre Maheu, "Le dieu canadien-français," *Parti pris* 4 (novembre–décembre 1966): 46–8; "Le rapport Parent," ibid., 2 (mars 1965), 7.

71. Maheu, "Que faire?" *Parti pris* 2 (mars 1965), 54; Piotte, "Sens et limites," 28.

72. "Manifeste 65–66," 20.

73. Ibid., 16; Piotte, "Ou allons-nous?" *Parti pris* 3 (août–septembre 1965): 68–9.

74. Paul Chamberland, "Les contradictions de la révolution tranquille," *Parti pris* 1 (février 1964), 4.

75. "Manifeste 64–65," *Parti pris* 2 (1964), 14.

76. Denis, *Lutte des classes*, 467–503.

77. Piotte, "Sens et limites," 36–7.

78. Gabriel Gagnon, "Vraie ou fausse indépendance," *Parti pris* 4 (novembre–décembre 1966): 9–10; Gilles Bourque et al., "Organisations syndicales, néo-capitalisme et planification," ibid., 4 (mars–avril 1967): 5–27.

79. Gaetan Tremblay and Pierre Maheu, "L'indépendance au plus vite!" *Parti pris* 4 (janvier–fevrier 1967): 2–5.

80. Bourque et al., "Pour un mouvement," *Parti pris* 5 (été 1968): 30–4.

81. Jacques Rouillard, *Histoire de la CSN, 1921–1981* (Montreal, 1981), 198.

82. CTCC and FTQ, "Les centrales ouvrières du Québec et l'assurance santé," *Relations industrielles* 13 (1958): 175–208.

83. Rouillard, *Histoire de la CSN*, 198; Denis, *Lutte des classes*, chap. 12, 287–308.

84. J.-J. Simard, "La longue marche des technocrates," *Recherches sociographiques* 18 (1977): 112–17, 129–32.

85. Réjean Pelletier, "Les parties politiques et l'État," in *L'État du Québec en devenir*, 241–61.

86. Carla Lipsig-Mummé, "Quebec Unions and the State: Conflict and Dependence," *Studies in Political Economy* 3 (Spring 1980): 136–7; Carol Levasseur, "De l'État-Providence à l'État-disciplinaire," in *L'État du Québec en devenir*, 315–25.

87. Bernard Solasse, "Les idéologies de la Fédération des travailleurs du Québec et de la Confédération des Syndicats Nationaux 1960–1978," in *Idéologies au Canada français 1940–1976*, II: 233–44, 255–67.

88. Levasseur, "De l'État-Providence," 317–22; Rouillard, *Histoire de la CSN*, 236–42.

89. Cf. Edmond Orban, *La modernisation politique du Québec* (Montreal, 1976), 15.

90. Jacques Grand'Maison, *La nouvelle classe et l'avenir du Québec* (Montreal, 1979), 263–72.

91. Cf. Dominique Clift, *Quebec Nationalism in Crisis* (Montreal, 1980).

SECTION 2

THE QUIET REVOLUTION: ORIGINS AND IMPACT

The term *Quiet Revolution* was used first by a journalist to refer to the administration of Jean Lesage's Liberal Party, which narrowly defeated the Union Nationale in June 1960 and retained power until 1966. Yet it is now becoming increasingly clear that the social, economic, and ideological forces that set the Quiet Revolution in motion were not dissipated with the defeat of the Liberal government in 1966. Those forces found expression in successive governments, the most prominent being the Parti Québécois. The Quiet Revolution had two dimensions, the first internal and the second external. Achieving reform within Quebec proved considerably easier than enhancing Quebec's power within Confederation or in international affairs. The first dimension involved using the Quebec state to modernize, as quickly as possible, Quebec's outmoded social, economic, administrative, and political institutions at all levels. The years between 1960 and 1966 were exhilarating and challenging ones for the Liberal cabinet of Jean Lesage, especially for reform-minded members, such as René Lévesque, Paul Gérin-Lajoie, and Georges-Émile Lapalme.

These ministers had the strong loyalty and active support of a new generation of deputy ministers and economic advisers such as Guy Frégault in culture, Arthur Tremblay in education, René Tremblay in commerce and industry, Michel Bélanger and André Marier in hydraulic resources, as well as Jacques Parizeau, a politically astute economist, and René Paré, followed by Roland Parenteau, who headed up the government's new Economic Council. Within four years, this group had managed to reform the civil service, granting its members the right to strike, establish a ministry of education, which quickly assumed control over all levels of education and introduced dramatic reforms, nationalize the remaining private hydro-electric companies into a dynamic and powerful Hydro-Québec controlled, in time, by Francophone specialists in all fields. The government also established numerous Crown corporations, including the General Finance Corporation, which set out to enhance the Francophone presence in the private sector by providing financial, technical, and managerial support for troubled Francophone companies, a task that proved far more difficult than anyone had anticipated. Many of the economic and social reforms introduced by the Lesage government were completed and even expanded upon by subsequent administrations. Indeed, many of the mandarins that had served the Lesage government remained in place to complete the reforms underway and to begin new ones.

Marc Renaud, in "Quebec's New Middle Class in Search of Social Hegemony," attempts to explain the distinctive character of state intervention during the Quiet Revolution by pointing to the emergence of a new middle class, which displaced the Church in health, social welfare, and education through the use of an expanded state apparatus. This new middle class also created numerous Crown corporations in order to expand career opportunities and structural mobility in all sectors of the economy for the baby-boom generation of highly educated Francophones. In the second essay, Kenneth McRoberts locates "the sources of neo-nationalism in Quebec" that underlay the Quiet Revolution in a series of inter-related developments. Such developments include the complex nature of the linkages between Quebec's economy and the Canadian and North American economies, the longstanding cultural division of labour, and the emergence in the 1950s and 1960s of a new middle class capable of articulating a Québécois neo-nationalism.

QUEBEC'S NEW MIDDLE CLASS IN SEARCH OF SOCIAL HEGEMONY: CAUSES AND POLITICAL CONSEQUENCES†

MARC RENAUD

Introduction

In the last three decades, Quebec has experienced social change to an extent and with a depth perhaps unparalleled in western countries. As a Canadian ambassador to Paris suggested, the recent transformation of Quebec society seems to be "the most rapid industrial, social, educational and religious revolution in the Western world."[1]

An overview of the most often cited indicators will permit an appreciation of the thoroughness of this change.[2] While two-thirds of the Quebec population lived in cities in 1950, more than 80 percent did in 1971, with the largest increases in the Montreal region, which half the population now inhabits. The Catholic Church was in 1960 the key institution of social control well as the moral authority and often, indirectly, the political authority. It was also the power holder, if not always the owner, in health, education, and social-welfare organizations. Ten years afterwards, it had been almost totally relegated to its spiritual role, with a sharp decline in the number of people engaging in religious orders, a drastic drop in the level of religious practice, and the state takeover of the health, education, and social-welfare fields. While there were about 2,000 new sacerdotal vocations per year in the late 1940s, only about 100 were recruited in 1970.[3] While roughly 80 percent of the population practised its religion in 1960, in urban areas only 15 percent to 35 percent still do so now. This was paralleled by a substantial and extremely brusque decline in the birth rate, moving from 30 births per 1,000 population to 28 in 1959, to 14 in 1974. During the same period (1950–1974), the divorce rate increased eighteenfold and the suicide rate increased to 4.4 times the 1950 rate!

The organization of the polity also profoundly changed. Provincial government expenditures multiplied by 32 during this period, with the most visible and important increments due to massive state interventions during the Quiet Revo-

†*International Review of Community Development*, New series, 39/40 (1978): 1–36.

lution (1960–65).[4] The traditionally dominant political party, the Union Nationale — which held power from 1936 to 1939 and from 1944 to 1960 — gradually lost its importance in the popular vote, to be replaced by the Parti Québécois, which with an entirely different political base took power in November 1976.[5] In the 1960s, public administration was totally reshaped: from parochial and paternalist in style and highly decentralized in its structures, it became centralized, bureaucratic, and typically "modern." A series of events accounts for this change: the growth of the human-service sectors (education, health, and welfare), the government takeover of these sectors, the reorganization of all ministries, the greater involvement of the state in the economy (for example, creation of state enterprises, government involvement in industrial sectors, and the creation of planning agencies), and the creation of a multitude of other government boards and agencies. In 1960 the Quebec provincial public sector employed 36,000 people, while in 1971 almost 350,000 people were employed in its administration, in public enterprises and in health and educational services — that is, an increase from 2 percent to 15 percent of the labour force. And this is a gross underestimate of the number of people paid by provincial tax money and by state enterprises. The expenditures of the federal, provincial, and municipal public sectors in Quebec have grown, according to recent estimates, from 33.4 percent of the Quebec GNP at market prices in 1961 to 45.8 percent in 1970, with the Quebec public sector accounting for 31.8 percent of the GNP in 1970 as compared to 17.9 percent in 1961.[6] The most noticed result of this febrile growth has been a democratization of the access to the previously Church-controlled and highly elitist educational system and a substantial improvement in the access of poorer strata to health services,[7] along with an extremely intense, although not necessarily successful, reshuffling of jobs, personnel, and organizations.

Position of the Question

Except for the brusque character of these changes and the dramatic downfall of the Catholic Church, Ontario, the neighbouring and comparable province, has experienced similar transformations. In particular, contrary to what is often believed, the expansion of the provincial and municipal public sectors for the economy has followed quite similar paths in all provinces and has meant a similar quantitative development of the state. Further, this expansion was in all provinces associated with a change in the ideologically dominant institutions, from religious and rural ones to secular and urban-based political and social ones.

In general, however, in all provinces except Quebec, this expansion did not mean much more than a change in the organization of the economy linked to the worldwide transformation of capitalism into its "post-industrial" or "advanced" stages. The state directly employed many more people, social security policies were much more extensive and progressive, Keynesian economic policies became widespread, the state organizational apparatus was modernized, and the coercive legal and fiscal powers of the governments were increased. But, all things considered, this expansion did not fundamentally alter the basic matrix of interest groups and class relationships within each province. Therefore, it did not look "revolutionary," as it seemingly did in Quebec.

In fact, although the tangible outputs of governmental actions have not markedly differed among provinces, these same actions in Quebec have taken on a colouring that contrasts sharply with what has occurred in the Anglophone provinces. What is particular to Quebec is not the changes per se, but its style of problem solving. In other words, Quebec has evolved what may be termed its own distinctive strategy of reform. The growth of the presence of government in Quebec was accompanied by a rhetoric so strongly social democratic, stated objectives of reform so sweeping, and such legislative authoritarianism, that one is forced to recognize the distinctive character of government intervention in Quebec.

In all countries where the structure of the economy is monopolistic, the technocratic point of view that everything needs administrative rationalization is bound to emerge and to confront individualistic, entrepreneurial, or market-oriented points of view. As many have said, the state is bound to grow and to institutionalize more and more aspects of social relations. In Quebec after 1960, not only did the technocratic point of view emerge, but — contrary to elsewhere — it gradually totally dominated and penetrated the state along with social-democratic ideals. Reform after reform, the heralding of fundamental objectives, the systematic recourse to the powers of coercion, and reorganization of the state permitted this point of view of take over the political management of problems and crises, thus determining the emergence of unique political dynamics and of a distinctive political culture.

This strategy of reform boils down to a typical three-act play for government actions.[8] The characteristic initial reaction of the Quebec government to the various social ills or to heavy public pressure has almost always been to arouse seemingly boundless hopes and expectations. Unlike the other Canadian provinces, Quebec has summoned numerous commissions of inquiry and policy-making bodies to elaborate, often in enough detail to be convincing, policies inspired by the desire to rationalize the allocation of resources and by the great social-democratic ideals of our times — equality of opportunity, heritage preservation, collective ownership of natural resources, democratization and regionalization of decision-making, comprehensive medical care, and so on.

The second step in government action, following the policy recommendations and the resulting expectations and co-optations, consists in implementing with lightning speed extremely ambitious plans of total reorganization, restructuring, and reshuffling. This has been done almost solely through the coercive mechanisms of legislation, without extended public debate, pilot projects, or other unusual procedures for gradual change. Here again we can see at work a style of political problem solving that is radically different from anything to be found elsewhere in Canada, where the accent is put on pilot projects and other ad hoc or "muddling through" procedures.

According to the scenario, the third act opens a few years later, when it turns out that the reforms have fallen short of their objectives, not only because they bore few solutions to the social problems they were supposed to solve, but also because they were far removed from the many social-democratic ideals they promised to fulfill. The often gaping void separating the ideal from the actual objectives and their operationalization would then become the yeast for the increasingly complex crises to come.

Clearly, this is what happened for the reforms in the education, health, and welfare fields. Whatever the political party in power, the same technocratic and highly ambitious, yet only partially successful, crisis-solving style has by and large pervaded government actions in these fields. The story is different for economic reforms. During the Quiet Revolution, exactly the same scenario was followed. Electric-power companies were nationalized. State financial enterprises were created, along with many public enterprises in the productive sectors. And central and regional planning agencies were set up — all of this in a context of profound economic reform. Afterwards, with the Johnson, Bertrand, and Bourassa administrations (1966–76), these organizations, except for a few, received much less support from government officials. A move away from the development of an indigenous state capitalism seems to have occurred: the overall government strategy shifted back to subsidizing foreign-owned enterprises, as incentives for their investments, thus lending credence to the hypothesis that the political base of these administrations was quite different from the one that supported the Liberal Party in the early 1960s and the Parti Québécois in the 1970s.

If this analysis is correct, the important question is the following: how can we explain the distinctive character of Quebec state interventions? How can we understand that, in general, technocratic elites and ideologies have had in Quebec an unparalleled status and legitimacy? How does one explain that, after so many years of passivity and conservatism, the Quebec state suddenly decided with such determination to pursue social-democratic objectives that undoubtedly present a leftist outlook by North American political standards?

There is an emerging consensus among Quebec sociologists to view the Quiet Revolution and later government reforms as the result of two interacting factors. First, there was the deeply felt need in various segments of the population to upgrade Quebec infra- and superstructures to catch up with the rest of North America economically, politically, and culturally. The 1957 economic depression, combined with the political pressures emerging from a structurally rapidly changing population, forced the Quebec government to modernize society to insure economic growth, full employment, and social peace. Second, a newly formed petty bourgeoisie could take advantage of this situation and more or less consciously manoeuvre to replace the Church as the locally dominant hegemonic group.[9] This search for hegemony would be the key feature of class relationships in Quebec in the 1960s and the 1970s. Within this new petty bourgeoisie, two segments are often distinguished: one, the neo-capitalist faction, is linked to private capital and is represented by the Liberal Party in the 1970s; the other, the technocratic faction, is tied to the new managerial roles in a monopolistic economy and can be found in Quebec especially in the top echelons of the public sector. The Parti Québécois is its political representative.

The purpose of this paper is to further specify this hypothesis, especially for understanding the distinctive reform strategy of the Quebec government. For reasons of conceptual clarity,[10] I prefer the term, "new middle class" to "new petty bourgeoisie." Needless to say, my argument here will be a highly tentative one. As Barrington Moore has stated, "All that the social historian can do is point to a contingent connection among changes in the structure of society." And, given the complexity of the issues to be addressed, their contemporary character and the lack of systematically gathered data, we can only hope to develop a plausible interpretation of the exceptional dominance of technocratic ideologies and elite groups, coloured as they are by social democratic ideas, in Quebec's political arena.

Summary of the Argument

The most plausible and all-embracing hypothesis to explain the distinctive problem-solving style of the Quebec state during the 1960s and 1970s is the emergence of a new middle class with a definite stake in the expansion of the state apparatus and the latter's legitimacy in society. The following summarizes this hypothesis.

Contrary to Anglophone provinces, the expansion of the state in Quebec occurred in a political and economic context that radically altered the pattern of class relations. Quebec's political economy can be schematically characterized by the following idiosyncratic elements.

First, there have been profound structural changes in Quebec's economy since the end of the Second World War, with the numbers of white-collar workers and skilled manual labourers growing in leaps and bounds compared to the number of unskilled and agricultural jobs. The result has been an impressive surge in the upward mobility of the French-speaking segment of the Quebec population, and an equally impressive increase in the college and university enrolment figures. This trend gathered momentum and, by the mid-1960s, thousands and thousands of young graduates were out looking for jobs.

Second, the private sector of the Quebec economy is less dynamic than in Ontario or British Columbia in terms of productivity, ability to attract new investment, and job-generating power. There is a general agreement among economists[11] to say that the Quebec economy has suffered a relative decline since the Second World War, compared to other Canadian provinces, especially because of this weak manufacturing sector and its heavy reliance on the primary and tertiary sectors for economic growth.

Third, the doors to upper and middle management in the largely English-Canadian and American private corporate world have remained for the most part shut for those who are of French origin, even when they have the same qualifications as their English-speaking colleagues. Several reasons have been suggested for this: the private economy was not expanding quickly enough, many enterprises were absentee owned and controlled, and the institutionalized networks of the business community systematically favoured the recruitment of people speaking the language of the incoming capital.

Unlike most other Canadians, French-speaking Quebeckers have been determined to work in their own province whatever the job situation may be. The politico-economic conjuncture in the 1960s and 1970s consequently conferred on the growth of the state apparatus in Quebec dynamics that are distinctive in the Canadian context. Given that the state turned out to be one of the only sources of job openings for the growing proportion of university graduates among the French-speaking population, had the civil service and public sector not expanded, the gap between English- and French-speaking Quebeckers would have continued to widen, since the already scarce upper- and middle-echelon jobs of the private economy were closed to the Francophones. The Quebec state was therefore the only institutional base capable of providing prestigious and well-paid jobs for educated French-speaking Quebeckers. In other words, these people had no choice but to orient themselves toward the state sector of the economy—that is, government, government-owned corporations and autonomous state-managed agencies, and industries or organizations directly or indirectly dependent on the state. In the other Canadian provinces, more and more individuals also became university educated, but, contrary to Quebec, the state was not the almost sole purveyor of jobs for them. They could also work in the private sector of the economy and, if they could not find job satisfaction within their native province, they could always go elsewhere in English-speaking North America.

University- or technically-trained Francophones can in fact be said to constitute a class in the sense that their academic capital provides them with commonly shared levels of market capacity and with a set of objective common interests in seeing the state evolve, by various means, interesting (i.e.,prestigious, powerful, and well-paid) jobs for them. Although this class is by and large composed of the people classified by census statisticians as "professional and technical labour," it is not merely a statistical aggregate. It is not simply the addition of individuals with certain attributes, such as a certain level of education, certain types of occupations, a given level of income, and so on. It is in fact a social collectivity grounded in the material order in a fairly identifiable fashion: specifically, by the similar symbolic skills brought by its members to the labour marketplace. Such a new middle class exists in all Canadian provinces, but in Quebec it has the supplementary cohesiveness-inducing constraints of a relatively closed and declining private economy. That is, contrary to its English-speaking counterpart, it is bound to view and use the Quebec state as its only leverage for survival.

The Quebec new middle class is not a "ruling class" or a "bourgeoisie" in the Marxist sense. That is, it is not part of this core group of families who own not only the larger part, but also the socially and culturally most determinant part of the world economy, the monopoly sector. It does not own the means of production in the private economy. The ruling class is for the most part foreign in origin, either English Canadian or American, and its enterprises often are absentee-owned and controlled.

The Quebec state with varying intensity throughout its history has had to act in ways that support foreign dominance, either directly (for example, subsidization of multinational enterprises for their investments) or indirectly (socialization of certain costs of production on public works, for example, to compensate for the lack of dynamism of the private economy). State spending has to behave in such a way in order to maintain the growth of the economy and low levels of unemployment.

This reality is undoubtedly harmful for the immediate interest of most of the fractions of the new middle class, but the latter are hard pressed to express their opposition lest they undermine the Quebec state itself. From time to time, when the economic context permits, some of these factions succeed in manoeuvring themselves into the position of being able to allocate resources in the manufacturing or the financing sectors of the economy, by socializing the purchase price or the investment capital necessary for creating this or that enterprise and nationalizing its profits. Such state actions may have the effect both of providing some new-middle-class elites with the power to allocate resources and of stimulating employment and economic growth to the satisfaction of both the general population and of the capitalist bourgeois class. Generally speaking, however, the new middle class most forcibly seeks to acquire real (if limited) hegemony at the local level in those sectors—especially human services—where the state has the freest hand.

Any action that has the effect of extending the quantitative and qualitative influence of the state serves the interests of this class. The new middle class has consequently produced a political culture that favours high-profile wide-ranging reorganizations that draw on, in the highly politicized context of Quebec, broad social-democratic and nationalist aspirations. Even though state intervention sometimes provokes short-term conflicts among petty-bourgeois factions (among "technocrats," "professionals," and "neo-capitalists," for instance), there is a common class interest in the self-preservative and self-promoting virtues of increased state initiative, and they spare no pains to impress on the population the idea that the Quebec state is the only collective lever it has. As an ex-Minister of Industry and Commerce said, given the weakness of the private economy and the general leverage of the Quebec state, Quebec would now be on the verge of creating a "socialism by default." This means the appropriation of key economic enterprises by the state and the enactment of thorough bureaucratic reforms aimed at equalizing the distribution of wealth and income in the society.

Against such a backdrop, when technocratic elite groups such as the dominant members of the Parent (education reform) or Castonguay-Nepveu (health and social-welfare reforms) commissions appear for one reason or another on the scene and formulate policies involving highly visible organizational shakeups, premised on larger social-democratic policies for Quebec society, they are automatically greeted with broad social support and open arms in civil service circles. No matter what short-term tensions these elite groups may cause, general class interest dictates that they be provided sweeping power and the legitimacy they need, inasmuch as they contribute to the quantitative *and* qualitative expansion of the state apparatus. This is why these groups have little trouble in obtaining broad cabinet and National Assembly approval for speedy and far-reaching reform, however authoritarian the legislation and regulations enacted may be.

In the very different context of Ontario, for instance, comparable groups have not been legitimized in this way nor received comparable powers. Of course, a new middle class also exists in Ontario, but the state apparatus is not its only means of survival and thus there are no social forces that push for unconditional support to technocratic elites whose aim is to extend state control. To put it another way, it is inconceivable, in a context like that of Ontario, that an elite group like the Castonguay-Nepveu Commission could succeed in completely controlling an entire sector of government activity and imposing its own blueprint for change and its own way of doing things. Again, this is not to say that such groups do not exist in Ontario — quite the contrary. But, given the politico-economic conjuncture in this province, their social status could not be as high and their ideologies could not penetrate the state as thoroughly as they have in Quebec.

To clarify the maze of numbers and events that will now be presented in support of this argument, figure 1 diagrams the structure of the argument just summarized: each point in figure 1 will be documented in the alphabetical order presented.

FIGURE 1

The Development of the New Middle Class

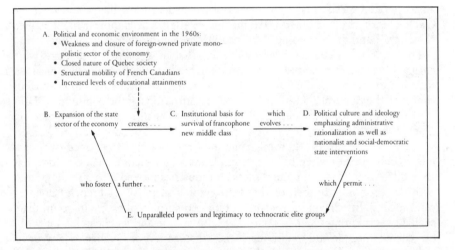

The Evolution of Quebec's Political Economy

The discussion of the evolution of Quebec's economy will use the classification categories developed by James O'Connor in *Fiscal Crisis of the State*.[12] I will distinguish among the *monopolistic* sector, the market or competitive sector, and the state sector. The first sector is highly monopolistic in concentration of ownership and in economic behaviour (like uses of price fixing). It requires large amounts of fixed capital invested per worker and it is involved in wide-scale markets. Important features of this sector are the high wages and salaries paid, the stable levels of employment, and the tendency toward vertical as well as horizontal integration of production and distribution processes. The market or *competitive* sector was once the largest economic sector, but it is now declining in importance. It is characterized by its lower levels of productivity, smaller-scale production, local or regional markets, lower ratios of capital invested per worker, lower unionization rate, lower wages and salaries, and more unstable levels of employment.

Agriculture, construction, retail-trade, and personal-service enterprises are typically part of this sector of the economy. O'Connor also divides up the *state* sector into two categories: production of goods and services organized by the state itself (for instance, mail, education, public health, welfare, and other social services) and production organized by industries owned by the state (state industrial enterprises) or under contract with the state (such as military equipment and supplies, highway construction).

1920–1945: Competitive Capitalism and the Arrival of Foreign Industry

It was not until the end of the Second World War that fundamental changes in the Quebec economy began. After the war, a massive migration took place to the major cities and foreign — especially American — monopoly capital moved in at an accelerated speed causing the occupational structure to change considerably. Quebec history from about 1900 to the mid-1940s has been thoroughly described elsewhere[13] and there is no need for us to discuss it in other than outline form.

This period was characterized by the fact that most French Canadians were engaged in petty commodity production, mostly in agriculture but also in small-scale industry. Priests, doctors, and lawyers were the local elites, in control of almost all the political, social, and cultural organizations of the community. During this period, foreign capital and its industries began to install themselves in Quebec, but this did not have any impact on the social organization of Quebec.

In fact, till the late 1940s, foreign and local capital largely remained two separate worlds, as they were fulfilling complementary functions. As Guindon has argued,[14] Anglo-Canadian and American industries moved into a society faced with the economic burden of the demographic surplus[15] of French-Canadian rural society. In relieving this acute population surplus, they could accumulate capital by exploiting Quebec's natural-resource base and its cheap labour without encroaching on the traditional social organization of Quebec society or its traditional elites. Furthermore, the foreign group could itself fill the management and technical levels of industry with little conflict, for French Canadians provided only the semi-skilled and unskilled labour.[16] As for French-Canadian society, the absorption of surplus labour by foreign industry permitted its distinctive political and religious elite, its political and social institutions anchored to the rural parish, and its petty commodity-production economy to survive despite the changes in the surrounding material order.[17]

1945–1960: The Growth of the Monopoly Sector and its Consequences

With more and more Francophones working within foreign industry and with the increasing monopolistic characteristics of this industry, the complementarity of functions and the convergence of interests between Quebec's traditional elites and foreign entrepreneurs gradually disappeared. By the early 1950s, the Quebec economy had changed so much that the traditional social order had stopped being reproduced, despite the length of time it took for this fact to be politically and socially felt.

By the early 1960s, while French Canadians comprised more than 80 percent of Quebec's population and owned 50 percent of the enterprises, they controlled only 15 percent of the value added in Quebec industry while some of the 13 percent of English Canadians and a few Americans controlled 85 percent.[18] In other words, French-Canadian ownership and control was almost entirely limited to the much less profitable competitive sector of the economy, while English-Canadian and other foreign interests owned and controlled the profitable monopolistic sector.

The ex-president of the Economic Council of Canada, André Raynauld, has done research on industrial enterprises in Quebec in 1961. His results confirm that the Quebec economy is characterized by a French-Canadian competitive sector and a foreign monopolistic sector. He writes:

> French-Canadian establishments were at the one extreme in every respect. Foreign establishments were at the other extreme in every respect and Other Canadian establishments were in between. With regard to *size*, Foreign establishments were seven times larger than French Canadian, and four times larger than Other Canadian by *value added*. The *average output* per man was 6500, 8400, and 12000 dollars respectively for French-Canadian, Other Canadian and Foreign establishments. *Wages and salaries* in French-Canadian establishments were 30 percent below those in Foreign, and 12 percent below those in Other Canadian establishments. . . .[19]

French-Canadian-owned enterprises, with few exceptions in 1961, were within the competitive or market sector. French-Canadian ownership was concentrated in agriculture, construction, retail trade, and services. According to the Royal Commission on Bilingualism and Biculturalism:

> Francophones are owners and proprietors in large proportions in agriculture and to a lesser degree in the service fields and retail trade. In wholesale they play a still smaller role, while in finance and manufacturing they account for about one-fourth of the total. Moreover, within manufacturing itself, the pattern of ownership is also uneven. In small-scale manufacturing, such as the production of wood products, Francophones predominate; but in fields requiring large capital investment and highly advanced technology, such as the manufacture of chemicals and petroleum products, they play virtually no role in ownership or control.[20]

Foreign-owned enterprises constituted Quebec's major enterprises, in terms of value added and outputs. These enterprises can be classified in three main categories. First, from this earlier phase of industrialization, largely created by the National Policy of the federal government in the 1870s, Quebec has inherited secondary industries in labour-intensive sectors (textile, wood, shoes, and other finished products). Second, in the mid-1930s, primary industries began to appear exploiting Quebec's natural resources (pulp and paper, primary metallic industries). Finally, later on, some large American high-technology enterprises (automobile, electrical equipment) came in, but at an extremely slow pace compared to Ontario.[21] Almost all these enterprises are owned and controlled by American and English-Canadian interests.[22] The second and third categories are largely part of the American monopolistic sector. The first category shows to a lesser extent similar monopolistic features.

Weakness of this Economy

This general structure of the economy in the early 1960s (much of it is still the same) had key economic and social consequences. The economy had two overwhelming characteristics. In the first place, as just seen, the profitable monopolistic sector was almost entirely owned by foreign interests, while the fairly large and unprofitable competitive sector was French-Canadian owned. Second, since the monopolistic sector, with the complicity of Quebec traditional elites, was built on the requirements of foreign interests and their industries, it appeared almost only where high profits could be made. Foreign enterprises therefore exploited Quebec's natural-resource base and cheap labour. In those industrial sectors where labour was abundant and therefore cheap, labour-intensive light consumer-goods industries developed. The dynamism of these enterprises has now considerably declined. Extremely few durable-goods and producer-goods industries have replaced them, even though such enterprises would have been necessary to generate new investments and create new jobs. The combination of a fairly large competitive sector and a partially weak monopolistic sector in light consumer-goods industries means that a relatively large proportion of workers are employed in slow-growth and low productivity industries.

This situation accounts for the general weakness of Quebec's economy in contrast to that of Ontario. Here are a few indices of this relative decline of Quebec's economy. Fewer people worked in the Quebec manufacturing sector in 1971 than in 1961, while this number has increased on the average all over Canada.[23] In fact, as a task force to the Department of Industry and Commerce recently noted, new jobs in Quebec tend not be created in the nonvalue-producing tertiary sector alone, contrary to Ontario:

> About 230,000 jobs have been created between 1966 and 1971, among which 133,000 are in "personal social service- and others" and 22,000 in the public administration. More than 90 percent of the new jobs are due to the growth of the tertiary sector. During the same period, approximately 50,000 jobs have disappeared in equal parts in construction and in the primary sector, in particular forestry and mining. This means a net creation of 180,000 jobs; that is 36,000 on the average each year in comparison with 85,600 for Ontario (428,000 total for this five-year period).[24]

Further, Quebec consistently had 50 percent of the bankruptcies in Canada, while its GNP accounted for only 25 percent of Canada's GNP.[25] Quebec always had a 20 percent to 50 percent higher unemployment rate than the Canadian average, usually twice as high as Ontario. Over the last two decades, the personal income per capita in Quebec has been 12 percent to 15 percent lower than the Canadian mean, and between 23 percent to 30 percent lower in Ontario. The discrepancies between Quebec and English Canada are even clearer if we disaggregate according to ethnicity. André Raynauld has shown that French Canadians were among the most poorly paid workers in Quebec in 1961, ranking twelfth in labour income in a list of 14 ethnic groups. He writes: "The most remarkable fact . . . is that French-Canadian labour income was 12 percent below the overall average in every province except Quebec, where it was 40 percent below the overall provincial average. In absolute terms, the gap was about 1000 dollars a year in Canada as a whole, and 2000 dollars in Quebec."[26]

Eliminating the effects of several factors (age, sex composition of labour force, education, occupation, employment status, region, and labour-force participation) on this discrepancy, he found that ethnicity still accounted for more than 50 percent of the income differential. French Canadians, because they are French Canadians and for no other reason, earn much less than their English-Canadian counterparts in Quebec.

The Closure of the Top Corporate World to French Canadians and the Closed Nature of Quebec Society

Not only was this structure of the economy weak for generating investments and for creating employment, but is also did not provide employment for university- or technically trained Francophones. On the one hand, the competitive sector does not possess high-income, high-prestige, and high-power jobs. The competitive sector is largely composed of small enterprises of self-employed individuals and a few workers. On the other hand, the top corporate world was and is closed to Francophones. Entries at the top of the occupational hierarchy were and are blocked to French Canadians, whatever their level of education. This has both historical and sociological grounds.

Both because of the "language" of the incoming capital and in view of their earlier higher levels of education, successive English-Canadian generations have always been better placed in the occupational hierarchy. As a consequence, they are still at an advantage over French Canadians for high-income and high-power jobs in the monopolistic sector. English Canadians have systematically preceded French Canadians in their patterns of social mobility, thus blocking the entry of French Canadians in the top jobs of the private economy. Whatever the levels of education now achieved by French Canadians, the institutionalized networks of the big-business community tend to omit French Canadians. Examples of these networks are the well-known links between Anglophone universities and enterprises in the monopoly sector. The Royal Commission on Bilingualism and Biculturalism has noted:

> Because of their higher educational level, their position in the occupational
> structure, and their original position as leaders of Quebec's industrialization,
> the Anglophones have always been better prepared than the Francophones
> to enjoy the benefits of the province's economic development. Once
> socio-economic patterns have been established, they tend to be
> self-perpetuating; the momentum favouring the Anglophones was never
> matched in the Francophone community.[27]

As a consequence, very few French Canadians could be considered part of a corporate elite. Porter[28] estimated this group to be 51 persons in 1951 (or 6.7 percent of the Canadian corporate elite at that time). Milner and Milner[29] and Clement[30] estimate that in 1971, while French Canadians constituted a third of the Canadian population, this group included only 65 persons (or 8.4 percent of the Canadian corporate elite). In Milner and Milner's words:

> We looked at those Quebec firms controlled by French Canadians, borrowing the results of a study[31] which selected from these firms a sample of the two largest banks, the two largest trust companies, the six largest industries, the three largest insurance companies, and the three largest finance companies. There are 216 positions on the boards of directors of these enterprises held by 163 persons. Of these 163 persons, 65 (40%) hold 118 (54%) of the 216 positions. These men hold among themselves 50% of the directorships of the insurance companies, 68% of the trust companies, 43% of the six industries, and 72% of the banks. These 65 persons thus are a good approximation of the French-Canadian economic elite. . . . Over half of this elite was educated in two schools: Collège Sainte-Marie and Jean de Brébeuf.[32]

It is important to add here that, notwithstanding the enormous fiscal and legal efforts of the Quebec state in the late 1960s to raise the level of education among Francophones and to enforce French as the language of work in Quebec, the private economy remained closed to Francophones. This runs counter to the popular belief that, with the increased levels of educational attainments of the Quebec population and the corollary rejection of the self-defeating rural and Catholic ideology, French Canadians could be in a position to make significant inroads into the private monopolistic economy.

Wallace Clement has presented convincing evidence to counter this belief. Noticing that the number of French Canadians in the economic elite had risen only from 51 to 65 from 1951 to 1971, he writes:

> This means a net increase of only 14 more French Canadians or 1.7 percent more of the elite population over the last 20 years. These have not been uneventful years in French-Anglo relations; quite the contrary, they were supposed to contain the "new awakening" (a loaded phrase which somehow assumes the French have themselves been their own barrier to gaining equality and not their position vis-à-vis the dominant Anglos) and the "quiet revolution" of the 1960s and the not-so-quiet revolution of recent years. In spite of ideological statements to the contrary, the French have not made significant inroads into the economic world.[33]

He then cites the research of Presthus[34] to show that not only have the French not made it to the very top of the corporate world, but they also did not make gains in the middle range and smaller corporations:

> A recent study based on 12,741 names of executives from some 2,400 companies operating in Canada listed in the 1971 *Directory of Directors* found only 9.4 percent to be French Canadians. This is only about one percent more than are to be found in the economic elite and includes many

corporations much smaller than the 113 dominant ones which are the basis of this study.[35]

Further evidence of the restricted mobility of Francophones into the private economy is provided by a study of the Institut International d'Économie Quantitative. It shows that, in 1971, 28 percent of the top management jobs in the private economy earing above $20,000, 28 percent of the middle management occupations earning between $15,000 and $19,999, and 48 percent of lower-level management positions earning between $5,000 and $14,999 were held by Francophones, while French Canadians constituted 75 percent of the labour force in 1971.[36] In other words, the proportion of Francophones occupying any level of management in the private economy is considerably smaller than the proportion of Francophones in the overall labour force. An analysis of the 1971 census has even shown that, at a same level of mangerial occupation, French Canadians earn 11 percent less than their English-Canadian counterparts.[37]

To sum up, university- and technically trained Francophones were in the early 1960s and still by the mid-1970s confronted with the following situation: a fairly large competitive economy with practically no appropriate job for their training and a monopolistic economy with only a few job outlets, either because enterprises are absentee owned and controlled or because some of them are in such obsolete industrial sectors that they do not expand enough to provide new jobs. When a position does open up, because of the historically determined linkages between the Anglophones and the business community, it tends to be given to an Anglophone. Almost the only job outlets therefore seem in the state sector of the economy.

One could object that, given this situation, French Canadians have incentives to go to work elsewhere in Canada or North America, as was the case for many French-Canadian unskilled labourers during the 1920s and the Depression years, but the situation was quite different then. In the 1920s and 1930s, the surplus labour of rural Quebec was such that is could not be entirely absorbed by incoming industry. In the 1960s and 1970s, we are talking about a different kind of people, individuals who have over 15 years of formal education and who correctly believe that they have the skills necessary for the top jobs at least as much as their Anglophone counterparts. In such cases, cultural barriers impose considerable restrictions on geographic mobility much more than they did in the 1920s or 1930s. The French-Canadian situation is different from that experienced by Canadians in the poorer Atlantic provinces. Maritimers who do not find jobs in their native province will tend to look for jobs anywhere on the North American continent. A corresponding Québécois, unless he or she accepts the disturbing emotional consequences of becoming an expatriate, is almost glued to Quebec's territory, whatever the job outlets.

Evidence for this phenomenon is overwhelming. For instance, reporting on a study of Quebec engineers, the Royal Commission on Bilingualism and Biculturalism wrote:

> Although 80 percent of the Francophone engineers in our Montreal sample thought Quebec offered them the best opportunities, only nine percent of

the Anglophones agreed with them; almost half the Anglophone engineers named the United States instead. There are indications that the situation is changing, but the evidence is consistent in showing a lower mobility rate and a lesser willingness to move on the part of Francophone engineers and their wives. If they work for a large corporation, the consequence of this difference is the same for the managers—a slower rate of promotion. For those who work in small firms of Francophone-owned institutions, this effect, though not as pronounced, is still at work.[38]

Further, if we look at some aggregated migration statistics,[39] the same phenomenon is visible: Quebec loses proportionally fewer inhabitants than any other province and received the smallest relative proportion of internal migrants. Ontario receives many more internal migrants and few leave the province, because of the economic wealth and immense job opportunities it offers. If these data could be analysed by ethnic origin, it is probable that even fewer Québécois would appear to be leaving the province.

In this sense, Quebec is a closed society for the Francophone segment of its population. However unfulfilling the job opportunities and whatever one's political opinions, Quebec, in a real sense, is a nation, the borders of which are not easily passed.

The Structural Mobility of French Canadians and the Increased Levels of Education

After the war, the politico-economic situation in Quebec changed somewhat. A great number of French Canadians had left the agricultural rural world to become unskilled or semi-skilled labourers in foreign industry. Many of the small commodity producers who in a former era had derived quite a good standard of living from their farms, retail stores, or crafts shops also joined the ranks of the increasingly urban working class. None of them was educated enough to occupy managerial, professional, or technical positions. During this period, English Canadians occupied the entire top managerial, professional, and technical occupations within industry.

From the 1930s to the early 1960s, two parallel phenomena took place. On the one hand, since Francophones increasingly filled the bottom positions of the occupational hierarchy and since more and more Anglophones filled the top positions of this hierarchy, French Canadians as an ethnic group were in fact getting proletarianized, in the sense of increasingly having nothing else to sell but their labour power. On the other hand, with the expansion of the monopoly sector and the corollary changes in the occupational structure (technical, clerical, and skilled tasks becoming quantitatively more important than unskilled and primary labour) came a structural mobility of French Canadians. That is, quite independently of their own volition and uniquely because of changes in the structure of the demand for labour, many French Canadians began to perform better-paid and somewhat more prestigious tasks. With such a structural mobility, French Canadians began to enjoy better standards of living and began to aspire for better jobs for themselves and their children. More and more people enrolled in school and great pressure was put on the state to facilitate the financial and geographical access to education.

The data that follow are unsatisfying because of the varying definitions of occupational categories used in different research studies and because of the lack of built-in comparability between the studies; however, they are the only published data available. However crude, they provide approximate empirical evidence for the phenomena just described.

The widening of the gap in the occupational hierarchy between Anglophones and Francophones in Quebec is well illustrated by an analysis performed by John Porter.[40] He compared the percentage of over- or underrepresentation of French and British males in various occupational categories, according to census data in 1931, 1951, and 1961. I have corrected for some slight computational errors in Porter's results and I have computed the same information for 1971. Because census statisticians have redefined certain occupational categories during this period, the results have only an indicative value.[41]

These data show that from 1931 to 1961 Quebeckers of British origin have increasingly been overrepresented at the professional and technical levels, moving from +5 percent to +7.2 percent. Conversely, the French have become more and more underrepresented in this group, moving from −0.9 percent to −1.5 percent. A similar evolution also seems to have occurred in the category "manager" between 1951 and 1961. For primary and unskilled jobs, although the gap has not been widened as much between 1931 and 1961, French Canadians have been constantly overrepresented, moving from 0.3 percent to 1.1 percent in 1961, to 1.3 percent in 1971. For the other occupational levels, there seems to have been a levelling off of the differences between the two groups, both increasingly tending towards the overall male labour-force distribution.

In other words, between 1931 and 1961, there seems to have been a widening gap between Anglophones and Francophones. This view is also confirmed by Rocher and de Jocas' analysis[42] of intergenerational mobility of sons in 1954. It showed that the relative proportion of English Canadians was increasing in nonmanual tasks and decreasing in manual jobs. In Rocher and de Jocas' sample, the gap in the top two categories (liberal professions and high management; semi-professionals and middle management) was, in 1954, increasing from 9.5 percent for the father to 15.2 percent for the sons, in favour of the Anglophones, while manual workers were increasingly French in origin, the gap moving from 14.3 percent to 29.3 percent.

In the 1971 census, the overall picture changed considerably. For all the occupational categories listed, the distribution of Anglophones and Francophones tended towards the overall labour-force distribution. While the gap for "professionals and technicians" had been widening between 1931 and 1961, it is reduced by more than a half in 1971, the British moving from an overrepresentation of +7.2 percent in 1961 to only +3.2 percent in 1971, the French moving from an underrepresentation of −1.5 percent to −0.8 percent, for a reduction of the difference from 8.7 percent in 1961 to 4.0 percent in 1971. Although this might only be an artifact of the census redefinitions, a similar, yet less drastic, phenomenon seems to have occurred for "managers." The gap between Francophones and

Anglophones in primary and unskilled jobs diminished from 7.0 percent to 3.6 percent.

The same phenomenon has been noticed by Jacques Dofny and Muriel Garon-Audy,[43] who studied the intergenerational mobility of sons in 1964, which they compared with the identical study of Rocher and de Jocas for sons in 1954. In 1964, the gap between Anglophones and Francophones was significantly reduced for all categories except "semi-professionals and middle managers," for "skilled and semi-skilled workers," and for "personal services." They concluded:

> In summary, for reduction of the gaps between French Canadians and
> English Canadians from the generation of fathers to the generation of sons
> in contrast to what was observed in 1954 (in 1954, in 6/8 cases the gap was
> increasing between the two ethnic groups; in 1964, on the contrary, the gap
> is decreased in 5/8 cases) would underline an acceleration of mobility for
> French Canadians.[44]

Sociologists call this phenomenon "structural" mobility, as opposed to "individual" mobility. Dofny and Garon-Audy have attempted to quantify its importance. French Canadians have recently experienced an enormous social mobility, much more so than the French Canadians studied in 1954 by Rocher and de Jocas or the English Canadians surveyed in 1964: 75.1 percent of the French Canadians studied in 1964 (with 50 percent upwardly mobile, 15 percent downwardly mobile, and 10 percent mobile to approximately equivalent jobs) have been mobile with respect to their fathers' occupational status, as compared to 64.1 percent in 1954 (35 percent upwardly mobile, 20 percent downwardly mobile, and 10 percent mobile to equivalent jobs) and to 66.0 percent of the Anglo-Canadians in 1964. Yet, this recent social mobility of French Canadians is to an important extent solely attributable to changes in the occupational structure — from primary and unskilled labour to skilled and white-collar tasks — that is, the mobility was structural rather than individual. Nearly half (45.0 percent) of the observed mobility among French Canadians in 1964 is structural, compared to a fourth (27.6 percent) of the observed mobility in 1954.

The Porter, Rocher/de Jocas, and Dofny/Garon-Audy data underline a key phenomenon. They seem to show that the gap between Anglophones and Francophones, which had been widening between 1930 and 1960, was transferred during the 1960s to higher levels in the occupational hierarchy because of the structural changes in the economy. The 1971 census data indicate that this gap has perhaps even begun to diminish, with proportionally more French Canadians entering managerial, professional, and technical jobs. In other words, while for a long time it looked as if the whole French-Canadian ethnic group was being increasingly proletarianized, the 1971 census shows, it seems, that an important class cleavage is appearing within the Francophone community in Quebec. Given the closure of the private monopolistic economy to French Canadians, this can only be attributable to the expansion of the Quebec state sector of the economy. The expansion of the state sector opened up new possibilities for mobility and thus probably did reduce the income, prestige, and power gap between Anglophones and Francophones.

But before we examine this specific issue, let us consider an important correlate of the structural changes in the economy: the rise of education among French Canadians. This phenomenon explains why proportionally more Francophones could by the 1960s aspire to professional, managerial, or technical jobs.

The transition of capitalism into its monopolistic advanced stages is associated with increased levels of education in the population. The increasing complexity of industrial tasks, the expanding needs for regulatory jobs, the growth of the human service sector, and so on all demand high levels of formal training. It took Quebec Francophones a decade or two longer than Anglophones to realize this, partly because their low-level jobs did not require many years in school; partly because it was culturally assumed that academic studies were valuable only to those who wished to become priests, doctors, or lawyers; and partly because of the extremely elitist structure of the Church-controlled educational system. In the 1950s, with the increasingly individually felt changes in the economy, things began to change.

Jacques Brazeau[45] has noted that between 1950 and 1960 the percentage of the population between the ages of five and twenty-four who attended school rose from 53 to 62; attendance in grades 9 to 12 more than doubled and, beyond Grade 12, it increased by more than 50 percent. Yet, the educational sector was incapable of coping with demands for massive school enrolment, as a consequence of the high costs and maldistribution of educational facilities. In 1960, Quebec had the tenth rank among Canadian provinces in secondary schooling (actually, one out of two Quebec adults had less than seven years of school), but it had the fourth rank for the proportion of its population holding a university diploma. That this system was ill equipped to fit the needs of children from low-income families is manifested by the fact that the retention rate in Quebec—defined as the enrolment in Grade 11 as a percentage of Grade 2 nine years earlier — was the lowest in Canada (33 percent).[46] The educational reforms of the 1960s resulted from such pressures and the retention rate jumped to 70 percent in 1967, placing Quebec in the fifth-highest rank among the ten Canadian provinces. Furthermore, while the Quebec education sector had been oriented for generations towards training in the liberal professions and in the humanities, proportionally more students now enrol in those fields that were not so long ago reserved for Anglophones (sciences, engineering, and the like), so that the overall school enrolment picture for Francophones increasingly tends to look more like Ontario's.[47]

To sum up, by the early 1960s, quite a few French Canadians had the formal training enabling them to fulfill top managerial, professional, and technical jobs in the economy and, after the educational reforms of the mid-1960s, their number considerably increased. In effect, a new middle class was born — that is, a social collectivity characterized by the fact that only the certified academic capital of its members, as opposed to the classical monetary capital provides them with bargaining powers on the labour market. This new middle class is, in essence, different from Quebec's old middle class and traditional elites whose power and status derived above all from their position vis-à-vis the religious order.

In the early 1960s, this new middle class was confronted with a private economy quite incapable of generating new job outlets and quite inhospitable to certified French-Canadian skills. The expansion of the state in this context came as a miracle. It provided job outlets to university- and technically-trained French Canadians, thus securing the survival of that class within Quebec.

The Expansion of the State Sector of the Economy

As we have seen, all over Canada, the 1950s and the 1960s witnessed an enormous expansion of the state sector of the economy. This expansion is mainly the expansion of the provincial and local state sectors. Both the provincial and the municipal governments have enormously increased their gross general expenditures[48] in comparison with the federal government: from $101.35 per capita on the average in 1954–55 to $802.54 in 1971–72 for the provinces; from $58.37 in 1952 to $437.64 in 1971 for municipalities; and from $314.99 in 1954–55 to $844.65 in 1971–72 for the federal government.[49] Provincial and municipal expenditures took an increasing share of personal income, while federal expenditures remained fairly constant. In seventeen years, the provinces and the municipalities increased their gross general expenditures by 800 percent, while the federal increased its by less than 300 percent.

The growth of the provincial level of administration is largely attributable to the expansion of state-controlled social services, which are taking an increasing share (from a half in 1950 to two-thirds in 1970) of an otherwise rapidly increasing total budget. In fact, the administration responsibility for social-welfare services has shifted almost entirely to provinces. While 34 percent of consolidated expenditures for health (after elimination of transfer payments between administrations) was assumed by the federal administration in 1947–48, only 2.8 percent was in 1970–71. The situation is identical for education (2.8 percent in 1970–71) but differs for welfare expenditures (where 73.4 percent were federal).[50] Overall, the priorities for provincial expenditures have shifted from roads and agriculture to health and education.

There is, besides governmental administrations, a second important element in the state sector: state enterprises. While the gross general expenditures per capita at the provincial level of government have expanded on the average in Canada by five times during the 1960s, the assets per capita of state enterprises have increased on the average in all Canadian provinces by four times during the same period.[51]

In general, these statistics underestimate the importance and the rate of expansion of the state sector of the economy, for they only partially include the economic activity derived from contracts of various private enterprises with the state. For instance, in Quebec, the economic activity — linked to Expo '67, to the massive construction of schools in the 1960s, hospitals, nursing homes, the Manic and James Bay projects, and the Olympics — is only partially accounted for in the previously presented statistics.

Now, if we compare the evolution of provincial finances, Quebec is strikingly different in three respects. First, because of Quebec's weaker economic structure, the share of provincial and municipal expenditures within personal income is considerably higher than in Ontario and in the other provinces on the average.[52]

The consolidated provincial-municipal expenditures represented a relatively equivalent per capita expenditure, but 34.9 percent of Quebec personal income in 1971, as compared to 27.5 percent in Ontario and 30.9 percent across Canada.

Second, the growth of the state sector in Quebec has really only begun in 1960 with the Liberal party administration, while the 1950s had been the take-off point for Ontario.[53] This is evident in the evolution of provincial and municipal expenditures. It is also evident in the growth of the assets of provincial state enterprises. In the 1960s, there was a sevenfold increase of these assets in Quebec, as compared with a threefold increase in Ontario and a fourfold increase on the average among Canadian provinces, so that these assets represented $6,604,432,000 in 1971 in Quebec (or $1095.63 per capita) and $6,443,001,000 in Ontario (or $836.43 per capita). As a result of this febrile creation and expansion of state enterprises in Quebec, their assets as of 1971, both in absolute terms and per capita, were the highest among all Canadian provinces.

Third, because the growth of the state sector in Quebec gained momentum only in the 1960s, the current public debt in Quebec is much higher than in Ontario. From 1960 to 1968, Quebec's direct debt (the government's) has increased by five times (Ontario, about 1.5 times) and the indirect debt (debt guaranteed to other parts of the state, such as state enterprises) by three times (while in Ontario it remained about the same).[54] In other words, the fiscal efforts were spread out over the 1950s and 1960s in Ontario, but they were condensed into the 1960s for Quebec.

These differences boil down to one sociological observation: the state sector of the economy is qualitatively, if not in strict quantifiable fiscal terms, more important in Quebec than in the other provinces. Since its expansion has been more sudden in its timing, more extensive in its nationalization and creation of enterprises, and more costly to its taxpayers, the state inevitably achieved a much greater presence in people's minds than anywhere else in Canada. This is to say that the state has expanded not only quantitatively, but also qualitatively. This has been well expressed by Claude Morin, a former high state official and minister of intergovernmental affairs in the Parti Québécois government:

> In the eyes of French-speaking Quebeckers, Ottawa and Quebec have no authority over each other; each administration is autonomous in its areas of jurisdictions; sometimes their activities are complementary, and if conflicts arise, the Government of Quebec is *a priori* in the right. . . . The common denominator of views in the other provinces is that the federal government is the "national" government; neither the Newfoundlander nor British Columbian questions this basic postulate. . . . An English-speaking provincial political figure, even a Premier, is considered to have received a promotion if he becomes a federal Cabinet minister. In Quebec, for a politician to move from the Quebec to the federal arena is no longer necessarily a promotion; the two are considered of similar significance.[55]

Because of this, the intensity of the feelings towards the actions of the Quebec government is incomparably higher in Quebec than elsewhere in Canada, as indicated by such things as the virulence of public debates, the much higher amount of press coverage, or the popular imagery surrounding political figures.

In this context, given the general ideology surrounding this expansion—which we will describe later—the Quebec state can easily appear as the collective lever for the upward mobility of all the Québécois people, independently of who in fact most tangibly benefits from this expansion of the state.

The Quebec State as the Institutional Basis for the New Middle Class

With more and more French Canadians being university educated but incapable of finding appropriate jobs, the gap between Anglophones and Francophones would have widened to a historically unparalleled, socially explosive proportion. But the state sector did expand and did provide job outlets for a vast proportion of the new middle class. In so doing, it became the institutional basis for the existence of this class.

The available evidence to support this hypothesis is quite scattered and unsystematic. Yet it describes the issue from so many different angles that it makes a rather convincing case for the assertion that the Quebec state has evolved into the main locus for the local hegemony of a Quebec Francophone new middle class.

A first line of evidence is the following. If we break down the 1971 census category "professional and technical" into occupational specialities, we notice that Anglophones are overrepresented in the natural sciences, engineering, architecture, mathematics, and related fields (+18.8 percent); the Francophones, underrepresented (−6.8%). Health and education are, however, significantly overrepresented by Francophones (+1.9% and +3.3 percent, respectively, for French Canadians; −7.6 percent and −8.4 percent, respectively, for Anglophones).[56] Because census statisticians presented disaggregated data of this sort only in 1971, longitudinal data are unavailable.

This pattern of over- and underrepresentation is not surprising. Health, education, and religion have traditionally been the only institutional sectors where mobility from bottom to top was conceivable for French Canadians. Similarly, because of their earlier association with monopolistic enterprises, Anglophones have until recently been more prone to specialize in and to work in hard-science fields.

What is important, however, is that the health and education fields are now almost totally under the jurisdiction of the Quebec state. With the hospitalization insurance plan, the educational reforms, the medical-insurance plan, and the reorganization of welfare services, almost all of the social services have become part of the state sector of the economy. The same has not occurred for the hard-science field. Further, the majority of the new jobs created within Quebec during the 1960s have been in social services. Health, education, and welfare employment has almost doubled, while the absolute number of people employed in manufacturing has slightly diminished. Making the reasonable assumption that the growth of employment in the state-controlled social services occurred for Anglophones and Francophones in proportion to their relative number in the overall population, this would mean that a large proportion of the Quebec new middle class went to work in these areas and thus in the state sector of the economy. In other words, the emergence of Quebec's new middle class was directly associated with the growth of the state's social-services agencies and departments.

A second line of evidence comes from the comparative examination of the location of work of various professional groupings of both ethnic origins. The Royal Commission on Bilingualism and Biculturalism investigated this question in the mid-1960s. It writes:

> Even among candidates with the educational qualifications suited to careers in industrial management, there appear to be substantial differences between Francophones and Anglophones as to where they actually choose, or are chosen to work. For instance, in 1964, commerce graduates of McGill were employed in industry to a greater extent than graduates of the École des Hautes Études Commerciales. . . . The membership list of the Institute of Chartered Accountants of Quebec showed a similar pattern of employment. More than 90 percent of the chartered accountants employed by the provincial and municipal government were Francophones; in industry and commerce less than 40 percent were Francophones. Among both commerce graduates and chartered accountants, however, there was a trend among the younger Francophones towards greater participation in the private sector. Even so, Anglophones still outnumbered Francophones to a considerable extent among the younger employees.

The same is true for engineers and scientists:

> The proportion of Francophone engineers working in private industry in 1963 was similarly low; only 25% of Francophone engineers compared with 78% of Anglophone engineers, were employed in this sector.... The pattern of employment of science graduates from Francophone universities among industrial sectors has many of the same features as that of Francophone engineers. Among scientists employed by provincial and municipal governments, 85% were Francophones. Their proportion was much lower in teaching (43%), the federal government (39%) and non-salaried professional services (32%). Like the engineers, they had low proportions in the large mining and manufacturing sectors (14%) and in construction, transportation, and communication (13%).[57]

The engineers' situation could be looked at from another angle. While one of the biggest electrical power companies employed only 20 Francophone engineers out of 175 in 1963 prior to being nationalized, Montreal Quebec Hydro (nationalized in 1944) had 190 Francophone engineers out of 243 at the same date.[58] We can reasonably assume that the nationalization of all electrical power companies has been conducive to the hiring of Francophone as opposed to Anglophone engineers. The situation in Montreal Quebec Hydro in 1963 has probably gradually been extended to the entire hydro field after nationalization. Again, this would show that the expansion of the state has served Quebec's new middle class.

This observation is strengthened by a third piece of evidence. The Centre de Sondage of the Université de Montréal conducted a study in 1973 on behalf of the Commission d'Enquête sur la situation de la langue française et sur les droits linguistiques au Québec (Gendron Commission). In this study, an inquiry was made into the location of work in a stratified random sample of Quebec university graduates. It showed that, on the aggregate, 25.6 percent of Anglophone university graduates in all fields worked for the Quebec government,[59] while 53.8 percent of Francophones did. In younger cohorts, the proportion is even higher: 65.3 percent of Francophone graduates and 33.8 percent of Anglophones work for the Quebec government. In other words, two-thirds of Francophones who graduated from university in the 1960s worked in the Quebec state sector of the economy, while one-third of Anglophones did. For those who had graduated from university before the early 1960s, the comparable figures were: about one-half of Francophones and one-fifth of Anglophones worked for the government.

Finally, not only has the expansion of the state provided, in gigantic proportions, job outlets to university-trained Francophones, but is also seems to have provided them with high incomes, perhaps even more so than if they had worked in a comparable job in the private sector of the economy. The relative income position of workers in the state sector considerably increased in the 1960s, while the income status of workers in the private sector either remained stable or decreased. It is remarkable that the entrance of a given occupational category in the state sector (for Quebec, physicians and surgeons in 1970, teachers in 1964, employees of institutions in 1961 for the most part) has meant a considerable amelioration of their relative income status in the following years. While workers in the state sector over the decade increased their declared incomes by at least one and a half times in constant dollars (two and one-third in current dollars), workers in the private sector have only very slightly increased their incomes.[60] Exactly the same phenomena occurred in Ontario, but, contrary to Quebec, they did not almost exclusively apply to a social collectivity whose survival depended on state expansion.

In short, all the evidence seems to point to the fact that state expansion has provided job outlets to the majority of educated Francophones within Quebec. It has created jobs that presumably were much more powerful, prestigious, and well-paid than the jobs the same individuals could have found in the private sector of the economy. To repeat, the expansion of the state and the creation of new job outlets within it are not unique to Quebec. The same phenomenon has occurred in all provinces and quantitatively perhaps to a comparable degree. What is peculiar to Quebec is that this expansion served as the almost sole institutional basis for the Francophone new middle class as a whole.

State Interventions and Their Ideology

It would be false to say that state expansion benefited only Quebec's new middle class. For one thing, it helped to modernize considerably the economic infrastructure, to the benefit mainly of the capitalist owning class. The Quiet Revolution can indeed by viewed partially as state interventions aimed at socializing the costs of production of the monopolistic sector, despite the fact that profits were to be privately appropriated in foreign hands. As Milner and Milner write:

> While the reforms of the period were genuine and did transform Quebec
> society, they operated only at the middle level. The basic pattern of

economic control, investment, and development was, except for a few adjustments, basically left untouched. Foreign interests were dominant and indeed many of the reforms were designed to encourage even further foreign takeover by providing the owing class with a modern economic infrastructure. As such there was a definite limit on the changes which the architects of the Quiet Revolution could accomplish, beyond what meant attacking the basic economic system root and branch. For the Liberals, being as always a party supporting and supported by big business, such a possibility was dismissed out of hand.[61]

In fact, never was this Quiet Revolution intended to go to the root economic causes of social inequalities between Anglophones and Francophones and among the Francophone population:

> From our vantage point today, we can make out the significant weaknesses at the base of Quiet Revolution. While it opened up the world of ideas to all possibilities, it limited changes in structure to those which meant catching up with North America. Those spheres of society which had been held back under the older order were permitted to expand and grow. The schools, the media, the arts, all experienced a renaissance and soon became the locus for the spread and discussion of the new ideas. The changes, though fundamental in relation to the older order, did not at any point challenge the underlying economic structure of Quebec. And when some intellectuals and writers were no longer content to rail against Ottawa and devise even more complex constitutional schemata, but instead choose to attack the economic system head on; and when these new ideas began to receive attention and consideration among the students and trade unionists — then the authorities decided that things had simply gone too far. "Law and Order" came back into style.[62]

Furthermore, many state interventions only derived from the imperatives to strengthen the economy and to maintain full employment: the government simply had to do something about the high rates of unemployment, the lack of investment, the comparatively declining growth of Quebec total production, and so on. As many economists have indicated, the Quebec GNP has progressed at a high rate despite a relative decrease in private investments, because of massive public investments:

> Let us remember that, during the period 1961–67, public works such as Manic-Outardes (important dam construction), the construction of the Montreal subway, and the preparation of Expo '67 have sustained growth and carried along the private sector. The construction of schools and hospitals between 1967 and 1970 has permitted to escape catastrophe. Finally, since 1971, the preparation of the Olympic Games, the prolongation of the Montreal subway, the construction of Mirabel airport, and the James Bay project are above all responsible for economic growth. Consumption has also been largely sustained by governments. Subsidies of all kinds (transfer payments) have increased, over the last 10 years, at the annual rate of 20% and they now represent in Quebec more than 15% of personal income.[63]

In consequence, two journalists were able to write that "every new brick put up in Quebec costs as much to the taxpayer as it costs the private investor."[64] In fact, a task force to the Department of Industry and Commerce estimated that in Quebec over three-quarters of the jobs created between 1966 and 1972 were linked to government actions, while the proportion is much smaller in Ontario.

Yet, despite these imperatives to maintain the growth of the economy, certain government interventions seemed to be more directly aimed at correcting the social makeup of the Quebec private economy and at providing top control jobs to members of the new middle class.

James Iain Gow has noted that, while the Duplessis regime in nineteen years (1936–40, 1944–1960) had created only five new departments (among which only two remained stable), eight regulatory boards, and one state enterprise:

> The 1960s have seen a much more febrile activity as far as the creation of new administrative institutions is concerned. In six years, the Lesage administration has created six departments, three regulatory boards, eight state enterprises and nine consultative councils. The impetus was followed by the Union Nationale Administrations between 1966 and 1970, with the creation of five new departments, seven regulatory boards, five public enterprises and three consultative councils.[65]

Jean-Jacques Simard has likewise tried to compute the quantitative growth of the state apparatus. He writes:

> The Quebec government includes 23 departments among which only one, the Department of Revenue, has not changed vocation since 1960, 55 consultative boards which were nearly all born in the same period, nine judiciary institutions, and 63 organizations aimed at economic management and regulation. Of the 148 para-governmental organizations, 126 date back only 15 years. The growth of the 250 school boards, the CEGEP, universities and schools, the thousand and more municipal councils, the thousand health and social welfare institutions . . . brought about in the name of coordination and coherence, was proportional to the increase of the financial, administrative and political dependency of these organizations on the upper echelons of government.[66]

All these councils, departments, boards, and enterprises provided previously unexisting high-prestige and high-power jobs for university-trained Francophones. This is indicated, for instance, by the number of people involved in new managerial tasks in the Quebec civil service between 1964 and 1971 (economists, sociologists, social workers, psychologists): it increased by more than 400 percent, while the traditional professional personnel of the government (like doctors and engineers) increased only by 20 percent.[67]

A similar job-creating process seems to have occurred through the economic reforms. To sustain production in some declining French-Canadian industries and to encourage an indigenous capitalism, the Société Générale de Financement was created. Electrical power companies were bought up. To create a public fund out of individual savings, the Caisse de Dépôt et de Placement was created. New enterprises were created to venture into value-producing sectors, such as steel, mining, petroleum, forestry, and so on. In all these cases, the costs of maintaining, buying up, or creating enterprises have been socialized, the profits (if any) nationalized, and the high-power control jobs appropriated by members of the new middle class.

Economist Albert Breton suggested in 1964 that the creation of such jobs may well have been their sole purpose:

> The nationalization of private assets is aimed at providing high-income jobs for nationals, rather than at other objectives connected with rasing social income, such as control of monopoly, increased investment in industries displaying external economies, or purchases of high-yielding public or social goods. This implication is borne out by the most important act of the new nationalist government of Quebec, namely, the nationalization of eleven private power companies. . . . This decision was not a decision about investing in electricity but one about investing in ethnicity. When the decision was made, it was not decided to consider the flow of rewards to society as a whole but only to a group within society . . . the new middle class in Quebec. . . . [The same is true for the Société Générale de Financement where] the resources which could have been invested to increase the social income of the community have been used . . . to keep already existing high-income jobs for the same middle class.[68]

In retrospect, this view is clearly an overstatement. As Carol Jobin has shown, the main impetus behind the nationalization of Quebec private electrical power companies was the inability of these companies to expand in a way that would have been profitable to them.[69] And yet the growth of Quebec's economy required such as expansion. That the new middle class benefited from this nationalization is secondary to the economically determined constraints imposed on the government to further expand the hydro field.

The creation of planning agencies and programs has also provided new job openings and a new mystique about the role of the state. During the 1960s, Quebec evolved broad programs and instituted highly advertised supervisory agencies. Their impact seems to have been negligible as far as tangibly developing Quebec's economy and reducing regional disparities, but they were important for creating prestigious jobs for Francophones. As political scientist Jacques Benjamin has written:

> Everything that has been undertaken in the last twelve years in the field of planning has only an emotive value; Quebec, it seems to me, must first control its economy in one way or the other (directly or indirectly) before creating plans. To first instigate a mystique of the plan and then to control the economy is the same as putting the cart before the horse. For the last twelve years, we have been working backward. We have consciously put the emphasis on the concept of planning while it would have been more fruitful to pay attention to the instruments; the "fever from France" has invaded the offices of the first planners; we wanted to apply the French model integrally to Quebec, while Quebec did not even possess some of the instruments enabling it to operationalize its plans, especially the control of the economy, the coordination between state departments and even political stability in 1968–70.[70]

The reforms of health, education, and welfare displayed gigantic reorganizations but a comparable lack of tangible benefits to the overall population. Although they did considerably facilitate the financial and, to a certain extent, geographical access to medical and educational services, they did not achieve the far-reaching social-democratic ideals that had been put forward. The education reforms were to be conducive to an extensive democratization of education, with new pedagogical relationships, the suppression of class differentials between types of schooling, a decentralization of management to regions, and parents' involvement in decision making. The changes actually implemented have fallen considerably below expectations. The health and social-welfare reforms were to institutionalize a new, more social approach to health and disease, decentralization of decision making to regions and institutions, and worker and consumer participation in the management of these institutions. The reality was again short of what had been promised. The net results of these reforms were huge reorganizations and administrative reshuffling that in a sense did rationalize the allocation of resources. But, above all, these reforms seem either to have maintained or reinforced the powers and privileges of various categories of Francophone professionals, or to have created new interesting jobs for university-trained individuals in the state bureaucracy.

The Unparalleled Status and Legitimacy of Technocratic Elite Groups

This overview of the main interventions of the Quebec state during the 1960s and the 1970s is rapid and oversimplifies several points. Yet, it underlines a key phenomenon. Because the Quebec state is virtually the sole institutional basis for the new middle class, this class has evolved a unique nationalist and social-democratic political culture. The old all-encompassing rhetoric of bishops in the Church has been superseded by an equally far-reaching rhetoric of elite members of the new middle class in the state, but with a different content. As the religious symbols of the past have helped traditional elites maintain their social status in Quebec traditional society, the nationalist and social-democratic ideals of new-middle-class elites now legitimize and reinforce their recently acquired dominance over an increasingly unionized and politicized population. Nationalism is not new in Quebec politics, but its association with social-democratic ideals is. It is this association between nationalism and a mild form of socialism that characterizes the ideology of Quebec's new middle class. Under different forms and with different emphases, both the Liberal party and the Parti Québécois — at different points in its history for the former and more consistently for the latter — have put forward such an ideology.

Such a political culture camouflages the objective interest of this class while at the same time legitimates intervention into more and more aspects of social life through an administratively rational problem-solving approach, thereby furthering its hegemony as a class.

This is not to say that this class manoeuvres in some conspiratorial manner, as if totally conscious of its interests or unconstrained by larger social, political, and economic forces. This is not to say either that administrative rationalization is useless. Quite the contrary: it is sometimes absolutely imperative. The point is that, because expansion of the state serves its interests, the new middle class will support all actions that will produce huge reorganizing, restructuring, reshuffling, *independently* of the objective necessity and feasibility of such transformations. This is so because both the quantitative (budget increase, growth of civil service employees and of the assets of state enterprises, and so on) and the qualitative (involvement in the greatest possible number of areas of social life, increase in the prestige and importance of professional expertise in the government, and increase of the visibility of the state) expansion of the state serves its search for jobs and a local hegemony. In this context, technocratic elite groups and ideologies that share the political culture of the new middle class are bound to be endowed with a status, a legitimacy, and political powers unseen in the rest of Canada, thus providing Quebec with a distinctive strategy of social change.

Conclusion

The combination of the objective material interests of a class in seeing the Quebec state sector of the economy expand quantitatively and qualitatively as well as its self-fulfilling ideological emphasis on nationalism and social-democracy, as argued here, is the most plausible explanation for the distinctive character of Quebec state interventions. There has developed in Quebec a systemic logic, so to speak, that has endowed the inevitable expansion of the state with hopes and expectations far beyond what could be delivered in a capitalist economy and under the present system of national government. Yet it did introduce new political dynamics, the results of which one would be hard pressed to predict. It introduced a new "social imagery" that could lead to a further technocratic and professional takeover or — because of the frustrations, inequities, and fiscal problems the reforms have brought on — it may lead to the tangible implementation of the ideals as advertised. Under the guise of deprofessionalizing through consumer and worker participation, of debureaucratizing through decentralization of decision making, and of repatriating the collective heritage and patrimony through nationalization and creation of state enterprises, government actions have in fact led to a further professionalization, bureaucratization, and concentration of powers and privileges. This contradiction may be managed to the advantage of those who benefit from it, but it may also, in the long run, assume a liberating character.

Notes

1. Quoted in Edmond Orban, "Indicateurs, concepts et objectifs" in *La modernisation politique du Québec*, edited by Edmond Orban (Quebec: Boréal Express, 1976), 7.

2. Unless otherwise noted, these indicators are taken from the various essays in E. Orban, ed., *La modernisation politique du Québec* and from Gary Caldwell and B. Dan Czarnocki, "Un rattrapage raté: Le changement social dans le Québec d'après-guerre, 1950–1974: une comparaison Québec/Ontario," *Recherches Sociographiques* XVII, 1 (1977): 9–58.

3. Denis Monière, *Le développement des idéologies au Québec des origines à nos jours* (Montreal: Éditions Québec-Amérique, 1977), 328.

4. For a discussion of these expenditures consistent with the argument developed in this article, see Daniel Latouche, "La vraie nature . . . de la Révolution tranquille," *Revue Canadienne de Sciences Politiques* VII, 3 (Sept. 1974): 525–35.

5. Here is the share of popular vote for the Union Nationale and the Parti Québécois in the last seven elections: 1956 (UN: 51.5%); 1960 (UN: 46.6%); 1962 (UN: 42.1%); 1966 (UN: 40.9%); 1970 (UN: 20.0%; PQ: 23.6%); 1973 (UN: 5.0%; PQ: 30.2%); 1976 (UN: 18.2%; PQ 41.4%). For analyses of these elections, see for instance Vincent Lemieux, ed., *Quatre élections provinciales* (Quebec: Presses de l'Université Laval, 1969); V. Lemieux, M. Gilbert, and A. Blais, *Une élection de réalignement* (Montreal: Cahiers de Cité libre, Éd. du Jour, 1970); or Robert Boily, "Genèse et développement des partis politiques au Québec," in *La modernisation politique du Québec*, 79–100. For a somewhat positive history of the Union Nationale and its leader, Maurice Duplessis, see Conrad Black, *Duplessis* (Montreal: Les Éditions de l'Homme, 1977).

6. Given the available data, it is impossible to regionalize the effects of federal spending and to estimate with any precision the total amount of spending by the public sector in a given year in a given province. Therefore, it is difficult to estimate the part of each province's GNP (or more precisely the Gross National Expenditure, which is equivalent) accounted for by government spending. For tentative estimates, see Kemal Wassef, "La situation du gouvernement du Québec dans les affaires économiques de la province" (unpublished manuscript, Confédération des Syndicats Nationaux, October 1971); and B. Roy-Lemoine, "The Growth of the State in Quebec" in *The Political Economy of the State: Quebec/Canada/U.S.A.*, edited by D. Roussopoulos (Montreal: Black Rose Books, 1973), 59–87.

7. For the health services, see A.D. McDonald, J.C. McDonald, and P.E. Enterline, "Études sur l'assurance-maladie du Québec," and André Billette, "Santé, classes sociales et politiques redistributive," both in *Sociologie et Sociétés: La gestion de la santé* IX, 1 (April 1977): 52–92.

8. I documented this scenario for health reforms in Marc Renaud, "Réforme ou illusion? Une analyse des interventions de l'État québécois dans le domaine de la santé," *Sociologie et Sociétés: La gestion de la santé* IX, 1 (April 1977): 127–52. Further evidence of the omnipresence of this scenario can be found in a variety of publications. See, for instance, *Une certaine révolution tranquille* (Montreal: Éd. La Presse, 1975); Kenneth McRoberts and Dale Posgate, *Quebec: Social Change and Political Crisis* (Toronto: McClelland and Stewart, 1976); Pierre Doray, "Une pyramide tronquée: les politiques de sécurité du revenu pour les retraités" (M.Sc. thesis, Département de sociologie, Université de Montréal, 1978); Diane Poliquin-Bourassa, "La réforme de l'éducation: phase II" in *Premier mandat*, edited by Daniel Latouche, vol. II (Montreal: Éditions de l'Aurore, 1977): 15–26; and Michel Pelletier and Yves Vaillancourt, *Les politiques sociales et les travailleurs, Les années 60* (Montreal: available from the authors, 1974).

9. Although present in the literature for a long time (e.g., Hubert Guindon, "Social Unrest, Social Class and Quebec's Bureaucratic Revolution" in *Social Stratification in Canada*, edited by J.E. Curtis and W.G. Scott (Toronto: Prentice-Hall, 1973), this hypothesis has been systematized by Gilles Bourque and Nicole Frenette in "La structure nationale québécoise," *Socialisme québécois* 21, 2 (1970): 109–56. A similar hypothesis has simultaneously been developed in Luc Racine and Roch Denis, "La conjoncture politique depuis 1960," ibid.: 17–78. Using different paradigms (in the sense of Robert R. Alford, "Towards a Critical Sociology of Political Power" in *Stress and Contradictions in Modern Capitalism*, edited by Léon Lindberg (Lexington, 1975): 145–60) a vast series of authors have expanded on a similar hypothesis. See, for instance, Anne Legaré, *Les classes sociales au Québec* (Montreal: Presses de l'Université du Québec, 1977); Pierre Fournier, *The Quebec Establishment: The Ruling Class and the State* (Montreal: Black Rose Books, 1976); Marcel Fournier, "La question nationale: les enjeux," *Possibles* 1, 2 (Winter 1977): 7–18; Daniel Latouche, "La vraie nature"; Denis Monière, *Le développement des idéologies au Québec*.

10. For a discussion of these terms, see Anthony Giddens, *The Class Structure of Advanced Societies* (New York: Harper and Row, 1973).

11. See, for instance, Pierre-Paul Proulx, ed., *Vers une problématique globale du développement de la région de Montréal* (Montréal: CRDE, June 1976); P. Fréchette, R. Jouandet-Bernadat, and J.P. Vézina, *L'économie du Québec* (Montreal: Les Éditions HRW Ltée, 1975); Ministère de l'Industrie et du Commerce, *Une politique économique québécois* (Quebec, Jan. 1974). This is also confirmed by the study of G. Caldwell and B.D. Czarnocki, "Un rattrapage raté."

12. James O'Connor, *The Fiscal Crisis of the State* (New York: St. Martin's Press, 1973); for further conceptual development, see his *The Corporations and the State: Essays in the Theory of Capitalism and Imperalism* (New York: Harper and Row, 1975).

13. See, for instance, the essays published in Marcel Rioux and Yves Martin, eds., *French-Canadian Society* (Toronto: McClelland and Stewart, 1964). See also Denis Monière, *Le développement des idéologies au Québec*, and Maurice Saint-Germain, *Une économie à libérer: le Québec analysé dans ses structures économiques* (Montreal: Presses de l'Université de Montréal, 1973).

14. Hubert Guindon, "The Social Evolution of Quebec Reconsidered" in *French-Canadian Society*, 137–61, and his "Social Unrest, Social Class and Quebec's Bureaucratic Revolution."

15. French Canadians had one of the highest birth rates in the industrialized world. Now it is among the lowest in Canada. See Jacques Henripin, "From Acceptance of Nature to Control: The Demography of the French Canadians since the Seventeenth Century," in *French-Canadian Society*, 204–15. See also Bureau de la statistique du Québec, *Tendances passées et perspectives d'évolution de la fécondité au Québec* (Quebec, 1976).

16. Some violent strikes have, however, occurred after the war. For a sociological analysis of these, see Hélène David, "La grève et le bon Dieu: la grève de l'amiante au Québec," *Sociologie et Société* I, 2 (Nov. 1969): 249–76, and "L'état des rapports de classe au Québec de 1945 à 1967," *Sociologie et Société* VII, 2: 33–66. On the beginnings of trade unionism, see Louis Maheau, "Problème social et naissance du syndicalisme catholique," *Sociologie et Société* I, 1 (May 1969), and Louis-Marie Tremblay, *Le syndicalisme québécois: idéologies de la CSN et de la FTQ 1940–1970* (Montreal: Presses de l'Université de Montréal, 1972).

17. Examples of the convergence of interests between the Church, political leaders, and "foreign" entrepreneurs abound. For instance, the Roman Catholic hierarchy supported simultaneously foreign corporations and French-Canadian workers in the development of trade unions. The actions of political leaders are even clearer as manifest in the proxy battle for the St-Lawrence Corporation, the 99-year leases to Iron Ore and others. For more examples, see the appendices to the manifestoes of the Quebec trade unions (translated in Daniel Drache, ed., *Quebec: Only the Beginning* (Toronto: New Press, 1972), and in *Quebec Labour* (Montreal: Black Rose Books, 1972). On the relations between political leaders and the corporate world, the most systematic study is Pierre Fournier, *The Quebec Establishment*. See also Union des Travailleurs du Papier et du Carton Façonnés, *Les Tigres de Carton* (Montreal: Éditions Québécoises, n.d.); Groupe de Recherches Économiques, *Les Compagnies de Finance* (Montreal: Éditions Québécoises, n.d.).

18. André Raynauld, *La propriété des entreprises au Québec* (Montreal: Presses de l'Université de Montréal, 1974), 78.

19. André Raynauld, "The Quebec Economy: A General Assessment" in *Quebec Society and Politics: Views from the Inside*, edited by Dale C. Thomson (Toronto: McClelland and Stewart, 1973), 152, my emphasis.

20. Report of the Royal Commission on Bilingualism and Biculturalism, Book III, *The Work World* (Ottawa: Queen's Printer, 1969), 447.

21. For descriptions of this industrial structure, see Gilles Lebel, *Horizon 1980: une étude sur l'évolution de l'économie du Québec de 1946 à 1968 et sur ses perspectives d'avenir* (Quebec: Ministère de l'Industrie et du Commerce, 1970); and P. Fréchette et al., *L'économie du Québec*.

22. For an examination of foreign dominance over the Canadian economy, see Kari Levitt, *Silent Surrender* (Toronto: Macmillan, 1970); R. Laxer, ed., *Canada Ltd., The Political Economy of Dependency* (Toronto: McClelland and Stewart, 1973); Wallace Clement, *Continental Corporate Power* (Toronto: McClelland and Stewart, 1977); T. Naylor, *The History of Canadian Business* (Toronto: Lorimer, 1975). For an examination of foreign dominance over the Quebec economy, see André Raynauld, *La propriété des entreprises au Québec*; Jorge Niosi, "Le gouvernement du PQ, le capital américain et le contrôle canadien" (unpublished paper, Département de sociologie, Université du Québec à Montréal, 1978); and Arnaud Sales, "La différenciation nationale et ethnique de la bourgeoisie industrielle au Québec," and "Le gouvernement du Parti Québécois et les pouvoirs économiques" (unpublished papers, Département de sociologie, Université de Montréal, 1978). As Niosi and Sales have convincingly shown, despite foreign dominance, an identifiable *grande* bourgeoisie exists among the Francophone segment of the Quebec population, but it is comparatively small and concentrated in specific economic sectors.

23. *Canadian Census*, 1961, vol. III, part 2, table 9; *Canadian Census*, 1971, vol. III, part 4, table 10.

24. Ministère de l'Industrie et du Commerce, *Une Politique Économique Québécoise* (mimeographed, 1974), 18.

25. Ibid., 9.

26. André Raynauld, *La propriété des entreprises au Québec*, 147.

27. Report of the Royal Commission on Bilingualism and Biculturalism, 81.

28. John Porter, "The Economic Elite and the Social Structure in Canada" in *Canadian Society*, edited by B.R. Blishen, F.E. Jones, K.D. Naegele and J. Porter (Toronto: Macmillan, 1961), 486–500.

29. Sheilagh Hodgins Milner and Henry Milner, *The Decolonization of Quebec: An Analysis of Left-Wing Nationalism* (Toronto: McClelland and Stewart, 1973).

30. Wallace Clement, *The Canadian Corporate Elite: An Analysis of Economic Power* (Toronto: McClelland and Stewart, 1975).

31. André Raynauld, *La Propriété des entreprises au Québec*.

32. Milner and Milner, *The Decolonization of Quebec*, 71.

33. Clement, *The Canadian Corporate Elite*, 233–34.

34. Robert Presthus, *Elite Accommodation in Canadian Politics* (Cambridge: Cambridge University Press, 1973).

35. Clement, *The Canadian Corporate Elite*, 234. As Pierre Fournier has argued in "Les tendances nouvelles du pouvoir économique au Québec," *Le Devoir*, 9 and 10 juin 1976, there is something intrinsically misleading in this approach. Generally, it tends to underestimate the importance of the French-Canadian bourgeoisie because it computes only the number of persons on corporate boards, a number likely to be substantially increased by legislation forcing French as the language of work in Quebec. Further, since these data are limited to the corporate world, they do not include this segment of the Quebec bourgeoisie linked to the co-operative movement (Mouvement Desjardins, Coopérative Fédérée, Coopérative agricole de Granby) and to state enterprises (like Sidbec, Dosco, and the Société Générale de Financement).

36. Tore Thonstad with C. Fluet and C. Ross, *Simulations de la pénétration des francophones parmi les cadres du secteur privé au Québec, 1971–1986*, Études réalisées pour le compte de la Commission d'enquête sur la situation de la langue française et sur les droits linguistiques au Québec (L'éditeur officiel du Québec, February 1974).

37. Dominique Clift, "French Elite Lags in Salary Scale," *La Presse* (1975).

38. Report of the Royal Commission on Bilingualism and Biculturalism, 488.

39. M.V. George, *Internal Migration in Canada: Demographic Analyses* (Ottawa: Statistics Canada, 1970).

40. John Porter, *The Vertical Mosaic: An Analysis of Social Class and Power in Canada* (Toronto: University of Toronto Press, 1965).

41. For reasons of space, all tables have been dropped from this article. For further detail, see Marc Renaud, "The Political Economy of the Quebec Health-Care Reforms" (Ph.D. thesis, University of Wisconsin, Madison, 1976), 411–28.

42. Guy Rocher and Yves de Jocas, "Inter-Generation Occupational Mobility in the Province of Quebec," *The Canadian Journal of Economics and Political Science* 23, 1 (Feb. 1957).

43. Jacques Dofny and Muriel Garon-Audy, "Mobilités Professionnelles au Québec," *Sociologie et Societé* I, 2 (Nov. 1969): 277–302.

44. Ibid., 287.

45. Jacques Brazeau, "Quebec's Emerging Middle Class" in *French Canadian Society*, 296–306.

46. Ian Adams, William Cameron, Brian Hill, and Peter Penz, *The Real Poverty Report* (Edmonton: Hurtig, 1971), 219.

47. See Hélène Ostiguy, "Statistiques détaillées relatives à l'enseignement supérieur" (unpublished manuscript, Université de Montréal, Département de Sociologie, September 1971).

48. Gross general expenditures reflect the administrative burden of a given level of government. Net general expenditures reflect the fiscal burden. From an accounting point of view, the difference is constituted by the following items: (1) All revenues of institutions coming under the government; (2) revenues in the form of interests, premiums, and discounts; (3) grants-in-aid and shared-cost contributions; (4) all capital revenue. These revenues are deducted from the corresponding gross expenditures to obtain the net general expenditures.

49. Statistics Canada, *Federal Government Finance, Revenue and Expenditure, Assets and Liabilities* (Catalgoue no. 68–211), *Provincial Government Finance, Revenue and Expenditure* (Catalogue no. 68–207), *Local Government Finance, Revenue and Expenditure, Assets and Liabilities* (Catalogue no. 68–204).

50. Research and Statistics Division, Department of National Health and Welfare, *Government Expenditures on Health and Social Welfare—Canada, 1927–1959* (Social Security Series, memorandum no. 16, Ottawa, 1961), 45; and Canadian Tax Foundation, *The National Finance 1973-74*, 24.

51. Statistics Canada, *Provincial Government Enterprise Finance* (Catalogue no. 61–204); *Federal Government Enterprise Finance* (Catalogue no. 61–203).

52. Statistics Canada, *Consolidated Government Finance — Federal, Provincial and Local Governments, Revenue and Expenditures* (Catalogue no. 68–202).

53. For systematic summaries of the evolution of Ontario, see a series of publications issued by the Ontario Economic Council and entitled *The Evolution of Policy in Contemporary Ontario.*

54. *Annuaire du Québec* (1971), 733.

55. Claude Morin, "The Gospel According to Holy Ottawa" in *Quebec Society and Politics: Views from the Inside,* edited by Dale C. Thomson (Toronto: McClelland and Stewart, 1973), 210.

56. *Canadian Census,* 1971, vol. 3, part III, table 5.

57. Report of the Royal Commission on Bilingualism and Biculturalism, 474–75.

58. Pierre-Paul Gagné, "L'Hydro et les Québécois: l'histoire d'amour achève," *La Presse* (13 June 1975), A-8.

59. The Quebec state is here defined as the provincial and municipal governmental bureaucracies as well as the electricity and the relevant parts of the education and health-care fields. It does not include state enterprises other than Hydro-Québec.

60. Department of National Revenue, *Taxation Statistics, Analysing the Returns of Individuals for the 1960, 1965, 1970, 1972, 1974, Taxation Year and Miscellaneous Statistics,* table 9.

61. Milner and Milner, *The Decolonization of Quebec,* 169.

62. Ibid., 191–92. A similar observation is expressed in Gérald Bernier, "Le cas québécois et les théories du développement politique et de la dépendance," in *La modernisation politique du Québec,* 19–54; and in Denis Monière, *Le développement des idéologies au Québec,* chap. 8.

63. Translated from Jean-P. Vézina, "Le développement économique: les enjeux en cause" in *Premier mandat,* 51.

64. Rhéal Bercier and Robert Pouliot, "Le pénible apprentissage de l'état québécois en matière de croissance: la charrue avant les boeufs . . ." *La Presse* (14 June 1975), A-7.

65. Translated from James Iain Gow, "L'évolution de l'administration publique du Québec 1867–1970" (unpublished paper, Département de Sciences Politiques, Université de Montréal), 37. See also his "Modernisation et administration publique" in *La modernisation politique du Québec,* 157–86.

66. Translated from Jean-Jacques Simard, "La longue marche des technocrates," *Recherches Sociologiques* XVIII, 1 (1977), 119.

67. Ibid., 122.

68. Albert Breton, "The Economics of Nationalism," *The Journal of Political Economy* (1964), 382, 384, and 385.

69. Carol Jobin, "La nationalisation de l'électricité au Québec en 1962" (M.A. thesis, Université du Québec à Montréal, 1974).

70. Translated from Jacques Benjamin, *Planification et politique au Québec* (Montreal: Les Presses de l'Université de Montréal, 1974), 114.

THE SOURCES OF NEO-NATIONALISM IN QUEBEC†

KENNETH McROBERTS

With the 1960s a new form of nationalism emerged in French Quebec. It professed to be territorial, defining the outer limits of the nation in terms of the established provincial boundaries of Quebec. While not necessarily separatist, its advocates sought a transformation of existing Canadian political institutions. They wanted a vast expansion of the powers of the Quebec provincial government, so that it could truly function as a "national state." Their vision of society was essentially secular, with advanced industrialism as the primary goal. Many of the new nationalists linked their national self-determination with "social democratic" or "socialist" ideals; in some cases national self-determination was seen as merely a precondition for class revolution.

In all these respects, the neo-nationalism of the 1960s differed markedly from the previous manifestations of nationalism among Quebec Francophones. But, in each of them, it was similar to many of the nationalist movements which arose during the same period in long-established Western European states. There too the new nationalism has been concerned with restructuring state institutions, to assure greater political autonomy, if not independence, for the "national" group. There too it has argued that central state institutions have worked against the economic interests of the "nation," depriving it of needed industrial and technological development. Frequently, these arguments have been tied to "leftist" social and political models.[1]

In Quebec, as in Western Europe, moreover, the recent wave of nationalism does not constitute a totally new phenomenon. Rather it is but the most recent manifestation of longstanding traditions of nationalist affirmation. These traditions are in turn based upon definitions of collective identity that were formed decades, if not centuries, ago.

†*Ethnic and Racial Studies* 7, 1 (Jan. 1984): 55–85. The author would like to thank Daniel Drache, Phillip Rawkins, and Glyn Williams for their comments on an earlier draft of this paper.

In the case of Quebec, a common identity was fashioned in the seventeenth century, while Quebec was still a French colony. The term *Canadien* was used to identify the colony's white settlers. It served to distinguish them not only from the settlers of the British colonies to the south but from metropolitan Frenchmen as well. While there was no movement seeking to restructure Quebec's linkages with France, let alone dissolve them through secession, there was open *Canadien* resentment over the appointment of metropolitan Frenchmen to top political and ecclesiastical positions within the colony.[2] During the subsequent century of direct British rule, initiated by the conquest of 1760, the primary function of the term *Canadien* was to distinguish the descendants of New France from the English-speakers who began to settle within the colony in increased numbers. Often the linguistic qualifier was added for good measure, as in *Canadien français*. This continued to be the practice after Quebec became linked with the three other British colonies in the Canadian Confederation of 1867. Within Canada, the *Canadiens* were very much the minority. But only in the 1960s did Francophones of Quebec adopt the more restricted, territorially-based identity of Québécois.

An important nationalist movement can be located in the early decades of the nineteenth century. During the 1820s, the *Patriote* movement emerged, under a largely liberal professional leadership.[3] Preeminently political, it demanded more autonomous political institutions that would be clearly responsible to the colony's population, with its heavily *Canadien* majority. These demands were justified by claims that the colony's English-speaking population, at times with the tacit support of the British colonial authorities, was threatening central *Canadien* institutions, such as the seigneurial system, the Civil Code and the French language itself. *Canadien* members of the legislative assembly managed to bring the colonial government to a virtual standstill. Finally, the *Patriotes* staged armed insurrections in 1837 and 1838, which were rapidly put down by British authorities. The failure of the rebellions marked the end of this first phase of *Canadien* nationalism, with its open confrontation with the established political regime.

In the wake of the rebellions, the worst fears of the *Canadien* leaders were realized. The British authorities formally adopted the goal of assimilating the *Canadiens*, determining that this was the most expeditious way to prevent further such occurrences. To this end, the colony of Quebec (Lower Canada) was joined with Ontario (Upper Canada). Nonetheless, the *Canadien* leaders were able to frustrate this assimilationist strategy as they established a working relationship with Upper Canadian reformers. Many elements of dualism emerged within the new government.[4] French and English were given legal status. For many government functions, separate administrative establishments were maintained for the two provinces. Hyphenated ministries were held by representatives of each of the two original colonies. After 1848, the capital was rotated regularly between Toronto and Quebec. A form of double-majority principle was observed in many instances (but violated in others), according to which issues of concern to a region could be decided only with concurrence of a majority of the region's members.

From the *Canadien* point of view, the United Canadas had become an advantageous arrangement, especially as Upper Canada's population began to exceed Lower Canada's. But, for precisely the same reasons, the arrangements were not popular among Anglophones (especially in Upper Canada). Thus, by the 1850s, Anglophones were spearheading a movement to merge Quebec and Ontario with other British colonies. Within this new arrangement, established through Confederation in 1867, the *Canadiens* were very much in a minority position. In fact, Confederation had been opposed by one faction of nationalist leaders who claimed that the terms of Confederation did not provide sufficient protection for the cultural distinctiveness of the *Canadiens*.

Despite the weakened position in which it put the *Canadiens*, relative at least to the United Canadas, Confederation was not seriously challenged during its first nine decades. Most descendants of New France continued to define themselves as *Canadiens* (or *Canadiens français*). Within Quebec, at least, they continued to use French as their primary language (usually having little or no command of English). French-Canadian nationalism persisted, and in some respects flourished, as intellectual and political elites continued to evoke the past glories of the *Canadien* nation and to call upon the contemporary generation to remain faithful to its cultural heritage. There were repeated instances of conflict between French Canadians and their Anglophone compatriots, often involving policies of federal or provincial governments. Typically, the French Canadians lost. At times, nationalists sounded alarms over what were seen as departures or violations of the original Confederation agreements. But it was not until the 1960s that large numbers of them began to place Confederation itself in question.

Confederation and French Canadians: The Limits to Accommodation

In attempting to explain this long quiescence and, by the same token, the neo-nationalist outburst of the 1960s, one might well begin with the political institutions that Confederation put in place. Many students have seen the functioning of state institutions as the critical variable in accounting for nationalist movements in other settings. To be sure, this literature has produced contradictory propositions. For some, tolerance of cultural diversity by the state facilitates and largely explains the persistence and growth of the nationalist movements.[5] Yet, this presumes the states can in fact choose to deny the existence of such groups, without incurring a blacklash of even greater proportions. The presumption may hold in some settings, but clearly not in all. The size and resources of the group at hand may be simply too great. In some cases, then, one must adopt the quite opposite presumption that, unless states seek to accommodate diversity in one fashion or another, they will face dismemberment. This, of course, is the underlying assumption of such theories of conflict management as Arend Lijphart's consociational democracy, in which through a series of devices political elites can achieve the degree of accommodation necessary for the state's survival.[6] Canada would seem to be such an instance, given the French-Canadian population's relative size (abut 30 percent of the total population) and its level of solidarity. Thus, one might expect that the explanation of Canada's long quiescence and the recent nationalist upsurge lies in the development and ultimate collapse of an elaborate political accommodation along the lines of consociationalism. After all, forms of consociationalism had been developed during the period of the United

Canadas and, as we have seen, had served to render the regime quite popular among *Canadiens*. In point of fact, however, Confederation provided a much more limited accommodation of the *Canadiens*.[7] Neither at the federal level nor at the provincial level (except for Quebec) did the new political institutions clearly function according to consociationalist norms. Accommodation of French Canadians was limited primarily to federalism, with the creation of an autonomous Quebec provincial government.

In part, as developed by Lijphart,[8] consociationalism entails proportional representation within political institutions. At the federal level, French Canadians have indeed enjoyed representation in the House of Commons, the Supreme Court, and, in most cases, the Cabinet, which is roughly proportional to their numerical presence in the Canadian population. (In addition, the BNA Act guaranteed the right to use French in Parliament and in federal courts, along with their Quebec provincial counterparts.) But in the Cabinet French Canadians traditionally were absent from the more important economic portfolios[9] and, until recent years, they were underrepresented in the upper levels of the federal bureaucracy.[10] In all of the provincial governments but Quebec, Francophones played a marginal role, or no role at all. Beyond mere representation, consociationalism also entails decision-making rules that require more than a simple majority, so as to afford adequate protection to "subcultures."[11] But in the House of Commons, decision-making is on precisely that basis. In the Cabinet, decision-making rules are less explicit. But there is no evidence that Quebec, or *Canadien*, members of the Cabinet enjoyed a formal veto (an important consociational device). Nor was the alternative consociational device of decision-making by "grand coalition" always followed within the Cabinet. There were instances of Cabinets being formed without significant Quebec representation, even when potential candidates existed among the government ranks in the House.

Not only does the historical role of *Canadiens* within federal institutions fall short of consociational standards, but there have been celebrated instances in which Anglophone and Francophone representatives took opposing positions with, in each case, the Anglophone position ultimately prevailing. Most important among these were the decision to hang Métis rebel Louis Riel, to contribute to the Imperial effort during the Boer War, and to impose conscription for overseas service in the two world wars. Each instance provoked a strong reaction within Francophone public opinion in Quebec. By the same token, Anglophone interests clearly prevailed in all of the provincial governments but Quebec. With the turn of the century, provincial governments severely restricted the provision of public education in French. Only within Quebec were education and other public services made available in French. The refusal of these provincial governments, and in many respects the federal government as well, to provide non-Quebec Francophones with French language services left these populations all the more exposed to assimilationist pressures. As a result, from the beginning of this century the Francophone minorities in most provinces declined markedly. In the process, the *Canadien* nation has become increasingly coterminous with the boundaries of Quebec.

In the end, it should not be surprising that consociationalism should be largely absent under Confederation. Within the United Canadas, where a semblance of consociationalism did exist, Quebec enjoyed a rough demographic parity with its partner. (In fact, Quebec's population had been slightly larger than Ontario's in 1840.) Thus, within the liberal presumptions of the day, it was quite appropriate that Quebec should be assigned half of the seats. The hyphenated ministries and double-majority principle followed from this. With Confederation the demographic balance was broken (in fact that had been a primary purpose of Confederation). Within the new political system, little more than thirty percent of the population was French-speaking; the rest was overwhelming English-speaking (in fact sixty percent of the total population was of British origin). As Lijphart notes, demographic "hegemony of one of the segments" is hardly conducive to consociationalism.[12]

To the extent that Confederation entailed an accommodation of *Canadiens*, the accommodation rested upon not consociationalism but federalism.[13] As such, it was a precarious one. Federalism provided Quebec with a provincial government, which would be responsible to an overwhelmingly Francophone electorate. (By the same token, of course, the other provincial governments would be responsible to essentially Anglophone clienteles.) An autonomous provincial government with jurisdiction over such matters as civil law, education and welfare may have been sufficient to forestall fears among Quebec Francophones of forced assimilation. Even if it were led by its Anglophone majority to do so, the federal government would not have the jurisdictional powers to stage a concerted assimilationist program. Yet, as the essential basis of accommodation of *Canadiens*, a Quebec provincial government was an ambiguous device. While it provided a certain security for Quebec Francophones it also provided the institutional base for a Quebec nationalism, in which the welfare of the "nation" would require a reinforced, if not sovereign, Quebec state. This possibility was all the greater given the demographic concentration of Francophones in Quebec, the hostility to Francophone interests of the other provinces, and the weak presence of Francophones in federal institutions. Yet, over many decades, despite repeated provocations, this potential was not realized.

In part, the ultimate emergence of Quebec nationalism can be traced to the rise of threats to Quebec's provincial autonomy, this essential concession to the *Canadiens*. In the wake of World War II, emboldened by Keynesian notions of state economic management, the federal state embarked upon a series of initiatives that involved spending within provincial jurisdiction. These programs touched upon areas that Francophone nationalists saw as critical to the cultural distinctiveness of French Canadians, such as education and social welfare. They provoked a strong nationalist reaction. But this reaction in itself cannot explain the nationalist upsurge of the 1960s. Rather than securing simply the retreat of the federal state to its own legislative jurisdictions, the neo-nationalists demanded a wholesale revision of the division of jurisdictions. As such, they seemed to be responding to more than simply the postwar centralization of Canadian political institutions. A more profound force appears to have been at work.

Over recent years, students of nationalism in many different settings have sought to locate this force in the underlying economic relationships in which ethnic groups find themselves. Within this perspective, political institutions are important not so much for their tolerance and recognition of cultural specificity, although this is important, as for their contribution to the underlying structure of economic relations among ethnic groups. Ultimately, neo-nationalist movements are seen as a response to these economic relations; it is economic discontent that reinforces ethnic economic relations; it is economic discontent that reinforces ethnic identity and makes it the basis of political movements. Several different patterns have been identified within this line of analysis.

Perhaps the best known application of this approach lies in Michael Hechter's notions of "internal colony."[14] For various reasons — economic, political, military — a stronger, more developed "core" region imposes itself upon another region. Through discriminatory practices, the core region ensures that the subsequent economic development of the peripheral region is geared to its needs. In effect, the peripheral region becomes an "internal colony" of the core. This "colonial" relationship between regions is paralleled by a "cultural division of labour." Since high-status positions are reserved for residents of the core region and periphery populations are related to lower-level positions, cultural differences that happen to distinguish the populations of the two regions also become criteria for admission to occupational categories. As a result of this cultural division of labour, interregional cultural difference become the primary basis of collective identity for the residents of the periphery. Over time, it may also become the focus of agitation for the autonomy and secession of the peripheral region.

As Tom Nairn has demonstrated, nationalist movements need not be restricted to regions that are "underdeveloped," let alone "internal colonies." Within a state whose economy is basically peripheral to continental economic centres, there may exist a more dynamic region that stands as a "middle-class enclave in a more backward country."[15] This "overdeveloped" region may come to resent the continued political domination of the backward state, finding it to be a drag on its own economic development. Catalonia and the Basque country have long resented the domination of distant capitals more attuned to the backward regions of their respective states. Ulster refused to join the new Irish state for what were essentially the same reasons (despite the "archaic religious dimension of the conflict.")[16] And with the decline of industrial England and the extraction of North Sea oil, Scotland has now joined this category.

Within one analysis it is only these "overdeveloped" regions that can produce serious nationalist movements. Peter Gourevitch has drawn a sharp distinction between economic and political leadership functions. He contends that if the two relationships coincide, with economic and political leadership functions being performed in the same region, then peripheral nationalism in other regions will be weak. In effect, then, with an "internal colony" the prospects of securing autonomy would appear to be too remote for a nationalist movement to attract substantial support. It is only if the two functions are located in different regions that there is the possibility of autonomist movements. The movements will appear in regions with "ethnic potential" that exercise economic functions but not political ones. (Presumably, there would be no incentive for a politically-dominant but economically-weak region to move towards autonomy.) This non-congruence of functions may be a longstanding condition, as with Catalonia, the Basque country, or Croatia, or of recent origin, as with Scotland, where England's industrial decline has been combined with the appearance of a new "trump card" of North Sea oil.[17]

In fact, however, the patterns of relations among regions may be even more complex than these various formulations allow. The notions of "over-development" and "non-congruence of functions" are found by the same bipartism that marks the "internal colony" model. The relationship lies between one region and another region (or a set of regions that all play the same role). Yet, in many cases, a region may be closely linked to several regions and these relationships may differ radically in character. A region may be bound as a periphery to one region, yet nonetheless succeed in reducing other regions to being peripheries of its own. This possibility is evoked by Immanual Wallerstein's notion of "semi-peripheries": "In part they [semi-peripheries] act as a peripheral zone for core countries and in part they act as a core country for some peripheral areas."[18] (While Wallerstein presents this pattern of relationships as one among countries, it obviously could include regions within a country as well.) Such complexity in interregional relationships is bound to affect the strength and direction of nationalist movements. For instance, if all the regions are within a single state, then assessing the desirability of regional independence would involve complex trade-offs in which the gains of disengagement from a core must be balanced against the costs of losing peripheries.

A second problem shared by much of this literature is a tendency, perhaps acquired from the nationalist groups under study, to see governments and government policies as the essential cause of economic difference among regions. In most cases, the actual role of government policy is more limited. Usually, continuing peripheral status will be to at least some extent due to the persistence of the very factors that had disadvantaged the region in the first place, making it vulnerable to incorporation by the core, whether they be access to world markets, to needed resources of to adequate pools of capital or the possession of a labour force with necessary skills. One could perhaps argue that incorporation into a larger political unit reduces the likelihood of policies designed specifically to rectify these deficiencies. But it would be difficult to demonstrate that the policies alone ("discriminatory" or not) had caused the region to remain disadvantaged. One could imagine discriminatory policies having a clear impact if the relative value of the periphery's economic base were somehow to be transformed through changing economic conditions, as in the case of resources whose prices on the world market were to change dramatically, and the core imposed policies that prevented the periphery from profiting fully from its new position. But, even then, there must be limits to what policies alone can accomplish. This is shown by the instances of "overdeveloped" regions, such as Catalonia, who have secured and retained core economic functions despite the fact that other regions controlled the policies of central political institutions and caused them to reflect their regional interests.

Both the need to conceptualize networks of interregional relations and the importance of specifying carefully the specific role of government policy in shaping these relations are demonstrated by the case of Quebec.

Quebec's Interregional Relations

There is no simple way to characterize the economic relations among regions. Different indicators can produce quite different results. The most straightforward way to assess regional advantage or disadvantage would be to look at aggregate measures of economic well-being, such as per capita income or levels of unemployment. But the concept of uneven development (let alone "internal colony") clearly involves some notion of difference in the economic functions of regions. Thus, it is important to compare the extent to which regions have been able to go beyond primary production to various forms of secondary manufacturing. Moreover, one would like to see whether these specializations were structurally related; in interregional exchange does one region tend to be supplier of resources and the other supplier of manufactured goods? Finally, the concept involves some notion of control of a region's economy from the outside. Thus, one should look at the extent to which enterprises (whatever their primary activity) are owned by residents of the region. Ideally, one would have data on the movement of profits that these enterprises generate: do these profits stay in the region or are they transferred to other regions whether as dividends to shareholders or as capital movements or in-house sales between the subsidiary and the head office? One might also look at the extent to which a region has been able to impose itself as a site through which other region's goods are transferred when they are exported to the world market.

On the basis of these indicators, Quebec has occupied a rather complex position throughout this century. The fact of the matter is that Quebec has been simultaneously linked to several different regions: parts of the United States; the other Central Canadian province of Ontario; the four provinces of Atlantic Canada; and the four provinces of Western Canada. In effect, Quebec has been involved in a whole system of linkages. Moreover, the nature of these different linkages varies enormously. Certainly, Quebec's position cannot be readily reduced to the type of simple core-periphery analysis that figures in the literature on nationalist movements. To some extent, but not completely, this complexity in regional position may explain some of the ambiguities that have marked the neo-nationalist movement in Quebec.

Since the beginning of this century, if not before, the Quebec economy has been very much in a dependent position vis-à-vis the United States. This is clearly reflected in measures of aggregate economic well-being such as income and unemployment levels.[19] But it can also be seen in the relative strength of manufacturing sectors, as revealed by the extent to which Quebec stands as a net importer of manufactured goods from the United States (while being a net exporter of primary goods).[20] Finally, it can be shown that US interests control a large part of activity within the Quebec economy. In 1970, 44.6 percent of the value-added of manufacturing in Quebec came from US-owned firms.[21] In short, by every measure Quebec stands as a periphery (or at least semi-periphery) in its linkages with the United States. As we shall see, this dependence on the United States is not particular to Quebec; it marks Ontario as well. There has been a vigorous debate over the cause of this pattern. But we will argue that American international superiority in technology has been a primary factor in creating and maintaining dependence.

With respect to the two regional extremities of Canada, Western Canada and Atlantic Canada, measures of economic well-being produce quite different results. Per capita income has been lower in Quebec than in Western Canada and unemployment higher. But by both measures, Quebec has fared better than Atlantic Canada.[22] Nonetheless, Quebec outscores both regions in terms of all the other measures. Quebec always has produced a much larger share of value-added in manufacturing (even in proportion to population) than have the other regions.[23] And it clearly has been the winner in the trade of manufactured goods with each of the two regions.[24] Moreover, Quebec continues to have a larger share of head offices than either of the two regions.[25] Thus, in its linkages with the two regions, Quebec continues to assume the role of a core.

In this case, governmental policies clearly have played an important role in shaping regional advantage and disadvantage. Through the imposition of tariffs on manufactured goods, the federal government has in effect forced Western Canadians and Atlantic Canadians to buy manufactured goods from Quebec at a higher price than they would be available elsewhere. Thus, without such policies Quebec would have been unable to assume as many core manufacturing functions. Moreover, Montreal enterprises were strongly aided by policies of the federal government in their successful bid to control Western Canada's economic development. The Canadian Pacific Railway drew upon enormous government subsidies to construct a railway line to the Pacific, and thus become the major transporter of goods to and from the Prairies. The Montreal banks were protected by federal legislation impeding the entry of foreign banks to Canada and by the federal government's refusal to charter banks based in Western Canada. Finally, the Quebec economy (along with the economies of Ontario and Atlantic Canada) has benefited from federal measures to maintain the domestic price of oil below world levels (at the expense of the Western Canadian producing provinces). Clearly, federal policies have made it possible for Quebec (and Ontario) to secure more of the core functions vis-à-vis Western Canada than would otherwise have been the case. In fact, one might argue that until the mid-1930s, if not later, Western Canada was quite literally an "internal colony" of Ontario and Quebec.[26] It would be harder to argue, however, that without these policies Western Canada would itself have been less of a peripheral economy, becoming for instance a significant manufacturing centre.[27] More likely, it would simply have been a periphery to an American core rather than a Central Canadian one.

On the other hand, in its relations with Ontario, Quebec emerges as the weaker economy. By such measures of well-being as per capita income and levels of unemployment, Quebec has been consistently weaker since the early nineteenth century.[28] With respect to manufacturing activity, throughout this century Quebec has had a lower proportion of its labour force concentrated in manufacturing than has Ontario.[29] Moreover, compared with Ontario its manufacturing tends to be in "softer," more labour-intensive industries. In 1974, Ontario was marginally the winner in trade of manufactured goods between Quebec and

Ontario.[30] As for the location of control functions, Quebec has seen a steady decline of its position for several decades now. At the beginning of this century Montreal was still the financial centre of the Canadian economy. Now Montreal's stock exchange is a mere shadow of the Toronto exchange. In recognition of Toronto's ascendancy as the Canadian financial centre, most foreign banks (who have recently been allowed to establish operations in Canada) are establishing their Canadian offices in Toronto rather than Montreal. Since the 1950s there has been a steady movement of the head offices of both American-owned and Canadian-owned companies from Montreal to Toronto.

Ontario's advantage over Quebec in manufacturing activity has been the focus of a wide-ranging debate among scholars over recent decades. Explanations have been offered in terms of differences in the impact of governmental policies, in the cultural traits of population, in relative geographical advantage, and in the timing of the commercialization of agriculture. Yet, in reviewing these arguments, we will show that none is satisfactory. Only an approach that situates the two provinces within the world economic system and traces their shifting relations with world economic centres can explain Quebec's disadvantage. Quebec's weaknesses can be best seen as a function of the weaknesses of what historically had been its core, Great Britain, and of the strengths of what has become Ontario's core, the United States. As for Montreal's decline as a head office centre, this too can be understood in these terms.

As we have seen, governmental policies (especially the tariff policies of the federal government) have ensured that there would be more manufacturing in Canada (at least for the Canadian market) than would otherwise have been the case. But it is difficult to show that governmental policies caused this activity to be concentrated in Ontario rather than Quebec. To be sure, one can argue that federal (and even provincial) policies could have better acted to offset Quebec's disadvantage in secondary industry. But it is hard to show that they were responsible for the disadvantage itself.[31]

Many different analyses of Quebec's disadvantage in manufacturing have focussed upon presumed cultural particularities of the French-Canadian population of Quebec that allegedly impeded the emergence of a significant entrepreneurial class. It has been argued that an "anti-business" ethic directed potential French-Canadian entrepreneurs into the liberal professions or the clergy.[32] Similarly, it has been argued that those French Canadians who did establish enterprises were handicapped by a strong family orientation, paternalism towards employees, and a fierce individualism, all of which served to keep French-Canadian enterprises small in size and thus unable to compete effectively with English-Canadian enterprises.[33] More plausible explanations of the weakness of French-Canadian entrepreneurs can be framed in structural terms, centring upon access to capital and markets.[34] Yet, however it should be explained, the weakness of French-Canadian entrepreneurs cannot in itself explain the weakness of the Quebec economy. The fact remains that since the late eighteenth century, Quebec has had an important Anglophone business community, centred in Montreal. Until this century, this community has been able to control the commercial and financial activity of Canada as a whole. Presumably, it could have offset any regional disadvantage stemming from the alleged entrepreneurial weakness of Quebec's French-Canadian population.

A different line of analysis seeks to explain Quebec's relative disadvantage in terms of the geography of the two provinces, most notably the initial access to resources needed for manufacturing. Allegedly, the reason that substantial manufacturing occurred in Ontario in the middle of the nineteenth century, but not in Quebec, was that Ontario had ready access to the essential resources of coal, which it imported from the American Appalachian fields, and iron. Lacking comparable access to these resources, Quebec had to turn to more labour-intensive forms of manufacturing. Ontario, for its part, was able to build upon its initial advantage thus conserving preeminence to the present day.[35] Nevertheless, recent studies have shown that Quebec was not handicapped in this way. In the 1870s, it could import coal from upstate New York. And it could import pig iron from Britain at a lower cost than could Ontario from its sources of supply. On this basis, "by 1870 Montreal was the leading large-scale producer of iron and steel products, equalling the combined production of Ontario's two centers: Toronto and Hamilton."[36] Thus, during the early years of industrialization Quebec was not handicapped by access to resources. In fact, in the case of iron and steel products, industrialization advanced at about the same pace in the two provinces.

Within a third line of analysis, the focus is upon the advent of prior stages of capitalist production. Allegedly, the mid-nineteenth-century inception of manufacturing activity occurred in Ontario rather than Quebec because there had already been a commercialization of agricultural production in Ontario. Through this process there had arisen in Ontario both the capital to underwrite manufacturing and the market to purchase manufactured goods (whether agricultural implements or consumer goods). There are several alternative explanations for Quebec's lag in the commercialization of agriculture. For some, the persistence of a pre-capitalist mentality, embodied in the seigneurial system that survived New France, blocked the production of an agricultural surplus for sale on a market.[37] Others point to class conflict within the seigneurial system.[38] But the most convincing explanation focusses upon the declining productivity of Quebec's agricultural lands, which had long been under cultivation.[39]

Yet, whatever the best explanation of Quebec's delay in the commercialization of agriculture, it is not clear that this delay can explain the present-day differences in the provincial industrial structures. Recently published evidence suggests that important manufacturing activity in Quebec did not await the commercialization of agriculture.[40] Manufacturing developed that was based not upon the local agricultural population (as was the case in Ontario) but upon urban Quebec and various export markets, most notably Ontario. On this basis, during the 1850s and 1860s Montreal was able to develop a large number of manufacturing enterprises that were able to sell a good proportion of their production on the Ontario market. It had not moved into two industries that would lead to more advanced forms of industry: farm implements (where there were no Montreal enterprises) and carriages (where Montreal enterprises catered only to the local market). But it had enterprises in shoemaking and textiles, which, while attracted by Quebec's relatively cheap labour, used "modern technology of a relatively capital intensive nature".[41] In addition, it had several "metal-based companies" that sold their production throughout Canada: "The largest, Moss and Brothers, employed 800 men and women and sold eleven-tenths [sic] of its production 'abroad'."[42] In this period, at least, Montreal had been quite successful in manufacturing for the Ontario market, and for foreign markets as well. To be sure, it had not established itself as a source of farm implements or carriages for the Ontario market. But it is not clear that the weakness of the market among Quebec farmers, as opposed to Ontario farmers, was alone responsible for this deficiency.

The most satisfactory explanation of Quebec's relative disadvantage lies in a dependence approach, which situates Quebec and Ontario within the world economic system, and traces how the evolution of the system has affected each of them. But the approach must be applied with care. While certain of its postulates are helpful, others are not. For instance, it has been argued by some, Tom Naylor in particular, that close dependence upon Great Britain tended to lock the Montreal bourgeoisie into certain economic roles, mercantile and financial, at the expense of others, especially manufacturing.[43] If the argument were valid, it would constitute a very straightforward explanation of Quebec's present day industrial weakness: Quebec, and Montreal in particular, was in the grip of a financial-mercantile bourgeoisie whose interests led it not only to shun manufacturing but to actively oppose its development in Canada. Ontario would have been less fully dominated by this bourgeoisie, and thus freer to move into manufacturing. The difficulty, however, is that, as McCallum has shown, during the 1850s and 1860s Montreal was heavily involved in manufacturing. Moreover this manufacturing was largely financed with the capital that the Montreal bourgeoisie had accumulated through its mercantile and financial activities. (In fact, some of its members were themselves directly involved in manufacturing.)

Dependence on Great Britain may have hindered Quebec's industrial development in another fashion: access to technology and, perhaps, even capital. In the latter part of the nineteenth century, British industry was no longer the centre of technological innovation it once was. Leadership had been lost to the United States.[44] Thus, Great Britain, Quebec's primary metropole, could not be relied upon as a source of industrial technology. If a region were to develop more sophisticated forms of manufacturing, but was not a centre of technological innovation itself (as neither Quebec nor Ontario were), better to be dependent on the United States. (The same would be true if it should need to import capital for these undertakings.) Here, Ontario was better placed than Quebec.

Ontario has the advantage of location. The peninsula of Southwestern Ontario is directly adjacent to the US industrial centres of Michigan and Ohio. And, of course, it is closer to the other Midwest industrial states than is Quebec. By the same token, Quebec's neighbouring states of New England and New York were much weaker as industrial centres than were Ontario's neighbours. Location was all the more critical in that most US investment in Canada has taken the form, not of portfolio investment as was the case with Great Britain, but of direct investment in which, in the case of manufacturing, an American enterprise would set up its own subsidiary in Canada to produce a line of products patterned after the American production. With such close integration of operations, proximity to the centre of a firm's activities in the US was the key to choosing a

Canadian site. The most dramatic illustration of this pattern is the concentration of the Canadian automobile industry around Windsor, just across the river from Detroit. But variants in the same patterns can be found in most US controlled manufacturing activities in Canada.[45] Moreover, US direct investment accounts for most of Ontario's present-day lead in manufacturing activity.

The long-term decline in Quebec's share of head offices, to the benefit of Ontario, can be understood in essentially the same terms. To the extent that US dependence explains the greater strength of Ontario manufacturing, it also explains why head offices of US-controlled manufacturing enterprises would be located in Ontario. And it explains why the head office of other types of enterprises would also be attracted to Toronto. Manufacturing strength meant greater prosperity and employment opportunities. Ultimately, it resulted in a larger population for Ontario. For many enterprises, then, Ontario was the most attractive market, and thus the logical location for a head office. It is primarily for these reasons, then, that banks, insurance companies and a wide variety of service enterprises that originally established their head offices in Montreal have been moving many, if not all, head office operations to Toronto and other parts of Ontario. Finally, it can be shown that US capital was instrumental to the initial growth of Toronto's financial institutions enabling them to challenge Montreal's status as financial centre. With the turn of the century, Toronto established itself as the Canadian centre for financing the mining of the Canadian shield.[46] Most of the capital that was funnelled through Toronto was American in origin.

To summarize our discussion to this point, Quebec's economic position has been closely defined by a complex of linkages. In some of these, Quebec has enjoyed the role of a core but in others it has been very much a periphery. Taken as a whole, these linkages appear to constitute what Wallerstein denotes as a semi-periphery. Thanks in large part to policies of the federal government, Quebec continues to play core functions vis-à-vis Western Canada and Atlantic Canada, in effect forcing them to buy its manufactured goods and housing some of the head offices that control their economic development. But it has increasingly assumed peripheral status in its dealings with Ontario. This disadvantage does not appear to be the direct result of federal government policies, "discriminatory" or otherwise. Nor do cultural or geographical differences between Quebec and Ontario afford a satisfactory explanation. It can be best understood in terms of Quebec's continuing status as a periphery of world economic cores. Historical dependence on Great Britain served Montreal well during the commercial era, but not when advanced industry became the key to economic growth. By the end of the nineteenth century the United States was the primary source of capital and technology for industrial development. Ontario was better situated than Quebec to attract American investment in industrial branch plants. Thus, it became the centre of advanced industrial activity in Canada. Through the same processes, Toronto was able to supplant Montreal as the dominant city in the Canadian economic system.

As such a "semi-periphery," Quebec does not fall readily into the different core-periphery models of nationalism that we outlined earlier. Certainly, it does not constitute a clear case of "overdevelopment," where "a middle-class enclave within a backward territory" resents political domination by the less developed regions of the system. Quebec is not the most developed region; and the political domination that it might resent is that of a stronger rather than backward region. Moreover, we have seen that Quebec is very much the winner in its relations with the remaining regions. Thus, it has little reason to abandon its relations with them.

By the same token, Quebec does not seem to fall into Gourevitch's notion of a non-congruence between economic and political functions. In the past, it enjoyed a leading role within the Canadian economy and this was paralleled by a leading political role within federal institutions, especially through the federal Liberal Party. Its relative economic decline has probably been paralleled by a decline in its influence within the federal government. (Some observers argue that the weakening of Quebec Anglophones' role in Ottawa has been offset by an augmentation of Quebec Francophone strength, but this probably is specific to the Trudeau regime.) Overall, the pattern has been one of congruence between economic and political functions. In fact, in his own analysis of the Quebec situation, Gourevitch traces the surge of Quebec neo-nationalism to both the decline of Quebec within the Canadian economic system and the new aggressiveness of Quebec Francophones in the face of Anglophone dominance of the Quebec economy.[48]

Finally, Quebec does not fall neatly within the pattern of underdevelopment, as represented by the notion of "internal colony." Elements of underdevelopment, as in relations with Ontario (and the United States), have been coupled with dominance of both Western Canada and Atlantic Canada. (On this basis, some scholars who are themselves highly sympathetic to Quebec nationalism have firmly rejected the notion that Quebec is somehow an "internal colony" of Canada.)[49]

While the various dimensions of Quebec's semi-peripheral status clearly have shaped and influenced the neo-nationalist movement, they do not fully explain the rise and subsequent course of Quebec neo-nationalism. Beginning with Quebec's linkages to Western Canada and Atlantic Canada, one would expect that Quebec's advantage here would restrain any movement to Quebec sovereignty or at least set outer limits to it. At a minimum, Quebec would want to retain tariff-protected markets for its manufactured goods. This was confirmed by the project of sovereignty-association, which the Quebec government produced in 1979, in preparation of the 1980 referendum. Within this scheme, a sovereign Quebec would maintain a customs union with the rest of Canada. But, in this version at least, sovereignty-association involves a much closer economic association than would have been necessary simply to protect Quebec's manufacturing activity. In addition to the free movement of goods, there would be a free movement of labour and capital, a common currency and the joint provision of a wide range of common services. As we shall see, other factors beyond the advantageous links with Western Canada and Atlantic Canada were apparently at work in narrowing the scope of the *souverainiste* project.

By the same token, Quebec's relations with Ontario, which do bear clear marks of "underdevelopment," can provide at best only a partial explanation of the neo-nationalist upsurge of the 1960s. First, they cannot explain its timing. As we have seen, Quebec's disadvantage in manufacturing dates from the late nineteenth century; it did not first emerge in the decades immediately preceding the Quiet Revolution. The movement of head offices can be traced to the 1950s, but it was not widely defined as a major public issue until quite recently. Second, while some of the economic initiatives were clearly linked to reducing Quebec's disadvantage vis-à-vis Ontario, such as the creation of a public steel mill complex in 1967 to break Ontario's monopoly of steel production, other initiatives such as the nationalization of privately owned hydro-electrical firms or the expansion of state support for French-Canadian owned enterprises (through the Société Générale de Financement), were more directly concerned with strengthening the role of Francophones within the Quebec economy. Thus "*l'épanouissement*" of the Quebec nation involved more than simply the elimination of its regional economic disadvantage.

There are also difficulties in explaining the *souverainisme* of the 1970s in these terms. Analyses of support for sovereignty-association show that Quebec Francophones are more likely to see sovereignty-association bringing improvement in Quebec's cultural development than in its economic development. If anything, perceptions of the economic consequences of sovereignty-association have been more likely to dissuade Francophones from supporting sovereignty-association than to attract them to it.[50]

As for Quebec's relations with the United States, where Quebec appears to be disadvantaged in most respects, they do not appear to have directly provoked the neo-nationalist movement. Grievance over American economic domination has not been prominent among the dominant elements of the Quebec neo-nationalist movement, although it certainly has been a concern of some elements on the left. Thus, in its program for a sovereign Quebec the Parti Québécois calls for major changes in the sectors where English-Canadian interests are important: finance, transportation and communication, but little change in the patterns of ownership in sectors where US interests are important: resource extraction and manufacturing.[51] If anything, the neo-nationalist movement has regarded the United States as a potential ally in its various economic projects. The most significant economic initiative of the Quiet Revolution, the nationalization of several English-Canadian-owned hydro-electrical companies, was financed through the sale of Quebec government bonds on the American market. English-Canadian financial institutions had refused to purchase the bonds, apparently out of resentment over the proposed nationalization.[52] The massive hydro-electrical development of the 1970s, the James Bay project, was also financed largely through American capital. In effect, the American linkage has been used to reduce Quebec's subordination to Ontario-based interests, as well as Anglophone interests within Quebec itself. One economic centre has been played off against another. Whether the result is a net reduction in Quebec's economic dependence is another question.

To summarize, the analysis of Quebec's economic position requires going beyond a simple bipartite model to envisage a whole complex of interregional linkages. The Quebec economy must be situated within not only the Canadian economic system, but the world economic system. On this basis, Quebec stands as a "semi-periphery" heavily dependent upon world economic cores while sharing with

Ontario certain core functions within the Canadian system. In fact, it is changes in the relative position of these world cores, the decline of Great Britain and the ascendancy of the United States, that can best explain why Ontario rather than Quebec now has the giant share of core functions within the Canadian economy. While these various interregional relationships continue to shape closely Quebec's economic development, their role in the resurgence of Quebec nationalism is far from clear. Underdevelopment vis-à-vis the United States has not directly fed this nationalism, although American capital has at time been used to finance its projects. Quebec's underdevelopment vis-à-vis Ontario may have helped stimulate neo-nationalism and *souverainisme* and its dominance over the other Canadian regions may have set limits to this nationalism, as in the coupling of sovereignty with an economic association, but they clearly cannot provide a sufficient explanation. Thus, it is necessary to look for other structural relationships that can contribute to a nationalist movement. These may exist within Quebec itself.

Cultural Division of Labour

The phenomenon of "uneven development" need not be simply a relationship among regions; it could also be a relationship among distinguishable populations within the same region. In the limiting case, it could be a relationship existing solely within a single city of a region. Here Michael Hechter's notion of a "cultural division of labour" is highly pertinent, providing that it is not viewed as a simple adjunct or outgrowth of core-periphery spatial relations but as a relationship among individuals that might take a multitude of spatial forms. Describing a cultural division of labour as "whenever culturally-marked groups are distributed in an occupational structure," Hechter is careful to go beyond the simple notion of hierarchy, or the extent that the "ethnic groups within it are differentially stratified." He posits a second "defining parameter" of segmentation or the extent that "the ethnic groups within it are highly occupationally specialized."[53]

Internally, Quebec has long been marked by a clear cultural division of labour. The terms of a specialization of functions, or segmentation, were established in the decades following the British conquest of 1760. The key positions within the colonial economy soon became the virtual monopoly of English-speakers. For the *Canadiens*, positions of power and influence were largely based upon the performance of services to the French-speaking population: religious, legal and medical. With time, political representation also became important as *Canadiens* assumed the predominant role within an autonomous government, the Province of Quebec (although they became bound by a hierarchical division of labour within the federal bureaucracy). The Anglophone dominance of economic functions within Quebec was to prove more tenacious. French Canadians did make some limited inroads into commerce, finance and industry during the latter part of the nineteenth century. But many of these were lost in the early part of this century.[54] In the course of this century, moreover, with industrialization, a hierarchical division of labour became more pronounced within the Quebec economy. It is only within the last two decades, due in large part to the neo-nationalist initiatives of the Quebec government, that the patterns have been broken, with hierarchy declining in Anglophone-owned enterprises and Francophone owners of enterprises becoming sufficiently important that scholars can announce the emergence of a French-Canadian or Québécois "bourgeoisie."[55]

The Anglophone capture of economic functions in the wake of the conquest can be seen as the natural consequence of Quebec's new dependence on Great Britain, rather than France. Government policies to that effect were not really needed. Nor, we argue, should the emphasis be placed upon alleged cultural or ideological differences between Francophones and Anglophones. As the colony had developed under the French regime, the primary source of profit was in the export of furs for sale on the French market and, to a lesser extent, the sale within the colony of consumer goods, which were obtained primarily in France. Now that the colony was linked to Great Britain rather than France, furs had to be sold on the British market and consumer goods had to be purchased there as well. Inevitably, British residents of the colony were better able than French Canadians to link up with buyers and suppliers in Great Britain. The same pattern persisted over subsequent decades, when wood replaced furs as the main export commodity. As British investors surveyed the prospects for investment in the colony, especially in the development of transportation facilities, they were bound to look to the fellow Britishers already established in the colony. In fact, given the dominance that (thanks to the British connection) Anglophone enterprises had already secured over the colony's commercial life, there would be little reason to look beyond them.

As canal projects and, later, railway construction, perpetuated and reinforced Montreal's role as a mercantile centre, large pools of capital were accumulated in Quebec. But they were essentially in the hands of the Anglophones. In this century, the new influx of American capital (which in the case of Quebec tended to be primary rather than secondary industry) did not alter this pattern. Usually it went directly into subsidiaries of US firms. By the same token, the recent emergence of a Francophone "bourgeoisie" can be understood in terms of a new availability of capital to Francophone businessmen, through the aegis of the Quebec state, along with an improvement in the markets of Francophone firms thanks to state purchasing policies.

The emergence of hierarchy within the Quebec economy, with managerial positions in large enterprises reserved for Anglophones, directly reflected Anglophone dominance of ownership. A variety of factors have been cited that might lead Anglophone owners to prefer Anglophone candidates over Francophone candidates for employment: Anglophone/Francophone differences in educational qualifications, proficiency in English, and values and norms; ethnic prejudice on the part of Anglophone owners; greater availability of Anglophone candidates through personal schooling and social networks, etc.[56] The apparent improvement in Francophone mobility in recent years can be traced in part to government policies, especially reforms of the educational system and government pressures to increase the use of French within enterprises. But, apparently, it also stems from a declining availability of Anglophone candidates, given accelerated migration out of the province.[57]

While historically excluded from major economic functions, *Canadiens* could nonetheless monopolize elite positions based on services to the French-speaking population. Their claim to these functions was recognized in the Quebec Act of 1774, which paralleled the 1707 Act of Union between Scotland and England in its acceptance of distinct religious and legal institutions. (Apparently, strategical considerations led to this redefinition of Quebec's mode of incorporation into the British empire.) The Act recognized that the French civil law applied under the *ancien régime* of New France should continue to be the civil law of the colony, thus ensuring that it was French Canadians who would provide legal services to the Francophone population. The Act also recognized the legal status of the Catholic Church and granted it the right to demand tithes from its parishioners.

With 1791, and the creation of a representative assembly, French Canadians could also pursue political careers. Nonetheless, these careers were heavily circumscribed. Appointive positions were still largely reserved for Anglophones. Clearly the colonial government did follow discriminatory practices with respect to its own personnel. This hierarchy within the colonial government helped to fuel the nationalist movement of the 1820s and 1830s. As we have seen, these restrictions apparently disappeared with the United Canadas. French Canadians enjoyed important roles within most parts of the new government. Under Confederation, however, a clear hierarchy emerged within the federal bureaucracy, thanks in particular to the preeminence of English as the working language. French Canadians enjoyed a more substantial role within the Cabinet, although even there a certain specialization of functions existed. Nonetheless, in the Quebec provincial government there were few restrictions. Instead, French Canadians played the dominant role. Moreover, the jurisdictions given the provincial government ensured that French-Canadian religious and legal elites would be protected from the intervention of the federal government, with its English-Canadian majority.

In sum, there has long been a clear segmentation of functions in Quebec with English Canadians monopolizing control of the colony's commercial and financial activities but French Canadians enjoying a protected position within religious, legal and political occupations. With the turn of the century, segmentation was joined by hierarchy as French Canadians were drawn to blue-collar positions within the English-Canadian managed industrial enterprises. The emergence and persistence of this cultural division of labour can best be seen as a function of Quebec's historical dependence upon Great Britain and, at a later point, the United States.

Clearly, the persisting cultural division of labour within Quebec was instrumental to the rise of neo-nationalism. Resentment over exclusion from major economic roles was a major theme in this movement. With the 1960s, Quebec political elites for the first time sought to use their control of the Quebec provincial government to challenge the Anglophone monopoly of controlling positions within the Quebec economy, claiming that Quebec Francophones had the right to be *maîtres chez nous*. With the nationalization of several English-Canadian-owned and -managed hydro-electrical companies in 1963, the Quebec government was able to carve out new management opportunities for Quebec Francophones. Also, in the 1960s various mechanisms were established to expand the pool of capital available to French-Canadian-owned enterprises. In themselves, these measures could have only a limited effect on the cultural division of labour, but they did serve to legitimize the idea that the Quebec government should intervene in the Quebec economy to improve the position of Francophones. The internal cultural division of labour also contributed to neo-nationalism in a second, more indirect manner. Largely as a consequence of Anglophone dominance of the economy, immigrant groups had tended to join the English-language community. By the late 1960s, a nationalist reaction had developed, calling upon the Quebec government to restrict access to English-language schools. Continuing dissatisfaction with the responses of Union Nationale and Liberal provincial administrations clearly reinforced nationalist sentiment. To the extent that these demands were not met, there was a continuing basis for attracting support for Quebec sovereignty.

Yet the persistence of a cultural division of labour cannot, in itself, explain the timing of the neo-nationalist movement. In part, the response to this question may lie with the changes we noted in Quebec's interregional relations. As we have seen, during recent decades Toronto has attracted many head offices from Montreal. In the process, Anglophone executives in Quebec have been increasingly reduced to the status of regional managers, following the instructions of head offices in Toronto. This change may, in turn, have undermined the prestige that Quebec Anglophones had always enjoyed within the Francophone population, making them more vulnerable to attack. This, at least, is the thesis of Clift and Arnopoulos:

> Aussi longtemps que cette communauté conservait son emprise sur l'ensemble de l'économie canadienne, sa situation au Québec était sûre et inattaquable. Mais dès que l'élite financière de Montréal devint simple exécutante de décisions entérinées ailleurs, la sitution devint peu à peu intenable. . . . Les élites anglaises, qui ne devaient leur situation prééminente à Montréal qu'a leurs réalisations historiques plutôt qu'à leurs qualitiés d'aujourd'hui, devinrent graduellement des rivaux encombrants dans la poursuite de carrières. C'est ainsi que commença l'offensive discrète de la class moyenne français pour les déloger des postes qu'ils détenaient collectivement aux échelons supérieurs des entreprises canadiennes faisant affaires à Montréal.[58]

Yet, this cannot be the whole explanation.

In sum, one can readily locate longstanding conditions that would support a nationalist movement among Quebec Francophones, centred upon the expansion of the Quebec state. Under Confederation, accommodation of Francophones within Canadian political institutions had been quite limited, falling well short of such prescriptions for ethnic accommodation as consociationalism. (The reforms of recent years were themselves a response to the rise of neo-nationalism within Quebec.) This clearly was the case at the provincial level, outside Quebec, where Francophone representation was minimal or nonexistent and French-language public services had been systematically denied. But even at the federal level representation was circumscribed and, at critical junctures, policies were adopted that Francophones had bitterly opposed. Thus, French-Canadian nationalists would have been well placed to argue for a transfer of powers and resources to the Quebec state, demonstrably the one government that Francophones could trust to protect their cultural distinctiveness. Quebec's semi-peripheral economy provided yet another set of potential arguments for a stronger Quebec state. While it might have been difficult to prove that federal policies had themselves created, or even heightened Quebec's disadvantage relative to Ontario, it would have been easy to show that there had been few federal efforts to correct it. Moreover, the availabilty to Quebec of American capital meant that a provincial government did not have to rely exclusively upon Ontario, or the English-Canadian bourgeoisie in general, for private and public investment. (To be sure, the clear advantage that Quebec drew from its dealings with Western and Atlantic Canada, plus the importance of the Ontario market, might preclude a movement to outright economic independence.) Finally, the cultural division of labour within Quebec, and Canada as a whole, provided yet another set of potential arguments. A strong interventionist state was an obvious instrument for carving out new roles for Francophones within the Quebec economy.

Nonetheless, these conditions alone cannot explain the rise of the neo-nationalist movement in the 1960s. After all, each of them had a long history. To be sure, they underwent changes in the post-war period, which might have made the nationalist diagnosis more compelling. Ottawa's attempts to influence the activities of provincial governments, often in the name of a pan-Canadian nationalism, may have heightened apprehension about the federal government. Increased American involvement in the Quebec economy may have reduced the sense of dependence upon Canadian capital. And the movement of decision centres from Montreal to Toronto may well have made Quebec Anglophones appear more vulnerable. But a satisfactory explanation of the neo-nationalist upsurge must go beyond these factors alone. Perhaps the key lies within Francophone society itself. New social categories may have emerged to make the neo-nationalist argument.

Social Change Within Quebec: New Classes and Neo-Nationalism

As it happens, from the early years of this century French Quebec underwent a profound transformation, from rural society to urban society and from primary industry to secondary industry. In the process, larger and larger proportions of Quebec Francophones must have become more fully aware and perhaps resentful of the structural weaknesses of the Quebec economy and of the cultural division of labour within Quebec society as a whole. But for these changes to give rise to a major neo-nationalist movement, focussed on the Quebec state, there had to be change at the ideological level: in the conception of the role that the Quebec state should play in economy and society. In particular, Francophone cultural and intellectual elites, including those within existing nationalist circles, had to discard their traditional disposition to look to private rather than public institutions, especially in matters of health, education, and welfare. This clearly was occurring by the 1950s, as intellectuals, professionals, union leaders, and various voluntary associations argued that urbanization had rendered inadequate Church-related institutions.[59] The Quebec state had to follow the example of other provinces and place health, education, and welfare services fully within the public sector. By the same token, it needed to diversify and strengthen the Quebec economy, eliminating its historical disadvantage, and to both equip Francophones for managerial functions and to ensure that positions would be available to them. In each case, it was argued, the Quebec state rather than Ottawa had to assume these responsibilities.

With the 1960s, under the Liberal regime of Jean Lesage, these ideas were put into effect. In the process, their neo-nationalist implications were to become much more clearly defined. Through a vast expansion of the structures of the provincial state, Quebec underwent its Quiet Revolution. Neo-nationalism became the official state ideology. Quebec officials argued that if indeed the Quebec state were to make Québécois *maîtres chez nous*, it would need strengthened jurisdictions, perhaps a *statut particulier*. In the wake of the Liberal defeat in 1966, the pressures for Quebec sovereignty acquired a new force. In particular, the Parti Québécois was formed in 1968, drawing together nationalist forces from several different organizations under the banner of "sovereignty-association." Elected to power in 1976, the Parti Québécois staged a referendum in 1980, on whether the Quebec government should be given a mandate to negotiate "sovereignty-association" with Ottawa. The PQ government was unsuccessful. A "Yes" vote was registered by only forty percent of voters (but by close to fifty percent of Francophones voters).

Thus, although the movement to Quebec sovereignty was ultimately unsuccessful, the basic themes of neo-nationalism heavily influenced and, in some respects, dominated Quebec politics over the 1960s and 1970s. Thanks to the new commitment to a dynamic, interventionist state, the potential for a nationalist movement, which lay in Quebec's political, economic, and social setting could finally be realized. If it were agreed that the deficiencies of Quebec's economy and the obstacles to Francophone mobility within it could be resolved through an active interventionist state and if the past record had shown that only the Quebec state could be entrusted with the distinct interests of Francophones in these and other areas, then it followed almost by logic it seemed, that the Quebec state must become a truly "national" state. To be sure, however, not all Francophones were drawn by this "logic." To grow as it did, the neo-nationalist movement must have drawn upon strata of Francophones that had a particular confidence in the capacities of state action to ameliorate problems and perhaps a special concern over such conditions as uneven development and cultural division of a labour. It is here, with respect to defining the social bases of the neo-nationalist movement that there has been considerable disagreement among scholars.

Recently, it has been argued with reference to the *souverainiste* campaign of the late 1970s that *souverainisme* has been based essentially among intellectuals, defined as the creators and disseminators of culture. Allegedly, they have dominated the leadership of the movement and have been its strongest supporters.[60] There are indeed good reasons to expect that intellectuals would be attracted to Quebec nationalism. Almost by definition, they are best able to fulfill their functions in French. Thus, they have a strong interest in the strength of French-language institutions within Quebec, and more generally, in the preeminence of French as the language of the Quebec residents. In an urban, industrialized Quebec these concerns provide compelling arguments for state intervention: to strengthen French-language schools and to ensure, by coercion if need be, that the children of Francophones (and immigrants) be educated within them rather than within English-language schools; to support French-language publishing, broadcasting, and film production; to reinforce the status of French as the primary language of work in Quebec; and to eliminate anglicizing tendencies within the French used in Quebec. These clearly have been concerns of the neo-nationalist movement, and of the Parti Québécois government. By the same token, the movement clearly has drawn heavily from Francophone intellectuals. But it may be misleading to see intellectuals alone as the core of the *souverainiste* movement.

In his recent analysis of the neo-nationalist upsurge in the industrialized world, Anthony D. Smith has called attention to another group. Restricting the term "intellectual" to actual creators of "ideas and paradigms," Smith identifies a second, much larger, stratum that he defines as consisting of individuals who have some form of higher education and use it to gain a livelihood.[62] Within this "professional intelligentsia" he distinguishes between liberal professionals and "technical professionals." The latter are understood as those who look for guidance and paradigms to the scientific intellectuals. Examples are engineers, economists, pharmacists, and laboratory technicians. Smith suggests that there may be a connection between the rapid expansion of the technical intelligentsia and the rise of Western neo-nationalism, with its concern over social and economic disadvantage, its "shift to the left," and its advocacy of various state programs of "social engineering."[63]

In the case of Quebec, many observers have characterized support for neo-nationalism in ways that are very similar to Smith's.[64] Typically, they have used the term "new middle class." Usually, the term is used to denote salaried individuals who possess educational or technical qualifications.[65] Emphasis in particular has been placed upon professionals within this category, who often are identified as bearing "technocratic" knowledge. There are strong reasons to expect that this group would be attracted to Quebec nationalism. As aspirants to managerial positions they would be especially likely to have resented Anglophone dominance of managerial positions in the Quebec economy and in the federal bureaucracy. By the same token, diversification and modernization of Quebec's industrial economy would bear the promise of new managerial openings for the Francophone new middle class. Professionals involved in such areas as health care and social services, who must look to public and para-public institutions for support, would also have a clear interest in the reinforcement of the Quebec state. In short, the neo-nationalist ideal of a strong interventionist Quebec state, supporting a large French-language public sector, should have had a strong appeal to several categories of the new middle class, beyond intellectuals alone. This would be especially so as the Quebec state expanded and became the employer of much of the Francophone new middle class, providing conditions that were difficult to match elsewhere. Perhaps in the early years of the neo-nationalist movement intellectuals were its essential bearers. But it would be surprising if other elements of the new middle class, especially those who are based in the public sector, did not come to play an equally important role. There are in fact some indications that this has been the case.[66]

Less persuasive is the argument made in some quarters that the centre of Quebec neo-nationalism, including the *souverainiste* movement, goes beyond the Francophone middle class to include a distinct Quebec bourgeoisie, or a Quebec-based fraction of a larger bourgeoisie.[67] It is difficult to accept these premises with respect to the conventional notion of a bourgeoisie, composed of owners of private property. Typically, owners of large financial, industrial, and commercial enterprises that are based in Quebec are seeking to expand their operations into other markets, both in Canada and in foreign countries. Thus, they have no particular interest in the fragmentation of the Canadian market, as could occur through secession.[68] And, as the case of Bombardier Industries, large Quebec-based and Francophone-owned enterprises are ready, and apparently quite able, to work closely with the federal government when their international efforts fall within its jurisdiction. In short, they have no clear interest in Quebec sovereignty. Moreover, the almost universal tendency of major Francophone businesspeople to support the forces for a "No" vote in the 1980 referendum suggests that they see no such interest.[69]

The proposition is more plausible if the notion of "bourgeoisie" is broadened to contain not only owners of property but managers of large enterprises, public and private. On this basis, a "Quebec bourgeoisie" could extend to key officials within the Quebec state and within state enterprises. They do indeed have an interest in strengthening the jurisdictions and resources of the Quebec state. Moreover, the officials of such state organisms as the Caisse de Depôt et de Placement appear to have secured a certain influence over the operations of some private enterprises, through using public funds to buy minority ownership within them. One might also include within a "Quebec bourgeoisie" key officials within the Francophone cooperative movement, as with the Mouvement Desjardins, who have amassed pools of capital through savings of Quebec residents. By and large, their investment activities are restricted to the territory of Quebec. In each case, the positions involve distinctly Québécois institutions. For that reason, they have often entailed conflict with economic and political institutions that are based in Canada as a whole or are lodged within other provinces. Thus, these "bourgeois" elements might indeed be supportive of the *souverainiste* movement, although probably not actively. But their "bourgeois" status is unclear. As managers, they would fall much more readily within the notion of "new middle class."

Conclusion

In sum, the 1960s saw the emergence of a new form of nationalism in French Quebec. This neo-nationalism transformed a centuries-old *Canadien* identity into one that is explicitly Québécois and it fuelled a new drive to secure for Quebec a truly "national" state, able to reinforce and strengthen distinctly Québécois social and economic institutions. Our analysis has demonstrated the long existence of several preconditions for this neo-nationalism.

Within the political institutions created through Confederation only the provincial government of Quebec, with its heavily Francophone electorate, proved to be a reliable defender of *Canadien* interests. In the process, the demographic strength of Francophones outside Quebec declined markedly. In its economic relations, Quebec has played the complex role of a "semi-periphery." While dependent upon a series of metropoles, it has been able to secure certain core functions within the Canadian economy. But by several indicators, Quebec has been less successful in this regard than Ontario. Moreover, its disadvantage has increased with the decline of Great Britain and the rise to world predominance of the United States, from which Ontario has drawn greater benefit than Quebec. In addition, since the late seventeenth century, Quebec's dependence upon English-speaking metropoles has created and helped to sustain a cultural division of labour within Quebec society, in which Francophones have historically played secondary roles both as owners and as managers.

It was only in the mid-twentieth century, however, that the potential for a neo-nationalist movement was finally realized. A "new middle class" of Francophones emerged, which had a strong commitment to state intervention and which argued that the circumstances in which Francophones had been placed dictated that this intervention be through the Quebec state. As a result, during the 1960s and 1970s the politics of Quebec (and to a large extent Canada as a whole) were dominated by the drive to transform the Quebec provincial state into a national state.

In terms of the formal goal of sovereignty, this drive has not succeeded. What, then, is its future? Presumably, the answer lies with the future impact of the specific conditions we have identified above. Here, quite contradictory tendencies emerge. Some of these conditions may become even more influential in the future, but others appear to be losing some of their salience.

With respect to political institutions, there has been an improvement in the role of Quebec Francophones within federal-level institutions and in the provision of French-language services by many provincial governments. But it is not clear that this is sufficient to weaken the longstanding belief of Quebec Francophones that only the Quebec government can be relied upon to respect and further Francophone interests. Under the 1982 Constitution Act, Quebec's powers were not substantially increased; in some respects they were actually reduced. As for the Quebec economy, trends within North America spell further decline. In a sequel to the initial shift of the centre of the American economy from the North East to the Mid-West, which led to Quebec's disadvantage relative to Ontario, the US centre is now shifting from the Mid-West to the Southwestern "Sun Belt." The further peripheralization of the Quebec economy can only mean that Quebec will draw even fewer benefits from dependence on the United States.[70] One might see a similar regional shift occurring within the Canadian economic system, once again at the expense of Quebec. Increasingly, Western Canada has become the focus of economic activity, based primarily upon resource development. Even Ontario sees its position as seriously threatened by this westward movement. Thus, in the future, dissatisfaction with Canadian political institutions and apprehension over the peripheralization and deindustrialization of the Quebec economy may be even more powerful in generating support for Quebec neo-nationalism.

Nonetheless, other conditions that had contributed to the neo-nationalist upsurge of the 1960s may not be as significant in the coming years. In certain respects Quebec's internal cultural division of labour has been attenuated, due in large part to the state reform of the 1960s and 1970s. The number of substantial Francophone-owned firms has been growing steadily; a new "Francophone bourgeoisie" has emerged. And there has been a marked improvement in the presence of Francophones at managerial positions within American and English-Canadian owned firms, and even an increase in the use of French at these levels. In effect, then, one of the strongest arguments for an interventionist Quebec state, as with sovereignty, may have lost some of its force.

More generally, the neo-nationalist model of an active, technocratic state may well have less credibility in the Quebec of the 1980s. The attack upon the state that liberals have waged throughout North America and Europe has certainly been echoed in Quebec. Rather than an instrument for the economic liberation of Francophones, the Quebec state, and its attendant state enterprises, is increasingly portrayed as a "dead hand" on the economy, stifling private enterprise, including Francophone-owned enterprise. The new Francophone bourgeoisie, more and more secure in its position, has been leading this attack upon the statist assumptions of the 1960s and 1970s. At the same time, disillusion with the Parti Québécois on the basis of its incumbency in the provincial government, may have undermined the confidence that middle-class and working-class categories of Francophones had had in the *souverainiste* project, at least as championed by the Parti Québécois. In particular, the new fiscal constraints on the Quebec state have led the PQ government to undertake a series of expenditure-reducing measures that have fallen very heavily upon public sector workers. The 1976 electoral victory of the Parti Québécois had been based upon the PQ's assurance that the issue of Quebec sovereignty would be dealt with in a separate referendum. PQ leaders had presumed that by providing effective government, they could sway many Québécois to their *souverainiste* option. This did not happen. Now, the precisely opposite dynamic appears to be occurring. Ultimately, then, the PQ has been bedevilled by the kinds of contradictions and moderating influences that confront any movement that, while committed to global change, assumes office within the established political system.

In sum, the emergence of neo-nationalism in Quebec in the 1960s reflected the confluence of several conditions. No one of these conditions alone can explain it. Thus, the case of Quebec clearly demonstrates the danger of reducing neo-nationalism to a single set of factors, whether uneven economic development, the biases of political institutions, the incidence of ethnic stratification, or the patterns of class relations with the "national" group itself. This danger is even greater when assessments are made of the future of neo-nationalism: quite contradictory propositions emerge. In Quebec, and elsewhere, the study of neo-nationalism will be a continuing challenge.

Notes

1. Anthony D. Smith, *The Ethnic Revival* (Cambridge: Cambridge University Press, 1981), chap. 9.

2. Michel Brunet, *La Présence anglaise et les canadiens* (Montreal: Beauchemin, 1964), 58; Denis Monière, *Le Développement des idéologies au Québec des origines à nos jours* (Montreal: Éditions Québec/Amérique, 1977), 71–72.

3. Fernand Ouellet, *Histoire économique et sociale du Québec, 1760–1850* (Montreal: Fides, 1966); Gilles Bourque, *Classes sociales et question nationale au Québec, 1760–1840* (Montreal: Parti Pris, 1970).

4. William Ormsby, *The Emergence of the Federal Concept in Canada, 1839–1845* (Toronto: University of Toronto, Press, 1974), 3, 122–25, as reprinted in *Consociational Democracy: Political Accommodation in Segmented Societies*, edited by Kenneth McRae (Toronto: McClelland and Stewart, 1974), 269–74.

5. Michael Hechter and Margaret Levi, "The Comparative Analysis of Ethnoregional Movements," *Ethnic and Racial Studies* 2, 3 (1979): 260–74.

6. Arend Lijphart, *The Politics of Accommodation* (Berkeley: University of California Press, 1968), and *Democracy in Plural Societies* (New Haven: Yale University Press, 1977).

7. While Robert Presthus (*Elite Accommodation in Canadian Politics* (Cambridge: Cambridge University Press, 1973)), argues that Canada does indeed conform to the consociational model, Kenneth McRae ("Consociationalism and the Canadian Political System" in *Consociational Democracy*, 238–61) and Donald Smiley ("French-English Relations in Consociational Democracy," in *Ethnic Conflict in the Western World*, edited by Milton J. Esman (Ithaca: Cornell University Press, 1977), 179–203) demonstrate otherwise. For his part, Arend Lijphart ("Consociationalism and Federation: Conceptual and Empirical Links," *Canadian Journal of Political Science* XII, 3 (1979): 499–516) sees Canada as "semi-constitutional."

8. Lijphart, *Democracy in Plural Societies*, chap. 5.

9. Frederick W. Gibson, ed., "Cabinet Formation and Bicultural Relations," in *Studies of the Royal Commission on Bilingualism and Biculturalism* 6 (Ottawa: Queen's Printer, 1970).

10. Christopher Beattie, *Minority Men in a Majority Setting* (Toronto: McClelland and Stewart, 1975).

11. Lijphart, *Democracy in Plural Societies*, chap. 5.

12. In fact, Lijphart is not too optimistic about the prospects for consociationalism in the demographic situation represented by the United Canadas: two segments of approximately equal size. He sees a "multiple balance of power" as more conducive to consociationalism than either of these (Lijphart, *Democracy in Plural Societies*, 55).

13. To be sure, beyond the three norms of consociationalism discussed above, Lijphart identifies a fourth: "segmental autonomy" (ibid., chap. 5). Federalism obviously can achieve this purpose. But, as Lijphart notes in a 1979 article, federalism itself is not sufficient to create consociationalism. For a federation to be consociational, the three other norms of consociationalism must be present in its central institutions (Lijphart, "Consociationalism and Federation," 513).

14. Michael Hechter, *The Celtic Fringe in British National Development, 1536–1966* (London: Routledge & Kegan Paul, 1975).

15. Tom Nairn, *The Break-Up of Britain: Crisis and Neo-Nationalism* (London: NLB, 1977), 203.

16. Ibid., 204.

17. Peter Gourevitch, "Politics, Economics and Nationalism: Some Comparative Speculations," *Comparative Studies in Society and History* 21 (1970): 303–22.

18. Immanuel Wallerstein, *The Capitalist World-Economy* (Cambridge: Cambridge University Press, 1979), 96–7.

19. Maurice Saint-Germain, *Une Économie a libérer?* (Montreal: Presses de l'Université de Montréal, 1973), 194.

20. Bernard Bonin and Mario Polèse, *À Propos de l'association Canada-Québec* (Quebec: École Nationale d'Administration Publique, 1980), 64–6; Pierre-Paul Proulx, Yves Rabeau, and Louise Dulude, *Études des relations commerciales Québec-USA et Québec-Canada* (Quebec: Éditeur Officiel du Québec, 1979).

21. Pierre Fréchette, Roland Jouandet-Bernadat, and Jean-Pierre Vézina, *L'économie du Québec* (Montreal: Éditions HRW, 1975), 345.

22. Economic Council of Canada, *Living Together* (Ottawa: Ministry of Supply and Services, 1979), chap. 4.

23. Ibid., 65; Gilles Bourque and Anne Legaré, *Le Québec: la question nationale* (Paris: Maspéro, 1979), 116.

24. Bonin and Polèse, *À Propos de l'association Canada-Québec*, 282.

25. Economic Council of Canada, *Living Together*, tables 5–20.

26. Donald V. Smiley, *Canada in Question*, 3rd ed. (Toronto: McGraw-Hill Ryerson, 1980), 261–4.

27. Nonetheless, Paul Phillips does indeed argue that without discriminatory freight rates on the Canadian continental railways, Western Canada could have produced manufactured goods, at least for local consumption (Phillips, *Regional Disparities* (Toronto: James Lorimer, 1978), 70).

28. Pierre Harvey, "Pourquoi le Québec et les Canadiens français occupent-ils une place inférieure sur le plan économique?" in *Le "Retard" de Québec et l'infériorité économique des canadiens français*, edited by René Durocher and Paul-André Linteau (Montreal: Boréal Express, 1971), 114.

29. Bonin and Polèse, *À Propos de l'association Canada-Québec*, 14.

30. Ibid., 284.

31. Ibid., 277.

32. Harvey, "Pourquoi le Québec et les Canadiens français occupent-ils une place inférieure?"

33. Norman Taylor, "The French-Canadian Industrial Entrepreneur and His Social Environment," in *French-Canadian Society*, edited by Marcel Rioux and Yves Martin (Toronto: McClelland and Stewart, 1964), 271–95.

34. Kenneth McRoberts, "Internal Colonialism: The Case of Quebec," *Ethnic and Racial Studies* 2, 3 (1979): 293–318.

35. Albert Faucher and Maurice Lamontagne, "History of Industrial Development," in *French-Canadian Society*, edited by Rioux and Martin, 257–71.

36. John McCallum, *Unequal Beginnings: Agriculture and Economic Development in Quebec and Ontario Until 1870* (Toronto: University of Toronto Press, 1980), 104.

37. Ouellet, *Histoire économique et sociale du Québec*.

38. Bourque and Legaré, *Le Québec: la question nationale*, 53–60, 111–20.

39. McCallum, *Unequal Beginnings*.

40. Ibid., chap. 7.

41. Ibid., 95.

42. Ibid., 94.

43. Tom Naylor, "The Rise and Fall of the Third Commercial Empire of the St. Lawrence," in *Capitalism and the National Question*, edited by Gary Teeple (Toronto: University of Toronto Press, 1972).

44. Glen Williams, "The National Policy Tariffs," *Canadian Journal of Political Science* XII, 2 (1979): 333–68.

45. D.M. Ray, "The Location of American Subsidiaries in Canada," *Economic Geography* 47, 3 (1971): 389–400.

46. D.G. Kerr, "Metropolitan Dominance," in *Canada: A Geographical Perspective*, edited by John Warkentin (Toronto: Methuen, 1979), 232.

47. Dominique Clift and Sheila McLeod Arnopoulos, *Le Fait anglais au Québec* (Montreal: Libre Expression, 1979), chap. 5.

48. Gourevitch, *Comparative Studies in Society and History*, 317.

49. Bourque and Legaré, *Le Québec: la question nationale*, 113–22.

50. Maurice Pinard, "A House Divided," *Report* (May 1980): 26.

51. Vera Murray, *Le Parti québécois* (Montreal: Hurtubise HMH, 1977); Kenneth McRoberts and Dale Posgate, *Quebec: Social Change and Political Crisis* (Toronto: McClelland and Stewart, 1980), chap. 3.

52. Clift and Arnopoulos, *Le Fait anglais au Québec*, 134–34.

53. Michael Hechter, "Group Formation and the Cultural Division of Labor," *American Journal of Sociology* 84, 2 (1978): 293–318.

54. Paul-André Linteau, "Quelques réflexions autour de la bourgeoisie québécoise, 1850–1914," *Revue d'histoire de l'Amérique français* 30 (1976): 64.

55. Jorge Niosi, "La Nouvelle bourgeoisie canadienne-française," *Les cahiers du socialisme* 1 (1978): 5–50; Pierre Fournier, "Les Nouveaux paramètres de la bourgeoisie québécoise," in *Le Capitalisme au Québec*, edited by Pierre Fournier (Montreal: Éditions Coopératives Albert St-Martin, 1978): 135–83; Bourque and Legaré, *Le Québec: la question nationale*.

56. McRoberts, "Internal Colonialism: the Case of Quebec."

57. Paul Bernard, Andrée Demers, Diane Grenier, and Jean Renaud, *L'évolution de la situation socio-économique des francophones et des non-francophones au Québec (1971–1978)* (Montreal: Office de la Langue Française, 1979), 132.

58. Clift and Arnopoulos, *Le Fait anglais au Québec*, 153–54.

59. Jean-Louis Roy, *La Marche des Québécois: le temps des ruptures (1945–1960)* (Montreal: Les Éditions Leméac, 1976); McRoberts and Posgate, *Quebec: Social Change and Political Crisis*, chap. 5.

60. Maurice Pinard and Richard Hamilton, "The Politics of Quebec Intellectuals: An Analysis and Some Comparative Perspectives" (unpublished paper presented to Joint International Seminar "After the Referenda: the future of ethnic nationalism in Britain and Canada," University of North Wales, Bangor, Wales, 5–9 November, 1981).

61. Ibid.

62. Smith, *The Ethnic Revival*, 108–11.

63. Ibid., 176.

64. Hubert Guindon, "The Modernization of Quebec and the Legitimacy of the Canadian State," in *Modernization and the Canadian State*, edited by Daniel Glenday, et al. (Toronto: Macmillan, 1978), 212–46; Louis Maheu, "La conjoncture des luttes nationales au Québec," *Sociologie et société* XI, 2 (1979): 125–44.

65. The "new middle class" is characterized in essentially these terms by Anthony Giddens, *The Class Structure of Advanced Societies*, 2nd ed. (London: Hutchinson, 1981), 107, 177.

66. These indications can be found both in data on the leaders of the Parti Québécois and in data on the social bases of a "Yes" vote in the 1980 referendum. With respect to the PQ leadership, our analysis of the occupational background of the members of the first Lévesque Cabinet shows that close to one third can be classified as "technocrats," given their past activities as administrators or economic advisors of governments. Among the remaining Cabinet members, an equal number would fall within the Pinard-Hamilton (but not necessarily Smith) category of "intellectuals": teachers, professors, and journalists. This second figure is much lower than that of Pinard-Hamilton. This may be due to the fact that many of the individuals in question have assumed more than one occupation. Some individuals who fall within our "technocratic" category have indeed spent some time teaching, and thus would qualify as "intellectuals," but we think that it would be misleading to do so. (Claude Morin, a long-term public administrator, Jacques Parizeau, a key economic advisor of successive Quebec governments, and Jacques Léonard, a university administrator and chartered accountant, are three examples.) We have tried to classify individuals in terms of their *primary* activity. With respect to the social bases of a "Yes" vote, we note that within the Pinard-Hamilton data *souverainisme* is also high among semi-professionals. Moreover, a recent analysis of survey data by André Blais and Richard Nadeau, in which administrators are analysed as a distinct category, shows that administrators within the public sector (unlike the private sector) "ont fortement appuyé le OUI." See André Blais and Richard Nadeau, "La clientèle de OUI" (unpublished paper, 1983), 10. They conclude about the Pinard-Hamilton argument: "la thèse doit donc être fortement nuance."

67. Bourque and Legaré, *Le Québec: la question nationale*, 203; Fournier, *Le Capitalisme au Québec*, chap. 5.

68. Niosi, "La nouvelle bourgeoisie canadienne-française."

69. Jorge Niosi, *La Bourgeoisie canadienne* (Montreal: Éditions du Boréal Express, 1980), 83.

70. Alain G. Gagnon and Mary Beth Montcalm, "Economic Peripheralization and Quebec Unrest," *Journal of Canadian Studies* 17, 2 (1982): 32–43.

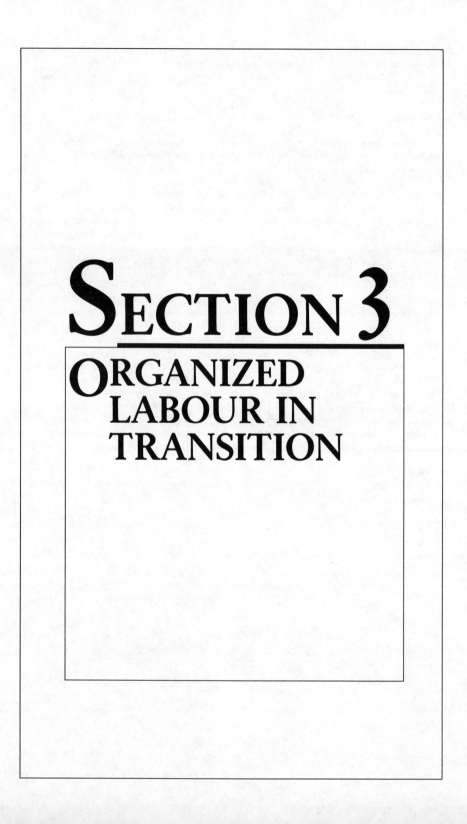

SECTION 3

ORGANIZED LABOUR IN TRANSITION

One of the more fascinating aspects of contemporary Quebec has been the ongoing radicalization of Quebec's three major labour centrals. The process started in the 1950s with the Catholic labour movement questioning and then denouncing traditional French-Canadian nationalism and its predominantly petty-bourgeois and clerical spokesmen and beneficiaries. Jacques Rouillard, in "Major Changes in the Confédération des travailleurs Catholiques du Canada, 1940–1960," analyses how this process of ideological renewal got underway after the war and what its consequences were. Spurred on by a small but influential group of liberal-minded Catholic priests involved with the labour movement, the Confédération des travailleurs catholiques du Canada (CTCC) abandoned its commitment to the right-wing ideology of corporatism and began to advocate the achievement of industrial democracy (that is, co-management, profit-sharing, and co-ownership) for Quebec's workers. In fact, when the CTCC's asbestos union requested a small measure of co-management during negotiations in late 1948, the American companies that owned the asbestos mines in the Eastern Townships adopted a hardline in defence of management prerogatives. The result was a bitter, sometimes violent, and very long strike during the first six months of 1949. Industrial democracy was going to prove far more elusive than Catholic labour leaders anticipated.

The CTCC, while remaining committed to its goal, began to advocate a more comprehensive range of liberal reforms that would humanize the capitalist economy. For the first time in history, the CTCC committed itself formally in the 1950s to the pursuit of fundamental human rights and genuine political democracy. The CTCC's primary objective was no longer the defence of the French-Canadian and Catholic nationality but rather the advancement of the rights and needs of the working class. This ideological shift toward liberalism resulted in a number of developments. One was the deconfessionalization of the CTCC, which culminated in the adoption of a new name, the Confédération des Syndicats Nationaux (CSN), in 1960. Secondly, the CTCC displayed its new-found militancy in several ways. Its leaders were aggressive in their denunciation of employers and engaged their central in a greater percentage of strikes than they had in the past. CTCC leaders also engaged in an informal alliance with Quebec's industrial unions to fight the anti-labour policies and practices of the Duplessis government. In fact, during the late 1950s it appeared to many that the CTCC might affiliate with the newly-formed Canadian Labour Congress.

Two of the most startling developments of the 1960s in Quebec included the growing support of the state for organized labour followed quickly by organized labour's commitment to a socialist and independent Quebec. In return for its support of the Liberal government's modernizing objectives, the CSN was able to gain, for large numbers of public and para-public sector employees, the right to form unions as well as the right to strike. To the chagrin of organized labour, the state proved to be just as formidable a foe as most of the large corporations. Increased confrontation with the state in the early 1970s provoked the leaders of Quebec's three union centrals to call upon their members to struggle for a socialist, independent Quebec by pursuing an aggressive strategy of general sympathetic strikes and by supporting the Parti Québécois. These developments provoked a chaotic but effective counter-offensive by the state and big business. Labour's radicalization also drove many private sector unions out of the CSN and further fragmented the Quebec labour scene.

Carla Lipsig-Mummé, in "The Web of Dependence: Quebec Unions in Politics before 1976," outlines the ever-changing relationship between unions and the state up to and during the Quiet Revolution. She demonstrates how coercion and neo-nationalism were employed by the Union Nationale after 1966 and the Liberal Party after 1970, often with the unwitting compliance of labour, to render organized labour increasingly dependent upon the state and thereby undermine and considerably weaken its political effectiveness. The serious recession of the 1980s and the return to power of the Liberals in 1985 will accelerate the erosion of the gains made by organized labour during the 1960s and 1970s.

The emergence of the modern feminist movement has influenced, to one degree or another, virtually every facet and every institution in our society. Women have been involved in organized labour since its inception, but their role has not, until very recently and only in a limited fashion, been one of equality. Mona-Josée Gagnon's article on "Women in the Trade-Union Movement in Quebec" provides a general overview of the ideological perception of women in Quebec society and within the three major Quebec labour centrals, the CSN, the FTQ, and the CEQ. The author outlines the extent to which a traditionalist ideology marginalized, until the 1960s, the role of women in these organizations. In the early stages of the Quiet Revolution, women were perceived as having a dual function — mother and paid worker — and emphasis was placed on the feminization of society. In fact, the unions adopted a protectionist attitude toward women ostensibly in order to defend their feminine qualities against the ravages of industrial capitalism. Only in the 1970s and in the face of continued opposition, has the traditional division of social roles assigned to men and women been contested, with some limited success, within the various union centrals and their federations and locals. Gagnon concludes her essay with some interesting insights into the factors conditioning the nature and level of the militancy of women within the bureaucracy of organized labour.

Major Changes in the Confédération des travailleurs catholiques du Canada, 1940–1960†

Jacques Rouillard

There is nothing really new about stating that the Confédération des travailleurs catholiques du Canada (CTCC) has undergone profound changes since the war. Historical works have repeated this and the leaders of the union have loudly proclaimed that there was a clean break between themselves and their predecessors.[1] For Jean Marchand, who was secretary general of the confederation from 1947 to 1961 and president from 1961 to 1965, the CTCC in its early days was clearly "nationalist, denominational and pro-corporatist, and chaplains also played a very prominent role." "Often," he wrote, "Catholic initiatives took precedence over those that were professional and specifically union-oriented."[2] Union leaders in the 1950s firmly believed they were breaking with the past and leading the confederation out of the dark ages.

No other work so strongly supported this argument than the book edited by Pierre Elliott Trudeau in 1956 on the 1949 asbestos strike. For one of the contributors, Reginald Boisvert, the CTCC for almost thirty years was not especially noted for its dynamism; the renewed vigour it had demonstrated during the strike reflected its rejection of "social conservatism" and its adoption of a "spirited doctrine that was fully conscious of the development of our milieu."[3] In developing their considerations further, some of the contributors to the book argued that the changes that the confederation had undergone had made it the agent for regenerating Quebec society. According to Trudeau, Boisvert, and Jean-Charles Falardeau, the CTCC workers had demonstrated the lack of realism in the Church's social doctrine and had substituted objectives that were closer to their real needs. More pragmatic, less dogmatic "because their life unfolds on a level of immediacy," the workers, Trudeau wrote, were the first to understand the meaning of industrialization, which had taken place during the war, and the

†"Mutations de la Confédération des travailleurs catholiques du Canada," *Revue d'histoire de l'Amérique française* 34, 3 (décembre 1980): 377–405. Translated by Henri Malebranche.

first to give free rein to the contradictions between ideology and the industrial reality.[4] For Trudeau, who rejected "proletarian messianism" and the "revolutionary mystique," this revival brought "liberty and justice" to Quebec society.[5] Believing that the workers constituted "a major force for purifying the laws and the democratic practices," he discovered within the workers' movement various elements of reform for which he had been fighting for a long time, namely a reformation of liberal democracy.[6] He interpreted the major changes that the CTCC had undergone as harbingers of profound changes in society, changes that the Quiet Revolution would put into concrete form.

It is not the intention, in the pages that follow, to prove the hypothesis that links the Quiet Revolution to the labour movement; rather, on a more modest scale, the transformations that led the Catholic confederation of trade unions to demonstrate greater militancy and to redefine its ideological orientation will be emphasized. Three themes will be considered: ideological evolution, denominationalism, and union action.

Ideological Evolution: From Corporatism to Liberal Humanism

Corporatism

Since it was first founded, the ultimate objective of the CTCC was to establish the professional corporation in Quebec. In organizing the professions into corporations, the Catholic confederation considered correcting the abuses of capitalism and restoring social order. The professional corporation, as conceived by the confederation, was composed of representatives of workers and employers who would look after the common interest of the profession. Issues such as salaries, working conditions, apprenticeship, production control, and even profit-sharing were to be discussed in joint committees by members of the corporation.[7] The corporation, at first, was to cover Quebec by industrial sector and then have overall responsibility for an intercorporative organization, composed once again of workers and employers, that would look after the general interests of the professions. It was felt that these structures would eliminate social conflicts and initiate permanent co-operation between workers and employers.

It is important to add that this system could only function insofar as a new spirit sustained all the social groups. Conflicting relations in the business world were to give way to a spirit of co-operation based on justice and charity. The Church took over the task of transforming attitudes by driving out the egoism of the employer and the mistrust of the workers. The adoption of corporatism not only included the establishment of a legal structure but it also fostered a moral transformation on the part of individuals.

Even though the CTCC's objective, up until the war, was to establish corporatism, we have already demonstrated that, from the 1920s on, its unions were negotiating with management, seeking to gain the balance of power.[8] Until such time as the employers changed their attitude, however, there was justification for defending as fervently as possible the professional interests of the workers, and no hesitation in resorting to a strike, if necessary. In their day-to-day activities, the international unions and the Catholic unions, in fact, came to resemble each other. The business of negotiating advantageous collective agreements required most of their energy, and even the CTCC's legislative program gradually aligned itself with that of the international unions. In fact, the CTCC had no other choice if it was to protect the material interests of its members. If it had acted otherwise, its followers would have abandoned it. And thus a rift appeared between the confederation's corporatist discourse and its union practices. While the leaders preached agreement and harmony with management, the unions were engaged in a power struggle in their negotiations with management.

In the 1920s and 1930s, the confederation was still not ready, however, to challenge the ideology that had prevailed at its founding. On the contrary, after the depression, when the Catholic intellectual circles, which were anxious to regain social order, restored the study of corporatism to a place of honour, the CTCC spelled out the ideas it had about its *raison d'être*. In 1939, the *bureau confédéral* [the executive committee of the CTCC and representatives of each federation and city council] was therefore given the responsibility of developing a program of corporatist reform. Held over until the following year, the report recommended that the professional corporation be built on a union base, that its Christian character be assured, and that the international unions be excluded.[9] As defined by the *bureau confédéral*, corporatism became a means of promoting Catholic trade unionism, since both international unions and non-union members were refused the right to be represented in corporations.[10]

After being discussed and amended, the program of the *bureau confédéral* was finally adopted at the 1942 convention. As in the initial plan, the resolution was emphatic about building the corporation on union organizations. As for international trade unionism, if it was not explicitly excluded, its presence was "signed away" with the requirement that the corporation be of Christian character and that the union party to its formation be incorporated.[11] Although rather vague in its application, the plan does reveal the CTCC's concern for setting aside projects, in vogue at the time, in which the corporation was not based on the union movement. The confederation also saw in its establishment the means for eliminating international unions, which, in any case, would never have co-operated in its formation since they denounced corporatism as a "fascist dictatorship over labour organizations."[12] Unfortunately for the theorists of Catholic trade unionism, the CTCC program made very little headway, for the war mobilized all of the confederation's energies.

After the war, pro-corporatist statements became increasingly rare; there was marked preference for substituting expressions such as "professional organization" or even "the democratization of the economy" for the term.[13] The soft-pedaling of the corporatist plan can be explained quite simply: the plan was associated much too closely with fascism, so that it became embarrassing to demand its implementation, especially at the end of a war against regimes that had, in fact, made it the basis of their social organization. Morever, for the proponents of free trade unionism, there was nothing commendable about the way corporatism was applied in these countries (Italy, France, Spain, Portugal, etc.).[14] Thus the CTCC gradually repudiated corporatism, which had been the industrial relations model at its founding. A question comes immediately to mind: what replaced it?

Business Reform

For several years the CTCC substituted for corporatism the idea of business reform that had been perfected after the war by French Catholic thinkers. Promoted in Quebec by younger members of the clergy, the idea gained validity among the new generation of CTCC leaders. The dissemination of this new interpretation of the Church's social doctrine fell to the Commission sacerdotale d'études sociales, which, in 1947, organized study days for chaplains and which also published a report in booklet form entitled *La participation des travailleurs à la vie de l'entreprise*.[15] Its works served as an inspiration for the Quebec bishops' pastoral letter of 1950 (*Le problème ouvrier en regard de la doctrine sociale de l'Église*) in which several paragraphs refer to the need for transforming the structure of private companies.[16] These new theorists of the Church's social doctrine, who were not yet formally repudiating corporatism, did criticize it for its globalism, maintaining that social reform must first start with the basic component of the economic system, the company.[17] They therefore proposed reforms within the company that would allow the workers a share in its profits, management, and ownership. For them, the employer's right of ownership of the factory was not absolute, for the company had a social character. Since production, profits, and the growth of the company all resulted from the contribution of capital and labour, they inferred a limited profit-sharing right for the workers as well as rights to the management and ownership of their company.[18] Even though, in practice, the new theorists watered down the scope of their principles to a large extent, nevertheless their premises were in direct opposition to the notion of ownership that prevailed in North America.

The CTCC adopted this plan for business reform and, at its 1948 convention, undertook to study and promote it among its members.[19] The new statement of principles, adopted as a preamble to its constitution in 1951, set this plan as a desired objective. "Within the company," it reads, "the workers must be considered to be collaborators participating in a common task. They must feel integrated and be able to participate in its management and its benefits."[20] Nevertheless, the idea in its original form was more or less abandoned two years later, when faced with resistance on every front.

Because it restricted the right to manage, the employer was particularly opposed to this plan for business reform. The issue divided the Catholic employer group, the Association professionnelle des Industriels (API), which was founded in 1943 as a counterpart to the unions in view of the establishment of the corporation. One of its founders, Father Bouvier, was even forced to resign as a chaplain because of his criticism related to business reform.[21] Although there are few allusions to this issue in the book edited by Pierre Elliott Trudeau, it was, in fact, at the centre of the dispute according to the employer.[22]

As far as the president of Canadian Johns Manville, Lewis H. Brown, was concerned, the origin of the strike did not concern salaries or working conditions but rather, an attempt on the part of the labour bosses to "assume the rights of management."[23] The union demands included an unacceptable clause as far as the company was concerned, namely one in which the union claimed the right of approval with respect to promotions, disciplinary measures and certain questions related to production, work methods, and rates of pay.[24] The idea of co-management advanced by the proponents of the plan for business reform had served as an inspiration for these union demands.[25] The company, who had made this a question of principle, considered these demands to be an attack on its right to manage. It may well be that these objectives were only window dressing to hide the real reasons for the company's opposition but it seems that this issue, at least in the first phase of the dispute, played a crucial role in the tough line taken by the employer. In the final agreement that ended the strike, the employer insisted that the union "acknowledge the right of ownership" and "agree to incorporate into the contract a clause called management rights."[26]

In other labour disputes, the CTCC also faced an equally stubborn resistance on the part of the employer to the idea of co-management, especially at the time of the textile workers' strike in 1947 (Lachute) and the aluminum workers' strike in 1951 (Shawinigan).[27] This resistance was a contributing factor to the CTCC's abandonment of its ideas in the 1950s. Very advanced for its time, the plan for business reform differed markedly from the usual union demands in North America. The American company, Canadian Johns Manville, very quickly became aware of this and asked the government to draw "a logical dividing line between what constitutes collective bargaining and what constitutes employer's rights."[28]

Liberal Humanism

After abandoning corporatism and encountering setbacks with its plan for business reform, the CTCC evolved on an ideological level towards what we would call liberal humanism. The confederation's statement of principles was developed in 1951 and 1960 along these ideological lines, which prevailed until the mid-1960s. At this time, the confederation started to generate an increasingly radical discourse.

After the war, when it became difficult for the Catholic thinkers to preach the virtues of corporatism, the Church became reconciled to a certain extent with both liberalism and democracy. It is significant to note that the Semaines sociales conferences, which reflected the preoccupations of Catholic social thinkers, devoted two sessions to these themes in 1942 and 1945.[29] The liberal ideas, which had until recently been rejected because they sprang from the French Revolution, no longer provoked the same censure. French Catholic thinkers such as J. Maritain, E. Mounier, and Father Delos and journals such as *Esprit*, *Témoignage Chrétien*, and *Économie et Humanisme* were all strong influences on French Canada's social thinkers. Several of these Catholics "of the left," as they were later called, drew their inspiration from personalism, a doctrine that proposed a happy co-existence between the autonomy and the social responsibility of individuals.

Rejecting individualism because it advocates inner directedness, personalism, on the contrary, encourages individuals to open themselves to others and to fit into a natural community. There is nothing very new about this aspect of personalist thinking in relation to the traditional teachings of the Church. This trend did open up new vistas, however, by proposing as a "fundamental affirmation" the existence of free and creative persons.[30] Although Mounier denied proposing "the freedom of liberalism," he nevertheless set forth the autonomy of persons as a postulate to his thinking and promoted freedom of choice, notions that were foreign to the traditional philosophy of the Church for whom freedom, far from being of value, was considered to originate from the weakness of human nature.[31] These new ways of thinking influenced the younger generation of clerics and laity of postwar Quebec who no longer displayed the same fears about the ideals of freedom and democracy. They were making a distinct effort to broaden the autonomy of the temporal sphere and to draw the Church closer to political and social democracy.

These tendencies, reflected in the speeches of the CTCC union leaders and chaplains, led the confederation to revise in 1951, for the first time in history, the preamble to its constitution. The authors of the text were buoyed by a democractic inspiration that was noticeably absent in the first version of the constitution, drawn up in 1921. In the revised constitution, they proclaimed the CTCC's faith in "true political democracy," a system that guarantees as much as possible the freedom of citizens, and they affirmed the equality of all persons as well as the confederation's opposition to "any unfair treatment on the basis of language, nationality, race, sex, or religion."[32] The confederation was proclaiming its support of fundamental human rights and even applied these to religion, thereby placing itself in direct opposition to its own doctrine since it was, in fact, denominational. The revised constitution of 1960 stresses even more strongly the CTCC's support of freedom and democracy.[33] That is why we have called this postwar ideological evolution of the confederation, liberal humanism.

This humanism sprang from the confederation's desire to humanize the economy, that is, to orient the production of goods first and foremost towards the satisfaction of human needs. The confederation felt that the value of "work" was more important than capital since the individual had to take priority over the accumulation of goods. Because liberal capitalism, based on the notion of maximum profit, depreciated human and spiritual values, the confederation renounced it, although it did recognize the legitimacy of the right to private property. Actually, what it condemned was not so much capitalism as its abuses, which had to be corrected by actively integrating workers into the life of the company and by appealing to the state to oversee economic activities.[34] The idea of participating in the life of the company, which had emerged shortly after the conflict on joint management, joint ownership, and profit-sharing, still remained one of the confederation's objectives, although it was somewhat vague in its specific applications. The company was still defined as a community of persons that, for this reason, called for the participation of workers.[35] It is not surprising that the CTCC criticized liberal capitalism since it had done so constantly from the time it was founded; what had changed after the war were its proposals for alternatives.

The liberal humanism of the CTCC also manifested itself in a new theme that appeared in 1958, namely, economic planning.[36] The humanization of the economic system required that the state plan its development. Anarchy, which until then had presided at its expansion, had created insecurity and inequality—causes of permanent social unrest. The symbolic intervention of the state through the development of a plan (with the co-operation of socio-economic agents) corrected certain abuses of the system and further directed the economy towards satisfying the real needs of individuals. Once again, the CTCC was influenced by the debates that had roused its French counterpart, the Confédération française des travailleurs chrétiens (CFTC), which had demonstrated its open-mindedness towards this reform as of 1957.[37] For these two confederations, the objective of the planning process was to humanize and democratize the economic system.

During the twenty years following the way, the CTCC lived through a period of profound ideological change. Since it was first founded, it had tried hard to offer workers a third path between capitalism and socialism. At first this was corporatism, and then after the war, it became business reform and liberal humanism. In another work, I demonstrated that employers, who had not committed themselves to the corporatist ideal were, in fact, the real reason for the failure of this ideology.[38] As indicated in the preceding pages, these same employers killed the idea of business reform since it did not meet the canons of their definition of free enterprise. This liberal humanism that succeeded company reform also advocated an ideal that was not easily reconciled with North American capitalism. Accordingly, the CTCC/CSN (Confédération des Syndicats nationaux) abandoned this option in the 1960s to devote its energies to democratic socialism — a model for society that it used to emphasize its criticism of capitalism.

The Nondenominational Character of the CTCC

Along with the changes in its ideological orientation, the CTCC gradually lost its denominational character after the outbreak of the war. At its founding, there were four characteristics that made it a Catholic confederation: the addition of the adjective "Catholic" to its name, the presence of a chaplain, its support of the Church's social doctrine, and the obligation that one had to be Catholic to obtain all the rights of a member. Gradually, the CTCC departed from each of these traits to become a nondenominational confederation, open to all workers. It is this progression that will be explored in the following paragraphs.

During the meetings that led to the founding of Catholic trade unions, the expectation was that only Catholics would have the privilege of being active union members. Although non-Catholics were not formally excluded, they were admitted as associate members only and could not vote or serve in a supervisory capacity.[39] In actual fact, however, few unions had associate members, and it soon became common practice in a city as cosmopolitan as Montreal, not to discriminate against non-Catholics. They were so few in number that there was no justification for being alarmed about their presence in the union. Moreover, the non-Catholics were hardly interested in joining unions that granted them, at least officially, an inferior status.

It was only during the war that the CTCC realized that this discrimination represented an obstacle for recruiting members. Because the war created favourable conditions for trade unions, the CTCC was very much aware of the fact that rival unions were progressing at a faster pace. In 1942, an inquiry ordered by Cardinal Villeneuve on this subject proposed the abolition of all discrimination in the recruitment of non-Catholics.[40]

The following year, other events outside the confederation forced the CTCC to review its position with respect to non-Catholics. In fact, the gradual implementation in Canada, in the war industries, of the equivalent in the U.S. Wagner Act placed the CTCC in a delicate position. Inspired by this act, the Canadian government passed several orders-in-council affecting labour relations in the war industries (which constituted seventy-five percent of all industry).[41] The government commissions responsible for applying these statutory orders recognized, as had their U.S. counterparts, the monopoly on representation that a majority union had in a company. Whenever two or more unions quarrelled over the membership of the workers, a vote of allegiance was taken to determine which union would negotiate the next collective agreement. Thus, the act led the unions within the CTCC to represent non-Catholics, to whom they still granted an inferior status.

This problem intensified in 1943 in the paper industry of the Saguenay region. The Price Brothers Company had granted two international unions a closed shop but they had subsequently become a minority union within the company's four factories. The company refused to negotiate with the Catholic unions, however, because they did not represent the workers practising trades essential to the operation of the factory and because its recognition of the Catholic unions would signify an obligation for non-Catholics to belong to a denominational organization.[42] The dispute degenerated into a strike, leading the government to establish a Royal Commission, which recommened that the "closed shop" clause be rendered null and void and the majority Catholic unions be recognized.[43] The government complied with the wishes of the Commission but also obliged the four unions within the CTCC to drop the word "Catholic" from their title and to grant equal rights and privileges to all their members.[44]

A few months later, CTCC president Alfred Charpentier invited the delegates to the confederation's convention to open up the movement "in a benevolent spirit of worker fraternity."[45] This suggestion created some conflict but led to a resolution that required, not that the members of the confederation be Catholic but rather, according to a somewhat vaguely worded dictate, that they "model their words and their actions as union members on the guiding principles of the CTCC."[46] Provided they supported the principles of the Church's social doctrine, non-Catholics could become full members of the confederation. The CTCC thus eliminated a first criterion of denominationalism by giving each member equal status regardless of religious affiliation.

A more important step towards nondenominationalism was taken sixteen years later, in 1960, when the CTCC abolished two more aspects of its denominational character: it dropped "Catholic" from its title as well as all direct references to the Church's social doctrine. In its statement of principles, the sentence that had previously said "to be inspired in its principles and its actions by the social doctrine of the Church" was replaced by another in which it recognized an allegiance only to Christian principles in its outlook and its actions.[47] In choosing between the Confédération des Syndicats chrétiens and the Confédération des Syndicats nationaux, the majority of the delegates rallied around the second name, thus eliminating the religious reference in the confederation's title.

Once again, at the end of the 1950s, the CTCC went through a difficult period in terms of recruitment, which it had hoped to avoid by being more receptive to non-Catholics. In a cosmopolitan milieu like Montreal, the CTCC had hardly penetrated into the larger companies because of its denominational character. When the bargaining units held a vote to choose the majority union, the CTCC faced a serious handicap since it had to deduct, right from the start, the vote of the majority of non-Catholics. Within the system of a union representation monopoly such as existed in North America, denominationalism imposed a major constraint on the CTCC. As the executive committee report indicated: "either the CTCC accepts the challenge and establishes a considerable number of majority unions or else it condemns itself to stagnation and, no doubt, it will eventually die out altogether."[48] Presented in this fashion, the dilemma was not difficult to resolve for the delegates at the 1960 convention, especially since the confederation had been studying this question for the previous four years and had received the assurance of the episcopate that it would not object, in principle, to any modifications to the CTCC's denominational status.[49]

The confederation's abandonment of two of its most important denominational traits raised more of an outcry among the chaplains than it did among the union members. In July 1959, five former chaplains published a brochure of fifty or so pages accusing the CTCC leaders of wanting to make the confederation a lay organization, that is, of allowing it to lose the traits that had been present at its founding.[50] They were right with respect to this point but the assembly of bishops, called upon to reach a verdict shortly thereafter, felt that the new plan "reflected sufficiently the social doctrine of the Church" so as to be acceptable. The bishops ended their letter by stating that it was the confederation's responsibility to change its constitution if it felt this was necessary.[51] In short, the episcopate acknowledged the full autonomy of the CTCC, a sign of how far the confederation had evolved.

This evolution reflected the changes that had occurred in postwar Quebec society. A new trend of thought had appeared within the Church among various clerics and laity who wanted to establish a much clearer distinction between temporal and spiritual actions and who wanted to restore to Catholic laity greater autonomy in social action. Unlike their predecessors, they thought that trade unionism and the co-operative movement were temporal activities that did not fall directly under spiritual authority. Not that they were rejecting that Christian principles had to guide social action but, rather, that their solution had to come from the judgment of the faithful and not from specific directives issued by the Church hierarchy. The Catholic laity engaged in social action, who assumed a greater role in the orientation of their movement, did not think highly of having to submit to specific rules governing their actions. Thus the chaplains played a much more discreet role within the CTCC unions after the war. And when the leaders of the CTCC decided, in 1960, to break free from the tutelage of the Church, the evolution that had gone on within the confederation had progressed too far for the bishops to stand in the way.

After the 1960 convention, only the presence of a chaplain still conferred on the confederation a semblance of denominationalism. It is obvious that the chaplain was to play an increasingly diminished role, so much so that, when he submitted his resignation in 1971, the *bureau confédéral* did not request that he be replaced.[52] The regional unions and organizations were, however, free to maintain a chaplaincy service, a practice that several had already abandoned or were soon to do so. This last episode in the process of nondenominationalism went unnoticed and heralded the extent to which the CSN had abandoned the principles present at its founding.

In sum, the CTCC's nondenominationalism occurred in two separate periods, in 1943 and especially in 1960. There are two major reasons to explain this process: the fear of stagnation in the growth of its membership and a desire for autonomy on the part of the CTCC leaders in the realm of temporal action. These changes came about very smoothly, a sure sign of the evolution that had gone on within the membership, and a sign that this evolution had already taken place within the affiliated body of the confederation.

Union Action

It is generally ackowledged that the CTCC became much more militant after the war. It openly supported numerous strikes, vigorously criticized management, and was to become one of the prime centres of opposition to the Duplessis regime. The major source of this turnaround stemmed from the change in CTCC union leadership after the war. According to former CTCC president A. Charpentier, in 1949 more than half the members of the *bureau confédéral* were new.[53] Several of these young labour leaders were recent graduates of the faculty of social sciences at Laval University where they had encountered the new trend in the interpretation of the Church's social doctrine.

As indicated in the introduction, these labour leaders felt they were injecting a new vitality into the confederation. They considered the pre-war CTCC to be more a movement for Catholic action than a professional defence organization. Under the influence of the clergy, the CTCC, they felt, was more interested in co-operating with management than in defending the interest of its members. And they felt that recourse to strike action was held in suspicion and members who were too militant were isolated from CTCC ranks. According to some calculations made by Jean Francoeur, one of the authors of a history of the CSN published in 1963, fewer than nine strikes out of a total of 507 reported in the province between the years 1915 and 1936 were apparently the work of the CTCC. He concluded, "One has to admit that a strike was almost completely outside this confederation's frame of reference for union action."[54]

In a review of national unions from 1900 to 1930, I questioned this image of the CTCC during its first ten years of existence. After an exhaustive analysis, I concluded that the Catholic confederation hardly differed from the international unions in its union practices. The two movements, with a fairly similar legislative program, worked towards signing good collective agreements, they sought to have the closed shop, and used the union label and the threat of strike action as a means of pressure.[55] In fact, contrary to Jean Francoeur's assertion, I tallied thirty-two strikes led by the Catholic unions between 1920 and 1930 alone. These represent thirteen percent of the strikes in Quebec during this ten-year period, at a time when the CTCC represented approximately twenty-five percent of Quebec trade unions.[56] Some of these strikes caused a considerable stir such as the 1921 strike of the Quebec policemen and firemen, the 1924 strike of the workers in the E.B. Eddy factory in Hull, and especially the 1926 strike of the Quebec shoe workers (88,677 lost work days).

The frequency of strikes is a good indication of union militancy. Research into subsequent years revealed that, between 1931 and 1940, the CTCC was responsible for at least twenty-one strikes, or nine percent of the strikes launched during these years.[57] The Catholic trade unions at the time represented approximately one-third of Quebec unions. Before concluding too quickly that the CTCC was non-aggressive, one must realize that several of the labour disputes were started by non-union members, and also that the CTCC, contrary to international unions, recruited mainly workers with minimal bargaining power: in the leather, textile, clothing, and service industries.[58] Because of these factors, the difference between the militancy of Catholic and international unions is less great than the numbers cited above would lead one to believe. Two of the strikes that the CTCC supported were among the major strikes of the period in terms of lost work days, namely the Dominion Textile strike (200,000 lost days) and the Sorel shipyard workers' strike (31,400 lost work days) of 1937. These facts contradict the image that one has had up until now of the CTCC's accommodating attitude towards management. Its corporatist ideology did not prevent it from rallying to the defence of its workers when the need was there. Chaplain-General Rev. M. Fortin noted in a letter to the bishops in 1925, that "the Catholic unions are not pious nor are they brotherhood associations; neither do they aim to exhort workers to practise abnegation, patience, or resignation...but their raison d'être is, like any trade union, to safeguard the interest of the working class."[59]

If such was the conduct of the Catholic unions prior to the war, were there any changes in the confederation's union practices after the war? Would the turnaround tend to be more ideological (the abandonment of corporatism) rather than falling within the realm of concrete union action? This hypothesis is considered by reviewing the CTCC's relationship with management, with rival trade unions, and with the provincial government.

Management

If one peruses the CTCC house organ, *Le Travail*, it is surprising to note how the tone of the articles changed in the 1950s: the writers of this magazine became more overtly aggressive towards management. Since its founding, the CTCC had denounced the abuses of capitalism and after the war continued to do so, but with unaccustomed vehemence. And its critics were aware of its desire to go beyond capitalism by means of business reform, at least at the beginning of the period. It must also be said that management had not spared the CTCC, having forced it into several long and difficult strikes, in particular those of Asbestos (1949), Louiseville (1952), the Dupuis Frères (1952), and Radio-Canada (1959). In December 1952, at the height of the Louiseville strike, the confederation's plenary committee decided on the principle of a general strike.[60] Although the leaders did not follow up this resolution, the gesture revealed their state of mind.

As with the previous periods, the percentage of strikes that the CTCC supported has been calculated. For the years for which we have statistics, namely from 1952 to 1960, thirty-four percent (99 of 287) of the labour disputes in Quebec involved unions affiliated with the CTCC.[61] When compared with the percentage of unions in Quebec, which was about one-third, the data clearly demonstrate the Catholic unions' fighting spirit. Considering that non-union members were responsible for several strikes, the CTCC had more than its share of disputes.

Anxious to find a means of fighting more effectively, the confederation approved the creation of a special professional defence fund in 1949, to assist a federation or union whenever there were "extraordinary circumstances."[62] Some professional federations had already set up a strike fund; others were invited to do so as quickly as possible. In 1951, the CTCC began to deduct union dues (10 cents a month) for its special fund, which it subsequently increased on a regular basis.[63] It was felt that both management and the government had placed restrictions on the confederation's exercise of its right to strike to such an extent that it had responded by adopting the means of ensuring a minimum of protection for its workers.[64]

This new and more serious wave of union militancy earned disapproval for the Catholic unions from several fronts including, as surprising as it may seem, the disapproval of some important international union leaders who repeated the accusation, and adopted it as their own, that certain sections of the CTCC had a revolutionary mentality similar to that of communists.[65] In presenting his report to the 1953 convention, the director of the confederation's organizational department, R. Harmegnies, admitted that the Catholic trade unions were no longer enjoying the support they had previously received from other social milieus, and added: "In several cases, this support has changed to open hostility."[66] Faced with this mounting opposition, the delegates at the 1953 convention, far from adopting a moderate approach, voted unanimously for a resolution stating that the CTCC would never be "party to the exploitation of the workers."[67] And indeed, the CTCC demonstrated this same willingness to fight in subsequent years.

The Union Centrals

If its ardour alienated the Fédération provinciale des Travailleurs du Québec (FPTQ), which was the Quebec central of trade unions that grouped together the international unions which, in turn, were affiliated with the American Federation of Labor (AFL),[68] the CTCC did have allies in the Fédération des Unions industrielles du Québec (FUIQ), which brought together the unions of the Congress of Industrial Organizations (CIO) and the Alliance des Professeurs de Montréal, who were exposed to the hostility of the Commission des écoles catholiques de Montréal and the Duplessis government. Founded rather late, in 1952, the FUIQ felt an immediate affinity with the CTCC. Both recruited a mass of workers who were similar in nature, the industrial workers; both wanted to go beyond business trade unionism; both hoped for increased intervention from the state; and finally, both condemned the Duplessis government. In fact, it was the anti–trade union stance of the provincial government that brought the two union groups together. Their co-operation started in 1948 when an inter-union cartel was formed to defeat Bill 5, and continued subsequently when they both opposed Bills 60 (1949), and 19 and 20 (1954).

The FPTQ also participated in these cartels but refused to join the march on Quebec that had been organized to protest against the last two bills. It felt that representations to government were more effective than mass demonstrations in obtaining modifications to the bill.[69] However, the real grounds for its refusal may be explained by an upsurge of inter-union rivalry among its affiliated unions and by the feeling it had that the CTCC possessed a revolutionary mentality.[70]

On the other hand, the CTCC's militancy pleased the FUIQ, and, within this union, a wave of sympathy developed that brought it closer to the CTCC. It lent the CTCC its moral and financial support for the strikers at Asbestos, Dupuis Frères, and Louiseville, and the CTCC reciprocated for the strikers at Noranda in 1953. The two movements had so much in common that, in 1956, it appeared much more likely that the FUIQ, rather than the FPTQ, would merge with the CTCC. But it was not up to the Quebec unionists to decide; rather, the choice depended on decisions made in the U.S. between the AFL and the CIO and their Canadian counterparts, the Trades and Labour Congress of Canada (TLCC) and the Canadian Congress of Labour (CCL).

Negotiations for the union merger were undertaken with the CTCC when the two Canadian confederations, the TLCC and the CCL, merged in 1956. As early as September 1955, before even being invited to merge with them, the Catholic confederation took the initiative by appointing a committee of nine members charged with the task of studying "the best methods of achieving complete labour unity within Canada."[71] After meeting with representatives from the Canadian Labour Congress (formed when the TLCC and CCL merged), the committee recommended, the following year at the CTCC convention, not a merger but an affiliation as a "national union" within the CLC. The Catholic confederation relinquished its status as a national trade union confederation to transform itself into one large union that would retain its affiliated unions.[72] For a number of CTCC leaders, including president G. Picard and secretary general J. Marchand, unity was essential, for division weakened the workers.[73] No doubt also, at this particular time when nationalism was viewed with suspicion, the CTCC felt the need to open up to the outside. But it was careful to cast constitutional unity aside, for the CTCC had certain characteristics it wanted to retain.[74]

Even with these reservations, the plan presented to the 1956 convention met with opposition once it was translated into concrete terms; it necessitated, in effect, a profound change to the structures of the confederation and the elimination of its denominational status.[75] With respect to this point, the committee for unifying the union received a rather feeble majority from the delegates and the special convention planned for June 1957, which was to rule on the affiliation, did not, in fact, take place, for tensions had appeared within the confederation. A group of trade unionists rejected affiliation since they thought that cohabitation with international unions would prove to be impossible and that it would signify the confederation's abandonment of its denominational status.[76] The issue was revived at the regular convention in 1957, where the affiliation plan of the committee for union unity was substantially amended by toughening its requirements towards the CLC. According to the plan that was adopted, the CTCC retained its autonomy with respect to its internal structures, its expansion, and the orientation of its doctrine; furthermore, it kept its central councils and remained independent of the Fédération des travailleurs du Québec (FTQ), even reserving for itself the right of legislative representation in the Quebec government.[77] Despite the amendments, which favoured the CTCC, the affiliation plan garnered only nominal support among the delegates (204 to 189), a sure sign that accord was far from being achieved within the confederation. Furthermore, the conditions underlying the affiliation rendered the CLC's accord almost impossible to obtain.

The CLC had also failed in its attempt to reduce the obstacles standing in the way of affiliation. At its 1958 convention, the CLC executive were refused the right — by the delegates — to negotiate an agreement with the CTCC without first obtaining the consent of each of the international unions that had rival professional jurisdiction with the CTCC unions.[78] The CLC's constitution required such consent, which rendered an agreement with the CTCC very problematic.[79] In short, the response to the CTCC's offer of affiliation was even more the concern of American rather than CLC decision-making centres, despite all the good intentions the CLC was able to demonstrate. The international unions had set aside the principle of jurisdictional exclusivity at the time of the AFL/CIO merger, but it is doubtful that they were ready to do the same for a union central as small (within the context of North America) as the CTCC. Thus, practically insurmountable obstacles stood in the way of an agreement between the two union centrals: the CLC had little power over its affiliated unions while the CTCC had laid down conditions for affiliation that were unacceptable.

Nevertheless, negotiations continued until 1961, with the CTCC making a number of concessions: it was ready "to encourage the elimination of duplicate organizations and jurisdictions" and it accepted the merging of its councils in the two years that followed the signing of the agreement.[80] There still remained the problem of overlapping jurisdiction which, in 1959, the CLC finally felt was impossible to overcome. It therefore withdrew its offer to grant the status of national union to the CTCC, leaving no other choice for the Catholic unions but to merge with the international unions.[81] As Jean Marchand stated, "The precarious scaffolding we had erected collaspsed like a building whose foundation suddenly gives way."[82] And carried away by the renewed spirit of nationalism that was asserting itself in Quebec at the time, the CSN ended its negotiations once and for all in 1961.

When one is aware of the long history of inter-union rivalry that existed between the CTCC and the international unions, it is surprising to see how the two labour bodies came so close to becoming affiliated. Even though there was no question that the Catholic confederation would disappear as an entity, the fact remains that the CTCC had undergone enormous changes since the war to draw so closely to the international unions. Setting nationalism aside, the ideological frontier that separated the two organizations narrowed considerably during the mid-1950s. The liberal humanism advocated by the CTCC was not so far removed from the ideology of the international unions. It is therefore not surprising that the CTCC drew closer to these unions and that it felt it had fewer and fewer valid reasons for dividing the workers.

The Provincial Government

In its dealings with the provinical government, the CTCC deserved its reputation as a centre for anti-Duplessis forces. Its relations with the government became so strained that the Catholic confederation stopped submitting its annual report to the premier in 1956. Until the Union Nationale came to power, the CTCC's relations with the Liberal governments, like those of the international unions, had been rather cordial. To the CTCC's great satisfaction, the Liberals had passed two acts that the CTCC had instigated, the loi des syndicats professionnels (1924) and the loi d'extension juridique des conventions collectives (1934). However, with the coming of Duplessis to power in 1936, the situation took a turn for the worse, for the government adopted and modified several bills that reflected unfavourably on the union movement. According to the CTCC president of the time, A. Charpentier, the government indulged in "a series of schemes indicative of the worst political attack against the very essence of the trade union movement in the province of Quebec."[83] The election of the Liberal Party in 1939 brought some respite although it did not last long, for the Union Nationale regained power in 1944.

What the trade unions especially disliked were the numerous pieces of legislation passed to restrict their activities and negotiating power. The government devoted itself to putting the public and semi-public sectors out of the reach of the trade unions (civil servants in 1938; rural municipality employees in 1949) and to taking away the right to strike (employees in charitable institutions, 1939; city employees, 1949), the right to arbitration (rural primary school teachers, 1946), or workers' certification if they went out on strike (Bill 20, 1954). In an attempt to substitute government action for the potential action of the unions and management, it gave itself the authority, in 1937 and 1938, to repeal or modify a decree granted under the loi des conventions collectives without consulting the parties to the agreement.[84] Duplessis' phobia about the closed shop became evident in 1938 in an act that provided for fines for anyone violating a salaried person's freedom to work; the draft labour code of 1948, which was withdrawn following protests from the unions, also contained a provision rendering the closed shop illegal, thus jeopardizing union security.[85] Moreover, while trying to appear to be fighting against communism, the Duplessis government was actually trying to weaken the union movement by sending various union organizers and leaders to jail, and even going so far as to deprive of union recognition an organzation that tolerated communist members among its officers and union organizers (Bill 19, 1954).[86]

Duplessis' anti-union leanings were also evident in his refusal to make any changes to the loi des relations ouvrières that would have resulted in more fair treatment of the unions. This act was passed in 1944 and had numerous deficiencies that the unions wanted to correct. According to the CTCC, this act, adopted to allow every worker to join a union freely, should have outlawed company unions and granted effective protection against dismissal for union activities.[87] The confederation particularly attacked the Commission responsible for applying the act, which, apparently in its interpretation, was unfavourably prejudiced against workers. Since the appointment of the majority of the commissioners was political,[88] it followed that their decisions often reflected the point of view of either the government or the employer. According, the CTCC developed a deep aversion towards the Commission as of 1953.

Duplessis also had the occasion to demonstrate his anti-union feelings during the course of several strikes, where his sympathy lay with management. He had a tendency to perceive a strike as an act of insubordination and an element of chaos and to attribute the responsibility for a strike to the intemperance of certain union leaders.[89] According to reasoning that still has a familiar ring, it was the union leaders who promoted the strikes and manipulated the workers. Hence, the premier accused them, numerous times, of being revolutionaries, saboteurs, and dictators. He suspected the CTCC leaders of wanting him to be defeated and of using a strike to satisfy their political resentment.[90] Whether the union leaders wanted him to be defeated or not, it is certain that his bias for management left them scarcely any other choice.

Duplessis' anti-unionism seems to have originated from two sources: the conservative ideology that sustained him, and the influence of North American union legislation. There is an interesting parallel between the content of the Taft-Hartley Act, adopted in the U.S. in 1947, and the labour legislation of the Union Nationale government. Both shielded the public sector from the reach of the trade unions, demonstrated the same anti-communist tendencies, and sought to outlaw the principle of the closed shop.[91] After the war, a particular idea seems to have gained a hold over government, namely that the concessions granted to the unions since the Great Depression had been too generous and that now the trend had to be reversed by restricting their freedom to manoeuvre. Coupled with this anti-union sentiment, which Duplessis shared with many governments, was his own paternalistic view of labour/management relations. He had difficulty imagining that these two social groups could maintain a relationship of equality. Rather, he felt that workers should be placed in a state of filial subordination. In a memo, he wrote in 1938:

> Employers must manage their industry with all due fairness, integrity, and kindness, but they must also be in charge, with workers, for their part, knowing how to obey orders and fulfill their duties to the best of their abilities. They too must be fair, honest, and kind. The unions, for their part, must protect their members, but not by persuading them that the employer is an enemy and not by intimidating those who do not wish to become union members.[92]

Based on such principles, one can understand how his government's legislation elicited the wrath of the trade unions, especially that of the CTCC, which was diametrically opposed to Duplessis from an ideological standpoint. While Duplessis perceived the company as a family, the CTCC, on the other hand, was promoting co-management and co-ownership.

The antagonism between the government and the CTCC prompted a new development within the confederation in terms of political action. Since its founding, the Catholic confederation had always opposed partisan political action and, in fact, its constitution of 1921 forbade it.[93] This political weapon had a socialist aspect that was not terribly compatible with a confederation that had been created to oppose this type of ideology. However, after events such as the asbestos workers' strike and the tabling of Bills 5 and 60, various union leaders questioned the wisdom of this position. Would it not be better to take the battle to where the shots were coming from, namely, to the political terrain?

At the 1949 convention, a cautious step was taken in this direction when the confederation formed a civil action committee (which became a committee with a political orientation the following year) whose objective was to educate the workers politically. It was carefully spelled out that the committee would not support any political party and that it would confine itself to influencing the government, to providing a civil education for workers and to directing "public opinion towards co-operation among the classes".[94] On the eve of the 1952 provincial elections, the committee received the authority from the *bureau confédéral* to communicate the CTCC's point of view on various programs the political parties had proposed and to clarify for voters the merits of the candidates running for office.[95] During the campaign, the committee promoted the confederation's legislative program and officially denounced four Union Nationale candidates for their hostility towards the CTCC.[96] This last gesture, which some delegates at the 1952 convention interpreted as a sign of political partisanship, prompted a long debate that ended with a resolution confirming the direction taken by the *bureau confédéral*.[97] At the same time that the CTCC was rejecting political partisanship, the majority of its members also realized the need for concrete political action.

For some, the political situation in Quebec demanded stronger political action. An official was finally designated to devote himself exclusively to the political education of the workers. And the idea of supporting, in co-operation with interested groups, various candidates who were concerned with the public's welfare was approved at the 1954 convention.[98] A further step was taken in 1959 when the convention amended the constitution so as to allow affiliated groups to adopt political attitudes they considered appropriate as long as these did not "run counter to the general interest of the movement."[99] However, the confederation did not commit itself further in this respect since it was encouraging strong opposition from among its members.

At the end of the 1950s, a number of events led the CTCC to question whether it should take the plunge into active politics. At its 1958 convention, the Canadian Labour Congress invited all union groups to agree on the creation of a new popular party. In response to this appeal, the *bureau confédéral* formed a committee and gave it rather vague terms of reference to "discuss political objectives of the labour movement."[100] However, at the convention several months later, two resolutions that were submitted, to the effect of studying the possibility of forming a Canadian political party, were both rejected by the resolutions committee, and the confederation reaffirmed its willingness to retain its independence from all political parties.[101] Several leaders of the confederation, G. Picard, M. Chartrand, and P. Vadeboncoeur, played a key role in the formation of the NDP in Quebec without overcoming, however, the reservations of the militant members within the CTCC.

It is remarkable to note that the Catholic confederation was extremely hesitant about going beyond educational political action to approach even indirect support of a political party. There was a deep-rooted opinion among Quebec unionists to the effect that union action was to be dissociated from partisan political action. In the truest Gomperian tradition, the ultimate goal of trade unionism, they felt, was economic; in politics, the worker acted in the role of citizen and not trade unionist. This deep-rooted opinion also had an impact on the international unions; their support of the CCF/NDP was rather diffident and, in any case, their members did not follow their guiding principles.

Faced with this sentiment, the CTCC, after the war, marked time by adding educational political action to its methods of lobbying and influencing governments. This development can be explained by the increased militancy of the confederation and especially by Duplessis' anti-unionist stance, which gave the CTCC leaders no respite. Several of them would have really liked to return, on political terrain, the blows that the premier was directing at them, but the majority of the members were not yet ready to involve the confederation in political partisanship.

It is apparent that the CTCC underwent enormous changes after the war. It abandoned the corporatist ideal as well as its own denominational character. On another level, it became increasingly militant towards both management and the government.

In conclusion, it is appropriate to ask: what are the underlying factors for this radical transformation of the Catholic confederation? In reply to this question, Louis-Marie Tremblay, in his book on the ideologies of the CSN and FTQ, indicated, as the principal factors for explaining this transformation, the development of the Quebec economy, the transformation of French-Canadian social thinking, and the changes in union leadership.[102] It is always risky to attribute to ideological trends or to union leaders changes that may, in fact, originate within the union base itself. I am aware of this but, owing to a lack of historical studies on unions for this period, I am forced to make do with explanations that are just as general. L.M. Tremblay cites the wave of industrialism that affected Quebec after the war as one of the reasons for the CTCC's revival, but I do not feel this was really a decisive factor. The international unions affiliated with the AFL, comprising the majority of unions in Quebec, did not wait until the war's end to display their militancy, which did not increase in the 1950s, except in the case of the various unions, few in number, affiliated with the FUIQ.[103] Similarly, the arrival of new leaders at the head of the CTCC does not seem to me to be responsible, in itself, for decisive changes; rather, it was the ideas they adopted that generated the revival.

What appears more significant to me are the ideological changes the confederation underwent. The postwar generation of Catholic clerics and laity rejected corporatism, which was associated too closely in their minds with fascism to be a valid alternative to capitalism. In Quebec as elsewhere, the victory of liberal democracies during World War II dealt a cruel blow to the right-wing ideologies that had given birth to corporatism. This victory also shattered the clerico-conservative ideology that the church had been promoting in Quebec since the nineteenth century. This more liberal spirit, which first came to prominence after the war, expressed itself in a clearer separation between the temporal and the spiritual and led to the CTCC's abandonment of denominationalism. In the area of labour relations, the younger Catholic clerics and laity, seeking alternatives to corporatism and capitalism, first advocated business reform and later, liberal humanism. This quest created the dynamics for change, which led to increased militancy on the part of the confederation. The CTCC's abandonment of corporatism created a favourable climate for the adoption of new ideologies and more radical union practices.

Notes

1. Examples of works that have adopted this point of view: CSN-CEQ, *Histoire du mouvement ouvrier du Québec (1825–1976)* (Montreal: CEQ, 1979), 124–131; Louis-Marie Tremblay, *Le syndicalisme québécois: idéologies de la CSN et de la FTQ (1940–1970)* (Montreal: PUM, 1972), 23–27; Hélène David, "L'état des rapports de classe au Québec de 1945 à 1967," *Sociologie et société* (novembre 1975): 33–65; Roch Denis, *Luttes de classes et question nationale au Québec (1948–1968)* (Montreal: Presses socialistes internationales, 1979), 128–134.

2. Jean Marchand, "La CSN a quarante ans," *Relations industrielles* 16, 4 (octobre 1961): 471.

3. Pierre Elliott Trudeau, *La Grève de l'amiante* (Montreal: Éd. du jour, 1956), 357 and 359.

4. Ibid., 89.

5. Ibid., 404.

6. *Cité libre* (décembre 1952): 66, in M. Behiels, *Prelude to Quebec's Quiet Revolution: Liberalism versus Neo-nationalism 1945–1960* (Montreal/Kingston: McGill-Queen's University Press, 1985), 127–28.

7. Related texts: J. Rouillard, *Les syndicats nationaux au Québec de 1900 à 1930* (Quebec: PUL, 1979), 199, 200, 228, 229, 310, 311; *La Vie syndicale* (août 1934), 6; (janvier 1940), 1; (décembre 1940), 5; Semaines sociales du Canada, *L'Organisation professionnelle* (Montreal: ESP, 1936).

8. This idea has been developed in Rouillard, *Les syndicats nationaux au Québec*, 240–50.

9. *La Vie syndicale* (decembre 1940), 5.

10. Jean Sexton, "La CTCC-CSN: du corporatisme à la reforme du l'entreprise" (unpublished Master's thesis, Laval University, 1979), 49.

11. CTCC, *Procès-verbal du congrès* (1942): 136–38.

12. *Le Monde ouvrier*, 7 août 1937, 4.

13. Sexton, *La CTCC-CSN*, 54.

14. In France, the policy of the Vichy government consisted, in 1940, of dissolving trade union confederations in order to facilitate, as it maintained, the integration of the workers into the corporatism of industry. This decision was all that was needed to discredit corporatism in the eyes of the Confédération française des travailleurs chrétiens (CFTC). *La C.F.D.T.* (Paris: Seuil, 1971), 11 and 34.

15. Commission sacerdotale d'études sociales, *La participation des travailleurs à la vie de l'entreprise*, Compte rendu des journées sacerdotales d'études sociales de 1947 (Montreal, 1949).

16. Quebec Bishops, *Le problème ouvrier en regard de la doctrine sociale de l'Église* (Montreal: Bellarmin, 1950), 26 and 27. As to the circumstances related to the writing of this letter, consult Gérard Dion, "La Petite histoire d'un grand document," *Perspectives sociales* 25, 2 (mars-avril 1970): 42–47.

17. Sexton, *La CTCC-CSN*, 69–133.

18. Commission sacerdotale, *La participation de travailluers à la vie de l'entreprise*, 13–45. Also consult articles on this subject by G. Dion, P.E. Bolté, and M. Clément in the *Bulletin des relations industrielles* (1947–1948) appearing under the title "Réforme de la structure de l'entreprise."

19. CTCC, *Procès-verbal du congrès* (1948): 225.

20. Ibid. (1951): 217.

21. Yvan Sénecal, "L'Association professionnelle des industriels" (unpublished Master's thesis, University of Montreal, 1954), 88–89.

22. Trudeau, *La Grève de l'amiante*, 173, 192, 385.

23. L.H. Brown, *La grève d'Asbestos*, brochure distributed by the Johns Manville Co. (1949), 9.

24. Ibid., 8. According to the union version, the only claim it made to management was that it consult the union in the case of all promotions, transfers, and dismissals (Trudeau, *La Grève de l'amiante*, 214).

25. A. Charpentier, *Les Mémoires d'Alfred Charpentier* (Quebec: PUL, 1971), 330–33; Sexton, *La CTCC-CSN*, 112.

26. Trudeau, *La Grève de l'amiante*, 230.

27. CTCC, *Procès-verbal du congrès* (1951): 36.

28. L.H. Brown, *La grève d'Asbestos*, 16.

29. *La Démocratie* (1942); *Liberté et libertés* (1945). It is surprising to note that there are no studies on the influence of personalism within French Canada except for, in a polemic spirit, Robert Rumilly's brochure, *L'Infiltration gauchiste au Canada français* (Montreal: the author, 1956). He has indicated very clearly how this new trend broke with the traditional thinking of the Church.

30. E. Mounier, *Le personnalisme* (Paris: PUF, 1950), 6.

31. E. Mounier, *Qu'est-ce que le personnalisme?* (Paris: Seuil, 1946), 97.

32. CTCC, *Procès-verbal du congrès* (1951): 215. In the same vein, as early as 1954, it formed a committee charged with the task of preparing a draft statement of fundamental human rights that was later to become part of the Canadian Constitution (CTCC, *Procès-verbal du congrès* (1954): 144).

33. Ibid. (1960): 131–38.

34. Ibid. (1951): 216–17.

35. J. Marchand, Rapport du président, CTCC, *Procès-verbal* (1961): 11 and 23.

36. Tremblay, *Le syndicalisme québécois*, 78–80.

37. G. Adam, *La C.F.T.C., 1940–1958* (Paris: Armand Colin, 1964), 286 and 293.

38. J. Rouillard, *Les syndicats nationaux au Québec*, 311.

39. Ibid., 231.

40. A. Charpentier, *Les Mémoires*, 401.

41. Ibid., 285.

42. Quebec, *Commission Prévost chargée de faire enquête sur certains différends survenus aux usines de Price Brothers & Company, Limited, et de Lake St. John Power & Paper Company, Limited* (août 1943), 1–10.

43. Ibid. 10–25.

44. A. Charpentier, *Les Mémoires*, 402.

45. A. Charpentier, Rapport du président, CTCC, *Procès-verbal du congrès* (1943): 26.

46. Ibid., 155.

47. CTCC, *Procès-verbal du congrès* (1951): 214; (1960): 131.

48. Ibid., (1960): 103.

49. Ibid., 110.

50. *Considérations d'anciens aumôniers fondateurs de syndicats catholiques* (Quebec, July 1959).

51. C.-O. Garant's letter to the secretary of the CTCC, 6 August 1960, CTCC, *Procès-verbal du congrès* (1960): 130.

52. Ibid. (1972): 186.

53. A. Charpentier, *Les mémoires*, 341.

54. In collaboration, *En grève! l'histoire de la CSN et de ses luttes de 1937 à 1963* (Montreal: Éd. du jour, 1963), 94.

55. J. Rouillard, *Les syndicats nationaux au Québec*, 249.

56. Ibid., 243.

57. Canada, Department of Labour, *Organisation des travailleurs au Canada 1931–1940*.

58. Canada, Department of Labour, *Labour Organization in Canada* (1931): 56–62; (1940): 20–37.

59. Maxime Fortin, *Mémoire sur le syndicalisme au Canada* (Montreal: Beauchemin, 1927), 17.

60. In collaboration, *En grève*, 164–76.

61. Canada, Ministry of Labour, *Grèves et lock-outs au Canada, 1952–1960*; Quebec, Ministry of Labour, *Rapport du ministère du Travail de Québec*, 1952, 1960; David, "L'état des rapports de classe au Québec," 63. I would like to thank my research assistant, Réjean Myre, who compiled these statistics.

62. CTCC, *Procès-verbal du congrès* (1949): 189–91.

63. Ibid. (1951): 188–89.

64. Ibid. (1952): 224.

65. *Le Devoir*, 29 septembre 1952, 3.

66. CTCC, *Procès-verbal du congrès* (1953): 141.

67. Ibid., 206.

68. *Le Devoir*, 16 juin 1952, 7.

69. Ibid., 21 janvier 1954, 3; *Le Monde Ouvrier* (juin 1954): 2.

70. *Le Devoir*, 11 juin 1951, 3; 4 octobre 1951, 3; 16 juin 1952, 7; 29 septembre 1952, 3.

71. CTCC, *Procès-verbal du congrès* (1955): 163.

72. Ibid. (1956), 238.

73. *Le Travail*, 23 mars 1956, 1; CTCC, *Procès-verbal du congrès* (1964): 14.

74. *Le Travail*, 14 octobre 1955, 1.

75. CTCC, *Procès-verbal du congrès* (1956): 224.

76. *Le Travail*, 4 octobre 1957, 3; 5 octobre 1956, 1.

77. CTCC, *Procès-verbal du congrès* (1957): 182–95; G. Dion, "La CTCC et au CTCC," *Relations industrielles* (janvier 1958): 57–61.

78. Louis-Laurent Hardy, *Brève histoire du syndicalisme ouvrier au Canada* (Montreal: Éd. de l'Hexagone, 1958), 137. We were not able to find the text of this resolution in the reports of proceedings of the 1958 convention. The resolutions presented to the resolutions committee and then rejected, are not all in the report of proceedings. J.-M. Bédard presented a similar resolution at the 1962 convention, which also met with little success (CLC, *Report of Proceedings* (1962): 76ff.).

79. CLC, *Report of Proceedings* (1956): 94–96, 616.

80. CTCC, *Procès-verbal du congrès* (1959): 104–11.

81. Ibid. (1960): 324.

82. Ibid. (1964): 16.

83. Ibid. (1937): 41.

84. J.R. Cardin, *L'influence du syndicalisme national catholique sur le droit syndical québécois* (Montreal: Les Cahiers de l'institut Social Populaire, 1957), 39–41.

85. *Le Travail*, février 1948, 8.

86. Ibid., 15 janvier 1954, 1.

87. Ibid., 14 décembre 1951, 4; 20 juin 1952, 1 and 3; 10 fevrier 1956, 1. It must be conceded with respect to this act that Duplessis, in 1945, decreased from sixty to fifty percent the number of company workers needed for a union to become certified, thereby obliging the employer to negotiate a collective agreement.

88. A. Charpentier, *Les mémoires*, 365.

89. Conrad Black, *Duplessis*, vol. II, *Le pouvoir* (Montreal: Éd. de l'homme, 1977), 501.

90. In collaboration, *En grève*, 170.

91. Henry Pelling, *Le mouvement ouvrier aux États-Unis* (Paris: Seghers, 1965), 215ff.

92. Robert Rumilly, *Maurice Duplessis et son temps* (Montreal: Fides, 1973), 1: 464.

93. CTCC, *Constitution et Règlements de la Confédération des Travailleurs Catholiques du Canada* (Quebec: Imp. L'Action Sociale Ltée, 1923), 25. For a review of the CTCC's political involvement, see Guy Lortie, "Évolution de l'action politique de la CSN," *Relations industrielles* 22, 4 (octobre 1967): 532–54.

94. CTCC, *Procès-verbaux du congrès* (1949): 95.

95. Ibid. (1952): 80.

96. Ibid. (1951): 81.

97. Ibid. (1952): 172–78.

98. Ibid. (1954): 178–80.

99. Ibid. (1959): 263; *La Gazette du Travail* (1959): 1318.

100. Ibid. (1959): 71.

101. Ibid. (1959): 262; *La Gazette du Travail* (1958): 1410.

102. Tremblay, *Le syndicalisme québécois*, 27–29.

103. In 1951 and 1955, the CIO had 53 and 112 affiliated unions respectively in Quebec, compared with 331 and 416 within the AFL (Canada, Department of Labour, *Organisation des travailleurs au Canada* (1951): 24–69, (1955): 30–104).

THE WEB OF DEPENDENCE: QUEBEC UNIONS IN POLITICS BEFORE 1976†

CARLA LIPSIG-MUMMÉ

The past decade has not been a propitious one for trade unionism in Quebec and elsewhere in North America. Regardless of ideological hue, trade unions have seen their political influence attenuated, their bargaining power undermined, their membership declining, their acquired rights threatened, their capacity to collect dues crippled, and, occasionally, their legal right to represent members abolished. For the first time since the 1920s, the unions' long-established role as champion of the underdog has come under attack. In a time of rising unemployment, government spokespersons in the United States, English Canada, and Quebec are manipulating the charged concept of labour aristocracy in order to set the unorganized majority to blaming the unionized minority for the present crisis. Quebec MNA David Payne's statement during the recent conflict in the education industry is typical: "It is truly unacceptable that a group of employees, already privileged in comparison to their private sector counterparts, takes the population as hostage and tries to force the government to pay the ransom."[1]

For the several North American union movements the recent attacks by the state, what David J. Bercuson calls the emergence of "scapegoat politics,"[2] signals the end of a long period of state-structured support for minority trade unionism. Scapegoat politics has emerged as a result of the fiscal crisis of the North American governments, a fiscal crisis triggered by a long-term international reorganization of the division of labour. The North American welfare state is being pressured on the one hand by private capital seeking extended subsidies to shore up unprofitable enterprises, while at the same time it imposes a private-enterprise model of cost effectiveness on the state itself. On the other hand, the state is being pressured by the ranks of the unemployed, swollen both in number and in need. In the face of these zero-sum pressures, North American

†From Alain Gagnon, ed., *Quebec: State and Society* (Toronto: Methuen, 1984), 286–313. The original version of this article appeared in *Studies in Political Economy* 3 (1980).

governments are turning on their union movements, cutting them off from the structural support — the enactment as government policy of threshold conditions which a minority union movement could not hope to win at the bargaining table — that has been the hallmark of labour policy since the New Deal in the United States, since the Second World War in Canada, and since 1960 in Quebec.

Setting the unions adrift goes hand in hand with a piecemeal dismantling of the welfare state. Unions have experienced the dismantling of the welfare state in ways that vary widely from industry to industry and region to region. But overall, the present crisis of North American trade unionism is structural rather than conjunctural. It is a crisis of outmoded union strategies cracking apart to reveal long-rooted self-deceptions, papering over political abdication.

In Quebec, as perhaps nowhere else in North America, the shift in government policy on organized labour is being experienced as a societal rather than a sectorial crisis, partly because it signals the end to the long process of consensual integration by which a modernizing state co-opted nationalist unions, party because it marks the end of the populist phase of the independence movement, and partly because it reveals the confusion and dependence with which the Quebec union movement confronts the problem of state power, even in a time when the class basis of state power stands clearly revealed.

This chapter is a return to source. It is an attempt to provide the background within which the present crisis may be evaluated, by exploring the historic patterns of Quebec labour's perception of politics and its relationship to the state, from the nineteenth century to 1976. To that end, it is divided into four parts: this, the introduction; a discussion of forms of union political activity; an analysis of the patterns of evolution of that activity in Quebec; and a conclusion, setting out the last century's developments as an explanatory framework for a subsequent analysis of the contemporary crisis of Quebec unionism.

The Political Arena: Forms of Union Intervention

All unions in developed capitalist societies are externally dependent institutions. "What they do," wrote V.L. Allen in 1971, "is always in response to well-established forces such as rising prices, unemployment, government action which influences living standards and over which they have little or no control. . . . Trade unions are patently not initiators."[3]

Worse, unions are not only dependent on an economic environment over which they have little control, they have also seen their powers progressively co-opted by the state. An essential aspect of the external dependence of unions derives from this policy of integration, which developed capitalist states have practised throughout the twentieth century. The essence of integration is that the state sets itself between capital and labour and "settles" the problem of class conflict by absorbing piecemeal the powers of one of the conflicting parties. In North America, the state has become omnipresent in the internal affairs of unions, setting narrow limits not only on administrative practices but on ideology and strategy as well. Labour legislation determines when, how, and for whom a union can act, who may hold union office and how a union may use its dues, what issues may be raised during bargaining, at what times and in what ways a union may enter into conflict with management, and how much a union may contribute to electoral politics. Over time, integration by the state (whether it be consensual or coercive) hollows out a union's organizational capacity for autonomous action, a capacity already circumscribed by the power of capital in liberal democracies.

North American unions have historically reacted in two ways to external dependence and integration. On the one hand, in an effort to increase their autonomy, they have chosen to *narrow* the terrain of their intervention in the hopes of *deepening* their margin of manoeuvre in a smaller area. "Narrowing the terrain" refers both to the population the union speaks for and to the issues it pursues in its membership's name: the union narrows its active defence to one craft or the workers in one industry, gives a priority to bread-and-butter issues, eschews organized politics, lobbies only when the bread-and-butter issues of its members necessitate it. (This was the logic by which skilled workers seceded from the Knights of Labor to form the American Federation of Labor in the 1880s; it is equally the logic of an industrial union like the United Steelworkers today.)

On the other hand, unions have sought to *expand* the population they speak for and the social goals they pursue, in an effort to reduce external dependence through a *broadening* of the fronts of conflict and the sources of alliance and the *addition* of political and social methods to the traditional economic ones. "Expanding the population represented" occurs on three levels: an expansion of the umbrella of membership to the multicraft, unskilled, multi-industry groups; an extension of the possibility of tactical alliance to other unionized groups; and extension of the offer of support to exploited groups outside the traditional limits of union membership. (This is the logic by which the United Autoworkers among others supported the civil-rights movement and the unionization of farmworkers in the United States; it is the logic by which the CNTU encourages and facilitates the growth of "groupes populaires" in Quebec today; it is also the logic behind English-Canadian union participation in the NDP.)

Historically, the narrowing or expanding of union objectives for social change has been determined indirectly by the constraints the evolution of capital places on the union's environment. But more directly, or conjuncturally, state policy on unions has influenced the choice of whether, how much, and in what way unions enter politics. Put otherwise, union goals have been more directly affected by capital's action in the economy; methods or strategies have been more directly influenced by state policy. Political action by unions is obviously influenced by a series of structural and conjunctural conditions that vary from society to society. But if we set aside for the moment the task of generalizing about societal preconditions for political action and look to the more descriptive task of defining types of union political action, it becomes possible to classify these according to the goals the organization articulates and the methods it uses to attain these goals. The intersection of these and the various forms of political action they produce are sketched in figure 1.

Union goals range from the narrowest (occupationally limited, bread-and-butter objectives) through the broadest (transformation of the entire system of power and property in the social system) passing through various types of reformist objectives. Union methods also fall along a spectrum, ranging from abstention (nonintervention in politics) through indirect intervention (political action through

FIGURE 1

Political Action by Labour Unions

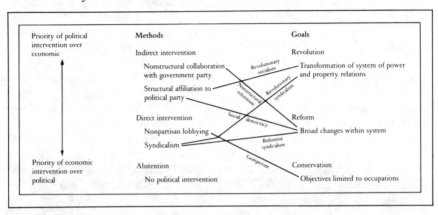

political parties), while passing through various sorts of direct intervention (syndicalism).

Many combinations of goals and strategies are possible and unions have experimented with most of them at one time or another. In Quebec, however, only a limited number of political strategies have been used. *Gomperism*, which combines craft-limited economic goals with nonpartisan lobbying, has historically been the most favoured form of political intervention of the Quebec craft unions affiliated to the American Federation of Labor and the Canadian Trades and Labour Congress, and of the unions affiliated to the Confederation of National Trade Unions before 1959. *Reformist syndicalism* — in which a union seeks to obtain limited reforms of the social order through direct intervention in politics in the form of political strikes, demonstrations, and the like—bypasses collaboration with or affiliation to a party. This form has been rather more popular with the rank-and-file and subcentral levels of union organization than with the centrals, and has its roots in the First World War period.

In addition, two types of political activity have occasionally been used and are now coming to figure increasingly in union strategy. These are *reformist indirect intervention* and *revolutionary indirect intervention*, involvement in politics through affiliation with a social-democratic or revolutionary socialist labour party. The Montreal Trades and Labour Council affiliated to or founded several short-lived labour parties from the end of the nineteenth century through the 1940s, while the Quebec affilates of the CCL worked towards the founding of a social-democratic labour party in the mid-1950s.[4] Increasingly today, the founding of some form of working-class party is being discussed in the centrals, but until 1980 the vaguely social-democratic platform espoused by the Parti Québécois had both blocked the founding of an independent social-democratic labour party and retarded the founding of a revolutionary socialist one.

In addition to reformist and revolutionary indirect intervention, to Gomperism and reformist syndicalism, two other sorts of political intervention were also employed by Quebec unions: *nonstructural affiliation with an existing party*, such as the Quebec Federation of Labour attempted with the Parti Québécois during the 1976 election; and *revolutionary syndicalism*, in which the union took the role of a revolutionary party regrouping a broad coalition of progressive forces under its own leadership and challenged the power of the state through a combination of economic and community confrontations. What forces have affected the choice of one or another strategy over time? The question required historical analysis. (See table 1.)

TABLE 1

Forms of Intervention

Period	Union	Primary	Secondary	State Posture
I. *1894–1907*	1. Knights of Labor	1. nonstructural affiliation to a party	1. —	Minimal intervention
	2. Trades & Labour Congress (TLC)	2. Gomperism	2. abstention	
II. *1907–1944*	1. Confederation of Canadian Catholic	1. Gomperism	1. —	Sporadic repressive intervention
	2. TLC	2. Gomperism	2. abstention	
III. *1944–1959*	1. CTCC	1. reformist syndicalism	1. nonstructural reformism	Repression and coercive integration
	2. TLC QFL 1957– 3. CCL	2. Gomperism	2. nonstructural reformism	
IV. *1959–1966*	1. CTCC–CNTU	1. nonstructural reformism	1. reformist syndicalism	Incomplete consensual integration
	2. QFL	2. reformist social democracy	2. —	
	3. CEQ	3. nonstructural reformism	3. —	
V. *1966–1972*	1. CNTU	1. reformist syndicalism	1. —	Coercive integration
	2. QFL	2. reformist social democracy	2. —	
	3. CEQ	3. nonstructural reformism	3. revolutionary socialism	
VI. *1972–1976*	1. CNTU	1. revolutionary syndicalism	1. revolutionary socialism	Coercive integration
	2. QFL	2. nonstructural reformism	2. —	
	3. CEQ	3. revolutionary syndicalism	3. revolutionary socialism	
	4. Confédédération des Syndicats Démocratiques	4. abstention	4. Gomperism	

Unions in Politics: The Temptation of the State

Union political activity in Quebec may be seen to have passed through a number of stages, distinguished from each other by changes in the nature of intervention and degree of strength manifested by each participant in the industrial-relations system.[5]

The first stage spans the 1800s, trailing off before the First World War. During this long period we see the founding of the first union in Quebec in 1827, the first cross-Canada mobilization of the unionized working class (the Nine Hour Movement, beginning in Toronto in 1872).[6] But it was not until the Knights of Labor established local assemblies in Toronto in 1881 and in Montreal in 1882, that unions began to look seriously towards influencing the state as a means of redressing their economic weakness.[7]

The Knights of Labor gave to the Quebec working class both its earliest style of political action and the first definition of union goals in the political arena. Politically, its objective was to convince the state to shore up labour's perennial weakness vis-à-vis capital. To this end it focussed on "educative lobbying" to create within the state both the precedent of and the mechanisms for regulation of child labour, factory safety, the control of the skilled labour market, and the limitation of immigrant workers.[8] It was modestly statist: it saw the state as capable and it looked to the state to reduce class tensions. At the same time, it recognized the state's hostility to strikes and sought to foster more positive government attitudes towards the working class by developing the state's role in bettering working conditions so that strikes could be (largely) avoided. Capital, not the state, was seen to be the linchpin in the system the Knights worked to transform.

As well as giving certain priority to educative lobbying, the Knights of Labor involved itself electorally. From 1882 onwards it focussed on municipal elections and supported working-class candidates for provincial and federal office, whether these were first endorsed by one of the traditional parties or stood as independents. At no time in Quebec did the Knights create a political party or an electoral organization that lasted beyond a particular campaign.

This form of two-pronged pressure-group politics was consonant with the Knights' worldview, with their view of the state, and with state policy itself at the time. The Knights' vision of the just society was nostalgic and preindustrial.[9] While it recognized that the state was no friend of the workingpeople, that recognition was harnessed ambivalently to a dependence on the state for support in the struggle against capital's excesses. And only because the state had intervened so little could the Knights believe that the election of workingmen might influence the form and content of state policy towards the "working classes." The Knights were militantly reformist and committed, if sporadically, to electoralism; they assumed that the election of a workingman's government would signal the profound and irrevocable transformation of labour's relations with capital.

In the United States the supplanting of the industrially and geographically organized Knights by the nationally linked craft federations of the American Federation of Labor (AFL) was largely completed by 1890. In English Canada the craft-oriented, pro-American tendency within the Trades and Labour Congress (TLC) did not emerge clearly as the stronger until 1894–95, and obtained supremacy only in 1902.[10] In both, the defeat of the Knights spelled the end to effective industrial organizing as well as to its unique form of political action on the municipal and local levels. In Quebec, however, in spite of loss of membership, expulsion from the TLC, and a real decline in importance to working-class organization after 1902, the Knights managed to retain some economic presence until 1921 and to continue its patterns of local political intervention which would, with modification, re-emerge as the distinguishing characteristic of union politics in Quebec during the 1960s and 1970s.

The triumph of the AFL tendency within the TLC during the late 1890s assured the ascendance of a strategy of electoral abstention and nonpartisan lobbying. From 1890 onwards, the TLC's Montreal Council refused to endorse or oppose any candidate.[11] It did, however, present various briefs to the federal government. Its rejection of electoral intervention was a luxury based on its assurance that, in the crafts it represented, its ability to maintain a scarcity of skilled labour would allow it to use no more than economic pressure to obtain the conditions it sought. Once "utopian" goals of societal transformation were set aside, the TLC could protect the job-related concerns of its members solely by intervention in the economic domain.

In the first stage of union activity in Quebec, workers also attempted to form working-class parties. In 1894, a Montreal branch of Daniel de Leon's Socialist Labor Party of America (SLPA) was founded; in 1899 and 1904 a Workers' Party (WPA) was established and re-established.[12] In 1904, the new pan-Canadian central Montreal branches formally affiliated to the Workers' Party and, although it elected a federal MP in Maisonneuve riding in 1906, by 1913 only two of its clubs were still in existence.[13] Neither the SLPA with its revolutionary socialist ideology nor the WPA with its reformist socialism seemed to cast down lasting roots or to set out a tradition on which later unions built.

A final note about the forms of union political action around the turn of the century. Whether reformist or revolutionary syndicalist, pressure-group electoralist or Gomperist, Quebec unions focussed their major (but not exclusive) energies on influencing the federal, not the provincial, state. However, the narrow and rudimentary forays of the province into regulation of industrial relations seemed to be paralleled for the most part by a sporadic and nonorganizational approach to politics by the unions.

A second stage of union political activity emerged slowly in the years before and after the First World War. While reformist and revolutionary direct action and nonstructural affiliation withered between 1900 and 1914, the TLC's Gomperism rooted and spread as the model of political inaction. It imbued, ironically, the emerging Catholic unionism with its philosophy of electoral abstention and came to characterize intervention in politics by the union movement in general until the end of the Second World War. Thus, a period of almost four decades in which American-based craft unions and Quebec-based Catholic unions of both craft and industrial structure, worlds apart in their vision of society and the workers' place therein, shared a Gomperist political perspective.

Catholic unionism grew slowly after its debut in Chicoutimi in 1907.[14] Indeed, one commentator asserts that it gained few adherents even outside Montreal before the First World War.[15] By 1921, however, the founding of the Confédération des travailleurs catholiques du Canada (CTCC) signalled the implant of a new view of industrial relations based on the principles of the "inequality of social classes, the harmony of capital and labour, and the right to national autonomy."[16] Its central objective was to offer Catholic workers an alternative to the (dangerously) radical, religiously neutral, American international unions affiliated to the TLC. By the 1930s, the CTCC had come to represent forty-five percent of all unionized workers, while the international unions represented twenty-three percent.[17]

Gomperism implies electoral abstention combined with legislative lobbying. During the years between the world wars, the TLC affiliates lobbied little — if at all — and played no organized role in elections. Instead, they restricted their activities to the purely economic domain, leading nearly all the strikes that occured during this period. The economic militancy of the TLC, however relative, thus stood in contrast to its political dormancy.

The CTCC, on the other hand, indulged in energetic Gomperism: it lobbied. Although it led only nine of the 507 strikes between 1915 and 1936,[18] it lobbied for and obtained passage of the law incorporating craft unions of white-collar workers and granting legal recognition to their collective agreements in 1923,[19] and of a law to extend collective agreements to cover all workers within an industrial sector in 1934.[20] It was thus moderately statist, appealing to the Taschereau, Duplessis, and Godbout regimes in turn to redress in the political domain the union's extreme weakness in the economic.

The provincial state emerged from the First World War prepared both to extract more powers from the federal in the domain of industrial relations and to use those powers vigorously. During the 1920s and throughout the Depression it intervened both legislatively and judicially in labour-capital relations; it enshrined the rights of capital in hiring, firing, suspensions, and decisions on the organization of production and the allocation of profit. The province also introduced measures defining the legal responsibility of each party to a collective agreement, restricted the rights of unions to intervene in politics, and defined itself as the ultimate arbitrator for an employer with labour problems. The Taschereau and the Duplessis governments saw the TLC as dangerously radical and the striking growth of the CTCC membership during the 1930s was in some measure due to the government's willingness to procure sweetheart deals between the CTCC and employers wishing to avoid unionization by the more militant TLC affiliates.

The late 1920s and 1930s saw as well a return to the use of verbal rather than written collective agreements, a rising proportion of strikes fought and lost over defence of previously acquired rights, and the establishment of a state tactic of playing off one central against the other, a tactic that continued to haunt the unions in the 1970s.[21] The TLC affiliates stayed out of both partisan politics and lobbying because they assumed they could do better through strikes and the threat of strikes. The CTCC eschewed electoralism because it felt politics should be outside the realm of a defensive workers' organization. Throughout the 1930s it too relied on economic means combined with lobbying to attain its modest economic goals. It was not until the Price Company strike during the Second World War (called to force the government to reformulate legislation governing the freedom of workers to choose which union they would affiliate with) that the CTCC began to see the necessity of more direct political action.[22]

To recapitulate, then, between the first decade of the twentieth century and the Second World War, unions faced a state that, regardless of which party was in power, interpreted its role as simply the protector of the employers' interests. It acted, in strike after strike, as the deployer of police rather than the conciliator.

Yet certain tactics of coercive integration made their first appearance in the 1920s and it was to that combination of repression and embryonic coercive integration that the unions responded. Regardless of the profound differences between the worldviews of the CTCC and the TLC, their methods of political intervention differed in quantity rather than nature. Both eschewed direct electoral action; both concentrated on lobbying. The CTCC simply lobbied more often and more energetically. And in a very real sense the reduction of the unions' economic power during the Depression ran parallel and contributed to retreat in the political arena. Fragmentation of political force between co-opting by the Church and abstentionism by the TLC further paralyzed union political action. It was only during the Second World War that the cautious use of economic pressure to obtain greater legal protection suggested to at least some unions that greater influence in the councils of state was essential to the safeguarding of prior economic gains.

A third stage of union political activity in Quebec began with the enactment of the Labour Relations Act of 1944 and ended with the death of Maurice Duplessis in 1959. This fifteen-year period, which has been called "la grande noirceur," was characterized by an intensification and refinement of the Quebec state's policy towards organized labour, by the introduction of militant social democracy by newly organizing industrial unions affiliated to the Canadian Congress of Labour (and to the American CIO), by the emerging economic militancy of the Catholic unions, by a series of not wholly unsuccessful attempts to create a common front among the centrals, and by the return to direct political activity by the unions.

Of these five characteristics of the industrial relations of this period, one is preeminent and stands in causal relationship to the others. The emergence of the Quebec state as an interventionist and quite partisan force in labour-capital relations transformed modest strikes into major confrontations between organized or organizing workers on one side and the full might of the state allied with national and international employers on the other. The hostility of the state forced the unions back into politics to preserve not only their autonomy but their very existence. The repressive legislation enacted by the Duplessis regime in the late 1940s and the early 1950s not only underscored the necessity for militant opposition to the regime and for collaboration among the competing centrals, but it also set the stage for the state to play off each central against the others. State policy during this period may be characterized as mature coercive integration larded with simple and devastating repression.

The 1944 labour code enacted by the Liberal Party transformed the principle of the state's regulative role in industrial relations in operational reality. Based on the American Wagner Act of 1935, La loi des relations ouvrières essentially established the state as the central force in industrial relations, delegating to its judicial, legislative, and executive arms the power to legitimate collective agreements and to control the formation of unions.[23] Under the 1944 Act, unions had to register with the government. The government could revoke the right of the union to represent its members at any time and the provisions of the Act allowed the case of breakdown of collective bargaining. In the same year La loi des differends was also enacted, forbidding teachers, firemen, municipal employees, civil servants, and communications workers from striking and submitting them to compulsory arbitration.[24] In other words, the state determined who would represent labour and the condition under which labour and capital confronted each other, legitimated the agreements reached, and the degree, type, and timing of sanctions each party could use against the other.

The return of Duplessis to power as the Second World War ended signalled the vigorous application of the new labour code. It should be noted that no break occurred in labour policy during the transition from Liberal to Union Nationale governments. Duplessis extracted from the new labour code the mechanisms to render the unions dependent on the state for their power to bargain and to service, and further refined them during the 1940s and 1950s.[25] Through a series of amendments to the code and lois d'exception introduced from 1947 to 1955, he created a repressive apparatus that was controlled directly from the premier's office and served to supplement the provisions limiting autonomy.[26]

Bill 5 — introduced in 1948, withdrawn the following year because of co-ordinated pressure from the centrals, and reinforced in fragments throughout the 1950s — ended any participation by unions in industrial-relations decision making.[27] Under Duplessis, the state interposed itself further between unions and their members, forcing unions to obtain the right to service and represent their members from the state rather than from their membership base. The substitution of government-granted recognition for worker-voted recognition, the revocation at will of the union's right to represent its members, the enforcement of compulsory arbitration, and the obligatory registration of union records — all aimed at reducing the unions' attempts at militant and autonomous economic activity. When, following the introduction of Bill 5, the three union representatives on the Conseil Superieur du Travail resigned in protest, they suggested that a veritable "statification" of the unions was taking place.[28]

The mechanisms of repression became more effective during the 1940s and 1950s. At Asbestos in 1949, Louiseville in 1952, Murdochville, Valleyfield, and Noranda, Duplessis used provincial police to break strikes and judicial intervention to cripple unions.[29] By 1952 it had become clear that the unions could not hope to use economic pressure to neutralize state policies hostile to their interests and that, ultimately, the use of the strike in pursuit of purely economic objectives had been defined by the state as political provocation.

It is within this context that the unions returned to direct political intervention. In 1955, there were three union centrals operating in Quebec. The provincial branches of the Trades and Labour Congress of Canada, affiliated to the American Federation of Labor, remained the largest numerically.[30] They intervened very little on the provincial political scene. During the 1950s they distanced themselves from the other centrals by their refusal to oppose Duplessis openly and benefited to some degree from his differential patronage.[31] The relatively tranquil relationship ended abruptly with the Murdochville strike and the formation of the Quebec Federation of Labour in 1957.[32]

On the other hand, the CTCC underwent a dramatic transformation after the Second World War. The series of violent confrontations that it became embroiled in, as the state moved repeatedly to break its strikes by use of the provincial police, transformed its understanding of the efficacy of political power. From the watershed Asbestos strike of 1948, the CTCC began to fashion two new interpretations of political intervention.

One interpretation, espoused by the central office under Gérard Picard saw increased political influence as a means of protecting acquired rights rather than as an objective in itself.[33] In order to obtain this influence, the CTCC set out during the early 1950s to demonstrate and lobby against Duplessis' proposed amendments to the labour code. It usually chose to work in common fronts with the CCL affiliates and, more rarely, with the TLC affiliates as well. Vigorous Gomperism quite naturally evolved towards a closer relationship with the provincial Liberal Party. As the opposition forces to Duplessis crystallized during the middle 1950s, the CTCC moved towards informal collaboration with the Liberal Party. The line between Gomperism and informal and nonstructural support for a political party is at best blurred and tends to shift erratically over time. Thus, throughout the 1950s the CTCC's official Gomperism was supplemented by informal support for the Liberals, on whose behalf it led a campaign of denunciation against Duplessis' minister of labour in 1956.[34] By that time, the CTCC's link with the provincial Liberals was just short of formal affiliation.

The second interpretation of political activity might be labelled reformist syndicalism. The deeply rooted syndicalist tradition of the CTCC, increasingly bypassed by the president's office, found new expression at the grassroots level in the regional and interindustrial groupings outside Montreal. Here, local unions moved towards *rapprochement* with locals affiliated to other centrals, concentrated on political education of the rank and file, and involved themselves in community problems of housing, health, and education. It might be said, then, that this philosophy, which defined the union as the logical instrument of all protective action undertaken in the interest of the working class, had its roots in the paternalism of the Church.

The third union organization in Quebec at the time was a relative newcomer, beginning mobilization in Quebec after 1940.[35] The industrial affiliates of the American Congress of Industrial Organizations (CIO) and of the Canadian Congress of Labour (CCL) were not so divided over the form and content of political activity. Their strength was drawn from basic industry and from textiles. Through a series of bitter strikes, by the mid-1950s they had established an unparalleled reputation for economic militancy and hostility to the Duplessis regime.[36] By 1954, affiliates of the CCL-CIO were advocating the formation of a social-democratic labour party. In 1955, their Joliette Congress issued a manifesto calling for the founding of such a party in Quebec and for a broad range of economic, political, and social reforms inspired by the CCF's program.[37] The call for an independent labour party was shortlived. During the 1956 elections, some of the CIO and CCL affiliates chose to support Liberal candidates who had incorporated several key planks of the manifesto into the Liberal platform.[38] Particularly in the area of industrial relations reform, the Liberal platform closely resembled the Joliette Manifesto.

The last years of the Duplessis regime, 1956–59, were of particular significance for labour. Following the merger of the AFL and the CIO in the United States in 1955, the TLC and CCL merged to form the Canadian Labour Congress in 1956 and began talks with the CTCC about the possibility of its inclusion.

When these talks broke down, a provincial branch of the new CLC was founded (the QFL), representing 36.8 percent of the CLC membership in Quebec at its inception.[39] The rest of the CLC's Quebec affiliates joined the QFL gradually over the next decade. The new QFL moved rapidly away from the CLC's implicit support for Duplessis, partly because of the influence of the social-democratic CCL affiliates in its ranks and partly because of the brutality of state intervention in the Murdochville strike of 1957.[40]

At Duplessis' death in 1959, then, organized labour had begun to evolve towards more effective political action. From the Gomperism and destructive competition of the 1940s, the unions had moved towards alternative forms of co-operation and had attempted the formation of a reformist labour party. By 1959, the union centrals, led by the CTCC, were assessing how best to extract maximum value from their informal collaboration with the Liberals. We may conclude, then, that the state's insistence on repressive and partisan intervention in collective bargaining after 1944 had forced the unions to move beyond traditional Gomperism to experiment with reformist syndicalism and to seek more direct influence in the political arena within which the rules of the workplace are determined.

We come now to the fourth stage of union political intervention: the experience of the Quiet Revolution. Between 1960 and 1966, the coercive integration characteristic of the Duplessis regime gave way to an incomplete consensual integration; the position of both the international and domestic fragments of capital came to be presented to labour through the medium of the neo-nationalist state. To understand the greatly transformed role of the state in industrial relations, however, it is necessary to locate it in relation to the more general changes in the relationship of both the state and the unions to Quebec society.

From 1945 to 1967, Quebec's economy experienced steady and unbroken growth. The GNP rose gradually, from $3 billion in 1946 to $19 billion in 1968.[41] In large measure, American sources had stimulated this growth. In Quebec both the relative and the absolute increase in American investment was made chiefly in the secondary sector, where the external dependence of the key growth industries deepened.[42]

The steady growth during the two postwar decades had two particularly pertinent results. First, the Quebec state was given the financial margin of manoeuvre necessary for modernization. Second, foreign investment, both new and established, remained so central to the primary and secondary sectors that any ideology of modernization would have to first come to terms with its hegemony.

The Liberal Party became the vehicle for this pragmatic ideology of modernization; its program was shaped by a new technocratic fraction of the old liberal professional stratum, which had been unable either to find a role for itself in the anachronistic structures of the externally dependent prewar economy or to transform the state into a vehicle for its own aspirations. Its philosophy of industrial relations, which remained largely unchanged during its six years in office, was set out by Jean Lesage in 1959.[43]

Lesage saw a "progressive statism" as the central method of modernization. Focussing on the transformation of the state itself — its takeover of medical and educational services formerly in the hands of the Church, its creation of a social-service network, the professionalization of the civil service, the multiplication of crown corporations — Lesage envisaged an expansion of the superstructure that was meant to modernize the labour force and, in some unspecified way, to "liberate" the economy from foreign domination. To accomplish this it was necessary for capital and labour to organize their members into province-wide organizations that would associate themselves with the state and participate in the elaboration of its strategy. For labour this did not mean unification of the three centrals, but the centralization of negotiating structures within each central at the province-wide level. For capital it meant the creation of a provincial council of business for which not only Lesage as head of government, but also Jean Marchand as head of the CNTU, lobbied repeatedly.[44]

The growth of the state triggered important shifts in the composition of the labour force. Over the long term the primary sector had been shrinking and the tertiary sector growing in terms of numbers employed. Quebec was no different in this regard from other industrialized societies. Thus, between 1947 and 1965, employment in the primary sector shrank from 24.2 percent to 9.2 percent, while employment in the tertiary sector rose from 44.5 percent to 58.1 percent.[45] In large measure, the growth of the tertiary sector occurred between the late 1950s and 1965, particularly in the public and parapublic sectors and in commerce. Public and parapublic services, between 1961 and 1969, expanded their employment by 65 percent; commerce, by 35 percent.[46]

This influx into the labour force of tertiary-sector workers had a massive impact on organized labour. First, the majority of the jobs created were white collar. Second, the large majority of the new workers were in the indirect or direct employ of the state. Third, the majority of those who filled the new state jobs were of blue-collar family origin.

The rapidity with which the public-sector jobs were created was paralleled only by the speed with which the new working class was unionized. Roughly 175,000 new unionists from the public and parapublic sectors entered the ranks of organized labour between 1960 and 1970. State employees now represented over one-third of all organized labour in the province.[47] The new state employees did not spread their affiliation evenly among the centrals. The CNTU benefited most directly from the expansion of state employment. In 1960 its membership was 80,075; in 1968, 199,102; and in 1970, it had risen to 205,783.[48]

The rapid expansion of the CNTU was the result of a complex series of changes both within the organization and in its relationship to Church, state, and the wider society. First, the deconfessionalization of the central, beginning after the Asbestos strike, allowed it to steadily ameliorate the quality of the services it offered to its members, as well as allowing it to embark on more militant collective bargaining. Second, the close collaboration between the CNTU and the Liberal Party made use of an instrumental neo-nationalism to identify the modernization program with the nation's destiny, and the CNTU with the natural leadership of the Quebec working class. Regardless of an official ideology which took the state to task from time to time, in the first years of the 1960s the CNTU operated as if it were the trade-union arm of a one-party state. Thus, the remarkable growth of the CNTU during the decade was largely a result of its participation in the Liberal vision. Of the 125,000 new members affiliating with the CNTU during the 1960s, some 106,000 were employed by the state, transforming the CNTU from a central three-quarters of whose members in 1960 were employed in the primary and secondary sectors to a central which, in 1970, represented members over 50 percent of whom were employees of the state. (However, the bulk of these were in what came to be known as parapublic sectors.)

The Quebec Federation of Labour fared rather less well during the Quiet Revolution. Created in 1957 out of the merger of the AFL and the CIO in the United States and the CCL and the TLC in Canada, it did not, during the first half of the 1960s, have the financial resources, structural freedom, or moral authority to operate as a Québécois central in its own right. It was rather, in Paul Bernard's phrase, a junior government to the senior government of the Canadian Labour Congress.[49]

As the provincial office of a Canadian central over 70 percent of whose members belonged to branches of American unions, the QFL suffered doubly from the conflicting nationalisms abroad in Quebec during this period. The neonationalism of the Lesage government and the affiliation of the QFL with the New Democratic Party combined to make it less than popular with the newly aware Québécois. Further, the close relationship between the CNTU and the government made it difficult for the QFL to compete successfully for representation of the new government employees. In one notable example, the passage of a special law barring unionization of civil servants by any central affiliated to a political party assured the QFL's defeat and the CNTU's success in affiliating some 30,000 provincial civil servants.[50]

Finally, the QFL was itself subject to a series of internal conflicts which reflected the contradictory nature of its membership and status in Quebec. The conflict between Quebec neo-nationalism and American nationalism expressed itself through repeated clashes between the entrenched bureaucracies of affiliated international unions and their members over issues such as francization of services, as well as through secession from pan-Canadian and American unions by Quebec locals.[51] The struggle to gain more organizational power for the QFL in order to operate as a more autonomous union central expressed itself in conflict between the QFL and its affiliated unions over the division of power, between the QFL and the CLC over provincial autonomy, and between the QFL and the CNTU over affiliation of new members.[52] In all, it is not surprising that the QFL's membership did not grow as rapidly during the 1960s. Its share of the new government employees was limited to some hospital workers, employees of school boards and municipalities, and certain categories of Hydro-Québec employees — in the large majority, blue-collar workers from the subcentral levels of government. The QFL remained a blue-collar central whose membership was employed in a large measure by the multinational sectors of private capital.[53]

It was the Teachers' Corporation (CIC-CEQ) that benefited most dramatically from superstructural modernization. The enormous expansion of public education coupled with a government-granted right to the obligatory membership of all teachers in the Catholic school system pushed membership from 12,000 in 1959 to 60,000 in 1968.[54] This 500 percent leap occasioned a transformation of the power relations within the central as urban, highly trained secular teachers took over positions of power. And the modernization of education triggered within the corporation itself a crisis concerning the relationship between professionalism and trade-union demands — although it would not be until 1967 that professionalism was identified with bourgeois affiliation and set in opposition to working-class consciousness, to alliance with the other centrals, and to confrontation with government.

By 1966, then, the portrait of union representation had changed as dramatically as had that of the state. The infusion of public-sector workers into the movement had forced major changes in affiliation patterns. Further, the modernization programs of the Quiet Revolution made the public-sector unionists potentially the most powerful bloc within the labour movement.

The transformed labour movement operated under a much liberalized labour code.[55] In 1964, after three earlier versions had been modified because of union pressure, a new labour code was enacted.[56] Its provisions, plus the modifications to the Public Service Act passed in 1965, created a veritable revolution of rising expectations. The right to strike was granted to all workers except firemen, police, and prison guards. The onus of compulsory arbitration and binding awards was removed and elaborate safeguards were provided against the coercion and takeover of newly formed unions.[57] In all, the changes in labour legislation during the Lesage era indicated, first, a growing role for the state as legislator in the industrial relations system; second, the crystallization of trade-union expectations concerning the rate at which conditions would be bettered and power shared; and third, the development of a role for the unions as state agents in the project of societal modernization. In place of the coercive integration of the Duplessis era, the Lesage regime attempted to introduce consensus. How fragile were its provisions would become clear when the economy began to contract. What was clear during the heyday of union modernization in the Quiet Revolution, however, was that the unions acquiesced to the strengthening of their dependence on the state.

The acquiescence was rooted in a profound and continuing union paralysis concerning the method of political intervention. From the mid-1950s on, under the impetus of the CCL, some elements in the labour movement had been advocating the creation of a workers' party. Certainly the QFL in 1960 refused support to the Liberals, suggested that its members destroy their ballots, and insisted that the founding of a workers' party was imminent.[58] When the Quebec NDP was founded in 1963, however, the QFL's affiliation took the form of a sort of moral support and passive affiliation rather than an active identification with the new party's future. And even this involvement was clouded by the founding of a rival Parti Socialiste du Québec (PSQ), attracting important trade-union figures unhappy with the NDP position on federalism.[59]

QFL affiliation to the NDP did not, however, stop it from supporting the Liberals on issue after issue during the period.[60] And if nominal affiliation to a workers' party contrasted oddly with conjunctural collaboration with the Liberals, it nonetheless gave form to a quite consistent stance on the part of the QFL vis-à-vis industrial relations. Less involved in the public sector than the CNTU, less enchanted with the nationalist program, and above all less historically committed to state intervention to shore up weak unions, as early as 1959 the QFL suggested that the state's growing role as an employer should push it to set an example for the private sector.[61] Between 1962 and 1966 it repeatedly announced that the state's historic role as third party was anachronistic;[62] its emergence as a major employer made the infusion of politics into collective bargaining inevitable.[63]

The CNTU, on the other hand, manifested an even more dramatic contradiction during the Quiet Revolution. Historically it had practised Gomperism, lobbying energetically while refusing electoral commitment. During the Lesage era it ceased to lobby any party but the Liberals. And, while it refused affiliation to the NDP and the PSQ as well as to the Liberals, its executive shared the vision of democratic planning and progressive statism that was the hallmark of state industrial policy.

Yet the CNTU could not avoid recognizing that the expansion of the state necessitated the politicization of its industrial policy. When strike after strike of its public-sector members pitted it against the Liberal government between 1964 and 1966, the CNTU found itself torn between collaboration in the national project and rejection of its implications for labour. The way out during the middle years of the decade seemed to be articulation of an increasingly sophisticated critique of the unchallenged structures of capital, but a critique that chose a co-operative and decentralized alternative, thereby avoiding explicit rejection of the Liberals' nationalism.[64]

In a very real way the national question paralyzed the unions' intervention in politics during the Quiet Revolution. While the state under Duplessis had practised repression and coercive integration, it had been relatively easy for the unions to work together and to recognize the need for a labour party. When a progressive nationalist regime came to power, however, it was able to divide the unions along the lines of structural-national affiliation (Québécois vs. international), to set them competing for state favours, and to make the prospect of autonomous union political action not only difficult but somehow disloyal. For each of the three centrals the crystallization of a more militant interpretation of power relations in the economic domain led to an increased political presence, but to relatively little evolution in the method used to articulate new objectives. The tension between the evolving and the stagnant methods — which characterized union political action at the level of the centrals — created a dead space at the heart of the movement which, after 1967, local and regional union groupings felt compelled to fill. In the struggle for concrete political power after 1967, the initiative passed to the rank-and-file and the lower levels of the union organization hierarchy.

The fifth stage of union political activity began during the last months of 1966. The Quiet Revolution's loss of momentum, the slowing down of Quebec's economic growth, and the explosion of expectations concerning union participation in social-policy formation all combined to polarize union hopes and governmental capacity. In this polarization, foreign capital was seen to play a large, but largely undocumented, role. Between 1966 and 1976 the state moved back towards coercive integration and the unions, after almost a decade of collaboration, were incapable of formulating a political defence.

On its return to power in 1966, Daniel Johnson's Union Nationale government began an immediate retreat from the privileged relationship with the unions that had characterized the preceding Liberal regime.[65] Between 1967 and 1972

Johnson, his successor Bertrand, and his Liberal successor Bourassa, refined and expanded the power of the state in industrial relations, expressly to revoke or restrict the gains unions had made in the first part of the decade. The immediate result was an explosion of strikes and lockouts: during 1966–67 alone, more workhours were lost in industrial disputes in Quebec than in Ontario, although the Quebec labour force was some 200,000 smaller. Some 60 percent of those involved in industrial disputes between 1966 and 1972 were employed by the state.[66]

The emerging state policy was a blend of juridical concern and legislative integration, ranging from the abrogation of collective-bargaining rights and the legislative imposition of contracts to the levying of massive fines on union members as well as unions. The CEQ, for example, lost its power to negotiate with local school boards and its right to secure a contract through free collective bargaining when in 1967 the government legislated a contract.[67] Following seven years of rising expectations concerning an expanded role for unions in educational modernization, Bill 25 first nullified the right to collective bargaining and then incorporated that right into the state's executive apparatus. Second, the state used its legislative powers to centralize responsibility for contract negotiation and enforcement within each central, reducing the autonomy of affiliated unions and federations and exposing the central to increased legal sanctions. Third, the state used its legislative powers to set the centrals to internecine competition. Legislation enacted during the last years of Bertrand's mandate and the first years of Bourassa's established the principle of the right of the state to rationalize representation within the industrial sectors by allowing no more than one central to bargain for workers within a particular industry, thus settling the centrals to really brutal competition for majority affiliation in those industries where they had traditionally divided the membership. (The construction industry is the most dramatic example.)

In the administrative domain, the government formulated an increasingly effective and standardized wage policy, which it began to enforce for the public sector after 1967. (The government had introduced this policy in 1964, but was not then prepared to push for it during negotiations.) The raises negotiated were popularly believed to derive from guidelines set for the public sector by the major employers in the private sector, and unions in the private sector took the public-sector settlements as an indication of what they could hope to obtain. Finally, the state enforced the principle of massive judicial sanctions against infringement of industrial relations law. Thus, in 1968 teachers affiliated with the SPEQ of the CNTU found a dozen of their leaders jailed after an illegal strike, while the defiance of injunctions issued for the hospital strikers during the celebrated Common Front strike of April and May 1972 resulted in large fines against refractory locals and eventually in the jailing of the presidents of the three union centrals.[68] Undoubtedly, the hardening of the state's position towards the unions, first viable in the late 1960s, began contributing to the very real regression the unions experienced during the 1970s. Several developments, both indications of and contributing factors to that regression, crystallized around 1972.

First among these was the breakdown of the CNTU-Liberal Party alliance. When the Liberals returned to power in 1970, they represented the fraction of the petty bourgeoisie who wished to continue the economic growth of Quebec by intensifying the ties with international capital. The fraction who had sought continued modernization through the repatriation of taxes paid to the federal state had left the Liberals in 1967, forming first the Mouvement Souveraineté -Association and then, in 1968, the Parti Québécois. In 1970 and again in 1973, the remaining Liberals under Bourassa pursued the policy of union domestication that had been the hallmark of their Union Nationale predecessor. Thus, between 1968 and 1976 the CNTU, facing a Liberal Party shorn of both the personnel and its ideological tendencies most amenable to union aspirations, looked towards the Parti Québécois as a possible political ally. That possibility, however, was approached with little clarity. When, during the 1970 election, the Montreal Council of the CNTU formally endorsed the PQ, it was discreetly reprimanded by the executive of the central.

A second development was the radical weakening of the CNTU. In 1971, 21,000 workers affiliated with the CNTU, the CEQ, and the QFL and employed directly and indirectly by the state, formed a Common Front for negotiations with the government. When these negotiations broke down in the spring of 1972, the Common Front went on strike, ignoring injunctions.[69] The strike having been broken by back-to-work legislation (supported by the Parti Québécois as well as by the more traditional parties) and the eventual jailing of the presidents of all three union centrals for contempt of court, the simmering ideological polarization within the CNTU exploded. During 1972 and 1973 the CNTU suffered the secession of approximately 60,000 of its members. This was an explicit rejection of the political nature of the public-sector strike, of its implications for relations with the Liberal Party, and of the Marxist interpretation of class relationships that the CNTU central office had been disseminating via working documents and political education sessions since 1971.[70] Some 30,000 of the secessionists, in the most technologically backward sectors, grouped together to form the Confederation of Democratic Trade Unions (CSD), which returned to political collaboration with the Liberal Party and to the narrowest of business unionism on the industrial scene.[71]

The additional 30,000 secessionists were members of the Civil Servants Federation (SFPQ); they simply disaffiliated from the CNTU, explaining that they thought they could obtain better material benefits for their members if they were not associated with a radical central.[72] Hard on the heels of this secession, the CNTU became embroiled in a debilitating internal struggle over raising the per capita contributions to the central strike fund. (The need to raise the contributions to the Fonds de défense professionnel arose out of the fines incurred during the Common Front negotiations in the first instance, then, during 1973 and 1974, out of the fines incurred during "illegal" strikes and walkouts held to reopen contract negotiations to take into consideration the steeply rising cost of living.) The debate over contributions, which stretched over several years, pitted the concept of the union as a radical social movement against the image of the union as a limited-issue, self-defence organization and resulted in the suspension of several thousand more members. It also revealed the prohibitive cost of confrontation with the state.

The fragmentation of the CNTU triggered a return to raiding between the QFL and the CNTU. And, while a minimal collaboration on short-term economic issues in the public sector was maintained, middle- and longer-term political co-ordination all but ceased. Particularly the competition between the two centrals for hegemony of representation in construction skillfully fanned during Bourassa's first mandate so envenomed relations among the centrals that the QFL in 1974 found itself the object of a Royal Commission of Enquiry on Industrial Relations in the Construction Industry, better known as the Cliche Commission. Within the CNTU, no one foresaw the dangerous precedent set by the invoking of such an inquiry until the Commission made its report public. In fact, the CNTU had called on the Bourassa government to intervene in construction locals to protect its minority position. The invitation by one union central to the state to intervene in interunion jurisdictional competition reveals both the depth of the confusions within the CNTU concerning the role of the state in industrial relations and the weakness of the QFL. It is not surprising that after 1973 the QFL began to look increasingly towards affiliation to or collaboration with the PQ as a way out of its seemingly perennial weakness. This allegiance culminated in 1975 with the disaffiliation of the QFL from the NDP, and its official endorsement of the PQ.[73]

In this deteriorating situation of rivalry, secession, and an increasing number of hard-fought but unsuccessful strikes in the private sector, the CEQ emerged as the arbiter of the union movement. It remained as an arbiter, however, only so long as it stayed out of jurisdictional disputes with the Canadian Union of Public Employees (QFL) over affiliation of nonteaching staff employees of the school commissions: in other words, until late 1975. Standing between the CNTU and the QFL, the CEQ mediated a truce in construction and their return to co-operation in the public sector. That co-operation began, haltingly, during later 1975, at just the time when the CEQ's own aggressiveness in affiliating nonteaching staff was beginning to place pressure on its relation with the QFL. On the executive level, the CEQ kept itself clear of collaboration with any party, although since the late 1960s it had been informally linked to the NDP.

To summarize, then, the contradictions of the Quebec economy after 1966 coupled with the defeat of the modernizing fraction of the Liberal Party under Lesage combined to turn state policy away from the luxuries of rapidly expanding state investment and the dream of union participation in state policy formation. Between 1972 and 1976, the disintegration of the union-Liberal alliance left the unions groping for a new channel of political influence. They faced a state prepared to extract their compliance forcibly, but seemed to have real difficulty seeing the state itself as the adversary. Each central pursued its own inadequate solution, with little collaboration among them. The QFL in this period set about establishing the informal but powerful ties of collaboration with the Parti Québécois, which had characterized the CNTU-Liberal relationship during the Quiet Revolution. Like the CNTU a decade earlier, the QFL eschewed formal affiliation, and certainly the PQ did not encourage it. And, like the CNTU during the 1960s, the QFL was to discover, once the PQ had been elected, that the party entertained no sense of responsibility to the class that had largely accounted for its electoral victory.

The CNTU, on the other hand, manifested an increasingly serious breakdown between ideology and method of political intervention. By 1972, the CNTU could trace the evolution of its perception of class relations in Quebec from social democratic to revolutionary socialist.[74] Marcel Pepin's address to the 1972 CNTU Congress was based on a systematic and sophisticated neo-Marxist interpretation of the double colonization of the Quebec working class. (This is possibly the only one of the major orientation papers issued by Pepin that stressed the issue of class domination over that of national domination in the hierarchy of oppression, in clearly Marxist terms.) Using André Gunder Frank's metropolis-hinterland formulation, he interpreted Quebec's external economic dependence and the revolutionary responsibilities of unions in ways that could lead to the formation of a radical labour party. However, the CNTU's actual method of political intervention throughout this period continued to reflect the traditional stagnation and confusion as to concrete options. Relations with the post-Quiet Revolution Liberal Party having been effectively terminated, the CNTU vacillated between an unstructured collaboration with the PQ, the formation of an independentist workers' party, and the unstable status quo.

In this vacuum of effective action, grassroots mobilization moved to the foreground. On the lower level of worker organization, innovative political solutions were being pursued. Since 1960, the democratization of internal union structures, which had occurred within all three union centrals, had the important result of rekindling a taste for participation in union and provincial politics by the rank and file. "Participation" was defined in terms of opposition: to the union's continued conservatism; to its control by foreign capital and American unions; to the agents of conservatism, capitalism, and colonization: the union leadership. No one group of rank and file focussed on all these opponents, and which opponent each focussed on determined its ideology. Thus, a determination to participate in union politics to end union control from Washington and the domination of American capital might ignore the problem of entrenched Quebec union leadership and would quite likely lead the adherents of this position to support the PQ. Concern with capitalism only, and with the alliance between the bourgeois provincial state and the collaborationist local union bosses, would lead a rank-and-file militant either to membership in one of the Trotskyist and Marxist-Leninist groups advocating the founding of a revolutionary party, or towards a syndicalist rejection of electoral politics, which by the 1970s had taken on a particularly revolutionary colour.

In the former case, the emphasis on union problems identified with national oppression, most marked in the QFL and the regional councils of the CNTU and the CEQ outside of Montreal, led towards nonstructural affiliation to the PQ for the subcentral union structures and the rank-and-file members themselves. Within the QFL in particular, adherence to this position tended to allow rank-and-file militants and the central leadership to make common cause to challenge those American unions they considered most undemocratic, corrupt, and controlled from the United States — in other words, an alliance of the central and local levels of union operation against the intermediary levels of affiliated union leadership, using nationalism to assert central control. In the latter case, emphasis on class issues, with national issues present but secondary, was of greatest significance in some regional councils of the CNTU, in some of its federation executives, and among rank-and-file teachers and hospital employees. (For a brief time in the mid-1970s, the Federation of Social Affairs of the CNTU was a central rallying point for Marxist-Leninist positions.) In the CEQ, support for the PQ was geographically based and an urban phenomenon restricted to Montreal and Quebec City.

To say that an emphasis on class issues from some sort of revolutionary perspective was present at various levels of the union movement, however, is not to argue that it was homogeneous. Before 1974, it was possible to distinguish between the impact of revolutionary syndicalism and revolutionary indirect action. Revolutionary syndicalists rejected electoral politics and saw strikes as their most effective political weapon. They concentrated on the occupation of factories, on political education, and on the creation of revolutionary consciousness by numerous methods of "formation." But contained within their orientation was the temptation of electoralism: could elections be entered as an educational device to undermine the credibility and legitimacy of bourgeois politics? Certainly the founding of the Montreal municipal party Front d'Action Politique (FRAP) by unionists and community organizers in 1969 partly reflected that view.[75] Within FRAP and in municipal campaigns elsewhere in the province, the revolutionary-syndicalist perspective before 1974 joined an electoralist nonsectarian socialism in which reformists and revolutionaries made common cause.

By 1974, however, the revolutionary-syndicalist perspective had largely disappeared from the rank-and-file level, fragmented and absorbed by the diverse leftist groups advocating some sort of revolutionary workers' party. Within the CNTU, the role of the revolutionary syndicalists in strikes was increasingly challenged by emergent Marxist-Leninist extra-central strike-solidarity committees outside the framework of any union central. The most important of these, Le Comité de solidarité aux luttes ouvrières, was founded by *En Lutte*. It went to the aid of striking workers in nonunionized industries, then continued to offer aid to unionized workers involved in long strikes that had begun to embarrass the central. By 1974, the Comité's success and militance had become an example to the centrals and had taken over the work of syndicalists within the centrals.

In local and regional politics, revolutionary-syndicalist intervention had the effect of weakening or destroying local electoral coalitions, so that outside of Montreal, at least, reformist direct action was left to nonsectarian socialists who could make common, if temporary, cause with the PQ. Around 1974, however, the field of rank-and-file and subcentral intervention in politics simplified and polarized. Before then, revolutionary syndicalism competed with reformist direct action and with a still-embryonic revolutionary left—each with its own prescription for the founding of a revolutionary workers' party—absorbed the revolutionary syndicalists and splintered the reformist direct action camp into social-democratic supporters of the PQ and socialists without an organizational base.

Conclusion

By November 1976, after almost ten years in the political wilderness, the union movement was still painfully divided between those who favoured that kind of collaboration with a governing party that would accelerate the process of integration into the state apparatus and those who, from a variety of perspectives, sought to retard or reverse the process. The lines were drawn between central and central and, within the CNTU and the CEQ between Montreal and other regions, between some of the regional councils and the executives, between hospital workers and teachers on the one hand and private sector employees on the other. Only the QFL avoided the divisiveness created by the question of the state, as the CNTU had done some fifteen years earlier, by denying the existence of the state per se, by focussing on government, and by casting its lot with a party it hoped would be friendly (if not committed) to working-class interest once in power. It might be argued that, if the 1960s were the decade in which the CNTU furthered the dependence of the union movement on the state through its relationship with the Liberals, after 1975 the QFL in its relationship with the PQ played a similar role. But regardless of which central occupied the leading position, the process of decreasing union autonomy continued apace, from consensual integration to coercion and back to largely unsuccessful attempts at consensus. Within the unions, the only strategy developed was the abdication of political leadership—the old reformist syndicalism with a vengeance. And its price was high: a hollowing out of the political centre, a polarization of membership, a reduction of the legitimacy of the organs of central union power. In some way, between 1966 and 1976, the unions came to be seen as the major institutional opponents to the state, but were incapable of either occupying the role or defending themselves against its consequences. Thus, when a party came to power in 1976 that was the choice of the large majority of the unionized working class, it could present itself as an alternative source of identification to the unions and challenge the unions for the ideological leadership of their own members.

And with the benefit of hindsight from the perspective of 1983, the emerging crisis of the Quebec trade-union movement (more severe than any this generation has known) is itself testimony to the deadly efficiency of integrational state policy orchestrated by a nationalist political party.

Notes

1. David Payne, "Les limites du pouvoir: Une question de conscience" (unpublished paper, Quebec, 21 March 1983), 1, my translation.

2. David J. Bercuson, "Ottawa Strikes Back," *Saturday Night* (March 1983), 48. He is referring to Canadian federal policies only.

3. V.L. Allen, *The Sociology of Industrial Relations* (London: Longman, 1971), 47.

4. Roch Denis, *Luttes de classes et question nationale au Québec: 1948–1968* (Montreal: Presses Socialistes Internationales, 1979), 160–67.

5. The *nature of intervention* means the form political activity takes and the worldview that informs that activity. *Degree of strength* is more elusive, but it entails the ability of one institutional participant to influence and/or determine the option(s) of the other(s).

6. Charles Lipton, *The Trade Union Movement in Canada 1827–1959* (Toronto: NC Press, 1973), 1–97.

7. Fernand Harvey, "Les Chevaliers du Travail," in *Aspects historiques du mouvement ouvrier au Québec*, edited by F. Harvey (Montreal: Boréal Express, 1973), 51, 87–89.

8. Ibid., 65.

9. Norman J. Ware, *The Labor Movement in the United States* (New York: Vintage Books, 1964), 320ff.

10. Harvey, *Aspects historiques du mouvement ouvrier*, 69–75.

11. Ibid., 107.

12. Alfred Charpentier, "Le mouvement politique ouvrier de Montréal (1883–1929)" in ibid., 151–58.

13. Ibid., 159.

14. Louis Maheu, "Problème social et naissance du syndicalisme catholique," in ibid., 119–46.

15. Denis, *Luttes*, 84–89.

16. Cited in ibid., 86, note 7.

17. Drawn from *l'Annuaire du Québec, 1968–69*, 399.

18. Black Rose Books Editorial Collective, *Quebec Labour* (Montreal: Black Rose Books, 1972), 15; Pierre Vallières, "Les grèves perdues" in *Aspects historiques du mouvement ouvrier*, 171–73.

19. Roger Chartier,"La création du Ministère du Travail, l'extension juridique des conventions collectives et les années d'avant-guerre (1931–39)," *Relations Industrielles* 18, 2: 215.

20. Ibid., 219–20.

21. Vallières, "Les Grèves," 169–73.

22. Leo Roback, "Les formes historiques de politisation du syndicalisme au Québec," in *La politisation des relations du travail*, edited by G. Dion (Quebec: Les Presses de l'Université Laval, 1973), 21.

23. Denis, *Luttes*, 73.

24. Ibid., 74.

25. Ibid., 79–82.

26. Ibid.

27. Roger Chartier, "Contribution à l'histoire de la législation québécoise du travail: 7," *Relations Industrielles* 18, 3: 346–62.

28. Ibid., 355.

29. Vallières, "Les Grèves," 169–73; Pierre-Elliott Trudeau, ed., *La grève de l'amiante* (Montreal: Éditions Cité Libre, 1956); Denis, *Luttes*, 135–39; *En grève* (Montreal: Éditions du jour, 1963).

30. Gérard Dion, "Les groupements syndicaux dans la province de Québec," *Relations Industrielles*, 1: 2.

31. Denis, *Luttes*, 142–44.

32. Ibid., 150–52.

33. Louis-Marie Tremblay, *Le syndicalisme québécois: Idéologies de la CSN et de la FTQ 1940–1970* (Montreal: Les Presses de l'Université de Montréal, 1972), 165–67.

34. Denis, *Luttes*, 177ff, discusses the complex relationships that influenced the CTCC's approach to the question of a third party vs. collaboration with the Liberals in the late 1950s.

35. The CCL affiliates did not, however, found a central Quebec organization to regroup its provincial affiliates until 1952.

36. Emile Boudreau, "Murdochville: douze ans d'organisation," *Socialisme* 64, 3/4: 3–30.

37. Michel Grant, "L'Action syndicale et la Fédération des Unions industrielles du Québec" (Master's thesis, Industrial Relations Department, Université de Montréal, 1968), 122–34.

38. Ibid., 140–49.

39. Paul Bernard, *Structures et pouvoirs de la Fédération des travailleurs du Québec* (Ottawa: Queen's Printer, 1969), is the best detailed study of the QFL during the 1950s and 1960s.

40. Boudreau, "Murdochville," 6–9.

41. Diane Ethier, Jean-Marc Piotte, and Jean Reynolds, *Les travailleurs contre l'État bourgeois* (Montreal: L'Aurore, 1975), 17–22.

42. Ibid.

43. Jean Lesage, *Lesage s'engage* (Montreal: Les Éditions politiques, 1959). The following discussion is drawn from Denis, *Luttes*, 232–42.

44. Jean Marchand, "Il est urgent que le patronat s'organise au niveau national," *Le Travail* 39, 2 (fevrier 1963).

45. B. Roy Lemoine, "The Modern Industrial State: Liberator or Exploiter?" *Our Generation* 8, 4: 73.

46. Ibid., 91.

47. Ethier et al., *Les travailleurs contre l'État bourgeois*, 24.

48. Ibid., 22–24.

49. Bernard, *Structures et pouvoirs*, 175.

50. See Jean Boivin, "La négociation collective dans le secteur public québécois, une évaluation des trois premières rondes, 1964–72," *Relations Industrielles* 27, 4: 679–90; J.R. Cardin, "La création d'un carrefour syndical dans la fonction publique du Québec," *Relations Industrielles* 21, 2: 251–57.

51. Cardin, ibid., 252.

52. Of the 11,261 workers involved in changing union affiliation in 1964–65, some 10,000 passed to the CNTU.

53. For the best summary of union membership before 1970, see Herve Gauthier, "La syndicalisation au Québec," *Québec Travail* (Quebec: Government Printers, 1972). For more recent summaries see Fernard Harvey, *Le mouvement ouvrier au Québec* (Montreal: Boréal Express), 287–89.

54. Recent work on the CEQ includes a project in progress: James Thwaites, "L'enseignement québécois: 1937–1973" (Université Laval); also *Histoire du mouvement ouvrier du Québec 1825–1976* (Montreal: Coédition CSN/CEQ).

55. *Le Code du Travail 1: Des relations du travail*, 8th ed. (Quebec: Government Printers, 1964).

56. Louis-Marie Tremblay, "L'évolution du syndicalisme dans la révolution tranquille," *Relations Industrielles* 22, 1: 94.

57. Boivin, "La négociation collective," 682–83.

58. Discussed in Denis, *Les luttes*, 290.

59. Ibid., 308–52.

60. For example, the nationalization of hydroelectric power.

61. Tremblay, "L'évolution du syndicalisme," 317.

62. Ibid., 323.

63. Ibid., 324.

64. See, for example, Marcel Pepin, "Une société bâtie pour l'homme," *Rapport moral du président général de la CSN* (1966).

65. Ethier et al., *Les travailleurs contre l'État bourgeois*, 34, suggests that towards the end of their mandate in 1966 the Liberals were already beginning to harden their line towards the unions, so that Johnson's position in the watershed Bill 25 debate in 1967 was not a rupture with the recent past but a continuation of emerging Liberal policy.

66. Ibid., 25.

67. Boivin, "La négociation collective," 682.

68. Ethier et al., *Les travailleurs contre l'État bourgeois*, 101–08.

69. The best work on the Common Front is by Ethier et al., ibid.

70. The best known of these was *Ne Comptons que sur nos propres moyens*, commissioned by the executive from an outside economist, 100,000 copies of which were distributed during 1971 and 1972.

71. R. Daigneault and M. Rioux, *La Grande Tricherie* (Montreal: CSN, 1973).

72. Jean-Louis Harguindeguy, Intervention during the Plenary of the CNTU Congress at Quebec City (June 1972). For the timing and immediate impact of the secession on the CNTU, see Ethier et al., *Les travailleurs contre l'État bourgeois*, 111.

73. *Proceedings*, Congress of the Quebec Federation of Labour (Montreal, 3–7 Dec. 1975).

74. Marcel Pepin, *Pour Vaincre, Rapport moral du président général de la CSN* (Montreal: CSN, 1972).

75. Cf. FRAP's platform, *Les Salariés au Pouvoir* (1970).

WOMEN IN THE TRADE-UNION MOVEMENT IN QUEBEC†

MONA-JOSÉE GAGNON

It took the resurgence of the feminist movement to interest researchers in the role played by women in various organizations, including trade unions. Research on the role of women in all sectors is bound to become more intensive over the next few years because of the topical nature of the discussion on the status of women. But there is precious little for the Quebec researcher to work on, and this is especially true in the field of trade-unionism. Very few historians have devoted their efforts to the Quebec trade-union movement as an entity. The subject of women in trade unions has inspired only a very small number of theses and inquiries and trade-union publications that never found a wide readership. Neither has much been written on the subject of Québécois women in the workplace: a few statistics (mostly from the federal government), a trickle of articles or monographs dealing tangentially with the subject. If serious works have been written in other countries about women in the workplace, studies on the role of women in the trade-union movement are, as a rule, only beginning to be published.

This bibliographical vacuum called for the publication of an article devoted to the role of women in the trade-union movement in Quebec. Since one has to start somewhere, at the risk of saying nothing at all, this article will try to posit hypotheses within a feminist framework and in the light of information we have on trade-union organizations. We hope that it will lead to more research papers, for women can no longer afford to be absent, either physically or at the ideological level, from discussions on the status of women, from the trade-union movement in Quebec, and from the other organizations that revolve around the latter. Fortunately, the affirmation of the presence of women in the trade-union movement seems to be a current trend. But this alone is not enough to confer on female trade-unionists as a group of political weight they have not yet earned.

†"Les femmes dans le mouvement syndical québécois," *Sociologie et société* VI, 1 (mai 1974): 17–36. Translated by Henri Malebranche.

Quebec Society: Ideology and Dynamics of the Trade-Union Movement

It is impossible to study the dynamics of the trade-union movement without parallelling it with the society in which it takes root. Even if the trade-union movement, through its leaders and activists, defines itself more and more as an agent of change within our society and the organ that challenges and questions the established order, it is nevertheless true that it has been sadly remiss in formulating its attitude towards women (ideological level) and stating what role it reserves for women (political level) in this same society. Proceeding from these premises, we will draw the balance sheet of societal ideologies that, in various degrees, have left their marks on the trade-union movement in its attitude towards women.[1]

The Place of Women in Quebec's Societal Ideologies

The perception of women in the workplace is but one aspect of a wider topic: the definition of the social roles attributed to men and women, these roles usually being defined in a complementary manner. For the same reason, the perception of women's militancy in the trade-union movement is connected to the perception of women in the workplace. This is why the following remarks on Quebec's ideologies cover the whole question of the status of women.[2]

A study of the place held by women in our ideologies gives us an insight into our ideological history. Such a study brings out very vividly the anxieties and the fears of Quebeckers when they had to face industrialization and urbanization. It is quite possible to make certain connections between wider ideologies and those specifically concerning women.

If it is difficult to determine the exact moment when an ideology emerges or disappears, it is nevertheless possible to determine the period when an ideology predominates. Until the 1960s, a traditionalist ideology centring on the women as a homemaker was unchallenged in Quebec. Such an ideology is part and parcel of the wider ideological system that can be called conservatism. Just as Quebeckers, at that time, refused, in the name of French-Canadian authenticity, to accept the changes and progress due to the transformation of the industrial structure, they rejected any change whatsoever in the status of women. Since the family was then considered not only the nucleus of Quebec society but, furthermore, the very reason for its miraculous survival as a nation, it was deemed unacceptable that women might have a vocation other than serving the family, the bulwark that protected Quebec against the Anglo-Saxon and materialist invader. It was therefore assumed that women were not fitted for activities outside the home, and they were resolutely kept away from the workplace.

The nationalist and clerical elites did not fail to sound the alarm when women workers moved in droves into the munitions factories during World War II. The very real need of the labour market for women workers, caused by the political and economic conditions of the time, appeared as an anti-French conspiracy aimed at killing off the family as an institution and spreading materialist and selfish ideas among women workers. These women were portrayed by Québécois elites as calculating, forsaking their children, thinking only of earning money,

⌐and little, if at all, interested in procreating. Over and over again, the presence of women at home was presented as the underlying and indispensable condition for Quebec's national survival. And it was for a whole set of religious, moral, and political reasons that women were refused admission to the workplace.

With the Quiet Revolution and the end of the Duplessis regime, the nationalist ideology had to make room in the 1960s for a broad ideology of liberal modernization, an amalgam of diffuse ideas. Its upholders shared a desire to adapt to reality and to reject the purely traditionalist conception of the role of women in society. However, fundamental values were not questioned, and the family and the traditional division of roles were never seriously challenged, either by the traditionalist or the liberal modernization ideology that idealizes a "symbiotic woman." While women's place is still defined by her role within the family, the liberal modernization ideology demands a lot from women. They are expected to be accomplished housewives and mothers, like those of preceding generations. But they are not to be confined, either physically or mentally, to the home. Women are expected to be socially aware, informed, and intelligent.

In keeping with some elements of the definition of feminine virtues and aptitudes in which the architects of the traditionalist ideology indulged, it is deemed that it is women's duty to make a specifically "feminine" contribution to the world. Women's softness, their love of peace, their spirit of sacrifice, their altruism, their sense of work well done, their understanding of child psychology, their maternal instinct, and so on, all these qualities fit them to particular social vocations. Women are thus called upon to make a contribution to society that will be accepted insofar as it is made within the framework of femininity. Even the feminist movement insists on the eminently "feminine" character, in the traditional sense, of women's contribution to political life (the women's movement for peace, for example). . . .

This ideology of liberal modernization, while still predominant, has now come under attack by an ideology that rejects differentiation between the sexes and challenges the very division of social roles between men and women. Because of this fundamental challenge, the notions of masculinity and femininity become void of content and are limited to observations on the physiological differences and on the differences in reproductive function. This ideology leads to a society of individuals, and to a complete transformation of the labour market and of the family as an institution as well.[3]

Quebec society has revolved around these three ideological systems over the last few decades. The trade-union movement has defined itself in relation to these ideologies; even though there has been little research done on the trade-union movement, it is generally possible to classify it, for analytical purposes, within these ideological systems.

Position of the Trade-Union Movement in Quebec Vis-à-vis Societal Ideologies

Even if the trade-union movement in Quebec now appears in the form of three main groupings[4] — the CSN (Confédération des syndicats nationaux), the CEQ (Centrale de l'enseignement du Québec), and the FTQ (Fédération des travailleurs du Québec) — origins are diverse: Québécois, American, as well as Canadian. Enough has been written on the sociological particularities of Quebec on the North American continent so that we need not dwell on the influence of the country of origin, along with all this implies in terms of differentiation in values, on Québécois trade-union confederations. These differences in values become obvious when one compares the attitudes of the FTQ and the CSN towards the status of women. We explained earlier the central character of the social role bestowed on women by the ideological architects in Quebec. The importance given to women and the family manifests itself clearly in the CSN and less so in the FTQ. We will return later to these differences in our analyses of the trade-union confederations. First, we will study the trade-union movement with origins in Quebec, and then later the trade-union movement of Canadian or American origin. Beyond the fundamental identity at the membership level — the members of all these confederations were, after all, Quebeckers and, as such, shared the same values and the same ambiguities — very sharp differences quickly emerged. These differences are now becoming blurred, if they have not completely disappeared, and it seems that the CSN and the FTQ, once so different, are now going to travel along parallel roads as concerns the question of the status of women.

We believe that the trade-union movement, like the political left in Quebec, was unable to formulate an ideology to challenge the accepted views on the status of women in response to the traditionalist ideology and then to the ideology of liberal modernization. To be more precise, there is a considerable difference, in time, between the challenge to our political and economic system and the challenge to the traditional division of sexual roles, and the realization that these two are somehow related. Thus, we witnessed how the trade-union movement, or at least some of its elements, started to challenge the whole social structure, to question its foundations, while continuing to uphold values relative to the status of women that were objectively related to a traditionalist ideological system. We will return to this hypothesis in the following sections.

The Québécois Trade-Union Movement

Ideology of the CTCC-CSN[5] on the Status of Women[6]

> As far as the CTCC-CSN is concerned, the family is the basic social unit. It transcends the individual. Socio-economic policies must be subordinated to its needs. It is considered that any society that does not show a special concern for the family and the home cannot pretend to be either a Christian or a civilized society.[7]

In the beginning, the CTCC-CSN appeared as the upholder of a double tradition that confirmed its Québécois authenticity: Catholicism and nationalism. Its foundation, in 1921, facilitated the consolidation of the trade unions that had emerged in Quebec, thanks to the active support of the clergy, in response to the penetration of trade unions of foreign origin, which were considered to be materialistic (non-Catholic) and even communist. The workers who were members of the CTCC presented themselves as members of a cultural collectivity (religious, ethnic, linguistic) that also included the employers, in accordance with the corporatist ideology that had a strong influence on the CTCC until the 1950s. The workers who belonged to trade unions of Canadian or American origins were, on the other hand, organized in opposition to their employers.

The CTCC quickly concerned itself with the question of women in the workplace because of the repercussions this was bound to have on the family as an institution. The CTCC always paid careful attention to working conditions for women, who were not considered "ordinary" workers.[8] The CTCC quickly departed from its somewhat relaxed attitude once it confronted the reality of women in the workplace during World War II. It then went along with the clerical and nationalist (bourgeois) elites in denouncing the hiring of female workers. The CTCC was opposed to the presence of women in the workplace in the name of family and moral values, denounced the day-care centres established by the government, and demanded a "family" salary that would be enough to relieve women of the obligation to work.

> The hour is serious. Our country is threatened at the very source of its vitality: the family. Measures meant to save us might in the end lead us to perdition if they are applied without taking God's plan into consideration.[9]

> Finally, the married woman with young children should not be admitted into the war factories. . . . The primary task of our mothers is to give a good education to their children. . . . On behalf of French-Canadian women, we are petitioning the provincial minister of labour and we are asking him to use his authority to exempt women from all types of work that, by their very nature or duration, might prove to be too strenuous for them or might expose them to grave moral dangers.[10]

In 1942, the delegates to the CTCC congress came out strongly in favour of giving priority to able-bodied men over women in hiring practices. At the same time it advocated pay equity for women. The congress also asked the government to classify men's and women's jobs, a measure bound to keep the female workers' salaries at a very low level. At the end of the war, the CTCC campaigned, along still with the clerical and nationalist elites, for women to return home, and it even asked the government to take action to this effect. In a publication that appeared after the war, the CTCC stated quite clearly that the presence of women in the workplace was abnormal but, for humanitarian reasons, it could not be forbidden to all women (abandoned mothers, young women with a family to support, widows). "The CTCC deems that it is impossible to reconcile the natural order of things with the presence of women in industrial and commercial activities. Social circumstances will no doubt mitigate the above statement."[11]

This fundamental rejection of the idea of women in the workplace was to dominate the CTCC until 1953 and leave its mark until 1964. This did not prevent the CTCC from occasionally looking after its female members, by demanding equal pay for equal work, and from pushing a protectionist policy as far as women were concerned (shorter working hours). If one takes a look at the CTCC's newspaper of that period, one realizes that, until 1960, the women's section and the articles for women were meant exclusively for the wives of the union members and dealt with the woman's duty to her family and her home.

The period from 1953 to 1964 represents a period of discussion within the CTCC on the question of women in the workplace. These discussions found an echo at the level of the congress: creation of a committee, reports on the question of women in the workplace, the non-representation of women in the executive circles of the CTCC. From 1953 to 1964, however, these discussions seem due more and more to the action of some individuals (Jeanne Duval, vice-president of the CTCC, in particular) than to the confederation itself. Not until 1964 did the CTCC, through its president, Jean Marchand, officially concern itself with this question:

> We are not against the presence of women in the workplace. It would be of no use. We only ask that their nature be respected. Working women are entitled to a status that not only gives them protection as salaried individuals but also takes into consideration their special needs as women with family responsibilities.[12]

It was in the 1960s also that the newspaper of the CNTU turned away from the wives of its members,[13] from recipes and housekeeping tips, to concern itself with the problems experienced by one-third of its members: female workers.

In 1964, the CNTU took a resolutely protectionist attitude towards its female members. This attitude was based on women's responsibilities to the home and their families: since women working outside the home had to bear the additional burden of the housework, they should be entitled to a certain number of privileges in negotiations and as regards labour laws as well. The presence of women in the workplace was still presented in a negative light: women who worked outside the home were said to do so out of necessity and, although female employment was essentially an abnormal situation, one has no choice but to accept it.

From 1953 until 1966, the CTCC-CSN frequently discussed, first in its congresses and later in the pages of its newspaper (from 1960 on), and often through a women's committee, the issue of women in the workforce. At this level, the action of the CSN was truly innovative in Quebec society; it was the first union to deal squarely with the practical problems caused by having women in the workplace and to denounce the inequalities suffered by women in the labour market. In 1966, however, the CSN's women's committee was officially dissolved, its members arguing that, female members not being fundamentally different from male members, they would have to adhere to the mixed structures of the CSN.[14] Since that time, the CSN, as a trade-union confederation, has not taken up a position on the question of women in the workplace except for its brief to the Bird Commission,[15] a brief that did not really give rise to discussions within the movement. This brief was drafted from a protectionist perspective.

> We should aim to do away with the living conditions or low-income situations in the family that force the married women to go out to work, so that her decision might be entirely a matter of personal choice and not bound only to financial circumstances. Women will then be able to participate fully in, and take a better interest in, the labour world since their participation will be of their own free volition. . . . But, as stated by the ILO [International Labour Organization], once this choice is made, women

should be in a position to do their work without any discrimination whatsoever and without prejudice to the health and the welfare of their family.[16]

From this position, the brief asked for measures in favour of women working outside the home (day-care centres, maternity leave, etc.). Nevertheless, it was true that female workers were defined as women first, with all that implied in terms of family and maternal responsibilities. Working women had to acquit themselves of these family functions. The attribution of these functions was not challenged. On the whole, the perspective was protectionist—that is, supporting laws or regulations taking women's additional responsibilities into consideration.

To sum up, the progression of the CSN's ideology on the question of women in the workplace can be divided into three stages. Up to 1953, the negative attitude was predominant: the presence of women in the workplace was against nature, anti-Christian, morally dangerous, and harmful to the family. The CTCC echoed at the trade-union level the traditionalist ideology expounded by the clerical and nationalist elites. The period from 1953 to 1964 saw intense discussion on the question of women in the workplace, at the instigation of influential women in the movement. In 1964, the question of women in the workplace became an official concern, and the presence of women in the labour force was officially sanctioned. At the same time, there was a formulation of a protectionist ideology within the framework of the ideology of liberal modernization. However, with the dissolution of the women's committee in 1966, the question of the status of women faded from the picture. Hopefully, in view of its break with anything even remotely connected with the traditionalist ideology, the CSN, by its silence, is approaching an ideology that rejects differentiation between the sexes, and is casting away its own protectionist perspective.

Presence of Women in the CSN

Until the mid-1960s, except for the year 1942, less than ten percent of the delegates to the congress of the CTCC-CSN were women, although they made up one-third of the membership. It was, however, for a long time customary to have a woman vice-president. One woman in particular was for many years vice-president of the CTCC-CSN and it was under her impetus that the discussion on the status of woman took a positive turn. For the last few years, however, the executive board of the CSN has been composed exclusively of men; the dissolution of the women's committee effectively confirmed the CSN's silence on the status of women. It was certainly not what the members of the women's committee had in mind when they argued for the dissolution of the committee; the little interest subsequently aroused in the CSN by the problems associated with the presence of women in the workplace shows that perhaps the sensitization process had not advanced far enough to allow the federation to do away with a catalyzing committee that had started discussion on the issue.

Figures dating back to 1948 show how women were represented within the CSN. Women always made up one-third of the membership and were predominant in a few sectors (garments and hospitals). At the executive level, one out of eleven persons was a woman; at the central office, there were eleven women out of 130 persons (eight percent). In 1968, there were eight women (thirteen percent) among the sixty presidents, secretaries, and treasurers of the central boards (regional structures), and only two women (six percent) among the thirty presidents, secretaries, and treasurers of the federations and sectors (trades structures). Finally, out of two hundred permanent employees of the unions, only five were women (2.5 percent), of whom two were at the CSN and the remaining three at the FNS (Fédération nationale des services).

Figures that were compiled in September 1973 from the CSN are shown in table 1. After the number of positions on the executive board was reduced from eleven to five, and later changed to six, there have been no women on the board. Lastly, there has been a very slight increase in female participation at the level of the permanent employees of the federation: 170 men and 10 women, that is from 2.5 to 5.5. percent.

TABLE 1

Representation in CSN Offices by Sex

Office	Women	Men	Percentage of Officers Who Are Women
Central board	17	109	13
Central office	4	13	23
Executive committees of the federation (presidents, secretaries, treasurers)	1	24	4
Executive committees of the central boards	15	48	24
Presidents of local unions	145	865	14
Secretaries of local unions[17]	418	593	41
Treasurers of local unions	190	720	29

Teachers' Unions: CIC-CEQ[18]

The CEQ has been legally considered a union only since the mid-1970s. However, well before that it was considered an integral part of the trade-union movement in Quebec. Teachers began to unionize around 1936, within the framework of rural and urban organizations. One woman, Laure Gaudreault, started the most militant organization in this field, the Fédération catholique des institutrices rurales. The teachers' trade-union movement was established along the lines of the Catholic trade-union movement, and it was, like the CTCC, and for a much longer time than the latter, open to the influence of the corporatist doctrine.

Up to the end of the 1950s, there were enormous disparities in the salaries paid to male and female teachers, as well as to those who worked in the cities and those in rural areas. Because of its corporatist character, the CIC never had to take a stand on the question of the presence of women in the workplace in general. Its campaign was limited to claiming pay equity for men and women.

Out of the eleven persons at the executive level in 1974, only two were women, in spite of the fact that women made up two-thirds of the membership. Of the 125 members of the provincial board of the organization, the supreme authority between the congresses, only twelve were women (ten percent). At the end of

1973, there were three women out of the forty-two presidents of the regional unions of the federation (seven percent), and only five women out of forty-six held a permanent position in the federation (eleven percent).

It was during its 1973 congress that the CEQ decided to examine in earnest the question of the status of women. A whole afternoon was devoted to the study in committee of the status of women.[19] In the plenary session the following day, a resolution was adopted that confirmed the CEQ's concern with the women's liberation movement along with workers' liberation. This resolution also mentioned day-care centres, salaries for homemakers, and the liberalization of abortion laws. It is noteworthy that the CEQ is the only union to have taken a stand on the abortion question, and even to have discussed it. On the practical side, a study committee was set up at the end of this congress: research budgets were approved; female teachers were given leave to take part in the committee's work. The committee is to carry out a study on how women are portrayed in school books; the committee will also hold sessions on this question in local unions and will promote the creation of women's committees.

The Quebec Trade-Union Movement of American or Canadian Origin

Ideology of the Fédération des travailleurs du Québec on the Status of Women

The FTQ was born in 1957 from the merger of the two Quebec branches of American and Canadian unions, the Fédération provinciale du travail du Québec (FPTQ) and the Fédération des unions industrielles du Québec (FUIQ). Affiliates of the American Federation of Labor and the Congress of Industrial Organizations, these two organizations represented the traditional trade unions and the industrial unions respectively; there were nevertheless some industrial unions within the FPTQ. The lack of thorough research on the ideology of these two organizations, combined with the fact that their weakness reduced them for all purposes to the status of co-ordinating committees, does not allow us to draw any inference whatsoever as far as they are concerned.

Besides, the FUIQ did not exist for more than five years; in spite of its social-democratic orientation, and although it challenged the whole social structure, which made it the most politically active federation, it does not seem that the question of the status of women was ever seriously debated within its ranks. On the other hand, the FPTQ, which was mostly a federation of traditional trade unions that in most cases controlled the hiring process and kept female workers away, had a very "masculine" profile and did not really discuss the presence of women in the workplace.

As a matter of fact, if one compares the number of times this issue of women in the workplace is mentioned in the pages of the FPTQ's newspaper or during its congresses with the big debate that took place in the CSN from World War II until the mid-1960s, one could almost accuse the FPTQ of indifference towards women. This attitude is all the more striking since all Quebec was at the time in the throes of a vast pro-family campaign that was directed against the presence of women in the workplace. This shows that the FPTQ was relatively impervious to the opinion campaign waged by the bourgeois elites and the CTCC. The latter, of course, demanded pay equity while deploring the increase in the number of women in the workplace. But a resolution to this effect, taken at the 1939 FPTQ convention, never gave rise to official speeches appealing to nationalistic, moral, and religious arguments, as was the case at the CTCC. The members of the FPTQ were solely interested in denouncing the use of cheap labour.

If we look at the present FTQ, which has been in existence since 1957, this indifference was prevalent until very recently. From 1957 to 1973, one notes the ritual resolution on pay equity and a denunciation of piece work done in the home. The newspaper included a column written by an influential woman in the movement who often offered her personal views on women's issues. In 1965, the FTQ refused, along with the CSN, to take part in a government commission of inquiry on night work by women in factories; pleading that the mandate of this commission was too limited, the FTQ, on the occasion of its congress, asked the government to initiate an investigation on the question of the presence of women in the workplace as a whole.

In 1968 the FTQ submitted a brief to the Bird Commission. This brief, like any other, remained unnoticed within the federation and did not give rise to any debate. It ascribed the problems connected with the presence of women in the workplace to the traditional division of social roles and was opposed to any kind of special measures (part-time work, for instance), in favour of women; night work for women, a ticklish topic, was never broached. The report of the women's committee tabled at the 1973 congress followed along the same lines, reconfirming the 1968 orientation and above all rekindling the discussion in the movement.

In 1972, therefore, a study committee on the status of women was set up in the FTQ. Composed exclusively of women who were either militants or employees of the affiliated unions, the committee was to single out the reasons why women were practically absent from the leadership and power structures of the FTQ and its affiliated unions. It was not, therefore, until 1972 that the FTQ decided to look in earnest into the question of the status of women in a way that would inevitably start discussions within its ranks. One should note that the representation of women within the FTQ—even in the mid-1970s, women only made up twenty percent of its membership compared to thirty-three percent in the CSN—is a relatively recent phenomenon that increased in the mid-1960s with the unionization of the public and semi-public sectors.

The report submitted by this committee in 1973[20] was the object of discussions in the congress and even of a session in committee for all delegates; this was a rather radical departure for a federation that had never really concerned itself with the question of the status of women.

After some lively sessions in committee, during which women expressed themselves more volubly than usual, the congress of the FTQ was to ratify the general orientation of the document in the plenary session, namely the following points:

—association of the traditional division of social roles with the discrimination suffered by women in the workplace;

—denunciation of the traditional division of roles;

—denunciation of the ghettoization of women into traditional occupations;

—adoption of an egalitarian attitude by the trade union towards women, as opposed to protectionism (negotiation of privileges, of special measures);

—recognition of the connection between the politico-economic system and the oppression of women.

A series of negotiation policies were later adopted in this perspective, policies that especially denounced the ghettoization of women into traditional occupations. The congress also passed a resolution condemning a policy calling for an eventual salary for homemakers in the name of the basic principles contained in the report: the need to recognize that women have the right to work, opposition to the traditional division of social roles, freedom for parents to bring up their children as they see fit, and so on.

With this report, the FTQ made a geat leap forward in acknowledging the issue of the status of women. But one should bear in mind the structural weaknesses of the FTQ (voluntary affiliation, financial and human resources reduced to a strict minimum); the FTQ is effectively powerless without the active and militant support of its affiliated unions.

Presence of Women in the FTQ

Women are underrepresented in a shocking manner in the leadership of the FTQ and its affiliated unions. To date, no woman has ever sat at the executive level in the federation; on the general board (the highest authority between congresses) there are two women out of eighty-five people. Women do not make up three percent of the 680 permanent staff members of the affiliated unions. Statistics updated by the study committee prove this underrepresentation over and over again. At the level of the local trade unions, however, women frequently sit on the executive board. This proportion decreases regularly at the level of the provincial boards.[21] It is noteworthy that even when, in some cases, women are achieving breakthroughs at the executive level, the full-time, permanent positions remain almost exclusively a male preserve. However, even if they are not part of the formal power structure, permanent employees have an enormous influence on the orientation of the unions' negotiation policies and constitute in this respect a kind of "parallel power base." Furthermore, there is no more room among the permanent staff members for "honorary" candidates; there is only room for confidence in leadership abilities and technical qualifications. Women, thus, still have a long way to go before they can take their rightful place within the ranks of the FTQ.[22]

Participation of Women in the Trade-Union Movement in Quebec

Unionization

Whereas the overall unionization rate for salaried workers in Quebec reached thirty-nine percent, which is far higher than the Canadian average, only thirty percent of the salaried women and forty-five percent of salaried men were unionized.[23] This low rate of unionization among women can be explained, albeit superficially, by the fact that women are proportionally more numerous in the sectors with a low unionization rate (tertiary sector and services in general). The question one should logically ask is the following: "Why is the unionization rate so low in those specific sectors?" The reasons are multifarious, from the practical difficulties in forming a union (small enterprises, labour relations along paternalistic lines, etc.) to the indifference and incompetence of the union structures, without forgetting the reluctance of women to unionize. This problem has been studied elsewhere.[24]

To make up for the unionization problems inherent in certain sectors, especially those where women workers are most numerous, the trade union movement, the FTQ in particular, has sought accreditation for each sector. This system, which has never been put effectively into practice and which might conceivably lead to an important expansion of the trade-union movement, could restore the balance between the unionization rate of women and their importance in the labour force.

As concerns unionization, it would be interesting to see to what extent the urban-rural opposition, as expressed by the FTQ and the CSN, has had an impact on the question of the status of women. On the one hand, in the 1940s the CSN had achieved solid breakthroughs in the small industries in the semi-rural areas dominated by small French-Canadian employers; the FTQ, on the other hand, through its predecessors, the FUIQ and the FPTQ, was represented in force in the large urban centres, the big factories with Anglo-Saxon or foreign ownership. Furthermore, the urban populations have always seemed to be ahead of the people living in rural or semi-rural areas (small towns) as regards accepting the realities of industrialization and urbanization, and the presence of women in the workplace was an integral part of this process. An additional explanation to the different attitudes in the debate on the status of women could be found in this urban-rural opposition that is reflected in the ranks of the FTQ and the CSN.

Women's Militancy

Historical Evolution

We have already described the massive influx of women into the labour market during World War II; not that they were absent before that, but they had been active in sectors that were relatively little unionized. Entering, thanks to the war, industrial sectors with a high productivity and a high unionization rate, women left their mark as ardent militants in many places. A series of women militants, in the tradition of the communist trade-union movement, worked within the trade unions of American origin. In many cases, these militants had come to the union movement through the channel of their political militancy (the Communist Party) and carved out a place for themselves in the trade-union movement. Many of these militants were swept away in the postwar "purge." Except for some isolated cases of political layoffs (for instance, Madeleine Parent, textile union), the departure of the women occurred in an almost "natural" fashion; the men, back from the war or from the army, resumed the places they had vacated in the labour market and in the union organizations.

The massive unionization of the public and semi-public sectors in the 1950s, and in particular in the 1960s, was to lead to the emergence of a new generation of women militants, and it is mostly these women whose voices are now heard in the labour federations. The affiliated unions of the FTQ, in particular, experienced a dramatic influx of women into their ranks in the 1960s. However, women are still by and large absent from the formal and informal power structures within the trade unions and labour federations.

Data on Women's Militancy[25]

Beyond the differences and similarities between the labour federations that we have already mentioned, and that are rooted in the ideologies and attitudes of the (male) union leaders, it is possible to isolate certain factors that are directly responsible for women's militancy. These should be considered as hypotheses, since, in our opinion, one cannot draw final conclusions from a single monograph. These conclusions are drawn from a study on the participation of women in the Fédération nationale des services (FNS) of the CSN, known nowadays as the Fédération des affaires sociales (FAS).

There are factors that can, according to our research, promote militancy. The available information has enabled us only to cross-check the local union officers' positions with the sex and marital status of the holder. In this context, "militancy" should be understood to mean accession to the executive level of a local trade union. There seems to be a positive correlation between the proportion of women in a union and the number of women holding executive positions. The odds are that more women will be found at the executive level of a union whose members are mostly women.

There seems to exist a positive correlation between the union's size and the participation of women in the executive circles of the local unions. The proportion of female members is not significantly different whether the local union in question is big or small. However, in terms of the executive, very large unions (a thousand members or more) have an extremely low proportion of women officers, while very small unions (49 members or less) have four times more women holding executive positions.

There seems to be, in the case of women, a positive correlation between marital status and union militancy. Whereas single women made up 45 percent of the women members of the FNS, they held 78 percent of the executive positions occupied by women. The available information unfortunately does not give any indication as to the dependants (number of children) of the women officers.[26]

Our research also led us to realize that the participation of women decreases the further one climbs the ladder of power and/or responsibility within the FNS. Fewer and fewer women are to be found at each level, so that their number at the top is practically negligible. Roughly speaking, women comprise 70 percent of the FNS membership.[27] Let's assume that the first level of participation consists in being an active member of one's local union: 51 percent of the members[28] taking part in the congresses were women. This figure is an approximation of the true proportion of militant women (we opted for a lower figure since we assumed a woman with children is more likely to be daunted by the prospect of a trip to a union congress). Already, a sizeable discrepancy is noticeable between the number of women members and the number of women militants.

This discrepancy becomes more and more pronounced as one goes up the hierarchy. A second level of participation consists of occupying an executive position in a local union and/or being an official delegate to the congresses of the FNS. According to the different measurement methods utilized, 36 to 42 per-cent of these positions were occupied by women. At the next level, for the years from 1964 to 1970, 32 percent of the positions at the federal office (the supreme authority between the congresses) and 30 percent of the positions on the execu-tive board of the federation were occupied by women. At the level of permanent delegates to the FNS, the percentage of women falls off drastically to barely 10 percent.[29] The course that women's militancy follows is thus strewn with obsta-cles and difficulties because this militancy does not necessarily bring along power and responsibility. These are the principal conclusions of our research study. Only other studies will confirm these trends, irrespective of the industrial sectors under study.[30]

The Trade-Union Movement in Quebec and its Attitudes Towards Women

Beyond attitudinal differences rooted in different union traditions, the labour federations share some positions: they are likewise confronted with the same alternatives and the same dilemmas. We will now try to bring into relief the positions they have in common.

The Traditional Demands

At the end of the 1930s, all the branches of the trade-union (workers') move-ment in Quebec jumped on the bandwagon of equal pay for equal work. Although the unions never budged from their position, this particular demand never met with the expected success. The union leaders admit that, in many cases, they still have not succeeded in raising the wages of women workers to the level of those earned by male workers; unionized male workers even occasionally challenge this principle.[31] If, in the beginning, trade unions were against women being paid lower wages, it was because their protectionist mentality caused them to oppose any form of cheap labour, which, in their opinion, represented a threat to the jobs of their members. The demand for pay equity became especially virulent during World War II, when there were extremely large numbers of women workers employed in sectors that, until then, had been male bastions. Official statements by the leaders of the CTCC make no bones about the reasons behind the stand taken by the union on the question of pay equity: a woman's place, they argued, was at home. The FPTQ passed a resolution in congress in favour of pay equity, "considering that able-bodied men are unemployed while women are working. . . ." (The union knew that, if forced to pay women the same wages as men, employers would hire male workers.) Once the war trauma was over, once the women, at least some of them, had returned to the home, the demand for pay equity became gradually institutionalized within a framework more relaxed and less charged with emotion. For many years now, the trade unions have been demanding pay equity for reasons of fairness and justice. It is still reported that some employers, once they have been forced by negotiations to pay the same wages to male and female workers, limit themselves to hiring men: however, the promotion and seniority clauses of the collective agreements can, to a great extent, counter these employers' attitudes.

Ghettoization of Women into Traditional Occupations

The efforts of the unions to ensure that women be paid decent wages were limited to those cases when they performed the same jobs as men; this gave the employers the opportunity to "invent," to their advantage, women's jobs that were as poorly paid as they were uninteresting. The employers were clever in their tactics; aware of the male hegemony in trade-union circles and of the fact that the unions only grudgingly tolerated the presence of women in the workplace, it was easy for employers to foresee that union demands could more easily be met if a position was seen as a female job. The notion of "acceptable wages" varies widely whether it is question of a male or female worker.[32] Even if the employers were responsible for creating this job classification and wage scale, the fact that the unions refrained from denouncing women's occupational ghettoization that permitted employers to pay women lower wages on the whole, makes the trade-union movement effectively the accomplice of the employers.

This silence on the part of the unions is all the more striking since they were demanding pay equity for reasons of justice and fairness. It was nevertheless easy to realize that this demand for pay equity was constantly being sidestepped by the employers through occupational ghettoization, the smallest difference between two jobs justifying a huge gap in wages, with women occupying, of course, positions at the bottom of the wage scale. Even in those industrial sectors dominated by unions (the garment industry, for example), the most prestigious and the best paid jobs (tailors, for instance) were exclusively a male preserve. Moreover, the traditional trade unions (FPTQ-FTQ) hampered, along with the employers, the hiring of women workers.[33]

The Temptation of Trade-Union Protectionism

On the whole, and until very recently, the labour federations tended to adopt a protectionist attitude towards women. This attitude, quite pronounced at the CTCC-CSN, but more blurred in the FTQ, rested on the double burden that most of the women workers have to carry: work outside of the home and work at home (children and housekeeping). It was on account of moral and familial reasons that the CSN came out against night-shift work by women.[34] It also demanded a lighter schedule for women workers in 1968.[35] The FTQ was the first to outgrow this protectionist attitude. It had never unequivocally opposed night work by women. In 1968, the FTQ came out against special demands by unions on behalf of women workers.[36] This trend was to be confirmed at the 1973 congress.

Conclusion

It seems that the various components of the trade-union movement in Quebec, in particular the CEQ and the FTQ, have resumed their dicussion on the status of women. However, as of 1973, women were still pathetically underrepresented in the union structures.

If, in the past, the CTCC-CSN and the FTQ, on account of their very different origins and traditions, have adopted distinct attitudes towards the question of female workers and the status of women, it is easy to foresee that these differences will become increasingly blurred, since both federations tend to take their political inspiration more and more at the same source and in keeping with similar social analyses. The trade-union movement — and this is especially true in the case of the CSN — tended to overlook the feminist dimension in developing its "political project"; while making critical analyses of our society and challenging its very foundations, they referred to plans regarding the status of women that were taken straight from the traditionalist ideology. Some re-adjustment needs to be done by the trade-union movement in this respect; furthermore, it will have to incorporate the feminist dimension in its daily practice and in the ideology that it represents.

The question of the status of women is not an isolated phenomenon that stands alone, and it cannot be approached as such. Any discussion on the presence of women in the workplace must include discussion on a wider scale that challenges the very orientation of a society. In this context, the trade-union movement will have to choose between protectionism and egalitarianism within its ranks. We believe that the ideology that reflects an absence of sexual differentiation should inspire the trade-union movement in Quebec in its future orientation. In so doing, the movement will be far ahead of the society in which it is rooted — but this is the true role of an agent of change, which it is playing at every other level in the political context. Furthermore, the defence and the promotion of the interests of its women members go through this channel.

Notes

1. It is clearly difficult to establish in these few pages the distinctions between "official trade-union movement" and the individual attitudes of trade-union leaders and militants. These two levels of analysis overlap often because of the personal involvement required by a subject such as the status of women and the masculine hegemony in the trade-union movement. Unless stated otherwise, we will limit ourselves in this article to the official positions adopted by the trade-union movement.

2. This section of the paper is inspired by the author's master's thesis (industrial relations) "La femme dans l'idéologie québécoise et dans la CSN: étude idéologique et monographie syndicale" (Université de Montréal, 1973).

3. See the *Rapport de la Commission royale d'enquête sur la situation de la femme au Canada* (Ottawa: Information Canada, 1970).

4. We will not talk in this article about the Centrale des syndicats démocratiques (CSD), which is interesting from a political point of view but does not deserve a special mention for the purpose of a study on the trade-union movement and women. In this context, it is connected to the Catholic trade-union movement and to the CTCC-CSN.

5. The CTCC (Confédération des travailleurs catholique du Canada) and the CSN are the same organization. The change of name and the dissociation from the church took place in 1961.

6. This section is inspired by a chapter of the author's master's thesis.

7. Louis-Marie Tremblay, *Le syndicalisme québécois* (Montreal: Les Presses de l'Université de Montréal, 1972), 99–100.

8. Lucie Dagenais, "Participation des femmes aux mouvements syndicaux," *XXIIe Congrès des relations industrielles de l'Université Laval sur le travail féminin* (Quebec: Les Presses de l'Université Laval, 1967): 146–57.

9. Speech on the question of women in the workplace, delivered by Alfred Charpentier, president of the CTCC on the occasion of the congress of the CTCC in 1942.

10. *Procès-verbal du congrès CTCC*, 1942, 132–135.

11. CTCC, *tract no. 8* (no date [after the war]), 10.

12. *Procès-verbal du congrès*, 1964, *Rapport du président*, 8.

13. For years, the editors of the women's section were effectively the "wives" of militants and wrote in this capacity.

14. The women's committee of the Confédération française des syndicats démocratiques (CFDT), a French, formerly Catholic trade-union federation, suffered the same fate.

15. Briefs submitted by the FTQ and the CSN to the Royal Commission on the Status of Women in Canada, June 1968.

16. Brief submitted by the CSN to the Royal Commission on the Status of Women in Canada, June 1968, 18.

17. If there is a post that has traditionally been allocated to women, whether at an intermediate or lower level, it is surely that of secretary.

18. The acronyms stand for, respectively, la Corporation des instituteurs et institutrices catholiques and la Corporation des enseignants du Québec, later la Centrale des enseignants du Québec.

19. This committee held its sessions at the same time as other committees. The participants were thus for the most part women and it was not therefore possible to sensitize all the delegates to these problems.

20. *Travailleuses et syndiquées*, FTQ, congrès 1973, rapport du comité FTQ sur la situation de la femme (Montreal, 1973).

21. SCFP is the union, within the FTQ, in which women are most numerous: 30 000 members of whom 13 000 are women (43 percent); 20 percent of the local officers are women; 2 out of the 10 members of the executive board of the provincial leadership are women; the full-time, permanent staff members are exclusively male. The figures are somewhat more encouraging in another union, the Union des employés de service. Eighty percent of the members are women; 15 of the 20 members of the general board are women; and there are 4 full-time, permanent female staff members out of a total of 20.

22. At the last conference, a woman (the first woman candidate ever) was defeated in the vice-presidential race. Some of her supporters had argued that "a woman is needed at the FTQ," a tactic that was denounced by some members of the women's study committee.

23. Data culled from Quebec statistics and the estimations of the union confederations enable us to make up the following table:

Total number of women employees:	35% of 2 100 000	735 000
Female union members:		
CSN-CSD	33% of 230 000	75 000
QFL	20% of 275 000	55 000
CEQ	66% of 70 000	45 000
CTF (not affiliated to the QFL)	25% of 125 000	30 000
Independent	25% of 100 000	25 000

Total: 230 000, a unionization rate of 30% for women and 45% for men.

24. Patricia Marchak, "Women Workers and White-Collar Unions," *La Revue canadienne de sociologie et d'anthropologie* 10, 2 (mai 1973). In this article, the author suggests that those female office or clerical employees who are not unionized are more interested in becoming unionized than their male counterparts. On the other hand, among unionized office and clerical employees, men are more satisfied with their union status than women. This can be explained on two counts. On the one hand, the income gap between the

sexes is wider than the income gap between unionized and non-unionized employees. On the other hand, unionization seems to have resulted in the institutionalization, rather than the abolition, of inequalities between men and women.

25. This section is inspired by the conclusions of the author's thesis.

26. These relations have not been confirmed statistically.

27. The figures used cover the period from 1964 to 1970.

28. These are union members who are not official delegates of their unions.

29. Data relative to the unions affiliated to the FTQ tend to corroborate this trend of underrepresentation of women among the permanent, full-time staff members.

30. Although I do not wish to assume this as a hypothesis, I cannot help noticing a phenomenon regarding women's militancy. Among women workers, it is the so-called "career women workers," those who are thirty-five or forty years of age or older, who are most militant; the younger ones either have children to look after, and thus have little free time, or consider their work as essentially transitory, temporary, or not very rewarding, and are therefore not interested in the union. Among the white-collar workers (hospitals, offices), however, the young women who are under thirty are just as militant as their elders, if not more so.

31. See Renée Geoffroy and Paule Sainte-Marie, *Le Travailleur syndiqué face au travail rémunéré de la femme*, study no. 9, prepared for the Royal Commission of Inquiry on the Status of Women in Canada (Ottawa: Information Canada, 1971).

32. The use of women as part-time workers (business, secretarial help, etc.) is a phenomenon that should be dealt with in the context of occupational ghettoization.

33. If nowadays women are to be found within the ranks of typesetters (FTQ), it is not on account of the union but rather because of the employers who hired women to work for lower wages in non-unionized workshops. Women were incorporated into the union when these shops became unionized. The hiring of women came in the wake of significant technological changes and the introduction of new machines that are operated more or less like typewriters. This does not prevent the operators of these machines from falling under the authority of the typesetters' union.

34. Brief submitted by the CSN to the Royal Commission of Inquiry on the Status of Women in Canada (Bird).

35. Brief submitted by the FTQ to the Royal Commission of Inquiry on the Status of Women in Canada (Bird).

36. Especially against the association of shorter working hours with the presence of women in the labour market.

SECTION 4

QUEBEC VERSUS OTTAWA: THE STRUGGLE FOR EQUALITY

At the heart of the "Quiet Revolution" was the neo-nationalists' determination to achieve political equality for the French-Canadian majority of Quebec. This struggle began in the mid-1950s with the publication of the Tremblay Report. Its traditionally nationalist commissioners called upon Quebec's political leaders to seek either the devolution of significant taxing and social powers to all the provinces or, failing agreement on this objective, the devolution of such powers to the province of Quebec, which comprised the homeland of the French-Canadian nationality. The intentions of the Tremblay commissioners were fundamentally conservative in that they wanted to prevent the imposition of the new social-welfare state, which was being elaborated by a new generation of English-Canadian nationalists in Ottawa, on the French-Canadian Catholic society of Quebec.

Neo-nationalists at *Le Devoir* and in the Liberal Party supported the constitutional objectives of the Tremblay Report but for very different reasons. They wanted to use the enhanced powers of the province of Quebec to create a Francophone-inspired and administered welfare state in Quebec. The Lesage administration, during its first four years in office, made some headway in what was to become a prolonged and bitter struggle for political equality for the Francophone majority of Quebec. Quebec retained complete control over the funding of its universities and opted-out of many of Ottawa's shared-cost programs in return for increased direct taxing powers. Quebec also managed to maintain control over its own pension scheme. Encouraged by these gains, neo-nationalists effectively pressured the Lesage government to reject the Fulton-Favreau amendment formula until enhanced power for Quebec had been entrenched in a renewed constitution.

By 1965, once Ottawa's politicians, reinforced by the newly-elected "Three Wise Men," Trudeau, Pelletier, and Marchand, realized that Quebec's appetite for new powers was insatiable, they decided to adopt a hard line. Ottawa's counter-offensive prompted René Lévesque and others to leave the Quebec Liberal Party and to create the Parti Québécois, a party committed to the achievement of sovereignty-association for Quebec. Under Daniel Johnson, Quebec sought increased status by pursuing a greater role in international affairs through a wide range of cultural and technical exchange programs with other Francophone countries. Once again, Ottawa intervened successfully in order to reassert its prerogative to speak and negotiate on behalf of all Canadians in international affairs.

When the Liberals, under the youthful leadership of Robert Bourassa, returned to office in 1970 they faced the rising tide of neo-nationalism symbolized, in part, by the Parti Québécois, which had garnered twenty-four percent of the popular vote but only a handful of seats in the National Assembly. Once again, the premier of the province of Quebec was pressured to reject a complex package of constitutional reforms referred to as the Victoria Charter, agreed to in 1971 by Ottawa and the other provinces after prolonged negotiations. Ottawa was prompted to reopen the constitutional question after the election of the Parti Québécois in November 1976. The PQ delayed its promised referendum hoping that the Trudeau government would be replaced by a Tory government more clearly identified with Canada's English-speaking majority. When Trudeau agreed to return as Liberal leader after the defeat of Joe Clark's minority Conservative government, it was with the intention of resolving the constitutional question. The defeat of the Parti Québécois in the referendum of 1980 gave Ottawa the opportunity to act. Trudeau decided to forge ahead unilaterally with a package that included patriation of a Canadianized BNA Act, an amendment formula, and an entrenched Charter of Rights. A coalition of opposition forces, which included seven of the provinces, the national Conservative Party, and women's and native movements, all aided by the intervention of the Supreme Court, forced Trudeau to negotiate significant changes to his package. The new accord was signed by Ottawa and all the provinces except Quebec. Ironically, a process of constitutional renewal, inaugurated by the neo-nationalists in the late 1950s, ended abruptly in 1982 with the exclusion of Quebec from the new accord, which, in some respects, constituted a diminution of the traditional constitutional prerogatives of Quebec.

Gérard Bergeron, a political scientist, demonstrates in "The Québécois State Under Canadian Federalism" how, at every stage in the constitutional debate between 1960 and 1976, Quebec's pursuit of political equality was thwarted effectively by a recalcitrant Ottawa and Anglophone premiers who supported Quebec only to the extent that the powers of their respective provinces were also enhanced. In "Quebec and Canadian Federalism," Claude Morin attempts to demonstrate how the federal system not only prevents the Québécois from being masters over their own affairs but contributes to their ever-expanding dependency upon foreign political, economic, and cultural powers over which they can exercise little or no control. Gil Rémillard, now the minister of intergovernmental affairs in the new Liberal government in Quebec, sets out in some detail the conditions under which Quebec might conceivably sign the Constitution Act of 1982. It will be interesting to see if he can meet his own challenge.

THE QUÉBÉCOIS STATE UNDER CANADIAN FEDERALISM†

GÉRARD BERGERON

A complete history of the relations between the Quebec government and the central power of the Canadian federal state would be distressingly monotonous without the occasional dramatic episode, which the media of the day exaggerate. These crises have been settled as much by historical delays as by structural and partial arrangements; however, the usual situation of underlying crisis or general uneasiness has tended to be self-perpetuating. The resolutions of tension involving the Quebec governments of the past quarter-century have all headed in the same direction: affirmation of the place and role of the Quebec state in the Canadian federal system.

— The Duplessis government's 1954 provincial legislation on personal income tax radically revised the wartime fiscal arrangements — nearly a constitutional *coup d'état*.

— The Lesage government in 1964 decided to set up the Quebec Pension Plan and in 1965 refused to accept the Fulton-Favreau formula for repatriating the Constitution.

— Daniel Johnson, in 1967, made an impassioned presentation of the viewpoint of *"Egalité ou Indépendance"* at the interprovincial Confederation of Tomorrow Conference, then sharply and candidly debated with Mr. Trudeau, then minister of justice, in front of the cameras at the nationally televised constitutional conference in February 1968.

— The Bourassa government, in June 1971, ultimately rejected the Victoria Charter on the Constitution after four years of hard work on constitutional revisions.

But the most "dramatic" of these events, and the most portentous, was the Parti Québécois' foreseeable yet unforeseen taking of power on 15 November

†"L'État du Québec sous le fédéralisme canadien," in *L'État de Québec en devenir*, edited by Gérard Bergeron and Réjean Pelletier (Montreal: Boréal Express, 1980). Translated by Denis Bousquet.

1976. This date marks more than just an episode: it represents the beginning of one era and the end of another. Since then, everything federal has been called into question, beginning with the principle of federalism itself.

The aim of this necessarily condensed chapter is to relate the evolution of attempts by successive Quebec governments to improve their constitutional position within the federal structure, where they have felt restricted and uneasy, and which they have sought to reform radically. It is not so much — or, at least, not immediately — a matter of the *social* dynamic in the Quebec state. It is an *intergovernmental* matter of the Quebec state in the Canadian federal structure. It is a question of the system's environment, or even "confinement"; a problem of the mutual maladjustment of the province in the federal state; a calling into question of conditions that have become less and less acceptable to the other party to the point of breakdown. During the last twenty years, enormous social and cultural energy has been spent on this uneven intergovernmental feud with a power that is both central and "external" but not "foreign." It has therefore been an ambiguous and asymmetrical feud of which the people of Quebec, before the referendum, were more witness and object than prime mover. This feud has itself been the locus and source of the ambiguity, which seems to be its nature.

The social dynamic of the Quebec state has many components: since the inception of the Quiet Revolution, the federal-provincial dimension has been its most striking external manifestation, considered by Ottawa and the other provincial governments to be the most threatening. And, without doubt after the Quebec referendum, the federal-provincial dimension has remained the most immediately decisive, possibly even the most crucial, element affecting the internal social dynamic itself.

The Shaking of Federalism

What came to be called the Quiet Revolution was also seen as a series of assaults on the workings of the Canadian federal system, which was about to be shaken more than ever before in its history. Under Jean Lesage, the Liberal Party of Quebec presented itself as the party of positive autonomy, as opposed to Duplessis' negative "defending our own." Furthering predecessor Georges-Émile Lapalme's favourite theme of "positive autonomy," the new Liberal leader declared in 1959, "Under our government, autonomy will be the vision of our people."

Besides the now-obsolete term "autonomy," two of the three concepts over which constitutional confrontations still occur were alluded to by the Quebec government as early as the July 1960 federal-provincial conference: "repatriation" and "sovereignty" (of Quebec). (The third concept, "association," first appeared in René Lévesque's *Option Québec* in 1967 and has not left the constitutional vocabulary.) In fact, three weeks after appointing his cabinet, Premier Lesage set out for Ottawa to present his new government's constitutional point of view. Manoeuvring with, but not forgetting, the topic at hand, regaining taxing powers, he presented ideas for the Constitution that had already been articulated: the proposal to include in the constitution a declaration of human rights and a constitutional court "conforming to the principle of a federal system" as well as the proposal to establish a permanent federal-provincial secretariat, pending the resumption at the end of 1960 of interprovincial conferences, which had not been held since 1926.

Such language had not been heard from Quebec delegations at past federal-provincial conferences. In the same sentence, the plan for "repatriation" was emphasized by a call for "federal and provincial sovereignty."[1] Indeed, "a sovereignty that, without effort, confines itself to opposition can survive only temporarily"; moreover, if "the sovereignty of Quebec recognizes the needs and realities of interdependence, it obviates dependence." Obviously one must make allowance for the rhetorical bombast of the moment and perhaps extend this observation to Mr. Bourassa's "cultural sovereignty" and to the poorly defined concept of "sovereignty-association"; but the persistence of the topic of sovereignty, ambiguous, to say the least, in a federal system, takes on a great deal of meaning with the recall of this early usage. These elevated deliberations did not obscure the more pragmatic worries over tax dollars, which, in the view of the Quebec delegates, were too scarce and, worse, subject to conditions set by the federal government. The Quebec delegates also took a clear stand against the general policy on subsidies and shared-cost programs that encroached on provincial jurisdiction. They also served notice that provisional arrangements would soon be challenged.

The Quebec government was no longer content to claim its autonomy (or its "sovereignty"); it assumed its autonomy. By establishing new ministries, it took over responsibilities and jurisdictions that the federal government could not then easily occupy: hence the risk which was to materialize, of new conflicts. It reaffirmed jurisdiction over natural resources at the October 1961 conference on "Resources and Our Future" and went so far as to refuse to participate five months later in a federal-provincial conference that established a national electrical grid.

The first Lesage government also took the initiative in two great rediscoveries: the mother country overseas and the other provinces at home. The opening of Quebec's General Delegation in Paris in October 1961 was an occasion for lavish receptions; it showed a profound desire to renew ties with genealogical and cultural origins; at the same time, the occasion introduced Quebec into the international French-speaking world.

It is known now that the resumption of interprovincial conferences, which were expected to take place annually, did not have a major impact on the Constitution. However, at the conference the new Lesage government demonstrated its interest by asserting (as early as 1960), "The provinces are no longer submissive to the federal government. They have now reached maturity and their relations with Ottawa are based on equality." This was not quite Mr. Johnson's "*Egalité ou Indépendance*," but the first word of his slogan was in. For that matter, the participants were careful not to "gang up" against Ottawa; however, several premiers shared Quebec's view that it was natural at these conferences to discuss the federal-provincial issues of repatriation and amendment methods as well as, in a general way, the functioning of federalism. But they did carefully avoid making policy decisions. The participants deferred the idea of a permanent interprovincial secretariat and they were satisfied to be a "permanent, although informal, institution of Canadian federalism."[2] The organizer of the conference demonstrated great diplomacy by inviting representatives of the federal government; its official observer remained silent. The part played by Mr. Frost, Premier of Ontario and organizer of the 1962 conference in Charlottetown, suggested, with only slight exaggeration, a parallel with the Mercier-Mowatt alliance of 1887. While the nationalist press in Quebec tended noticeably to amplify the event and its possible consequences,[3] the English-Canadian press praised the spirit that moved the participants.[4] In short, the new Quebec government attracted attention on the interprovincial plane, which subsequently faded out.[5]

In the wake of the July 1960 federal-provincial conference, the first part of what was to become famous as the "Fulton-Favreau formula" was finalized. The Quebec government then proposed the resumption of discussions on repatriation and the amending formulas of the Constitution. The first draft of the "Fulton formula" finally emerged from a series of four conferences between Mr. Fulton (the federal minister of justice) and the provinical attorneys general. The formula provided for the unanimous consent of the provinces for all amendments likely to affect their areas of jurisdiction. The Quebec and Saskatchewan governments opposed this provision: Quebec, because the federal government failed to consider beforehand the restrictions placed on the province in the 1949 amendment on matters of constitutional reform; Saskatchewan, because of the right of veto provided for *all* provincial governments.[6] The repatriation and amendment formula, revised to become the Fulton-Favreau formula a few years later under the Pearson government, was rejected at the last minute by the Lesage government in 1965. The point to remember is that, as early as 1960–61, the Quebec government proved to be extremely careful not to deny its constitutional future — an unfailing constant to this day.

However, the new nationalism was in favour during this post-Duplessis period. It was a question no longer of "the province" or "the province of Quebec," but of "Quebec" or "the state of Quebec," expressions made popular wherever Jean Lesage spoke. The Rassemblement pour l'indépendance nationale (RIN) was formed in September 1960 in Montreal. A public conference held that autumn at Laval University had a resounding impact on public opinion.[7] The question of independence for Quebec was debated for the first time in the public arena. As one historian said, "The first term of the Lesage government achieved within a few months a modified political relationship between Quebec and Canada. Lesage had compelled constitutional discussion, renewed interprovincialism in Canada, and integrated reference to the French into Canadian politics."[8] During the second of the Lesage government, from 1962 to 1966, it would be realized that the Quiet Revolution was not quiet from the constitutional standpoint.

During those years, Quebec politics was especially fraught with emotion. Four major conflicts occurred between Quebec and Ottawa. Moreover, government initiatives were taken to allow study of the general malaise that was degenerating into crisis, with the view to devising corrective policies. In Quebec on 23 March 1963, the Legislative Assembly unanimously passed a resolution to establish a

Parliamentary Committee on the Constitution; in Ottawa, the Royal Commission on Bilingualism and Biculturalism was created shortly after Pearson's Liberal Party formed a minority government on 8 April 1963. Meanwhile, on 5 June 1964, after some internal squabbling amid party and government reorganization, the Liberal party of Quebec split from the provincial wing of the Liberal Party of Canada, which was proportionally weaker and which had been vacillating for the past year in its minority government position. About fifteen months later, three of Quebec's best-known opinion leaders (Jean Marchand, Gérard Pelletier, and Pierre Elliott Trudeau) joined the national Liberal Party "in order to defend federalism,"[9] as one of them said. All these actions must be interpreted against the backdrop of serious confrontations between the Liberal governments in Quebec and Ottawa.

After repeated demands over three years for better revenue-sharing arrangements, the Quebec premier resorted to an "ultimatum." In his budget speech of 5 April 1963, Lesage set one year as the deadline for agreement on a formula that allowed Quebec to collect twenty-five percent of personal income taxes and estate duties. His tone at the November 1963 federal-provincial conference was pressing, even threatening. After joking about "co-operative federalism, as they [in Ottawa] sometimes like to call it," the premier emphasized that "the way Confederation works ought to be reconsidered" and that "we shall even be called on to transform it, since reality will inevitably lead us to question it." He blamed "a framework designed for an obsolete situation." This charge received "nearly total denial" from federal officials: "We had the impression that they did not condescend to listen to us."

In these emotional circumstances, the pension plan issue flared up. One of the Pearson government's legislative priorities was a huge contributory and universal pension plan to provide a secure retirement income and to protect transient workers. Especially sensitive to whatever involved social security, the Quebec government flatly objected and even announced its intention to set up its own plan, not only to maintain this jurisdiction but also to have, eventually, at its disposal the public funds accumulated in the plan. A long and occasionally bitter debate between the two governments ensued.

The watchword was firmness for the federal negotiators at the opening of the federal-provincial conference in Quebec City on 31 March 1964. There was no question of yielding to Quebec's arguments on the family allowance plan or on withdrawing from shared-cost programs. For its part, the Quebec government boosted its retirement insurance plan along with a general increase in fiscal resources, the lack of which could have resulted in double taxation, for which the federal government would incur the public's wrath. After two days of extremely tense confrontation, Lester Pearson's genius for diplomacy inspired a compromise: Quebec could have its own pension plan, its demands concerning family allowances would be satisfied, and a committee would be set up to study all the problems resulting from the Canadian fiscal system. Some observers were alarmed by what appeared to be a sudden reversal of the federal course. Indeed, it was an important victory for the Quebec government, whose brief, moreover, was of exceptional quality.[10] Federal spokespersons saw this compromise as an example of "co-operative federalism," which could also be conciliatory, even if belatedly so.

The Quebec leaders seized the moment and reopened the debate on shared-cost programs. In most cases these programs had been drafted without consulting the provinces, therefore they could not take the provinces' priorities and special circumstances into account. It was an old story. In breaking with the strict policies for grants under the St-Laurent and Diefenbaker governments, the Pearson government was agreeable to allowing provinces to opt-out of shared-cost programs in return for financial compensation either in the form of a larger share of tax revenues or an increase in equalization payments to the have-not provinces. The application of this opting-out formula allowed the federal government to retain control over national standards, but at least Quebec, with increased fiscal resources, was in a better position to define the corresponding programs that it agreed to implement.

The most sensational bone of contention in the relationship between Quebec City and Ottawa was the issue of Quebec's external relations: whenever foreign states were involved, the disputes tended to make headlines. Lacking a department of external affairs, the Quebec government reached the point of using its newly created Departments of Education and Cultural Affairs to wage legal and diplomatic guerilla warfare on Ottawa's Department of External Affairs. Beyond the sensational aspect of these guerilla tactics and some comical incidents, what was involved was far from amateurish and was nothing less than the principle of sovereignty: in the current meaning of international rights and, from that point of view, the federal government's sovereignty is entrenched; in the interpretative meaning of federal constitutional rights, the sovereignty of Quebec is more questionable but not without grounds.[11] The years of the Liberal government's second term were highlighted by the sumptuous formality of new meetings between DeGaulle and Lesage in Paris in 1963 and 1964 as well as a series of joint France-Quebec initiatives, especially in the areas of culture and education. La Commission permanente de coopération franco-québécoise, established for this purpose, held its May 1965 meeting in Quebec City; since then, meetings have been held periodically.

Taken aback by the speed and cunning of the Quebec government, the federal government had no alternative but to appear as a good loser as long as the symbols of its international sovereignty were respected: first by ratifying the France-Quebec ententes (neither treaties nor agreements) of February 1964 and February 1965 by the exchange of notes between the French ambassador and the Department of External Affairs; subsequently, on a higher level, by a general agreement between the two countries to cover future ententes. These precautions, taken to safeguard Ottawa's honour and to respect Quebec's relative freedom to make agreements, did not prevent discord in the following years; but let us not anticipate events.

After the Quebec government came within a whisker (the premier himself urged it) of accepting the Fulton-Favreau formula on repatriation of the amendment formula for the Constitution, in the last months of his second term the Quebec premier postponed agreement "indefinitely."[12] The formula complemented and elaborated on the Fulton formula rejected at the end of 1961 and in early 1962 by the governments of Quebec and Saskatchewan, respectively. The circumstances of 1964 and 1965 seemed better: Prime Minister Pearson and his minister of justice, Guy Favreau, were particularly well disposed to take Quebec's requirements into consideration. Laboriously negotiated at the federal-provincial and interprovincial conferences of 1964, the new formula restricted the federal government's authority to change the Constitution in accordance with the amendment agreed to in London in 1949, thereby erasing the major objection raised by Quebec in 1961. Further, the old formula stipulated that unanimity of the eleven governments would be required for issues involving the so-called fundamental sectors;[13] for other powers, a two-thirds majority of the provinces provided for two-way "delegation of legislative powers," from the federal government to the provinces and vice versa.[14] For the first time since 1927 an attempt at repatriation was on the way to succeeding.

The Pearson government soon had to lower its sights. In the Commons, John Diefenbaker found the formula contrary to the spirit of the Fulton formula of 1961. New Democrat Andrew Brewin denounced the replacement of a "colonial relic" with a "straitjacket." Jurist Bora Laskin, a future chief justice of the Supreme Court, opined that the formula was "a complete constitutional disaster."[15] In the Quebec Legislative Assembly, the debate grew severely confused over the Lesage government's determination to limit the power of the Legislative Council, which was dominated by Union Nationale appointees. Opposition leader Daniel Johnson stood firmly against the proposed formula: he went so far as to accuse the premier and his colleague Paul Gérin-Lajoie of treason. While the premier held that "nothing prevents Quebec from achieving a particular status," the leader of the Union Nationale argued exactly the opposite. Nationalist groups and students' associations protested vigorously and organized special meetings. Two men who later took opposite sides, Jacques-Yvan Morin and Claude Ryan, denounced the compromise, which Quebec could not decently accept: repatriation, as a question of process should follow the questions of the redefinition of Quebec's status and the protection of minorities.

Jean Lesage argued vehemently against the flood of protest: repatriation was a prerequisite to constitutional change; the proposed formula maintained Quebec's power to unilaterally amend its own constitution; and "Quebec had a right to veto not only on its own constitutional evolution but also on that of Canada as a whole." Two of his most nationalistic ministers, René Lévesque and Pierre Laporte, were called in to rescue the premier, but they were booed by an audience of students in Montreal. The strong government of the Quiet Revolution was being shaken and divided, the opposition was gaining ground, and public opinion was being stirred up more and more. Jean Lesage had to yield. In January 1966, he replied to Prime Minister Pearson that the Quebec government had to postpone indefinitely the consideration of the proposed constitutional amendment. After the unsuccessful attempt of 1960–61, this failure was felt with consternation in Ottawa and some provincial capitals. It signified the defeat of the strongest nationalist government that had been seen in Quebec; paradoxically, it was also a personal defeat for Jean Lesage, to whom his former mentor, Lester Pearson, had hinted that he had a chance to succeed Pearson as leader of the Liberal Party of Canada.

This controversy had triggered an enormous nationalist turmoil over the constitutional future of Quebec; it was not to be hindered by a new and completely

"Canadian" Constitution. A man and a party who had tried for five years to move left toward the nationalist faction took advantage of the situation: Daniel Johnson and the Union Nationale.

Defeat of the Attempts at Renewal

By the time the Union Nationale recaptured power in June 1966, it had become commonplace to refer to the chronic crisis of the Canadian Constitution. The previous year's preliminary report of the Royal Commission Inquiry into Bilingualism and Biculturalism mentioned this diagnosis: "At present Canada is passing, without always realizing it, through the major crisis of its history. . . . Everything goes on as if the circumstances set in 1867 and not seriously questioned since then were not rejected for the first time by the French Canadians of Quebec." During a less than triumphant tour of Western cities in September 1965, Jean Lesage repeated several explanations and warnings, one of which was a declaration of intent: "We want the equality of the two groups that founded this country. . . ."[16] Another was this earnest plea for history's judgment: "If ever Confederation collapses, it will not be because Quebec, the native land of French-Canadians, will have separated. It will be because the means of keeping Quebec in the fold will not have been found."

Even though the Quiet Revolution had started to falter fifteen months earlier, its course was nearly impossible for the Union Nationale government to reverse. It was even less possible to retreat from the previous government's strongly autonomist positions because, through electoral alchemy, the new government probably owed its unexpected victory to the *indépendantiste* vote.[17] Before that, had come the remarkable success of the Union Nationale's meetings in March 1965 at the first convention in the party's history. Further, the bitter struggle waged by Daniel Johnson against the Fulton-Favreau formula had won him the reputation as a strong and shrewd defender of the future rights of the state of Quebec.

The new premier's constitutional doctrine was contained in a booklet bearing the pompous and ambiguous title *Egalité ou Indépendance*. In the various meetings that followed, the governments of Johnson and then Bertrand tended to promote a special status for Quebec and recognition for the equality of the collective rights of Canadians of both languages. The Liberals, who disposed of René Lévesque's *Option Québec* fairly quickly at their 1967 convention, also proposed the special status option in the report of the committee on constitutional affairs (called the *Rapport Gérin-Lajoie*) in order to decisively defeat Lévesque's *Option*. The report has been consigned to obscurity.

For the sake of completeness, at this point it should be possible to analyse events as diverse as the visit of General de Gaulle, whose famous words reached around the world; René Lévesque's departure from the Liberal Party, which has been called "a fact fraught with future"; the publication of the first volume of the so-called B and B Commission; the five years of deliberations by the Parliamentary Committee on the Constitution, whose work and status were vague; and the huge organization of the États généraux du Canada français, with its preliminary meetings in 1967 and 1969. All these events contributed to general constitutional debate and promoted the various "options" presented to the people of Quebec.

The festivities of the centennial celebration and the cosmopolitan exhibition at Expo 67 provided euphoric diversion during a wonderful summer, shaken only by one thunderbolt — "*Vive le Québec libre!*" Serious issues returned with autumn. The wind carried solemnity and a sense of responsibility tinged with optimism. First, the provinces met without the federal government, which had opportunely refused to participate.[18] Premier John Robarts of Ontario had initiated this Confederation of Tomorrow Conference. It was specifically convened to discuss the federal system. To match this initiative, the Pearson government convened a federal-provincial conference on the Constitution in February 1968; its deliberations assigned to various levels over three years culminated in the sinking of the Victoria Charter by a belated but definitive "no" from the Quebec government.

The premier of Ontario had clearly identified the objectives of his interprovincial conference: (1) the place and role of Quebec in Confederation and of French Canadians in federal institutions, along with the protection of French-speaking minorities outside Quebec, and (2) the examination of the existing functioning of federalism at its two levels so that it would not hinder a society of two languages and regional diversity. But Quebec's position went much further: in a document entitled *Exposé préliminaire* and tabled at the beginning of the conference, Premier Johnson developed the concept of a dual Canada and the urgency of a completely new Constitution. His general program contained thirty fundamental propositions that amounted to a new division of powers. No one was willing to undertake a task of that magnitude. One group of premiers listened more intently than the others to the presentation of Quebec's point of view: the group consisted of the premiers of Ontario, New Brunswick, and Nova Scotia. The opposite group consisted of the premiers of Saskatchewan, Alberta, British Columbia, and Newfoundland. The premiers of Manitoba and Prince Edward Island were slightly more understanding on some points. So much for the overall picture; on the details of various points, many other alignments could be seen.

At the time of what journalists dubbed "the escalation of separatism" during the autumn of 1967, Daniel Johnson told his fellow premiers of his fears: "The acts, these constitutional processes, along with a certain cast of mind have had the effect of sealing the French-speaking into the province of Quebec. Unless we are rid of this ghetto complex, no declaration, no wish, no request by any politician can check the course of events."[19] The premier was the central figure at the conference: with his sincerity and charming personality he managed to dissipate much of the apprehension created by his disturbing *Egalité ou Indépendance* slogan. He portrayed himself as mandated to gain, point by point, equal status for the French-Canadian nation, not to attain independence. The initial euphoria of goodwill paved the way for raised consciousnesses of responsibilities before engaging in the next round of federal-provincial constitutional conferences. The experience suggested some form of group dynamics for heads of government at the same level, without a higher-level mentor, in preparation for the decision-making process of constitutional organization.

Peter Newman may have passed the soundest judgment on the somewhat fluid results of such a meeting: "It will no longer be possible for very long to equate Canada with Confederation as we now know it."[20] The comments from the Anglophones varied from the measured optimism of John Bird, who referred to a "conference on reconfederation,"[21] to the cutting irony of Leslie Roberts, who described it as "the great Centennial non-event."[22] But as never before, a premier of Quebec expressed in a nationally televised speech the scale of Quebec's political culture and the direct continuity from the past to the imperatives of the future. Within a few days, he had mitigated the distrust caused by the verbal excesses of the opposition leader, which Johnson had been shortly before. With the support of his only French-speaking colleague, Premier Robichaud of New Brunswick, who urged the other participants to understand Johnson's touchingly difficult situation, Premier Johnson sounded the alarm of the national emergency: "The French-Canadian population will not wait as long as before. We are patient, yes, but with the means of communication, things move more quickly in Quebec. This is not an ultimatum. There is no blackmail possible with English Canadians, just as there is none with French Canadians. But we will not wait ten years."[23]

Despite elements of dissatisfaction — for everyone — the Confederation of Tomorrow Conference was a useful preface to the systematic work on the revision of the Constitution that would soon be undertaken by the Canadian government. The other favourable factor was the publication of the B and B Commission's report; it was difficult for the federal government to ignore the principles underlying the Commission's recommendations. The work of constitutional reform was to last close to four years, only to end with the Quebec government's rejection. What was to be called the Victoria Charter contained the starting point for the eventual new Constitution. It consisted of an assortment of diverse proposals that had not been worked out in one hundred years of constitutional history. At the beginning, the federal government recommended as a preliminary step the drafting, by itself, of a declaration of the fundamental rights of Canadians. At the insistence of the Quebec government, this point was to be "studied in the context of an overall examination of the Constitution"; at the insistence of the Nova Scotia government, regional disparities were also to be examined. The federal government acquiesced. Such an expansion of the agenda required a complex organization of the working mechanism and the allotment of a long period to finish the studies.

The study of the results of the work and negotiations at various stages would be the subject of a long and winding tale, too ponderous to be told here. The examination of the working mechanisms of constitutional revision would be an interesting case of technical analysis of a special category, quasi-constituent, of negotiations. It will at least be remembered that the centrepiece consisted of the seven federal-provincial conferences between February 1968 and June 1971 — four public sessions televised at least in part and three closed-door sessions. Occasionally, as they saw fit, the premiers talked in private without their experts. The "permanence of the revision" was secured by the Permanent Committee of officials who held fourteen sessions and who could specialize their tasks in subcommittees (fundamental rights, official conferences, sales tax, and estate duties). In addition, seven departmental committees were formed to investigate a corresponding number of areas of activity,[24] but they did not seem to have the importance of the Permanent Committee, which was the real hub of the work.

The setting in motion of these mechanisms at various levels showed a firm desire to succeed, which endured through changes in government and personnel turnover. Nineteen heads of government participated in the conferences, but only four attended all the sessions. Four provinces changed governments during this period. Pierre Elliott Trudeau, who became prime minister in April 1968, chaired all the federal-provincial conferences except the first one in February 1968, which Lester Pearson presided over and to which he delivered an impassioned and partly prophetic declaration of policy principles. The Quebec government was represented successively by premiers Johnson, Bertrand, and Bourassa.

The Victoria Charter was a composite of diverse provisions, most of which had been agreed to in principle with great difficulty. Provisions concerned an updating of the wording of amendments to section 94(a) (control of social policy) of the British North America Act, the withdrawal of the rights of reserve and disavowal, fundamental rights (political and linguistic), the organization of the Supreme Court and federal courts, processes dealing with regional disparities, and finally the federal government's consultation procedures with the provinces on these issues. This mixture of sixty-one clauses listed under ten headings was to be dealt with as a whole — a package deal — at Prime Minister Trudeau's insistence. With approval by the eleven governments before the deadline of 28 June 1971, it would then be possible to proceed with the repatriation of the Constitution, following which the revision process could be started.

The amendment formula in the Victoria Charter was called the Trudeau-Turner formula, which was substantially different from the obsolete Fulton-Favreau formula. The Trudeau-Turner formula specified that the majority be made up of a province with twenty-five percent of the population of Canada (Ontario and Quebec), at least two Atlantic provinces, and at least two Western provinces with at least fifty percent of the population of the region. This was a refinement of the Fulton-Favreau formula, which had improved on the Fulton formula.

The ensuing battle in Quebec over the Victoria Charter was fought on much wider ground than just the clause that revised the formula for a majority vote, even though it provided Quebec and Ontario with a veto. The major objection was obviously over Quebec's basic right not to abdicate its constitutional power before the redistribution of powers was carried out. The limited objective espoused in this campaign to refuse to ratify the Charter was the strongly held contention that the Quebec government's jurisdiction over all social policy must be recognized. And the addition of sections on social matters to the Charter, accidental in a way,[25] allowed Quebec to reject the entire document: in short, a procedural Cleopatra's nose . . . .

The public opinion campaign against acceptance of the Charter was shorter (because of the short time prescribed) and more hectic than the campaign that had forced Jean Lesage to defer "indefinitely" the consideration of the Fulton-Favreau formula. The same opinion leaders as those of the Fulton-Favreau formula years expressed their views: Jacques-Yvan Morin, Claude Ryan, Marcel

Faribault. A common front of opposition was organized, protest meetings were held, and petitions were circulated. The three opposition parties unanimously supported rejection. The Bourassa cabinet was divided, but the strongest ministers argued for a negative response. On the one hand, there existed the obligation of respecting the requirement, unfailingly advocated by Quebec premiers, to redistribute powers before repatriation; on the other hand, *indépendantistes* were not to be provided with polemics because of political uneasiness a few months after the October Crisis of 1970. Most criticism focussed on the heavy-handedness of the take-it-or-leave-it package deal that seemed unnecessarily like an ultimatum. Since a satisfactory resolution of the key social-policy issue had been denied, the chances of a new Constitution suitable for Quebec had diminished. The announcement of Premier Bourassa's negative response was formulated to be sober and moderate.

> This [negative] decision stems from the existing necessity of agreeing as much as possible on clear and accurate constitutional clauses in order not to transfer to the judiciary a responsibility that is primarily a political one — that is, a responsibility of the elected representatives of the people. Thus, the clauses dealing with income security allow some uncertainty, which is incompatible with the objectives inherent in any concept of constitutional revision. If this uncertainty were removed, our decision could be different.

What Marcel Faribault called a "gigantic bluff" had ultimately failed.[26] The prime minister's inflexible policy had been harshly denounced. The more undecided but forseeable[27] stand by Premier Bourassa, who had that February subscribed to an agreement in principle but had eventually changed his mind, was finally praised by all "for understanding and expressing the voice of his people at the decisive moment."[28] However, his attitude was criticized throughout English Canada: from its utterly different perspective, and with the information available, it had collectively misunderstood his rejection! After this rejection at the last minute, like that of the Fulton-Favreau formula, many English-speaking circles gave credence to the notion that a premier of Quebec could not be counted on to impose on his legislature and a vigilant public whatever agreements he had made at the bargaining table.

Without doubt, analyses of method at this time are more valid than criticism of the men involved. For example: "M. Trudeau and M. Bourassa moved as far apart and even as close together as they could, against all the others. Yet they could not be reconciled because the reasoning behind their respective responsibilities is incompatible."[29] Or, "The failure of the Victoria agreement rests not only with the Quebec government but also with all the heads of government who stood solidly behind the senseless procedure to which Quebec alone had the courage to say 'no' . . . . When English Canada admits that no miracle worker exists to deliver Quebec on a silver platter, the real discussions can begin. Then they will be more fruitful."[30] In his own way and in more clear-cut circumstances, a Quebec premier, in this representative role, had illustrated Daniel Johnson's prophetic announcement to Pierre Elliott Trudeau: "Even if I disappeared tomorrow morning, my successor at the bargaining table, if he were premier of Quebec, would speak the same language."[31]

Final Efforts at Revival

When a government cannot make a decision on a large issue that is liable to question the foundation of the state's organization, it is always possible to recommend an in-depth study that is also a noble diversion, in the form of a royal commission inquiry such as the Rowell-Sirois, Massey-Lévesque, Laurendeau-Dunton commissions in Canada and the Tremblay, Parent, Gendron, Castonguay-Nepveu commissions in Quebec. When a government encounters an impasse or is unable to take or think of action and if, as well, it must demonstrate interest, it can find a makeshift solution by establishing a special parliamentary commission, which is less impressive than a royal commission and no more binding, yet still convenient to use for the official good conscience.

That is what happened with the Parliamentary Committee on the Constitution of Quebec, which, after five years of sporadic and almost secret activity, disappeared without leaving behind a report and hardly any other trace. It happened with the Special Joint Committee of the Senate and House of Commons on the Constitution between 1970 and 1972 and in 1978. As an intermediate solution between commissions of inquiry and parliamentary committees, it is always permissible to set up a special working group, the task force, which can extend a hearty welcome to all sorts of proposals that come from outside and are suitable for updating the facts of a problem that goes round in a circle. In Ottawa, the Task Force on Canadian Unity, also called the Pepin-Robarts Commission (or Task Force), was one of them.

In all these cases, the government of the day maintained total freedom to decide what to retain from the submissions. Since not all conclusions are equally suitable, the government selected whatever fit the general course of its policies and could be put into practice without too much risk. By and large, the result has not been useless, since many people have been put to work or have been listening. Usually time has not been gained, but it has at least been occupied. But, as a rule, it has been spent to such an extent that, when proposals and recommendations are made public, they are outdated by new events about which the government has already reached a decision or taken a different stand. But at least studies are carried out and testimony is given that would not be aired otherwise. For the sake of consultative democracy, it is good that the "general public" can interact with the "parliamentary caucus"; they must appear to communicate with each other.

As a trained constitutionalist, Pierre Elliott Trudeau has safeguarded above all things the principle that constitutions should be tampered with as little and as late as possible. Shortly after his arrival in the House of Commons, Trudeau, then the prime minister's parliamentary secretary, said that he could not understand why some members of the House should be "fascinated" by the "notion of a joint parliamentary committee for discussing constitutional problems here" (after the fashion of the Parliamentary Committee on the Constitution of Quebec). After demonstrating with a triple-exclusion dialectic[32] the uselessness of such a task, he concluded that "this idea is essentially the idea of an emergent middle class that wants to change the rules of the game without concern for fundamental needs."[33] Four years later, having been minister of justice and then, for a longer time, as prime minister, sponsored the hard work that was to lead to the failure of the Victoria Charter on the Constitution, he finally agreed to the establishment of the Special Joint Committee of the Senate and the House of Commons on the Constitution. But, like everyone else, he did not have high hopes for the eventual usefulness of the results of the committee's work. It can even be assumed that, as head of the federal government, he personally had little inclination to be swayed by it.

The Joint Committee consisted of ten senators and twenty MPs. Under the chairmanship of Senator Molgat and MP Mark MacGuigan, it tabled its report in Parliament on 16 March 1972, two years after its creation. It was close to a year after the Quebec government had rejected the Victoria Charter; the committee had not been able to finalize a preliminary report before the decisive meetings of February and June 1971. The work of the committee progressed as if it were operating in isolation from the main federal-provincial constitutional negotiations; by the time the committee bore its fruit in the form of an elaborate report, the question had been "frozen" following the impasse that ended four years of intensive intergovernmental work on constitutional issues. Even though the report did not provoke any general debate in the House after publication, it is useful to look over its contents. The extent of the work achieved in 145 meetings is also noteworthy; half of those meetings were held in 47 different communities in Canada; hearings and written statements ran into the hundreds, attendance was outstanding, and the work was intensive.

In the matter of federal institutions (the Governor General, the Senate, and the Supreme Court), the joint committee did not produce much innovation; it took into account the reforms that had already been widely advocated for some time, such as the appointment of the justices of the Supreme Court generally in accordance with the Victoria Charter. The committee embraced the same conservatism over the matter of dividing the powers between the two levels of government; it stressed the necessity of "continuing to use the lists of exclusive federal and provincial powers" but also increasing "the list of common powers" (Recommendation 49). Regarding the latter powers, "issues mainly of national interest should be deferred to the federal government; those of primarily provincial interest, to provincial legislative assemblies" (Recommendation 50). Proposals on the power of taxation as well as the federal power over expenditures and shared-cost programs were restricted to the means of preventing possible uses by the federal government (Recommendations 54–57). Nothing of the foregoing was earth shattering. One group, recruited from the two legislative houses and composed of members from all political parties, clearly indicated its intention to reach a difficult consensus on the ways to remedy some ills, such as the institutionalization of federal-provincial relations,[34] but without weakening the authority essential to the federal government.

The hottest topic, self-determination for Quebec, defied consensus. This result was a sign of the times: the joint committee could not avoid mentioning, but in extremely cautious terms: "The preamble to the Constitution should acknowledge . . . that the existence of Canadian society depends on the free consent of citizens and on the common will to live together; any difference between them should be settled through peaceful means" (Recommendation 6). But, "if at a given time the citizens of one part of Canada declare democratically in favour of a historical policy that would be opposed to the retention of the existing regime, that difference should be settled through political negotiations, not recourse to military force or any other form of coercion" (Recommendation 7). This was, without doubt, the best that could be achieved, given an organization of that nature, of that composition, in that place. The principles were a minimum for only two members of the committee, Liberal MP Pierre de Bané and Conservative Senator Martial Asselin, who insisted in a minority report that the Constitution should contain formal recognition of Quebec's fundamental right to self-determination. These two parliamentarians also requested the recognition of a common principle for the distribution of powers in the federal system — that is, contrary to the Canadian Constitution, the exclusive powers would go to the federal government and the residual powers to the provinces, which would have to consent explicitly to any expansion of the federal government's areas of jurisdiction. The minority report was not mentioned in the committee's report; the committee refused to table the minority report in Parliament. In any case, for the first time in the history of Canadian politics, Quebec's right to self-determination had been debated freely and at length in the Canadian Parliament. At the right moment, will Recommendations 6 and 7 of the Special Joint Committee of the Senate and the House of Commons on the Constitution resurface?

During the two difficult years of minority government between 1972 and 1974, Prime Minister Trudeau took no major initiative on constitutional reforms. The report of the joint committee was left on the shelf. After receiving a comfortable majority in 1974, the prime minister prepared to launch a new offensive for repatriation, a project that appears to have been one of his two "great plans"; the other one was the recognition of the two official languages. It was the fourth time since 1961 and the tenth time in fifty years that an attempt was made to repatriate the Canadian Constitution. In April 1975, the prime minister obtained an "agreement in principle on the suitability of repatriating the Constitution" according to the amendment formula set down at the constitutional conference at Victoria. In other words, out of the ten headings in the constitutional charter, only nine with a bearing on the "modification of the Constitution" remained. This time, the governments of the Western provinces objected to the majority clause that affected them, namely, two provinces with fifty percent of the region's population. Their objections were satisfied. Further, some provincial governments insisted on the addition of the subjects of the Supreme Court and regional disparities to the formulas for repatriation and amendments that had been agreed to in Victoria. For his part, the premier of Quebec laid claim to constitutional guarantees for French language and culture.

On 5 March 1976, the prime minister met with the premier of Quebec in order to become acquainted with the latter's intentions before making another move. This tense interview[35] revealed that repatriation was not a priority for Quebec and that the nature of the guarantees that the Quebec government would insist on would determine the matter of the distribution of powers; this issue was to be excluded, according to the federal proposal. The same evening, in front of supporters of the Quebec wing of the federal Liberal Party, the prime minister, in an infuriated and sarcastic tone, tore apart the Bourassa government's policy concerning Bill 22 and the Constitution.[36]

Once more, in 1976, after 1961, 1965, and 1971, the Quebec government had halted the process of repatriating the Constitution. In his historic speech, Prime Minister Trudeau reiterated his intention to repatriate the Consitution unilaterally, if need be. "It is not only possible but perhaps desirable to act unilaterally. After 110 years of waiting . . . someone will have to summon up enough courage to go and get it!" One month later, he described in the House of Commons the three possible options for the unilateral process of repatriating the Constitution. Pierre Elliott Trudeau seemed determined to ignore Robert Bourassa's "nebulous theses of cultural sovereignty." Then he assembled a file for "the formal constitutional independence of the country."[37]

The unanimous response of the provinces was set down in Premier Lougheed's letter on behalf of his fellow premiers and made public on 14 October 1976. The provinces again raised the substance of several agreements in principle, assented to at the time of the Victoria Charter, in the areas of culture and communications, the federal government's powers over expenditures in areas of provincial jurisdiction, and the method of Supreme Court appointments. By thus asserting their rejection of unilateral repatriation, the provinces again pecked away at several provisions of the Victoria Charter and even raised new points, such as immigration policy and taxation of natural resources. The unanimity of the provinces, after the paralysing reluctance of the Bourassa government, reinforced the Trudeau government's will to proceed unilaterally to "the formal constitutional independence of the country." In Quebec's wake, the other provinces had extended a debate that could no longer go on.

The date is to be remembered: it all happened in October 1976, and, one month later. . . . The tale that had begun fifteen years earlier with Quebec's concern for repatriating the Canadian Constitution and ended with Quebec's fourth rejection of the proffered proposal is rather strange. And the country where these events took place along two conflicting imperatives has a constitutional regime that is also strange, to say the least.

Notes

1. ". . . that this conference decide to resume discussions on repatriation and the amendment formula of the Constitution in order to lift the major restrictions on federal and provincial sovereignty involved in the reversion to London."

2. According to Jean-Charles Bonenfant's phrase in "Les conférences interprovinciales," *L'Action catholique* (11 juillet 1966).

3. "A new force is born. It is not intended to oppose the power of Ottawa, but it will be able to neutralize it." Pierre Laporte, "La glace est brisée entre les provinces," *Le Devoir*, 5 décembre 1961.

4. "The heads of the provinces, prompted by the best intentions, have analysed the problems with more comprehension and harmony; they have created a climate of understanding that will be priceless for better revenue sharing and settling financial problems." *The Globe and Mail*, according to a survey of the press by *Le Soleil*, 12 décembre 1960.

5. On the possible role of interprovincial conferences in revising the Constitution, see chapters 23 to 27 of my book, *Incertitudes d'un certain pays* (Quebec: Les Presses de l'Université Laval (PUL), 1979).

6. Preference for the provision of a two-thirds majority and a special provision in the case of Quebec, the consent of which would be required for any matter affecting its property system and civil law.

7. See *Le Canada, expérience ratée . . . ou réussité?* (Quebec: PUL, 1961), an account of the first conference of the Institut des affaires canadiennes.

8. Jean-Louis Roy, *Le choix d'un pays: le débat constitutionnel Québec-Canada 1960–1976* (Montreal: Leméac, 1978). This book provides an indispensable reference for the subject at hand.

9. Pierre Elliott Trudeau, *Le fédéralisme et la société canadienne-française* (Montreal: HMH, 1967), v.

10. Estimated in some Ottawa circles even higher than the federal project. See Judy LaMarsh, *Memoirs of a Bird in a Gilded Cage* (Toronto: McClelland and Stewart, 1968), 126.

11. "Why would the state that implements an agreement not itself be able to negotiate and finalize it? Is not an agreement made for the essential purpose of being applied and are not those who will implement it responsible for its terms? . . . It can no longer be conceded . . . that the federal government can exercise a sort of surveillance and control of opportunity over the international relations of Quebec," argued Paul Gérin-Lajoie in a conference before the corps consulaire de Montréal (12 April 1966).

12. Which meant "without limit," as Jean Lesage would say later, on 4 February 1966.

13. The use of English or French, the law-making power of legislatures, and the rights and privileges guaranteed to legislatures by the Constitution.

14. In both cases, in consideration of the agreement by the four provinces.

15. Quoted by Jean-Louis Roy, *Le choix d'un pays*, 46.

16. Again the theme of equality . . . .

17. It is worth recalling the strange results: with nearly forty-seven percent of the popular vote, the Liberal Party had to cede power to the Union Nationale, which had received forty-one percent, its worst performance since 1944. It was believed at the time that the small margins of victory by Union Nationale candidates were made possible by the votes cast for the independentist parties, le Rassemblement national and le Rassemblement pour l'indépendance nationale; the latter parties received 9.3 percent of the vote in the metropolitan areas.

18. It was the first time that a province took the initiative of calling a federal-provincial conference. On the one hand, the Ontario government accepted the interprovincial character of the proposed conference; on the other, the federal government was compelled to call a federal-provincial conference on constitutional issues according to protocol and in the shortest possible time.

19. *La Presse*, 29 novembre 1967.

20. "Search for a consensus," *The Montreal Star* (27 Oct. 1967). A few days earlier, the paper said: "There is something slightly absurd in the fact that, after a century of Canadian existence, ten intelligent men have to meet to discuss the survival of their country." (*Montreal Star*, 25 Nov. 1967.)

21. *The Financial Post*, 2 Dec. 1967.

22. *The Montreal Star*, 2 Dec. 1967.

23. *La Presse*, 2 décembre 1967. These words take on particular resonance when they are read in 1980.

24. Fundamental rights, official languages, the Senate, judicial organization, the fiscal system, regional inequalities, and the National Capital Region.

25. Claude Morin, a veteran of that type of meeting in his capacity as deputy minister of intergovernmental affairs, narrates the incident: "Indeed, at one point during the conference, the Charter included no provision for social policy. It was the object of a separate document that was not acceptable to Quebec in any case. During a momentary hesitation, the premiers and their advisors wondered whether it would be preferable to combine the two documents into one. No one voiced a formal opinion and the matter was left hanging for a few seconds. Then suddenly some Quebec delegates proposed a single document. The suggestion was accepted at once. That is how the portion of the document dealing with social policy was included in the Victoria Charter. Seven days later, Quebec cited these passages to reject the Charter of which it was an integral part." *Le pouvoir québécois . . . en négociation* (Montreal: Boréal Express, 1972), 154.

26. "Il n'en tient qu'au Québec de tirer parti de sa position," *Le Devoir*, 26 juin 1971.

27. Premier Bourassa declared to the Parliamentary Committee on the Constitution on 27 May 1971: "I am not in a position to say if Quebec's reservation expressed in February will turn into a definite refusal. But clearly the anxiety voiced by Quebec in February remains."

28. Claude Ryan, "Le 'non' d'un gouvernement et d'un peuple," *Le Devoir*, 25 juin 1971.

29. Jean-Paul Desbiens, "La signification d'un non," *La Presse*, 23 juin 1971.

30. Claude Ryan, "Le 'non' d'un gouvernement et d'un peuple."

31. Quoted by Jean-Louis Roy, *La choix d'un pays*, 278.

32. "Either the Opposition or the Independentists have no thoughts on the Constitution and this committee can serve only to provide them with some and consequently this committee is no longer useful; or they have thoughts on the Constitution and they do not agree with the government and then again this committee is of no use; it can serve only as a forum to bring constitutional problems down to the level of political chicanery and partisanship." *Debates of the House of Commons* (21 June 1966).

33. Ibid.

34. Through the establishment of a Department of Intergovernmental Affairs and a permanent Federal-Provincial Secretariat as well as by instituting "the holding of a federal-provincial conference of the premiers, convened at least once a year by the Prime Minister of Canada, unless the majority of premiers decides not to hold it." (Recommendations 61, 62, 60.)

35. As for the atmosphere of that meeting, see the narrative by Robert Bourassa in Raymond St-Pierre, *Les années Bourassa* (Montreal: Héritage, 1977), 208–9.

36. The following comments by Michel Roy on that speech were published in *Le Devoir*, 8 mars 1976: "He was not arrogant, as his opponents often claim. He was just scornful and dramatic, to the point that his arguments, although they were well founded in some cases, seemed more like droll and coarse accusations. They were not surpassed by his words and excesses but by his feelings, impulses, and profound exasperation that could overwhelm the mind, exploding like bombs launched haphazardly, spattering the clique that runs Quebec."

37. It asserted, among other things, "that eight of the fourteen major amendments to the Constitution were not preceded by any consultation and that it is not rare for the federal government to ask for and obtain from the Parliament at Westminster the adoption of an amendment to the Constitution despite the opposition of some of the provinces" because "the provinces have no right whatsoever to be consulted on amendments to the Constitution submitted to the Parliament at Westminster." *Notes de référence sur le rapatriement de l'Acte de l'Amérique du Nord britannique* (Ottawa).

Quebec and Canadian Federalism†

CLAUDE MORIN

When economic or political systems are judged according to the higher principles that guide them or the virtues that theoretically sustain them, it is always possible to find that they possess intrinsic qualities that would make any system seem potentially flawless. Pure federalism (or the "ideal" federalism) has its fair share of advocates in Canada. As for the federalism that exists in reality, its deficiencies can all too easily be attributed to the fact that the model has been improperly applied; it would suffice to respect its principles and make use of its intrinsic virtues in order for everything to run smoothly. This attitude brings to mind those classical economists who regard unemployment as a chance aberration in a system that shows an otherwise normal trend towards equilibrium and full employment. . . .

The following remarks are those of a practising Canadian federalist concerning the political system in Canada as we know it today and have known it in the past. No attempt has been made to define ideal standards.

The Québécois have dealt with Canadian federalism for more than a century. This long experience permits the following fundamental proposition to be drawn: *To the extent that the Québécois[1] want to control their own affairs, the Canadian federal system not only represents an obstacle to the fulfilment of this objective, it also inevitably increases Québécois dependence upon outside political, economic, and cultural powers over which they could only, in the best of circumstances, exert a fortuitous and short-lived influence.*

†"L'expérience québécois du fédéralisme canadien," in *La modernization politique du Québec*, edited by Edmond Orban (Montreal: Boréal Express, 1976): 79–100. Translated by Jane Parniak.

More Than a Century of Misunderstanding

To start, let us consider the Québécois desire for autonomy. In this context, the history of Quebec since well before the advent of confederation has been characterized by an instinctive[2] and frustrated quest for political independence.

Paradoxically, Québécois politicians have frequently been heard to support what they call the "true federalism,"[3] and to profess their belief in the necessity for harmonious collaboration with the central government.

But it is necessary to go beyond mere words and look at the implicit connotations of the expression "true federalism." This is obvious in the case of such premiers as Mercier, Duplessis, Johnson, and Bertrand. For each of these men, federalism was practically synonymous with federal non-intervention in matters that the Québécois considered important.[4] In other words, the federal system was better insofar as it limited the action of the central government; it became invalid or misrepresentative if Ottawa was granted a wide and varied scope of action. It is no exaggeration to say that almost all our politicians have clung to a negative conception of federalism in the sense that they have seen it as a source of obstacles to federal ambitions. Often, they have criticized certain actions on the part of Ottawa under the pretext that the central government was violating the "principles of federalism."

At the same time, for the other nine provinces, these "principles of federalism" justify rather than prevent the action of Ottawa in almost any domain; this situation clearly shows the depth of the continual misunderstanding that has haunted Canada and Quebec since confederation took place in 1867.

It might even be suggested that the Québécois of 1867 were open to confederation — inasmuch as the issue interested them and they were able to express an opinion — because certain politicians had succeeded in convincing them that confederation would effect no disturbances in their everyday lives. From this perspective, the new political system was all the more acceptable because the Québécois thought that their habits, customs, and institutions were to remain unchanged.

Based on their understanding of the principles of federalism, Québécois politicians have waged an ongoing battle against a federal takeover that was activated by Canadian federalism itself. It has been a verbal battle for the most part; moreover, even when concrete results have been achieved, the "autonomist" victories have only been temporary. Federal expansionist ambitions have never been definitively blocked, and never has Quebec been able to exercise federal prerogatives completely and uncontestedly. From the beginning of federation to the present, with varying intensity at different periods of time, Canadian federalism has been established and functions at the expense of Québécois political power.

We thus face a situation that borders on the absurd. Traditionally, the Québécois put their faith in federalism because they believed that, if its principles were respected, the system would guarantee them a certain degree of political independence. Basically, it was the most "secure" system. On the one hand, it was supposed to ensure a form of independence. On the other hand, Quebec would not be completely alone. What more balanced combination could be imagined?

However, the English-Canadian majority has never viewed the situation in this way. This became especially obvious during the attempt at constitutional revision, 1968–71, and it had certainly been noticed well before that time. English Canadians feel that federalism guarantees national unity by allowing a strong central government to co-exist with regional administrations (provincial governments) that are better equipped to handle local issues.

Quebec has never accepted this kind of "national unity." On the contrary, almost each time the idea has been expressed, our politicians have taken great pains to emphasize the dangers represented for Québécois power and the profound lack of understanding shown by English Canada towards Québécois aspirations.

In English Canada, federalism was welcomed because it led to a "national unity" sustained by an omnipotent federal government and submissive provincial governments. In Quebec, federalism was accepted just because it was believed that it formed an obstacle to such a "national unity." Thus, federalism was favoured on both sides, but for conflicting reasons.

The Importance of the System

These parallel conceptions of federalism could co-exist and supply ample material for discussion and governmental stances just so long as they remained parallel. However, as soon as they had to be compared in the context of resolving practical problems, one conception necessarily had to prevail, after a rather long period of tension and hesitations. Two complementary factors, whose influence is likely to be overlooked in a purely theoretical treatment of Canadian federalism, had to be taken into account. These factors are the demography and the balance of power in Canada.

Demographically, French Canadians, and particularly Franco-Québécois constitute a minority in Canada. In such circumstances, it is only natural that the English-Canadian majority should exert more influence than the French-Canadian minority over decisions that affect Canada as a whole. But at the level of daily decision making that governs the division of governmental power in Canada, the federal-provincial balance of power is probably more significant than the demographic factor.

In this connection, over and above all the subtle nuances that might be emphasized, an indisputable fact is brought to light: the federal government and every province except Quebec are normally and habitually ready to entrust any decisive governmental responsibilities to the central power. These responsibilities have varied throughout the years but, at present, the following domains could probably be considered decisive: economic growth, the fight against regional inequality, social security, communications, culture, scientific research, energy, urban affairs, environmental issues, and consumer affairs. The central government and nine out of ten provinces in these areas fall primarily within the scope of the federal power, although it must be assured of the collaboration of the provinces.[5] It has never been, and never could be, a question of entrusting primary responsibility to the provinces. Such action would contradict both the objective of "national unity" that was discussed earlier and the tendency towards centralization of governmental control that results in the type of strong central government desired by English Canadians.

On the whole, English Canadians share the view of federalism that has just been outlined. From their point of view, they are certainly correct. In effect, it is pointless to confer decisive responsibilities upon nine governments when the most effective way to avoid anarchy and ensure efficiency is to place them directly in the hands of the central power.

It is important not to be misled by the more or less incisive statements against federal takeover that are occasionally proffered by Anglophone provincial politicians.[6] Often, these statements are only aimed at hindering a federal government of opposing political allegiance, or they spring from the understandable frustration that politicians can feel towards a too innovative central government. These negative attitudes have never long endured or formed a definitive obstacle in the way of federal policies. Basically, the Anglophone provincial governments have never tried to retain their decision-making autonomy to the point of provoking federal-provincial crises capable of weakening the system, because they realize that public opinion would not support such action; they are content to be given some allowance and to be consulted by Ottawa. Their concerns are mainly administrative when they are not simply partisan. Futhermore, these governments are not interested in regaining federal power; on the contrary, they are often more interested in relinquishing some of their responsibilities to the federal government. And this quite often occurs.

The Choice Between Futile Conflicts and Peaceful Surrender

As a general rule, it is supposed that the Québécois stance differs radically from that of Ottawa or the other nine provinces. We say "as a general rule" because it sometimes happens, when a Québécois government is mainly controlled by Ottawa, the actual Bourassa administration or the Godbout administration of 1941,[7] for example, that the traditional autonomist viewpoint is discarded. But these are exceptional cases. Normally, Quebec is not prepared to accept that the decisive domains mentioned above fall naturally within the scope of the central government. On the contrary, due to the permanent feeling in Québécois politics that they must control their own affairs as much as possible, there is a tendency to immediately entrust almost all governmental control to the Québécois power, expecting only certain areas of public responsibility that must without a doubt be entrusted to the central power. This point of view is so firmly rooted that practically any instance of intervention by Ottawa in any domain during the previous two or three generations has been considered by Quebec as a more or less illegitimate federal intrusion. At any rate, this is the attitude shared by most of the Québécois who are concerned with the problem of federal-provincial relations.

One of the most obvious consequences of this situation is the periodic recurrence of overt or latent conflict — conflict, not just friction — between Ottawa and Quebec. Two opposing conceptions of Canada have arisen between Ottawa and Quebec. Firstly, there is a marked difference in understanding as far as Canadian federalism is concerned. Furthermore, Franco-Québécois feel that they form a nation, a unique attitude that is not shared by the citizens of Saskatchewan or Nova Scotia.

Obviously, each province has its own distinct outlook, but this feeling of belonging to an individual community, a nation, is found only in Quebec.[8] Insofar as this community, aided by its government, wishes to preserve or increase its autonomy, it will inevitably oppose the tendency, which prevails in Ottawa and the rest of Canada, to entrust the control of all Canadian matters, including those of Quebec, to the central power. As a practical consequence, within present-day Canada, Franco-Québécois can only conduct themselves politically as a nation at the price of successive conflicts, which are costly in time, energy, and resources. The dilemma is the following: either, anxious to preserve and increase Québécois power, the government of Quebec is forced to conduct frequent battles with Ottawa, or it no longer concerns itself with Québécois power, for tactical reasons, from discouragement, or because it is distantly controlled by Ottawa, thus automatically becoming a regional subdivision of the central power.

If the Québécois-Ottawa conflicts ended with permanent gains for Quebec, the struggle within the present political framework would be worth it. But this is not the case. Experience shows that a Québécois gain, when the case arises, is short-lived; this was clearly demonstrated during the period 1960–72. At best, the centralizing tendency can be slowed down; it has never yet been stopped.[9] The notorious swing of the pendulum that, according to some historians and jurists, governs federal-provincial relations in Canada—in other words, the alternation of periods of centralization and decentralization—simply does not exist. Certain periods, like the present, show a clear centralizing tendency, others less so; but there is never a period that seriously leans towards a lasting decentralization. We have only to ask ourselves this question: What are the significant powers held by Ottawa at the time of confederation that have since been relinquished to the provinces? The answer: none. We must then ask ourselves the inverse question: What are the significant powers initially held by the provinces in which Ottawa now regularly intervenes? The answer would include a whole list of responsibilities, ranging from social assistance to municipal affairs (notably housing and urban affairs) and cultural matters, and covering a significant portion of labour laws and environmental protection. And all the rest. . . .

The Establishment's Political Model

In English Canada, most of the politicians and specialists of federal-provincial relations follow a model that, although true in part, is seriously incomplete but nonetheless convenient for the political status quo. For them, Canada is comprised of one central government and ten provincial governments. There are obvious demographic, sociological, and geographical differences between the ten provinces. No two provinces are alike; there are many regional inequalities, different mentalities. Furthermore, Canada is afflicted with a linguistic problem, which distinguishes this country from other federations such as the United States, Australia, or West Germany.

This model forms the foundation of the policies of the current federal government. As well as assuming the responsibilities of a national government, with all the implications of legislative supremacy, Ottawa has been concerned with combatting two types of inequality mentioned in the model: the relative poverty of certain regions, and the inequality of the French language.

The situation is quite different in reality. Québécois want to have control over their own affairs. They are obviously aware that, in this interdependent world, no one is entirely independent — neither the United States, the U.S.S.R., nor any other nation. This does not prevent them from believing that there must be a way for them to at least take a bigger part in the political and economic decisions that concern them and from which they suffer the fortunate or unfortunate effects.

We reiterate: the Québécois want to be recognized as a nation! This is so true that nothing of the contemporary evolution of Quebec is likely to be understood if this particular aspect of the Québécois attitude is not taken into account. However, this aspect is wholly absent from the model that has been outlined. The official and semi-official spokespersons from English Canada have never seriously considered it in their analyses and recommendations. They have only gone so far as to recognize that Quebec is probably — not definitely — a province that differs somewhat from the others. No one has ever believed that an authentic nation was situated there. An enormous error in the interpretation of reality has thus been committed.

Certainly, each individual Franco-Québécois would not describe the situation exactly as it has been treated here; some would even appear to be indifferent to these matters. This lack of awareness, which strengthens the argument of those who would deny the existence of an authentic Québécois nation, stems from two major sources. Firstly, there is a world-wide phenomenon that in any society there is a variable proportion of people who are not yet aware of their actual situation, or who see advantages in the status quo.[10] Furthermore, the political system tends, by its values, its game rules, and its centralizing dynamic, to minimize or even cover up the true socio-cultural nature of Canada.[11] Canadian federalism, as it evolved, functions better if the preponderant role of Ottawa in comparison to Quebec is not called into question. In other words, as it now stands, the system would not accommodate the legal recognition of the Québécois entity, much less the practical consequences that would logically ensue from a division of responsibilities between Ottawa and Quebec. Canadian equilibrium demands that Quebec sustain relations with Ottawa that are identical to the relations that hold between the other provinces and the central government.[12] Furthermore, the inertia of the system and the balance of power between English Canada and Quebec does not permit this equilibrium to be changed in actual circumstances. The failure of the constitutional revision serves as proof of this.[13]

In the last analysis, without undergoing a complete transformation, the system can only go so far as to establish politics aimed at French-speaking individuals, but not at the Québécois nation as such: bilingualism at the federal level, subsidies to improve employment in certain regions (notably in Quebec), better integrated social security, etc. In other words, it is hoped that measures that are certainly not bad in themselves, aimed at individuals, will resolve a political problem situated at the level of a whole society. More to the point, it is hoped that these measures will allow the problem to be dismissed and forgotten. Yet it persists.

The problem persists and its symptoms persist, more so at certain periods, less during others. It is to be expected that eventually Ottawa will react and try to place even more emphasis on solutions the system will tolerate: more subsidies, more social allocations, but no political solutions liable to increase the status of Quebec within Canada. Ottawa will do nothing to substantially alter the federal-provincial balance of power to the advantage of Quebec.[14] Above all, it wishes to avoid overt consideration of the problem of division of power.

Automatic Dependence

The federal government pursues the objective of occupying more and more terrain. By multiplying initiatives on the levels of culture, regional development, social politics, etc., the central government tries to play an increasingly significant role in Québécois life. In this way, it hopes that Québécois citizens, as individuals, will be indebted to it for increasingly wide-ranging services. On one side, the demands of contemporary life direct the government towards a consistently more varied action, and on the other side, as the "national power," it wants to resolve problems attributed to the linguistic disadvantage suffered by French Canadians. Thus, Ottawa is led to promote policies that entail immediate financial and material benefits, ultimately resulting in an increased Québécois dependence upon the central power. Because its spending power and resources are undeniably more plentiful than those of the provinces, the central government, without being deliberately paternalistic, will be able to buy the support, at least temporary and certainly interested, of a considerable number of Québécois who are unaware of the manoeuvre. This "transaction" is devised to be carried out at strategic moments, so it may easily be supposed that federal "generosity" will succeed in influencing the course of events and thwart politically affirmative ambitions that are otherwise difficult to stifle.[15]

Thus the customary practices of the Canadian federal system and Ottawa's resistance to a marked Québécois affirmation lead to an aggravated state of Québécois dependence upon outside powers. In this perspective, the Canadian federal system plays a leading role in the traditional alienation of the Québécois people. This is the keystone of a whole system, which basically maintains and reinforces the subjugation of the Québécois people to outside powers who try to convince them that submission is a necessary step towards the achievement of material well-being. It has been said that Quebec is the most well-kept and well-treated colony in the world, probably the one which, globally, has the highest standard of living. In other words, we are comfortable colonists.

It is not unpleasant to be comfortable, even as colonists. Ottawa is well aware of this fact. The capitalists of each country investing in Quebec are also aware of it. Those who presently hold political power are aware of it, as were certain leaders known to the Québécois of former generations.[16] And a substantial number of the Québécois themselves, those who profit by the status quo, or imagine that they do, and those who hope to profit by it, are prepared to adapt to the current system and convince their compatriots that this is where their future lies.

It is always difficult to imagine what the average citizen thinks, for the good reason that nobody has yet encountered this statistical entity. However, let us try to survey the tableau offered by the established powers to the average Québécois.

At present, these powers hope to convince the Québécois of the following "useful truths":

1. The central government possesses both the knowledge and the resources required to advance the most suitable policies. Without the contribution of Ottawa, little could be accomplished in Quebec.

2. The Québécois need a provincial government capable of influencing the central government in the right direction, capable, that is, of inducing the government to develop policies that would bring better social benefits, more abundant subsidies, and all sorts of other financial generosities to the Québécois.

3. The Québécois form a small nation that could certainly never be self-sufficient and whose standard of living depends upon the enlightened generosity of a whole series of foreign investors who are liable, at any time, to invest elsewhere.

4. The Québécois must not attempt anything that might frighten off these foreign investors who, at the slightest alarm, will hasten towards friendlier climes. For this reason, it is necessary to avoid, among other calamities, high-pressure political disputes, strikes of any kind, and immoderate linguistic demands. The Québécois must be calm and docile; otherwise, they will lose investments and the employment situation will suffer.

5. It is common knowledge that the federal system is not perfect and is in need of major amendments. But these amendments can only be accomplished if the other partners in confederation also become convinced of the need for reform. Everything must progress gradually, little by little, programatically. Quebec cannot run ahead of the others; rather, the Québécois should endeavour to make their partners aware of the deficiencies of the federal system so that these shortcomings might subsequently be corrected, one by one, in a positive spirit devoid of any nationalistic claims unacceptable to the partners.

These useful truths — and there are many more — are interconnected. Quebec is dependent upon Ottawa. Federal subsidies depend upon the respect Quebec shows towards the rules of the current political system. Wealth depends upon foreign investors. Quebec's economic development is dependent upon the contribution of American capitalism. The progress of Quebec depends upon social harmony. Social harmony depends upon the upholding of traditional values.

We could continue to add all sorts of formulas in which "depend" would figure each time. The fundamental dogma that has always been fed to the Québécois is this: the more submissive the Québécois are, the happier they will be. The sort of happiness involved is never specified, except that it corresponds to the situation or to the values that the Québécois hold most highly at a given moment: standard of living, liberty, language, institutions, etc. The formula applies in any political, economic, or psychological circumstances. The only permanent idea found here is that of dependence. Throughout the course of their history, the Québécois have always been dependent in relation to some outside power. In a sense, the history of Quebec is nothing but the history of a long dependence.

Necessary Independence

In another sense, it is also the history of a long struggle towards independence, a struggle that has been both politically and economically unsuccessful to this point. In the context of politics and economics, we find a duality that has characterized the evolution of Quebec (particularly since 1867): the difficult choice between the "social" or the "national" as Québécois objectives. Briefly, it could be said that partisans of the "social" objective consider nationalist preoccupations as secondary and the surrounding political framework unimportant; they prefer to concentrate upon concrete reforms and benefit as much as possible from the constitutional status quo. Partisans of the "national" objective would rather change the system or pursue nationalist aims, without which they consider that concrete reforms are likely to be short-lived and Québécois institutions weaker.

At different periods of time, Québécois political powers have gravitated towards one or the other of these two poles. The Liberals have almost always leaned towards the "social" rather than the "national" (except during the period under Jean Lesage when the two orientations were reconciled), while the Union Nationale of Maurice Duplessis and Daniel Johnson leaned in the opposite direction.

In actual circumstances, the continued alternation between the "social" and the "national" constantly threatens to increase the dependence of the Québécois. In the present constitutional framework, neither option can reach its logical conclusion, whether it be economic or political freedom. The equilibrium of the system requires that those who adopt the "social" option drop all political disputes, because they would detract from economic and social objectives. Inversely, those who opt for the "national" perspective are led to neglect the fundamental material requirements of the population because their energy and resources will be used to other purposes. The Québécois, insofar as they wish to control their own affairs, seek economic and political freedom. Despite the imposition of the dogma of dependence throughout the generations, more and more Québécois are seeking, in a peaceful and orderly manner, to enjoy a better standard of living while assuming more responsibility for their present and their future. They are seeking, confusedly and intuitively at times, to reconcile the objectives that have always been presented to them as incompatible: independence and prosperity. Increasing numbers of Québécois believe, not that anything is possible for Quebec, but that more is possible than they have been led to believe. No longer is it only the minority of yesteryear who share this opinion. In other words, the Québécois are losing faith in the old dogma of dependence.

I am not claiming that the federal system is the sole, or even the main obstacle to the economic, social, or cultural liberation of Quebec. Nor am I claiming that the system is the major cause of all the problems that afflict the Québécois community. It is futile to substitute one dogma in the place of another. But our knowledge of the federal system is sufficient to allow us to pass judgment on it. Firstly, as we have seen, it has led to the degeneration of Québécois power, which is already sufficient justification for its rejection, at least as far as Quebec is concerned. Furthermore, it creates an enormous factor of dependence, thus strengthening the other kinds of dependence that affect the Québécois, if only psychologically. This explains the earlier statement that the federal system is the keystone of Québécois subjugation. It envelops Quebec, thus intervening politically between the Québécois, as a nation, and the outside world. In this way it offers them protection; such as the frequently heard argument of federalist defence. But it can also act as an intermediary, a channel deserving of trust and confidence. In this role of intermediary, the system becomes what sociologists term a "situational definer," and what is best for Quebec is determined by the institutions of federal Canada. In effect, the definer, which is controlled by a non-Québécois majority, determines what are acceptable attitudes and aims to safeguard a state of affairs that conforms to the wishes of the majority; otherwise the majority itself would quickly reject the system.[17]

The Québécois are only able to exercise federal power in a superficial and ephemeral fashion. They are unable to benefit at the provincial level from political attributes exclusive enough to guarantee a real autonomy of decision against a system that, by its game-rules and internal dynamics, nullifies the abilities of the Québécois government. Furthermore, they are deprived of an economic power that could compensate for their minority status within Canada. So what choice is left to them? On the one hand, there is habitual submission to external powers, on the other hand, the pursuit of independence. The consequences of the first alternative are already familiar to us.

A Step Towards Dignity

The pursuit of independence certainly evokes more questions than does submission. What kind of independence, and to what degree? Politicians like to envision all types of independence: economic independence, cultural independence, political independence, etc. In reality, independence cannot easily be subdivided. If a catalogue of all possible types of independence is required, then we insist that the Québécois must first of all pursue political independence; in other words, they must reach a state in which the government of Quebec would be their only government. Cultural independence will spring from political independence, and cannot otherwise be attained. Political independence will also engender all the instruments of action and social reform that the Québécois still lack, including economic independence.

How much political independence? Total, but not exclusive of the establishment of mutually advantageous relations between Quebec and Canada. A contradiction might be discerned here. How can we achieve independence while simultaneously joining forces with another? First of all, this would be a voluntary association, just as the European Common Market is voluntary, and not imposed. Secondly, it would be mutually advantageous in the sense that one side would not impose its institutions, its priorities, its methods, or its government on the other. Finally, a voluntary and mutually advantageous association would serve to strengthen the associates and would not be legally, economically, or politically detrimental to either.

Seen in this light, the political independence of Quebec is no longer that widely misunderstood separatism that some people are determined to present in a negative and exaggerated manner in order to deny Québécois aspirations that they refuse to accept. Rather, it is the proposition, made by Quebec to Canada, of a new association in reciprocal dignity.

Those who continue to talk about separatism also insist that English Canada would never agree to such an association. In fact, they are probably not aware of what they are saying. For the proposition is founded on the fact that the preservation of Canada depends upon the necessary independence of the Québécois people. Otherwise, Canada will force the Québécois to renounce their dignity. A country built in this way will never go very far, and the current status quo will threaten its progress even more than the proposed Canada-Quebec association.

We shall soon reach the point where, in order to survive, Canada, as much as Quebec, will have to change. For Canada, the independence of Quebec is basically a question of survival. For Quebec, it is also a question of dignity.

Notes

1. Who are these Québécois? In this article we assume that they are Franco-Québécois. It must be emphasized that this summary definition is not racist; it simply derives from the fact that the consequences of the Canadian federal system are entirely different for French-speaking Québécois than for their English-speaking fellow citizens, who are part of an Anglophone community that covers North America.

2. It is precisely an "instinctive" quest. Québécois opposition to Ottawa's takeover tactics has always assumed an intensity found nowhere else in Canada. Furthermore, the issue only interests the population of Quebec to such a degree, even if it is not a constant priority. The Québécois have always tried to safeguard the degree of independence that they believed the constitution of 1867 had guaranteed them. Until about 1960, they struggled to keep this independence. Since 1960, with the advent of the Quiet Revolution, they have endeavoured to increase it.

3. In effect, Québécois politicians have invoked federalism and its virtues more often than have their colleagues from the other provinces. Even now it is frequently referred to.

4. Cf. *Rapport de la Commission royale d'enquête sur les problèmes constitutionnels* (Quebec, 1956).

5. The Rowell-Sirois Report and the Massey-Lévesque Report have provided the central government, which lacked irrefutable constitutional arguments, with practical motives for intervening in domains not clearly, or not at all, contained within its competence.

6. The author has personally witnessed, during federal-provincial conferences, extremely vehement attacks on the central power, for example by B.C. (17 July 1958) and by Alberta (4 Nov. 1968). The first case involved an attack on the federal program of medical insurance. The charges laid against Ottawa were more severe, to the author's knowledge, than any voiced by Quebec in recent years. (See in this context Richard Simeon, *Federal-Provincial Diplomacy* (Toronto: University of Toronto Press, 1972).) More recently, in 1974 and 1975, wealthy Alberta took a severe stance against Ottawa concerning the oil issue.

7. The fact that provincial political parties are dependent upon federal parties of the same allegiance is neither surprising nor abnormal in a federal system. Federal and provincial parties are as interconnected in such a system as are the domains of competence. However, sometimes this dependence leads to arrogant conduct on the part of the federal party. In Quebec, except under Jean Lesage, federal Liberals have always treated provincial Liberals in a patronizing or even contemptuous manner. This was noticeable at the time of the Liberal opposition during the Duplessis era, when on two or three occasions the federal Liberal government practically undermined the provincial Liberal Party with its stances on tax distribution or the mining rights at the iron mines of Ungava. At the time of writing, the Liberals of Pierre Elliott Trudeau do not show a great respect towards the Liberals of Robert Bourassa.

8. This does not prevent federal spokespersons from putting Québécois nationalism on the same footing as the regionalist spirit found here and there in Canada.

9. The same phenomenon was manifest during the Duplessis era (1944–59).

10. Premier Bourassa alleges that the population lacks interest in the constitutional debate, precisely in order to justify the lack of priority that he himself shows towards the question. It is somewhat as though a decision were made to abandon scientific research on the pretext that the public does not express daily interest in the matter. They forget that, even if the masses do not continually follow the progress of cancer research, they are nonetheless affected by its results.

11. The "true socio-cultural nature of present-day Canada" could obviously be discussed at great length. One of the best existing definitions is to be found in the introduction to the first volume of the *Report of the Royal Commission on Bilingualism and Biculturalism*.

12. During the first meeting of the Constitutional conference in February 1968 at Ottawa, Pierre Elliott Trudeau, at that time federal minister of justice, spoke in order to demonstrate to what point the establishment of a particular statute for Quebec risked fundamentally altering the aspect of Canadian federalism and presented, concerning the role of Ottawa vis-à-vis Quebec, political and administrative disadvantages that he considered to be major and deleterious.

13. This experience (which lasted forty months) stood out from all other attempts at constitutional revision in that it summoned up the energy of a part of the political and administrative personnel of all the governments of Canada, as well as numerous advisors. It gave rise to more rigorous research than had any of the diverse constitutional changes. Although it did not get right to the heart of the matter, it at least progressed further than at any time in the past. The process was unsuccessful, however, essentially because of the profoundly divergent stances taken by the Québécois and the other governments. These divergences dated from the beginning of the revision, at the time of the Union Nationale. Starting in 1970, the Liberal government had to recognize their existence, but introduced a change of style that led momentarily to the belief that the discussion would re-open on a new footing; at least this is what the federal government expected. A change of style had already taken place with the decease of Daniel Johnson and the accession of M. Bertrand. All this to show that the revision experience was long enough, wide enough, and varied enough to be able to conclude without error that it is impossible to reconcile the political objectives of the Québécois power and the central power.

14. Several otherwise very well-informed individuals continue to think that, with a litttle effort, the Canadian federal system would succeed in transforming and satisfying Quebec, all with the approbation and participation of Ottawa. These individuals never specify which political circumstances would produce such a result, but they are convinced of its eventual occurrence. The author is confident that this will never happen. Not only does recent experience prove it, but only a profound misunderstanding of the forces at work in our federal system would lead to a belief in a transformation that would arise from the system itself, especially if, within the system, Quebec is content to formulate those sorts of verbal complaints that are generously and futilely scattered throughout Québécois political history of the last fifty years.

15. Since the early 1960s there exists a whole school of thought in Quebec according to which it is strategically convenient to brandish the "threat" of Québécois independence in order to obtain financial benefits from Ottawa. Preceding the creation of an *indépendantiste* party, political leaders would take the liberty of uttering "threats" themselves. Thus arose Daniel Johnson's slogan "Equality or Independence." For the same reason, in 1963, M. Lesage risked a fiscal ultimatum in his budget speech. With the advent of an *indépendantiste* party, the political situation changed so that the "threat" came not from the leaders themselves, but from the possibility that these leaders could be replaced by supporters of independence if Ottawa did not change its perspective toward Quebec, or was not sufficiently generous. Since 1970, the election of *indépendantiste* MNAs and the constant action on their part has further polarized political options. This has created a dilemma for the Liberals in power. If they threatened Ottawa but gained nothing, the *indépendantistes* would be provided with favourable political arguments. If, on the contrary — and this is what happened — they were docile for fear of providing the *indépendantiste* opposition with arguments, Québécois power would disintegrate even more rapidly than usual. The polarization following the provincial election of 1970 prevented the Québécois political parties from thereafter taking the middle road between independence and unconditional federalism. Henceforth, it was impossible for them to navigate in the "happy medium" that was exploited so well by the Union Nationale of Daniel Johnson.

16. One constant of Québécois politics in recent decades is the pursuit, in the service of decision centres outside of Quebec (mainly financial), of "advantageous conditions." It is almost never the case that the

Québécois will devote themselves, alone or in collaboration with others, to activities that they hope will be taken care of from outside: investment, extraction and processing of resources, etc. They are content to negotiate the most advantageous conditions, to look for marginal benefits arising from decisions made in New York, Ottawa, or elsewhere. From this perspective, almost all Québécois governments have played the role of intermediary between Quebec's natural resources and financial or technical resources that are automatically located externally. Although Quebec obviously cannot do everything alone, the constant outlined here bears witness to a revealing state of mind. In sum, we hope that "others" will bring us tangible benefits when they condescend to come and exploit our resources, and there is not much effort made to incite and guide the potential dynamism of the Québécois and their institutions so that they will take a more reasonable part in the exploitation of their own territory. In this perspective, the frequently affirmed confidence that is felt towards the virtues of private enterprise as opposed to governmental intervention, which is immediately judged to be either incompatible with our traditions or inefficient, provides a useful excuse for those who see the progress of Quebec only as a function of external aid; in effect, the only private enterprise that is likely to be profitable in actual circumstances, exploitation of resources, which requires massive funding, is of American "nationality." There are several exceptions to this phenomenon — almost all of which are situated within the domain of hydro-electricity — where we rely more upon proper Québécois organisms. Even in these cases, financing by loan has been accomplished externally. But the dependence that springs from a loan to Hydro-Québec from New York is infinitely less consequential than the direct implantation of foreign companies in Quebec.

17. The possibility apparently remains for the Québécois to assure for themselves the control of the totality of institutions and of federal policies. In this context, a question might be asked: How often will English Canada be willing to submit to Quebec? We have already seriously considered some aspects of the response to this question, so it will suffice to say that, at best, the Québécois, as a group, could only exert an entirely relative influence on the progress of Canadian affairs. To this affirmation, certain individuals will undoubtedly reply that the bilingualism policy of the present federal government [of Pierre Elliott Trudeau], as an example, is a direct result of age-old Québécois pressure, which would seemingly contradict the preceding argument. Thereupon, four comments: Québécois pressure dates back one hundred years (even more), which does not constitute a particularly obvious demonstration of French-Canadian political power; bilingualism is the unadapted response of the federal system to the political problem of Quebec; in any case, this bilingualism is strictly limited and kept from going beyond the frame within which it is supposed to work; finally, bilingualism and the struggle against regional inequality are far from comprising the totality of what could be called the "progress of Canadian affairs."

UNDER WHAT CONDITIONS COULD QUEBEC SIGN THE CONSTITUTION ACT OF 1982?†

GIL RÉMILLARD

The fact that the Quebec government has still not signed the Constitution Act of 1982 has no legal significance. From the political point of view, however, it is difficult to accept that what can be termed Canadian history's second federative compromise was carried out without Quebec, a founding member of the first compromise in 1867. Although the Lévesque government could be reproached for many errors in strategy, it nonetheless remains that no Quebec government, regardless of its political leaning, could have signed this agreement of 5 November 1981, any more than it could today. The 1982 Constitution Act could become acceptable to Quebec if certain modifications were made, however.

In fact, up until now the Lévesque government has, for four principal reasons, refused to sign the 1982 Constitution Act:

1. The peoples' right to free movement between provinces, guaranteed by section 6 of the Canadian Charter of Rights and Freedoms, could call Quebec's employment policies into question.
2. The right to education in the language of the minority, as per section 23 of the Charter, means a significant limitation to Quebec's power to legislate in matters of language and education.
3. The amendment formula is unacceptable because it does not allow for financial compensation in all cases of withdrawal.
4. The specificity of Quebec society and the equality of the two founding peoples must be recognized.

Let us look now at Quebec's grounds for refusal.

---

†"A quelles conditions le Québec peut-il signer la Loi constitutionnelle de 1982?" (1–3) *Le Devoir*, 26–28 fevrier 1985. Translated by Michael Menzies.

Free Movement of the People

The goal of section 6 of the Canadian Charter of Rights and Freedoms is to guarantee all Canadians the right to live in, to enter, or to leave Canada. The Supreme Court of Canada, in *Law Society of Upper Canada v. Skapinker* (3 May 1984), confirmed that section 6 guaranteed the right to move freely, to establish residence, and to work anywhere. These principles exist in many federal states including the United States of America. In addition, these principles are included in the international pact relative to civil and political rights and in the European agreement to safeguard human rights and fundamental liberties.

Are these principles unacceptable to Quebec? There is no doubt that they signify a certain constraint. For example, Quebec can no more limit access to its territory by other provincial labour forces than can the other provinces. Quebec cannot, for instance, stop Ontario workers from coming to work on a construction site in Hull. It is, above all, this aspect that provoked the Lévesque government's criticism. However, as a result of the parliamentary debates in Ottawa that followed the agreement reached that famous night of 4 November 1981, a restriction was brought to the application of section 6: if a province has an employment rate inferior to the national average, it can, for example, regulate access to its territory by out-of-province personnel. This restriction serves thus to delay the possible effects of section 6 while conserving its principle of application.

As long as one accepts federalism, the principles of freedom of movement and establishment of residence are self-evident and can only confirm the willingness of the federal states to have their populations profit from the advantages of a common territory. The disadvantages that these rights could entail for a federalist government are compensated for by the advantages that its citizens can gain. Section 6 of the Canadian Charter of Rights and Freedoms is thus more than acceptable to Quebec. However, the principle of freedom of movement and establishment of residence leads us, as a result, to the right to education in the language of the minority which, in itself, creates additional difficulties.

The Right to Education in the Language of the Minority

In its 26 June 1984 decision concerning Bill 101 — *Attorney General of Quebec v. Quebec Association of Protestant School Boards* — the Supreme Court of Canada concluded that "the constituent," so termed by the court, "had Quebec in particular in mind when it enacted section 23 of the Canadian Charter." This situates extremely well the context in which these language rights were written into the Charter of Rights and Freedoms. In fact, section 23 is the result of the long development of a certain idea of Canadian duality.

In 1979, the Pépin-Robarts Commission (on national unity) noted the existence of a new national phenomenon in Canada: the existence of the Québécois people. The commission thus gave a new significance to the concept of Canadian duality. No longer did this concept refer to the relationship between French and English Canadians, but rather to the one between the Québécois and the rest of Canada. Thus the very foundations of the theory of two nations, recognized by the Commission on Bilingualism and Biculturalism in 1969, were being questioned. Aware of this contradiction, the Commission on National Unity noted that "at the moment when the members of the B and B Commission were preparing their report, they believed in certain national realities which, today, we are obligated to contest."

This recognition of the existence of a Québécois people prompted the commission to recommend that language rights not be written into the Constitution, but rather left to the discretion of the provinces. The commission was thus taking a considerable risk, since it was entrusting the protection of the minorities to the goodwill of the provinces. Its reasoning was as follows:

— the French-speaking minorities, with the exception of the Acadians, were being rapidly assimilated;
— the English-speaking minority in Quebec was, despite Bill 101, well treated;
— Quebec had to be allowed the power necessary to protect its Francophone character.

Section 23 of the Canadian Charter of Rights and Freedoms is the result of a very different reasoning: the French-speaking minorities outside Quebec and the English-speaking minority inside Quebec must have constitutionally guaranteed rights in order to survive and develop within a bilingual federation. The return to the classic theory of two nations or of two founding peoples is thus sanctioned, from the point of view of language at least, by section 23.

This section establishes three criteria governing the right to enrol a child in courses given in his or her language:

1. the mother tongue (first language learned and understood);
2. the parent's language and place of education;
3. the child's language and place of education.

The Criterion of the Mother Tongue

This is the criterion of the first language learned and still understood. The application of this criterion poses many difficulties since it refers to norms of existence that are fundamentally subjective. For example, it is no easy task to determine the first language learned by the child of an Anglophone father and a Francophone mother, or vice versa.

However, by virtue of section 59, this criterion does not apply to Quebec, unless it is with the consent of the Quebec government or the National Assembly. This has not yet been given. That is to say, then, that Canadian citizens of British origin in the same situation, can have their children taught at a French school in the English-speaking provinces. Thus, the criterion of the first language learned and still understood does not pose a problem for Quebec.

The Criterion of the Parents' Language of Instruction in Elementary School

The second criterion gave rise to what is called the "Canada clause." Its precedence over the "Quebec clause" of Bill 101 was confirmed by the Supreme

Court on 26 July 1984 in *Attorney-General of Quebec v. Quebec Association of Protestant School Boards*. According to this criterion, parents who, for example, received their education in English at the elementary school level in a Canadian province are entitled to have their child taught at an English school in Quebec.

Does the Canada clause endanger the survival of the French language in Quebec? It appears difficult, according to currently available demographic studies,[1] to draw such a conclusion. Moreover, provided that one accepts federalism and freedom of movement as guaranteed by section 6 of the Charter, the Canada clause poses no obstacle. However, in order to grasp all its implications, the Canada clause must be situated in the context of a third criterion.

The Criterion of the Education Received by One of the Children at the Elementary or Secondary School Level in Canada

If a child has received or is receiving her or his elementary or secondary education in French or English, the child's education can continue in that same language anywhere in Canada, as can the education of the child's brothers or sisters.

This last criterion supplements and broadens the scope of the Canada clause. It could have consequences for immigrants and for those regions, like the Outaouais, that border on Quebec and Ontario. Francophone parents, for example, could enrol one of their children at an English school in Ottawa in order to, at some point later on, enrol the child as well as his or her brothers and sisters at an English school in Hull, contrary to Bill 101.

To a certain extent, this criterion could also apply to immigrants. Let us take, for example, the case of Greek immigrants who, immediately upon their arrival in Toronto, register their eldest son at an English school. After becoming Canadian citizens, they decide to settle in Montreal. They can then register their children at an English school, even if they themselves did not receive their education in English in a Canadian province.

Once might wonder if this broadening of the Canada clause will substantially affect Quebec's French-speaking reality. Certain people, like University of Ottawa professor Charles Castonguay, claim that it will.[2] It appears, in fact, very difficult to situate this broadening of the Canada clause in the context of its potential consequences. Prudence would demand that, in view of section 59, the criterion of the child's place of education be left to Quebec's discretion, as it was with the criterion of the mother tongue.

In addition, the opportunity should be taken to modify section 59 and to establish that the decision to apply the criteria of the mother tongue and the child's place of education be made by the National Assembly alone, and not by the government of Quebec. This is what Quebec specified, and rightly so, in its law concerning the 1982 Constitution Act (Bill 62). In fact, it is hard, for example, to imagine a minority government making such an important decision because, even if it were defeated on the question, the decision would, by the very terms of section 59, be irrevocable. Legally speaking, however, one wonders if Quebec can brush aside, with one simple law, a choice provided for in the Constitution.[3] It would therefore be better to amend section 59 in order to give this power to Quebec's National Assembly alone.

Thus amended, section 59 might read:

> 59(1) Paragraphs 23(1)(a) and 23(2) take effect for Quebec on the date set down by proclamation of the National Assembly of Quebec.
>
> (2) The present section is rescinded as of the date of the coming into effect for Quebec of paragraphs 23(1)(a) and 23(2), and the numbering of the present law is modified accordingly, by proclamation of the Queen and the Governor-General under the Great Seal of Canada.

Section 59 would thus stipulate that the criterion of the first language learned and still understood (mother tongue), like that of a child's place of elementary or secondary education, would only apply following a proclamation to that effect by the National Assembly. The situation would thus be clearer and the Canada clause would be the only applicable criterion for English-language education in Quebec.

This amendment to section 23 could be made in accordance with section 43 of the 1982 Constitution Act. That is to say that such an amendment, which applies to Quebec alone, would need only the approval of the Parliament of Canada and that of the National Assembly.[4] It is thus a matter of making a relatively easy modification, which would have the important advantage of leaving the application of this highly debatable broadening of the Canada clause to Quebec's discretion.

The application of these three criteria does not automatically confer the right to education in the language of the minority. There must also be, as is specified in section 23(3), a sufficient number of children for this right to become a reality. In addition, this sufficient number will entitle the children to either an elementary and secondary school education in the minority language at a minority-language school, or simply to register at a majority-language school in order to take courses there in the minority language, still paid for with public funds however.

Subsection (3) raises a lot of questions.[5] One might ask oneself, among other things: What is a sufficient number? Could the right granted by this section be limited simply to immersion classes? Does the expression "minority teaching establishments" imply the right of administration? The Ontario Court of Appeal recently answered some of these questions in what was, for the government of Ontario, a very interesting ruling.[6] As far as Canada is concerned, however, it does not appear that the Supreme Court will have to revise this decision in order to confirm its principles. It would thus be desirable for the Canadian government to ask for a Supreme Court opinion on these questions, as provided for in the law on the Supreme Court. Such a procedure would, for the moment, be better that a constitutional amendment, which, according to section 41, would necessitate unanimity.

It is in this context that the preponderance of the Canada clause over the Quebec clause must be situated, just as the Supreme Court ruled in the case of Bill 101. This decision certainly limits Quebec's authority to legislate in matters of language and education, but it may also mean an end to the ambiguity in the situation involving the Quebec government and the Francophone minorities outside Quebec. In fact, by means of the Quebec clause, Quebec's Anglophone minority was refused what Canada's Francophone minorities were demanding.

The Canada clause may permit or even encourage Quebec to regain and play to the full its role of national birthplace to French Canadians, without jeopardizing what the Pépin-Robarts Commission identified, much to its credit, as the national Québécois phenomenon.

The government of Quebec could thus play a determined role in this new lease on life that can be seen throughout Canada in French minorities that, not so long ago, were thought to be doomed to quick assimilation. The Supreme Court will have to give real meaning to these minority language education rights and it will take time to appreciate their real implications. From now on, however, it may be assumed that the risk posed to Quebec by section 23 of the Charter, limited to the criterion of the Canada clause alone, would be minimal in relation to the beneficial effects it could have for French Canadians as a whole. Under these conditions, Quebec could accept it enthusiastically and without hesitation.

The Amendment Formula

Both language rights and the Canada clause could have become acceptable to Quebec with an amendment requiring the approval of the Parliament of Canada. For the amendment formula, however, the consent of all the provinces would be necessary. The situation is thus more difficult.

Since the repatriation and the Constitution Act of 17 April 1982, our Constitution has contained an amendment formula. It provides for the modification of the Constitution in the Parliament of Canada and any seven provinces totalling at least fifty percent of the Canadian population (section 38). It also makes provision for unanimity in certain areas (section 41). In addition, only the consent of the Parliament of Canada and of those provinces concerned is required in certain other cases (section 43). Finally, the formula allows for the possibility of a province's withdrawal from an amendment "derogative of legislative jurisdiction, property rights or all other rights or privileges of a legislature or a provincial government" (section 38(3)). This withdrawal can result in financial compensation under the following two conditions: if the amendment is related to education or other cultural domains; or if it is a question of transferring provincial jurisdiction in these matters to the Parliament of Canada (section 40).

Let us take, for example, the case of higher education. The Turner government favoured action on Ottawa's part to establish so-called "national" standards in this sector. Certain provinces proved quite sympathetic to this idea, even if it does concern an area that comes under their jurisdiction. According to the amendment formula, the Parliament of Canada and seven provinces totalling fifty percent of the population could entrust this power to federal authorities. Quebec, which prizes this power, could use its right of withdrawal and, consequently receive full financial compensation. If it were a question of an amendment concerning the transfer of jurisdiction in the area of health, for example, Quebec could again avail itself of its right of withdrawal, but without financial compensation. The Québécois would thus be doubly taxed since they would have to finance their own health care system while contributing with their tax money to the system established by Ottawa for the rest of the country.

The negotiations underway that famous evening of 4 November 1981 concluded the next day, allowing the right of withdrawal, but without financial compensation.

Driven to the wall by the refusal of seven provinces to accept his right of veto formula, and threatened with the withdrawal of his principal ally, Premier William Davis of Ontario, Trudeau proposed a significant compromise by accepting a formula that implicitly included the possibility of special status, which he had always vigorously denounced. He rejected, however, the principle of financial compensation in all cases of withdrawal, considering it to actively encourage this possibility. Financial compensation associated with the right of withdrawal was subsequently written into the repatriation bill, but was limited to the transfer, from the provinces to the Parliament of Canada, of legislative jurisdiction in matters of education and culture. Thus, the compromise remains unsatisfactory. Such is the first weakness of the amendment formula. The provinces are granted the right of withdrawal, but those wishing to exercise it, except in the areas of culture and education, are penalized. The government of Quebec is therefore right to demand, before accepting this amendment formula, that there be financial compensation in all cases.

Furthermore, the principle of financial compensation, as it appears in section 40, is vague and ambiguous. What is the meaning of the expression "Canada provides the provinces with fair compensation"? A clarification of the evaluation method for financial compensation would be needed. One could refer to the tax point system that already exists in cases where a province withdraws from a joint federal/provincial program. It is not a matter of writing down in detail in the Constitution all the elements dealing with the application of the method of compensation, since it may vary according to the evolution of the tax system. Its basic principles should, however, be written into section 40 in order to clarify the meaning of "fair compensation."

The amendment formula has a second weakness fraught with consequences: section 42, which refers to the House of Commons, the Senate, the Supreme Court, the creation of new provinces, and the annexation of the territories to the provinces, provides expressly for the non-application of the right of withdrawal in these cases. It is difficult to see how a province could withdraw from an institution of amendment dealing with the acceptance of a new province into Confederation. That is to say, then, that the Parliament of Canada and seven provinces totalling at least fifty percent of the population could substantially modify the institutional foundations of Confederation, or even agree to the creation of new provinces, without Quebec's consent. That is an unacceptable situation that runs directly counter to the fundamental principles of our federalism.

Thus, the right of withdrawal, as it is currently worded, suffers from two major omissions that make it clearly unacceptable to Quebec:

1. there is no financial compensation, except in matters of education or culture where there is a transfer of jurisdiction from the provinces to the federal government;

2. it has no effect on amendments relative to federal institutions, the creation of new provinces, or the annexation of all or part of the territories to the existing provinces.

These omissions could be corrected without major difficulties — it would be a matter of completing the 1982 compromise. The compensation formula would necessarily have to apply in all cases of withdrawal and not just in matters of education. This is what the formula originally provided for when Quebec signed it on 16 April 1981. In addition, the meaning of "fair financial compensation" would have to be clarified. However, given that financial compensation may not apply in every case of modification, such an amendment would be insufficient. A veto formula should apply to section 42 for federal institutions and acceptance of new provinces exclusively. A return to the Trudeau resolution formula, a derivation of the 1971 Victoria formula, might be possible for this section alone. Thus, an amendment relative to the subjects enumerated in section 42, which include, among others, the Senate, the House of Commons, the Supreme Court, the acceptance of new provinces, and the annexation of the territories to the provinces, ought to have the consent of the parliament of Canada, every province that, as of 1982, totalled at least twenty-five percent of the Canadian population, two Western provinces totalling at least fifty percent of the region's population, and two Atlantic provinces totalling at least fifty percent of the region's population.

Quebec would thus have veto power in cases dealing with the reform of federal institutions, the admission of another province, or the annexation of territory to one of the provinces. As the Supreme Court decided on 6 December 1982, Quebec's right of veto has, as far as the Constitution is concerned, never existed. What did exist before the repatriation, however, was a political force that obliged Ottawa and the other provinces to respect Quebec's opinion. In this sense, the 1982 Constitution Act's amendment formula is already a substantial improvement, but it has yet to be completed. The repatriation is an unfinished compromise. What is currently unacceptable to Quebec could, without insurmountable difficulties, be changed. On the whole, what already exists in principle is very valuable and must be completed.

Two principal reproaches can be directed at the formula for withdrawal with financial compensation. To begin with, the formula is said to have the potential to create special status, which could call into question the very existence of Confederation. It should be noted that, first of all, it is only in the case of a transfer of jurisdiction from provincial to federal authority that the right of withdrawal with financial compensation would apply. It would not do, therefore, to exaggerate the quantitative importance of its possible application. Secondly, it is a good idea to bear in mind that the notion of special status is an intrinsic part of the concept of federalism. Moreover, the compromise of 1867 sanctions this special status principle, whether it be section 94, which does not apply to Quebec, or the famous section 133, which only affects federal and Quebec institutions. In addition, special conditions were also established for the six provinces that subsequently joined Confederation. Section 59 of the 1982 Constitution Act, concerning the criterion of the mother tongue, is also an example of Quebec's special status. It should be mentioned as well that this right of withdrawal with financial compensation and the special status that could follow have existed, without disrupting Confederation, since the 1960s in joint federal-provincial projects. It is important not to confuse special status and the danger of balkinization with the asymmetrical federalism advocated by the Pépin-Robarts Commission, which is the only possible solution to respecting Canada's duality as much as its regionalism and multiculturalism.

The right to withdrawal with financial compensation has been criticized because it does not offer any protection in cases of jurisdiction not involving disbursements. If a transfer of authority does not involve any expense for the province wishing to retain it, it is difficult to see why there should be financial compensation.

The only real limit to the right of withdrawal with financial compensation involves institutions, the acceptance of new provinces, and/or the annexation of territory to the provinces. This oversight could be corrected by our proposed amendment to section 42. If the amendment formula were altered in such a way as to include equitable financial compensation in all cases of withdrawal, and a right to veto for the subjects of section 42, Quebec could adhere to it with confidence.

The Recognition of the Specificity of Quebec and of Canadian Duality

Section 40 of the Constitution Act of 1982 provides for financial compensation in cases of withdrawal linked solely to education or culture. It is, in a way, implicit recognition of the specificity of Quebec society. The parliamentary debates on this amendment to the compromise of 5 November 1981 effectively demonstrate that it was introduced in order to satisfy Québécois demands. Prime Minister Trudeau refused the proposal of financial compensation in all cases but, by way of an accommodation to Quebec specificity, he did accept compensation in cases of education and culture. Another example of recognition of Quebec's specificity in the 1982 Constitution Act is section 59, which stipulates that the criterion of the mother tongue may only be applied with the consent of the Quebec government or Leglislative Assembly.

These articles are not, however, the explicit recognition of Québécois specificity that the Canadian Constitution should acknowledge. Formal recognition of the Quebec people's specificity in the Canadian Constitution, as acknowledged, much to its credit, by the Pépin-Robarts Commission, should be rendered by an amendment to the preamble of the 1867 compromise. This preamble, which can serve as a reference for the interpretation of the 1867 Constitution Act and all its amendments, including the 1982 Constitution Act, ought to reflect the constitutional aspirations of all Canadians. The preamble in its present form, which refers strictly to the situation in 1867, should eventually disappear. It could be replaced by wording more likely to express the socio-political composition of Canada and the general objectives of Canadian men and women living together in a federal regime in this territory called Canada.

It is in such a context that the Constitution must formally recognize the specificity of Quebec society. The modifications to the 1982 Constitution Act, which must be effected in order to make it acceptable to Quebec, are all based on this specificity. Legally, however, it is not necessary to demand explicit recognition of this specificity in order to sign the 1982 Constitution Act. Nevertheless, it would certainly be interesting to take the opportunity to do so by giving the 1867 Constitution Act a new preamble. The specificity of Quebec society is a principle that must apply to all constitutional matters and not just to those found in the 1982 Constitution Act.

The same reasoning can be applied in regard to the equality of the two founding peoples. This principle must be written into the preamble of the 1867 Constitution Act. While the principle of Québécois specificity refers to Quebec society as a distinct socio-political group, the equality of the two founding peoples refers to French Canadians who, along with English Canadians, established the federation of Canada. Constitutional recognition of these two principles could reconcile the different perceptions of Canadian duality. In fact, by recognizing these two principles, references to Canadian duality would be made as much in terms of the Québécois and the rest of Canada as in terms of French and English Canadians.

Although, from a strict legal standpoint, these principles are not essential to Quebec's signing of the 1982 Constitution Act, the opportunity should be taken to come to an understanding concerning modifications to the preamble of the 1867 Constitution Act. These modifications would be formal recognition of the specificity of Quebec society and of the equality of the two founding peoples: French and English Canadians.

All in all, the modifications that should be brought to the 1982 Constitution Act in order to make it acceptable to Quebec do not represent insurmountable difficulties.

History will remember that, in 1982, the intervening parties to the second Canadian federative compromise did interesting work, given the circumstances. Significant concessions were made on both sides. This compromise remains incomplete, however, and the important thing now is for us to complete it. It must be made acceptable to Quebec, and constitutional reform regarding our institutions and the sharing of legislative powers between the two levels of government must be pursued.

Given the referendum of 20 May 1980, the repatriation of the constitution must be seen in the context of the intense evolution of Québécois nationalism. Based at first on the protection of religion, Quebec nationalism at the beginning of the 1960s was stated in terms of language. The election of the Parti Québécois and the promulgation of the Charter of the French Language (Bill 101) resulted from this second stage. The repatriation marks the beginning of a third stage based on the only true measure of protection for any people whoever they might be: their excellence. The status of a language will always be directly proportional to the social, political, and economic situation of those who speak it. In the coming years, the Québécois, and French Canadians in general, will be confronted in more and more evident fashion by the challenge of excellence. It is up to us, as a people, to equip ourselves with the tools necessary to meet this challenge. It is in this sense that the 1982 Constitution Act must be amended as soon as possible so as to make it acceptable to Quebec.

The language question will always be worrisome to Francophones and will have to be re-examined regularly in the light of new demographic data, legal rulings, and the principle of minority rights protection. If, in a few years, the Canada clause were to pose serious problems, it would have to be called into question once again. The Supreme Court decision of 26 July 1984 concerning the preponderance of the Canada clause over the Quebec clause could be revised if the demographic situation were to prompt both a different evaluation of and a challenge to the principle of legitimacy cited by the Supreme Court itself in support of its judgment. A fundamental right or liberty must be situated in the context of societal evolution, so the notion of final decision does not have the same strict legal application as is normally the case.

In ten years or so, the language rights situation in Canada will have to be re-examined. Between now and then, however, Quebec will have to rise to the challenge represented by the 1982 Constitution Act. The challenge of excellence, as much in the framework of Canadian federalism as in an international context, is the only really effective guarantee of security for the Québécois as for all French Canadians. In addition, Quebec's signing of Confederation's second compromise will make it possible to broach the other stages of constitutional reform in order that federal institutions and the sharing of legislative powers conform more closely to our present-day reality.

As well, it must be understood that Quebec's conditions for signing the 1982 Constitution Act cannot be those of the government of Quebec alone. The Lévesque government was wise enough to get the National Assembly to pass a resolution by which Quebec opposed the compromise of 5 November 1981 negotiated without its participation. From the standpoint of legitimacy, it would be unacceptable for this same government, which is now at the end of its electoral mandate, to have Quebec broach such a fundamental subject without the consent of the National Assembly preceded by an in-depth study by a parliamentary commission. It is on these conditions that this unfinished compromise, which is what the 1982 Constitution Act is, can be completed and can serve as the foundation for the constitutional reform that is becoming more and more essential to Canadian unity.

Notes

1. See Henripin and Larochelle, *La situation démolinguistique au Canada; évolution passée et prospective* (Montreal: Institut de recherches politiques, 1980).

2. See Charles Castonguay, "Le recul du français dans l'Outaouais" in *Le Dossier Outaouais*, edited by J. Cimon (Quebec: Pélican, 1979), 64.

3. Superior Court Judge Jules Deschênes has already replied in the case of *Montreal Professors Alliance and Rodrigue Dubé v. Attorney General of Quebec* (judgment rendered 27 April 1983). The case is to be heard soon by the Court of Appeal.

4. It would even be possible to continue on without the consent of the Senate. If, after 180 days, the Senate has not adopted a resolution, section 47 allows for the House of Commons to pass the applicable motion despite Senate disagreement.

5. See Daniel Proulx, "La précarité des droits linguistiques scolaires ou les singulières difficultés de mise en oeuvre de l'article 23 de la Charte canadienne des droits et libertés," (1983) RGD 335–349; Joseph Eliot Magnet, "Minority-Language Educational Rights in The New Constitution and the Charter of Rights," *The Supreme Court Law Review* 4 (1982), 153.

6. "Education Act and Minority Language Educational Rights," 26 ACWS (2d) 146 (26 June 1984).

SECTION 5
THE POLITICS OF LANGUAGE

No other issue, except perhaps for the violence associated with the FLQ and the October Crisis of 1970, has aroused more public debate and created such a high level of social and political tension than the question of language. The language debate began shortly after the Second World War when an increasing majority of non-Francophone, non-Anglophone immigrants arriving in Montreal began sending their children to English-language schools, either Catholic or Protestant but usually the latter. Motivated by religious and nationalist concerns, a small minority within the Commission des écoles catholiques de Montréal (CECM) attempted for a decade to get the Duplessis government to create a bilingual sector for immigrant children. When, in the early 1960s, the Lesage government approved a trial program of bilingual schools, its implementation was effectively foiled by powerful Anglophone opponents both within and outside the Catholic school board. The issue remained dormant until 1968 when the Francophone-dominated Catholic School Board of St. Leonard proposed to phase out its English-language schools. The neo-nationalists were trying to force the Union Nationale government to legislate all immigrants into French-language schools while the immigrants, predominantly Italian Catholics, were trying to preserve the principle of freedom of choice. Montreal's Anglophones, wary of any precedent that might endanger their established educational rights, threw their considerable support behind the immigrant community. The resulting pressure forced the Union Nationale government to recognize freedom of choice in Bill 63. In so doing, it incurred the wrath of the neo-nationalist movement and suffered a crushing defeat at the polls in 1970.

The language debate dominated Quebec politics for the next decade and contributed, in part, to the defeat of the Liberal Party by the Parti Québécois in the election of 1976. The PQ's charter of the French Language, best known as Bill 101, received widespread support from Francophone society. The Charter improved on Bourassa's Bill 22 in that it abandoned the bureaucratic language tests for immigrant children and streamed them, as well as all English-speaking Canadians entering Quebec from other parts of the country, into French-language schools.

Richard Jones, in "Politics and the Reinforcement of the French Language in the Province of Quebec, 1960–1985," provides a comprehensive overview of the demographic, ideological, and political pressures and constraints that challenged the language policy of all three of Quebec's political parties since the late 1960s. William Coleman, in "From Bill 22 to Bill 101," demonstrates how and why the Parti Québécois was able to satisfy the neo-nationalists by adopting a fairly coercive approach to the use of language in the public sector while at the same time bowing to pressure from the Anglophone and Francophone business sectors to modify substantially the original Charter's coercive measures pertaining to the use of the French language in the private sector.

POLITICS AND THE REINFORCEMENT OF THE FRENCH LANGUAGE IN CANADA AND QUEBEC, 1960–1986†

RICHARD JONES

It is commonplace to affirm that language has been a political issue in Canada ever since 1760 when the British completed their conquest of New France, and the colony's approximately 70,000 French-speaking inhabitants came under British domination. The new masters hoped that time would enable them to transform the French Canadians into good English-speaking members of the Church of England[1] or that British immigration would eventually swamp them. Although the English language rapidly assumed a privileged place in Quebec and in Canada, the French did not disappear; indeed they multiplied prolifically.[2] When Canada assumed Dominion status with a federal form of government in 1867, Quebec, the territory inhabited largely by Francophones, became a separate province.[3]

Confederation did not open an era of linguistic harmony in Canada. Indeed, bitter language conflict burst forth frequently as French-speaking minorities outside Quebec saw their few linguistic rights, particularly in the area of education, curtailed or eradicated by English-speaking majorities.[4]

Until 1960, it could be said that the status of the French language in Canada was at best stagnating and that citizens who spoke French or were of French ethnic origin were clearly disadvantaged compared to those who spoke English or were of British ethnic origin.[5] This article seeks to show that, since 1960, the status of the French language in Canada, as well as the position of Francophones in Canadian society, has, in many ways, improved markedly. Governments, at both the federal and provincial levels, have played a major role in this evolution; they intervened because of powerful political pressures applied by Canada's French-speaking population.[6] Yet many of the changes at the federal level and in the

---

†This article has not been previously published. It is an adaptation of a communication delivered at the annual meeting of the Southwest Social Sciences Association in San Antonio, Texas, March 1986.

provinces with English-speaking majorities have been cosmetic or at least not very far-reaching. The really significant transformation has occurred in the province of Quebec.

The Federal Government and the English-Speaking Provinces

The Royal Commission on Bilingualism and Biculturalism was established by the federal government in 1963 in response to demands for greater linguistic equality that were being formulated by French Canadians. According to its terms of reference, the Commission was expected to "recommend what steps should be taken to develop the Canadian Confederation on the basis of an equal partnership between the two founding races."[7] During the 1968 federal election campaign, linguistic equality was one of the themes developed by Liberal Prime Minister Pierre Elliott Trudeau. Trudeau was convinced that the federal government had to demonstrate to French Canadians that it was the government of all Canadians, not of English-speaking Canadians alone. Trudeau's concern was that the government of Quebec would succeed in portraying itself as the real representative of French Canadians; this situation could only undermine national unity.[8] The following year, Parliament adopted the Official Languages Act whose objective was to increase the percentage of French-speaking civil servants, augment the use of French within the civil service, and make French-language services at the federal level available for most French-speaking Canadians.[9] Finally, in 1982, linguistic rights were enshrined in the Canadian Charter of Rights and Freedoms,[10] an integral part of the Canadian Constitution.

Fifteen years after its adoption, the Official Languages Act had, in the words of Language Commissioner d'Iberville Fortier, produced some remarkable achievements but fallen far short of creating the equality between the two official languages that, after all, was the stated objective of the legislation. In his opinion, Canada had reached a "kind of watershed between the solid accomplishments of the past and new challenges which will take us beyond mere statements of principle."[11]

Since the late 1960s, most of the nine Canadian provinces with English-speaking majorities, and particularly New Brunswick and Ontario, have taken measures to assist their French-language minorities. New Brunswick, approximately one-third of whose population is French-speaking, adopted its own largely symbolic Official Languages Act in 1969. Ontario, with nearly half a million citizens of French mother tongue,[12] has also extended French-language rights in areas such as education and the courts though, probably to avoid a backlash, it has refused to become officially bilingual. Other provinces have also taken initiatives although, in some important cases, they have acted only under judicial pressure.[13]

This flurry of linguistic activity in Canada has had no effect on the relatively rapid assimilation, into the English-speaking majority, of Francophones living in the eight provinces that are massively Anglophone. The Task Force on Canadian Unity, created in 1977 with a broad mandate to obtain and publicize the views of Canadians regarding the state of their country, waxed pessimistic in this regard. Attributing the phenomenon to, among other factors, relatively high rates of intermarriage of Francophones with Anglophones, the Commission concluded: "The rate of linguistic assimilation of French-speaking minorities is quite high, and appears to be accelerating in all English-speaking provinces other than New Brunswick."[14]

The 1981 census figures confirmed this sombre diagnosis, showing that 32.8 percent of Canadians of French mother tongue, living outside Quebec, had shifted to English as the main language of the home. The 1971 figure had been 29.6 percent. Thus, the French mother tongue group now represents only 5.3 percent of Canada's population outside Quebec, and the group for which French is the language spoken in the home constitutes an almost negligible 3.8 percent of the population.[15]

There can be no doubt that, without the presence of the province of Quebec, the situation of the French language in Canada would be bleak indeed.[16] Although the Francophone minorities outside Quebec have long been agitating for better treatment, the pressures they could exert on their respective provincial governments as well as on the federal government have been relatively modest. In addition to lacking economic clout, the group has been simply too small, too widely dispersed geographically and, until recently, too disorganized to wield much weight.

Quebec's presence, then, has been decisive for the French fact in Canada. Four out of five French-speaking Canadians live in that province, Canada's second largest in terms of population. Just as the rest of Canada has become relatively more English-speaking as the Francophone minorities retreat, Quebec has, in recent years, become increasingly French-speaking. The 1981 census showed that 82.4 percent of Quebeckers were of French mother tongue and that virtually the same proportion generally spoke French in the home.[17] In other words, languages in Canada seem to be undergoing a territorialization whereby Quebec becomes more French while the rest of Canada registers consistent gains for the English language.[18] Ultimately, this phenomenon could strengthen division within Canada.

The Beginnings of the Language Debate in Quebec

Respecting the reinforcement of the French language in Canada since 1960, Quebec has been a theatre of dramatic activity, and state intervention has been constant and has had measurable impact. The undeniable result has been to strengthen the position of the French language in that province, though the extent of that improvement and particularly its durability remain subjects of rather acrimonious debate.

By the late 1960s, the major political parties in Quebec were all debating the language question and attempting to conceive policies that would not only satisfy their members but also ensure wide support at the polls. The context, as we shall see, favoured the most nationalistic of the three major parties, the Parti Québécois, ideologically committed to a French Quebec. Although after coming to power in 1976 it had to contend with realities that it could neither change nor ignore, it was able to accomplish its objectives in matters of language to a considerable degree.

A series of factors contributed to transforming the issue of language into an increasingly controversial subject in Quebec and finally to forcing the government to legislate. From 1944, the very conservative rural-based Union Nationale had been maintained in power under the firm and, according to his foes, dictatorial hand of Maurice Duplessis.[19] Duplessis died in 1959 and, the following year, the Liberals under Jean Lesage gained power, promising to modernize Quebec. The pace of change became so breathless that a journalist soon baptized the new era the "Quiet Revolution."[20]

The reforms of the Quiet Revolution aimed at modernizing the institutions, developing the economy, and furthering the welfare state. But they also had considerable nationalistic content since they were designed to improve the lot of Francophones as well as the position of Quebec in Confederation. The nationalization of the private Anglo-Canadian and American hydro-electric power utilities,[21] Quebec's epic confrontations with the federal government over questions of money and power, and the province's ventures into the domain of international relations, notably with France, were at least partly based upon nationalist considerations.

The educational system, revamped at least structurally by the reformers of the Quiet Revolution, began turning out more and more graduates seeking employment. Certainly the expansion of the provincial government during these years created many new jobs for Francophones. In other fields, though, Anglo-dominated structures blocked opportunities. The federal civil service as yet offered few possibilities to Francophones unwilling to do virtually all their work in English. In addition, private enterprise, particularly the upper echelons, remained an Anglophone preserve that French Canadians had great difficulty penetrating. Social scientists have abundantly described the rise of this new Francophone middle class.[22] For its members, tangible and intangible objectives of an individual character linked to self-interest, questions of jobs, money and social status, were not the only motivations. Aspirations of a collective nature were also important. Many Francophones were less and less disposed, after the "cultural mutation"[23] of these years, to continue to accept what they perceived as second-class citizenship. This group would be the standard-bearer of the new nationalism.

Nationalists in Quebec were highly sensitive to the nationalist currents that in the early 1960s were sweeping parts of Europe and the newly-emancipated states of Africa and Asia. Some Quebeckers saw their province's status as akin to that of a colonized state and they began preaching Quebec's independence.[24] Naturally, an independent Quebec was to be a French state.[25]

The Quiet Revolution can be said to have marked the demise of the traditional Quebec, a Quebec whose identity was based on Catholicism, French language and culture, and ruralism. Of course, since the early twentieth century, the traditional society had been in decline; indeed, by 1921, Quebec's population was half urban. By the mid-1960s, Quebec was rapidly becoming a secular society as the Church withdrew from its temporal preoccupations. What remained to distinguish French Canadians from other North Americans?[26] Language and culture, no doubt, and the nationalists would give the promotion of these traits their full attention.

The preoccupation with language also stemmed from profound feelings of insecurity among Francophones. For example, the decline of the birth rate could have potentially disastrous effects on the proportion of the French population in Canada as well as in Quebec. As late as 1947, some observers, like Paul Sauriol, a journalist at the nationalist daily *Le Devoir*, foresaw the day when French-speaking Canadians would form the largest linguistic group in Canada.[27] Traditionally, a high birth rate was seen as a means of counterbalancing the influx of immigrants into Canada few of whom spoke French or learned that language. But, by the late 1950s and early 1960s, the birth rate began to decline precipitously. In 1954, the rate was still 30.4 per thousand. By 1965, it had dropped to 21.3.[28] The dream of the "revenge of the cradle" was apparently over.

Another worrisome trend was the fact that the great majority of immigrants settling in Quebec chose to send their children to English-language schools[29] and to integrate into the English-speaking minority. For them, English was simply the most "attractive" language. Should they leave Quebec, they would obviously require an excellent knowledge of English. Within Quebec, it did not appear essential for them to learn French, particularly for those living in the Montreal area. Some demographers hypothesized that Montreal would be close to having an English-speaking majority by the year 2000.[30] Not surprisingly, the increasingly vocal nationalist lobby urged that French be established, to a much greater degree, as the language of work and of education. Only the government could bring about the desired changes.

But the government, regardless of what party was in power, had to be forced to act. The nationalists suspected that, without powerful popular pressure, the parties committed to federalism, specifically the Liberals and the Union Nationale, would not dare adopt the bold pro-French measures that they deemed necessary. But there was another more attractive possibility. Perhaps the nationalists, now more and more favourable to independence for Quebec, could themselves ride to power within a party whose backbone they would form. Then they could write and apply the language legislation. This, precisely, was to come about.

Before studying the ways in which the three major political formations dealt with the language issue, a brief description of each is necessary. The Liberal Party, largely urban-based, was the force behind Quebec's modernization in the early 1960s. It was quite willing to promote nationalist causes; still, there were limits beyond which a party committed to maintaining Quebec within Confederation could not go. In addition to widespread backing among Francophones, the party enjoyed the support of big enterprise, mostly Anglophone, and of the Anglophone minority in general.

On the specific issue of language, the Liberals were disposed to taking modest steps to strengthen the position of French. They were, however, unwilling to risk alienating those groups relatively satisfied with the status quo, particularly their English-speaking supporters and the business community. Nor, in the years from 1960 to 1966 when the Liberals held power, was the nationalist lobby sufficiently strong to force it to go further. In their 1960 election program, the Liberals promised to take measures to assist the French language and culture and notably create an Office de la langue française.[31] Few could feel threatened by these proposals. In 1966, the Liberals went somewhat further, declaring themselves willing to make French "the main language of work and of communication in Quebec" in order to "guarantee the vitality of the language and at the same time enable the majority of [Quebec's] population to live in French." Reassuring the hesitant, they declared that this objective was to be accomplished "with full respect for the undeniable rights of the Anglophone minority."[32]

The Union Nationale, in power from 1966 until 1970, might have been expected to produce bolder policies than the Liberals. During the Duplessis years, had it not boasted of being the vehicle of nationalism and the ardent defender of Quebec's autonomy?[33] Moreover, it was less beholden to the English-speaking minority from which it received relatively few votes. Yet it was perhaps more the flag-bearer of an old-style nationalism in which the defence of language through government intervention was not judged necessary. Nor did it desire to rouse English-speaking Canada against it. Thus, in 1966, the party devoted just a single line in a twenty-page program to the subject, vaguely promising to give French the status of "national language."[34] Clearly, the nationalist lobby could not hope for satisfaction from this party!

The impetus for movement on the language question was to come from a new party, established in October 1968, called the Parti Québécois. This left-of-centre political formation was the vehicle of the nationalist aspirations of Quebec's new middle class, the intelligentsia that had come of age during the Quiet Revolution. Teachers, professors, professionals, students, and elements of the working class formed the backbone of the new group.[35] It proposed a modified form of independence for Quebec called "sovereignty-association," a sort of hybrid formula implying political sovereignty for the province coupled with an economic association with the rest of Canada.

The language policy of the Parti Québécois reflected both its orientation toward independence and its middle-class composition. The independentist option meant that it viewed Quebec as a separate entity. The Anglophone minority in Quebec was thus not perceived as part of a Canadian majority, a position that, in the eyes of the Liberals and the Union Nationale, justified special status for that group. Rather, Quebec Anglophones were simply another minority that would have to learn to participate in the life of a French Quebec. As for the party's middle-class power base, it implied that employers' views risked being given short shrift. Still, it should be noted that the Parti Québécois, mainly because of the powerful influence exerted by its charismatic leader, René Lévesque, did not propose to abolish the English-language school system. Its position on this question would provoke considerable tension within the party.

Language Legislation: From Bill 85 to Bill 22

All three parties ultimately had to wrestle with the language issue, both in opposition and in power. It was during the Union Nationale's mandate from 1966 until 1970 that pressures heated up considerably. In 1968, a local school council in the town of St. Léonard on Montreal Island voted the gradual elimination of schooling in English for the large number of Italian children enrolled in the district.

The Italian community protested vehemently while the nationalist camp welcomed the commission's decision. "What we need are ten, twenty, fifty St. Leonards," contended *Le Devoir* editorialist Jean-Marc Léger, echoing the campaign of the group that was spearheading the movement for obligatory French schooling.[36] The English-language community demanded that the government intervene to guarantee by law unimpeded access to English-language schools for any Quebec child. Obviously, Anglophones were concerned that this isolated incident could snowball into a powerful and dangerous trend and that the English-language school sector would be deprived of the not inconsiderable reinforcements furnished by the "Allophone" community.[37]

The Union Nationale government was thus obliged to come to grips with this very volatile issue. Many of its members in the National Assembly,[38] conservatives from rural districts, had little interest in this question that concerned mainly Montreal and they were primarily concerned with preserving social peace. Pressures from the powerful Anglophone community urged legislative action to guarantee what it contended were its rights.[39] But the Union Nationale also counted a few nationalists who were convinced that action was needed to defend the French language. The premier would have to arbitrate these differences.

Daniel Johnson, Quebec's premier from 1966 until September 1968, was assuredly a nationalist. He had frequently criticized the lack of rights of the French-speaking minorities in the other provinces, demanding "Equality or Independence" as well as additional legislative powers for Quebec in the framework of a new constitution.[40] Still, he was a shrewd politician and he found the subject of St. Leonard a slippery banana peel indeed. At a press conference held a few hours before his sudden death, he responded ambiguously to English-speaking journalists who queried him repeatedly on the affair. "We will take all useful measures, not by legislation but by other means, to make non-French-speaking Quebeckers part of Quebec so that they feel at home and learn French, the dominant language of Quebec." But he went on to say that language rights had to be protected and that it was inadmissible that local school commissions have the power to define them.[41] Just like the celebrated Marquess of Plaza-Toro, Johnson seemed to want to mount his horse and ride off in all directions at once. He certainly feared the political consequences of any action his government might take.

Johnson's successor, Jean-Jacques Bertrand, desired a rapid solution. A convinced federalist, he represented a rural district one quarter of whose population was English-speaking. Perhaps for those reasons he was less given to pushing nationalist themes. In any case, he indicated his intention to legislate "free choice" in respect to the language of instruction, hoping thus, vainly as it turned out, to gain Anglophone support in a by-election held to fill a vacancy in the Assembly.[42] Nationalist groups objected strenuously as did several Union Nationale legislators, and Bertrand decided to withdraw the proposed bill.[43] With the objective of gaining time, he also decided, in the tried and true Canadian manner, to have a study done. He thus set up the Gendron Committee whose mandate was to "make an inquiry into and submit a report on the position of French as the language of usage in Quebec."[44]

September 1969 brought riots opposing French and Italians in St. Léonard where the school commission struggled to find a solution acceptable to all sides.

The Prime Minister's office was besieged with letters and telegrams, and the English-language press urged: "Mr. Bertrand must act."[45] In the Assembly, the opposition Liberal Party also applied pressure, signifying that, although the Union Nationale appeared divided on the issue, the Liberals would support Bertrand.[46] Disorders in Montreal linked to illegal strikes provoked a veritable panic within the government, forcing it to move to repress the troubles, linguistic and otherwise.[47]

With the support of most of his Cabinet and the elected members of his party, Bertrand decided upon what he hoped would be perceived as a middle-of-the-road course. He presented Bill 63, entitled An Act to Promote the French Language in Quebec,[48] which proposed to give all new arrivals in Quebec a knowledge of the French language. But the really important part of the new law, the one relevant to the St. Leonard affair, was the clause dealing with the language of instruction: it recognized the right of any Quebecker to enrol his or her child in an English-language school.

In general, English-speaking Quebeckers were satisfied with this new law. The Liberals, with the evident intention of embarrassing the Union Nationale, criticized the bill on the grounds that it did not really make French the "priority language" of Quebec.[49] As for the nationalists, many of whom were already supporting the fledgling Parti Québécois, they were furious at what they perceived as a "linguistic Munich," an ignominious surrender on the part of the Bertrand government, a powerful encouragement to the anglicization of Quebeckers. Immediately, they began urging repeal of the law. Thousands of demonstrators converged upon the National Assembly in Quebec City to express their opposition. Strikes erupted in the colleges and universities. When the next provincial elections were called in 1970, the Union Nationale was defeated handily by the Liberals but the two-year-old Parti Québécois managed to garner one-quarter of the vote. It is difficult to judge the role of the language question in the Union Nationale's defeat but the relative success of the Parti Québécois indicated that nationalist sentiment was rising.[50]

Now it was the turn of the Liberals to open Pandora's box. After the Gendron Commission finally published its report in 1973 recommending strong measures in favour of French, they could no longer refrain from moving. Fearful of the rapidly improving fortunes of the Parti Québécois (which had obtained nearly one vote in three in the 1973 elections), the Liberals had to make proposals that would conserve the support of at least the less extreme nationalists. The nationalist camp was simply becoming too important to be neglected. Yet the Liberals also represented the non-French-speaking community in Quebec and business had considerable influence in the party. How could the Liberals hope to harmonize the rapidly polarizing positions on the language question?

Bill 22 was the Liberals' attempt to find a solution to the dilemma.[51] It clearly demonstrated their conviction that most French-speaking Quebeckers were now prepared to take strong measures to reinforce the position of the French language. Bill 22 thus proposed a series of measures designed to make French, at least to a greater degree, the language of work and of communication within Quebec. The means to bring this about were persuasive rather than coercive. More radically, though, the bill restricted access to schools in the English sector to Anglophones and to Allophones who had a sufficient knowledge of English, a level that was to be verified by tests. Moreover, a cap was placed on the size of enrolment in the English-language sector.

This measure showed that the Liberals were now willing to risk provoking the ire of the party's non-French-speaking supporters. Undoubtedly, they calculated that non-Francophones, even though unhappy, constituted a captive electorate. After all, they had never backed the Union Nationale in the past and there was certainly no possibility of their supporting the independentist Parti Québécois.

But the Liberals gravely miscalculated the extent of Anglophone discontent. A marathon radio program on the English-language station CFCF in Montreal brought 600,000 Quebeckers, mostly Anglophones, to sign a telegram-petition to Prime Minister Trudeau urging abolition of the law.[52]

Nationalists bitterly attacked Bill 22 because of numerous loopholes; they insisted that it would do little to bring immigrants into the French-language stream, and the statistics ultimately showed that they were right in this regard. Indeed, in 1976–77, the last year of operation of Bill 22, the percentage of Allophone children attending English schools actually increased by 6.4 percent.[53] Still, the Anglophone and Allophone communities were even more adamant in their opposition to the law, particularly the stipulations regarding the language of education. When, in 1976, the Union Nationale, traditionally the voice of Quebec nationalism, made the sensational promise that, if elected, it would restore free choice of the language of schooling, large numbers of non-Francophones rallied to it, deserting the now detested Liberal Party and its despised leader, Robert Bourassa.[54] For numerous other reasons unrelated to this paper, the Liberals lost ground while the Parti Québécois gained sufficient support to win the election and form the next government.

Bill 101: The Charter of the French Language

Contrary to the other two parties, the Parti Québécois had made no secret of its policy on language nor of the priority that it gave that question.[55] After all, the notion of an independent Quebec was predicated on the existence of a Quebec nation, of a separate identity, of a "personality at whose core is the fact that we speak French."[56] An independent Quebec would "make French the country's only official language," the party's 1971 program asserted. French would be the language of governmental institutions, it would be the working language of all enterprises, all new immigrants would be required to pass a French fluency test as a condition for obtaining a permanent visa or Quebec citizenship.[57] Since language was the fundamental value championed by the party, it was only natural that "Péquistes" be intensely concerned with the dangers faced by the French language in Quebec and committed to taking strong corrective measures. As befitted left-of-centre believers in a strongly-interventionist government, laws would be adopted to solve linguistic problems.

Parti Québécois adherents were undoubtedly far more united on language policy than were the supporters of the two rival parties. Nevertheless, the Parti

Québécois was on several occasions racked by acrimonious disputes concerning what rights or privileges, if any, would be accorded the province's English-speaking community.[58] For example, would there be a publicly-financed English-language school sector? Radicals within the party who favoured unilingualism, many of whom had been members of the separatist Rassemblement pour l'indépendance nationale, wanted the demise of English schools; indeed, during the 1971 congress, party president René Lévesque had to threaten to resign in order to have his more moderate position prevail. Again, in February 1973, the party's executive had to take a harder line on public financing of English schools, agreeing to place a permanent ceiling on funding, in order to convince party members to accept simply the principle of the existence of schools for the English minority.[59]

The party program, on language as on all other questions, was defined with impressive democracy by elected delegates during frequent annual or biennial congresses; it certainly reflected the membership's aspirations, though generally tempered by the leadership's more moderate positions. It did not necessarily constitute a shrewd and sound appreciation of the Quebec context in general and of political realities in particular. Thus, after its election in 1976, the Parti Québécois quickly came to realize that designing a general policy was much easier than drawing up specific regulations and applying them to everyday situations. Like the other two parties, the Parti Québécois faced numerous constraints in dealing with language. Specifically, the need to take account of certain pressure made it impossible to build a Quebec as unilingually French as the party had originally intended.

Shortly after its arrival in power, the Parti Québécois government issued a White Paper detailing the language policy that it intended to implement.[60] This policy was soon set out in proposed legislation, the symbolically numbered Bill 1. The bill proposed vigorous measures to make French the language of the workplace and backed these up with threats of fines and other penalties for non-compliance. It also proposed that, generally, only French could appear on signs in public and that hitherto English-language institutions would have to communicate with the government and among themselves in French. The English-speaking school sector was to be maintained but, in most cases, only children with at least one parent who had had his or her primary schooling in Quebec in the English language were eligible. It was clear that the English sector was doomed to atrophy.

Reaction of Quebec's Anglophones was uniformly negative although, contrarily to what they had said of the Liberals, they could not pretend that the Parti Québécois had abandoned them.[61] English-speaking Quebeckers had shown only negligible support for the Parti Québécois, the party of separatism.[62] On language, the party's platform had always been quite clear — and quite unacceptable from the point of view of the English-speaking minority.[63]

In particular, business circles denounced certain aspects of Bill 1 linked to the language of the workplace. Essentially, they maintained that the law's requirements would increase costs and put Quebec enterprises at a comparative disadvantage in relation to firms elsewhere in North America. They also contended that the law gave too much power to workers and unions. Finally, the clauses that severely limited enrolment in English-language schools caused deep concern: would recruiting efforts and transfers from outside the province not be hampered?

Certainly the Parti Québécois numbered few adherents in the business world. Business thus had to make special efforts to make its weight felt once the Parti Québécois came into office. In many respects, its remonstrances were successful in that the modified version of Bill 1, called Bill 101 (in particular, its final version) took heed of business criticism. Of course, the Parti Québécois could not, even had it so wished, have abandoned the key stipulations of its language project; closely surveyed by the party's membership, the government had to remain within bounds. On the other hand, the Parti Québécois could not afford to alienate irreparably the business world. A referendum on sovereignty-association had to be held during its first mandate in office and it was reasonable to assume that, if Quebec's economy floundered during this period, the electors would spurn the project.

Even with the amendments, Anglophone businesses clearly did not like the law. Many enterprises, particularly head offices, left Quebec, often blaming the language legislation. Sun Life was a noisy and well-publicized example of this exodus. Yet it is very difficult to evaluate the actual causes of these departures. For some, higher Quebec taxes were the important issue. For others, militant unionism made Quebec a difficult place in which to do business. For still others, it was important to be where the action was, and that meant moving west, to Toronto, or to Alberta during the oil boom of the late 1970s.

The Parti Québécois was thus forced to moderate its language legislation and to apply it less rigorously than might otherwise have been the case. For example, head offices and research centres were exempted from the law's provisions. Professionals who had no contact with the public would not have to pass a test of French proficiency.[64] Moreover, it was common knowledge that hundreds of students were illegally enrolled in the English Protestant schools; while denouncing the situation frequently, the government preferred that the law be flouted rather than use force to expel these students.[65]

The courts ultimately constituted an additional constraint. They declared unconstitutional certain sections of the language legislation, thus weakening Bill 101.[66] Since Quebec remains a part of Canada, the Supreme Court of Canada is the court of last appeal, a situation that the Parti Québécois did not foresee or did not want to imagine in the heady days of 1977. In addition, the new Canadian constitution, adopted without Quebec's consent in 1982, contains certain language guarantees with which Quebec is not in agreement but which nevertheless apply.

One new element that could well have an impact on the language question is the return to power, in December 1985, of the Liberals under their reincarnated leader, Robert Bourassa. The party has again become the advocate of the English-speaking minority, which counts four ministers in the provincial Cabinet. Yet interestingly — and this is surely an indication of the very considerable evolution that Quebec has undergone in matters of language since the early 1970s — the Liberals have indicated that, while they may make certain concessions and adjust Bill 101 to make it more flexible, they will not abrogate the law. Among the modifications envisaged should be mentioned the softening of the requirement that signs be in French only. Public opinion polls show an increasing percentage of Quebeckers willing to accept bilingualism on signs.[67] Still, it is apparent that

Quebec has adapted to the law and that the law has changed Quebec. More than half of all Allophone children are now enrolled in schools in the French sector.[68] The proportion of workers who say they work in French has increased significantly.[69] Enterprises under French control now furnish more than sixty percent of all jobs in Quebec, up from forty-seven percent in 1960.[70] Even the English-speaking minority, which has undergone a veritable revolution since 1970, seems able to live with the law.[71]

It was inevitable that the changes that occurred in Quebec in the early 1960s would eventually have an impact on language, a highly emotional issue. Within the federal government and the English-speaking provinces, these changes have certainly had some effect. The proportion of French-speakers in the federal civil service has increased and now approaches the proportion of Francophones in the total population.[72] French-language services have become more widely available. Bilingualism has become more popular among Canada's English-speaking population.[73] Still, a command of English remains a virtual necessity for Franco-phones outside Quebec since, with some exceptions, the concentrations of French-speaking population are insufficient to allow daily activities, notably work, to be carried out in French. It is thus not surprising that assimilation takes a large toll among the French-speaking minorities and that even the awakening of the federal and, at least, some provincial governments to the French fact does not seem to have stemmed linguistic losses.

The Quebec case is very different since that province has always had a strong French-speaking majority that controls the provincial government. Nevertheless, until very recently, the English-speaking minority in Quebec has wielded enormous economic power (and to a somewhat lesser extent still does)[74] and, in addition, has benefited immensely from the prestige accruing to speakers of Canada's and North America's major language. The Quiet Revolution of the early 1960s made Francophones aware of a linguistic disequilibrium that disadvantaged them.[75] But it was inevitable that any attempt to modify fundamentally the balance between the two languages in Quebec would provoke bitter disputes between the majority and the minority.

Three political parties faced the challenge of enhancing the status of the French language within Quebec and of improving opportunities for Francophones. Each party's actions in this regard were affected by particular constraints. For the two old parties, the Liberals and the Union Nationale, the language issue caused internecine strife within party ranks as well as considerable harm at the polls. In particular, the Liberals had to deal with the fact that their supporters included virtually the entire non-Francophone minority, a group whose conception of Quebec society was markedly different from that of most Francophones.

The Parti Québécois, as we have seen, proceeded differently. Far from trying to shy away from the issue and to seek some middle ground that would not alienate important factions, the party placed language reform in the forefront of its program and it hoped that its promise of a strong stand in favour of the French language would generate support among a majority of French-speaking Quebeckers. That hope proved realistic enough although, once in power, the

Parti Québécois could no longer ignore key sectors of opinion that had opposed its language policy.

What does the future bode for the French language in Quebec? The heroic exploits of the knights of language are now fading rapidly into the past. There are many indications that the younger generation of Quebeckers, those who did not fight the battles of the 1960s and 1970s, believe that the question has been permanently resolved and that French is now secure in the province.[76] This phenomenon is perhaps an indication of the relative success of Bill 101 in changing the face of Quebec. Other observers, perhaps more perspicacious, see continued dangers for the French language, regardless of the language legislation. The Conseil de la langue française, charged with advising the government on matters of language, affirms that French has still not become the "normal, habitual language of work, of teaching, of communications, of commerce and business."[77] The English language continues to surround and to penetrate Quebec. Communications, and notably cable television, have made English-language stations more numerous for most subscribers than French-language stations.[78] American culture and cultural practices will undoubtedly have a growing impact on Quebec as an open society. In addition, the tremendous advances of computer science since the late 1970s, a phenomenon entirely unforeseen by the writers of Bill 101, have been largely in English, whether it be manufacturers' manuals or software. Indeed, the three offices concerned with the application of Bill 101 see the francization of this sector as the major challenge of the near future.[79]

Other problems, though having no relation to Bill 101, certainly affect the future of the French language in Quebec. Education critics have decried poor teaching of French in schools.[80] Even business leaders have protested against graduates' insufficient mastery of the French language. Finally, demographic projections for Quebec indicate that the province's population will begin to diminish shortly after the year 2000. Declining births (the Quebec fertility rate now stands at 1.42, considerably below the Canadian average of 1.68), minimal immigration from foreign countries and, since the mid-1970s, a negative balance in population exchanges with other Canadian provinces, explain this phenomenon the repercussions of which could be dramatic.[81]

Language legislation in Canada, and particularly in Quebec, has undoubtedly had significant effects. Still, it appears certain that legislation alone cannot solve the major challenges that the French language must face if it is to maintain what has been acquired over the past twenty years.

Notes

1. The secret instructions accompanying the Quebec Act of 1774 are eloquent in this regard. For historian Hilda Neatby, the act and the instructions taken together signified "gentle but steady and determined anglicization." See her *Quebec: The Revolutionary Age, 1760–1791* (Toronto: McClelland and Stewart, 1966), 139.

2. Historian Fernand Ouellet calculates the birth rate at a very respectable 50 to 55 per thousand during the century following the Conquest. See *Histoire économique et sociale du Québec, 1760–1850* (Montreal: Fides, 1966), 142, 197, 468.

3. In 1851, 75.2 percent of Quebec's population was French-speaking. By 1901, this figure had climbed to 80.3 percent: *Annuaire de Quebec, 1968–1969* (Quebec: Bureau de la Statistique du Québec, 1968), 179.

4. For a generally good study of English-French relations in the nineteenth century, see A.I. Silver, *The French-Canadian Idea of Confederation, 1864–1900* (Toronto: University of Toronto Press, 1982). On the Manitoba School Question, Paul Crunican's *Priests and Politicians: Manitoba Schools and the Election of 1869* (Toronto: University of Toronto Press, 1974), is excellent. As for Ontario's attempts to suppress French-language education, consult Robert Choquette, *Language and Religion: A History of English-French Conflict in Ontario* (Ottawa: University of Ottawa Press, 1975).

5. The Royal Commission on Bilingualism and Biculturalism, in an oft-quoted and abundantly discussed table, showed that French Canadians in Quebec placed twelfth among fourteen ethnic groups by average labour income of male salary- and wage-earners in 1961. Those of British origin placed first, at a level 55 percent higher than that of the French. Even bilingualism did not appear a significant economic asset. Looking specifically at language, unilingual Anglophones were at the top of the ladder, well ahead of bilingual Francophones: *Report*, Book III: *The Work World* (Ottawa: Queen's Printer, 1969), 22–24. It should be mentioned, though, that by the 1980s the French had achieved virtual economic parity with the British in Canada: Jac-André Boulet and Laval Lavallée, *L'évolution des disparités linguistiques de revenus de travail au Canada de 1970 à 1980* (Ottawa: Conseil économique du Canada, October 1983).

6. Canadians whose mother tongue (i.e., the first language learned and still understood) was French accounted for 28.1 percent of the population in 1961, and for 25.7 percent in 1981: Statistics Canada, 1961 and 1981 Censuses and tables furnished in *Language and Society* 9 (Spring 1983), 20–21. Also, 24.6 percent of Canadians told government census-takers in 1981 that the language they most often spoke at home was French. This question, more indicative of the actual strength of the French language in Canada, was first asked in 1971.

7. Royal Commission on Bilingualism and Biculturalism, *Report*. Book I: *The Official Languages* (Ottawa: Queen's Printer, 1967), 173.

8. Daniel Johnson, premier of Quebec from 1966 to 1968, promoted the Two Nations concept. In this regard, he asserted: "French Canadians seek to identify themselves with the State of Quebec, the only state in which they can claim to be masters of their destiny, the only one that they can utilize to promote the development of their community." On the other hand, English-Canadians tend, for their part, to "consider Ottawa as their national state": Daniel Johnson, *Egalité ou indépendance* (Montreal: Éditions Renaissance, 1965), 24, 50.

9. S.C. 1969, c. 54, "An Act respecting the status of the official languages of Canada." The text and comments may be found in Commissioner of Official Languages, *First Annual Report, 1970–1971* (Ottawa: Information Canada, 1971), 105–14 and 1–11.

10. Sections 16 to 23 of the Constitution Act, 1982, specify language rights.

11. Commissioner of Official Languages, *Annual Report 1984* (Ottawa: Minister of Supply and Services Canada, 1985), preface.

12. This figure, however, represents a mere 5.5 percent of the total population of Canada's most populous province; Francophones tend to be concentrated in the eastern and northern portions of the province.

13. Such is the case of Manitoba, now obliged by the Supreme Court to translate its laws into French. The Francophones of that province proposed that, instead of translating thousands of laws, many of them inoperative, the provincial government offer certain services in French. In 1984, after having accepted the proposition, the government yielded to widespread Anglophone opposition and backed down from its commitment.

14. Task Force on Canadian Unity, *A Future Together: Observations and Recommendations* (Ottawa: Minister of Supply and Services Canada, 1979), 51.

15. Statistics Canada, 1981 census and tables furnished in Robert Bourbeau, "Canada's Language Transfer Phenomenon," *Language and Society* 11 (Autumn 1983): 14–22.

16. The most recent Statistics Canada report affirms that the French have maintained their positions, in relative terms, only in Quebec (figures quoted in *La Presse*, 26 janvier 1985).

17. Bourbeau, "Canada's Language Transfer Phenomenon," 15.

18. This phenomenon was first convincingly documented by Richard J. Joy in *Languages in Conflict* (Toronto: McClelland and Stewart, Carleton Library no. 61, 1972). Davidson Dunton, co-chairman of the

Royal Commission on Bilingualism and Biculturalism, has remarked on the popularity of the "two unilingualisms" solutions to the Canadian language question: "The Muddy Waters of Bilingualism," *Language and Society* 1 (Autumn 1979), 7.

19. See Richard Jones, *Duplessis and the Union Nationale Administration* (Ottawa: Canadian Historical Association, booklet no. 35, 1983) and reprinted in this volume.

20. This era has recently been chronicled by political scientist Dale C. Thomson in *Jean Lesage and the Quiet Revolution* (Toronto: Macmillan of Canada, 1984).

21. "Masters in our own house" was the theme of the Liberal election campaign in 1962. The major issue of the campaign was the nationalization of the private electrical power companies (*Manifeste du parti libéral du Québec*, 1962, 1).

22. For example, Hubert Guindon, "Social Unrest, Social Class, and Quebec's Bureaucratic Revolution," *Queen's Quarterly* LXXI, 2 (Summer 1964): 150–62; Roch Denis, *Luttes de classes et question nationale au Québec, 1948–1968* (Montreal: Presses Socialistes Internationales, 1979).

23. The expression is from Université de Montréal sociologist Guy Rocher, *Le Québec en mutation* (Montreal: Éditions Hurtubise HMH 1973).

24. The titles of some of the separatist books published in these years are revealing: Raymond Barbeau, *Le Québec est-il une colonie?* (Montreal: Les Éditions de l'Homme, 1962); Raymond Barbeau, *La libération économique du Québec* (Montreal: Les Éditions de l'Homme, 1963); Andrew D'Allemagne, *Le colonialisme au Québec* (Montreal: Les Éditions R-B, 1966).

25. The major independentist group of the early 1960s, the Rassemblement pour l'indépendance nationale, vigorously denounced bilingualism and objected to any legislative recognition of rights for Quebec's English-speaking linguistic minority (*Programme du R.I.N.*, octobre 1962, 2).

26. Université Laval sociologist Fernand Dumont was one of those asking this question. See: "Y a-t-il un avenir pour l'homme canadien-français?" in *La vigile du Québec* (Montreal: Éditions Hurtubise-HMH, 1971), 57–76.

27. "Programme d'immigration au service d'une politique raciste," editorial, *Le Devoir*, 7 octobre 1947, 1.

28. *Annuaire du Québec 1968–1969*, 255.

29. The percentage of New Canadians enrolled in French schools fell from 52 in 1931–32 to 25 in 1962–63, then to 11 by 1972–73: Gary Caldwell, "Assimilation and the Demographic Future of Quebec" in *Quebec's Language Policies: Background and Response*, edited by John R. Mallea (Quebec: Centre international de recherche sur le bilinguisme, Presses de l'Université Laval, 1977), 57.

30. Jacques Henripin saw Montreal as being between 53 and 60 percent French-speaking by 2000, a decline of between 6 and 13 percent, in "Quebec and the Demographic Dilemma of French-Canadian Society," *Quebec's Language Policies*, 43, 48.

31. *Programme politique du Parti libéral du Québec*, 1960, 2.

32. *Québec en marche. Le programme politique du Parti libéral du Québec*, 1966, 5.

33. The best history of the party is Herbert F. Quinn's *The Union Nationale: Quebec Nationalism from Duplessis to Lévesque*, 2nd ed. (Toronto: University of Toronto Press, 1979).

34. *Objectifs 1966 de l'Union Nationale, un programme d'action pour une jeune nation. Québec d'abord*, 3.

35. Of the nearly 90,000 members of the Parti Québécois in 1971, nearly 40 percent belonged to the liberal professions, including a very large number of teachers, nearly 25 percent were white-collar workers, mainly office employees and service workers, and 15 percent were students: *Le Parti québécois en bref* (Montreal: Les Éditions du Parti québécois, 1971), 21.

36. Jean-Marc Léger, "Il faut créer dix, vingt, cinquante St-Léonard," *Le Devoir*, 4 septembre 1968.

37. "Allophone," in the Canadian context, is the term used to describe persons whose mother tongue is neither English nor French.

38. Since 1968, Quebec's unicameral legislature has been called the "National Assembly," an appellation of obvious symbolical value. The other Canadian provinces use the term "Legislative Assembly."

39. From Toronto, a *Globe and Mail* editorial denounced what it saw as "cultural protectionism": "Turning Back the Clock," 2 Sept. 1968.

40. See, for example, Johnson's speech at the first meeting of the Constitutional Conference in Ottawa in February, 1968. Constitutional Conference, First Meeting, *Proceedings* (Ottawa: Queen's Printer, 1968), 53–71.

41. Text of press conference quoted in Paul Gros d'Aillon, *Daniel Johnson, l'égalité avant l'indépendance* (Montreal: Les Éditions internationales Stanké, 1979), 230–34.

42. This was the interpretation of journalists and even Bertrand admitted that there did seem to be a coincidence ("Des groupes francophones protestent: le bill sur les droits scolaires sera présenté aujourd'hui," *Le Devoir*, 26 novembre 1968). The election theme in the district of Notre-Dame-de-Grâce, an English-speaking constituency in Montreal, was "Remember St. Leonard" (*The Montreal Star*, editorial, 20 Nov. 1968).

43. This is the interpretation of Jérôme Proulx, a Union Nationale deputy, in his book, *Le panier de crabes* (Montreal: Éditions Parti Pris, 1971), 111–24. Journalists agreed ("Le bill sur les droits scolaires: l'opposition du caucus fait reculer Bertrand," *Le Devoir*, 27 novembre 1968, headline; Vincent Prince, "Le bill Bertrand renvoyé à un Comité," editorial, *Le Devoir*, 14 décembre 1968).

44. Order in council no. 3958, 9 Dec. 1968, quoted in Commission of Inquiry on the Position of the French Language and on Language Rights in Quebec, *Report: The Position of the French Language in Quebec; II: Language Rights* (Montreal, 1972), v.

45. Robert J. Macdonald, "In Search of a Language Policy: Francophone Reactions to Bill 85 and 63" in *Quebec's Language Policies*, 219–42.

46. Pierre Laporte's speech in Débats de l'Assemblée nationale du Québec, 10 octobre 1969, 3152.

47. Proulx, *Le panier de crabes*, 152–53.

48. The bill closely resembled Bill 85, presented a year earlier and withdrawn.

49. Opposition Leader Jean Lesage's speech in *Débats de l'Assemblée nationale du Québec*, 28 octobre 1969, 3376–78.

50. In the opinion of Jérôme Proulx, who resigned as a Union Nationale deputy to vote against Bill 63, the law destroyed the party. See *Le panier de crabes*, 153–54 and 193–94. A poll done for the Quebec City daily, *Le Soleil*, showed that the Union Nationale's stand on the language of education won it no support among Anglophones, 71.9 percent of whom proposed to vote for the Liberals while only 9.4 percent preferred the Union Nationale (*Le Soleil*, 18 avril 1970, 12). Other polling, done by political scientist Peter Regenstreif, showed that at least a small majority of Quebeckers were satisfied with the government's record on language while large majorities were dissatisfied with its record on issues like strikes, taxes, and unemployment. Quoted in Vincent Lemieux, Marcel Gilbert, and André Blais, *Une élection de réalignement: l'élection générale du 29 avril 1970 au Québec* (Montreal: Éditions du Jour, 1970), 86.

51. Official Language Act, Statutes of Quebec, 1974, c.6.

52. William Tetley, "The English and Language Legislation: A Personal History" in *The English of Quebec: From Majority to Minority Status*, edited by Gary Caldwell and Eric Waddell (Quebec: Institut québécois de recherche sur la culture, 1982), 381–97. Tetley was an Anglophone minister in the Bourassa cabinet that adopted Bill 22. For an informative study of Anglophone opinion, see Michael B. Stein, "Bill 22 and the Non-Francophone Population in Quebec: A Case Study of Minority Group Attitudes on Language Legislation" in *Quebec's Language Policies*, 243–65.

53. Michel Paillé, "The Impact of Language Policies on Enrolment in Public Schools in Quebec" in *Contribution à la démolinguistique du Québec* (Quebec: Conseil de la langue française, avril 1985), 139–40; Claude St. Germain, *La situation linguistique dans les écoles primaires et secondaires, 1971–72 à 1978–79* (Quebec: Conseil de la langue française, 1979), 12, 24.

54. Quinn, *The Union Nationale*, 279–80.

55. The party's "political action program," adopted during its third congress in February 1971, specifically promised to mount a campaign to fight for the repeal of Bill 63 (Parti Québécois, *Le programme — l'action politique — les status et règlements, édition 1971*, 35).

56. René Lévesque, *Option Québec* (Montreal: Les Éditions de l'Homme, 1968), 19.

57. Parti Québécois, *Le programme*, 21.

58. For Vera Murray, the Parti Québécois, even while in opposition, was rife with tension on virtually all aspects of its ideology. She sees the battles as pitting a "technocratic" wing, more moderate, emphasizing efficiency and planning, and controlling the party's executive, against a more radical "participationist" wing, representing a minority of the party's members, but very vigorous and noisy in the defence of its left-wing social-democratic positions: *Le Parti Québécois, de la fondation à la prise du pouvoir* (Montreal: Éditions Hurtubise HMH, 1976), 29–30.

59. *Le Devoir*, 26 février 1973.

60. Camille Laurin, *La politique québécoise de la langue française* (Quebec: Éditeur officiel, 1977).

61. Many Anglophone organizations and firms testified during government hearings on Bill 1 (Assemblée nationale, Journal des Débats, Commission permanente de l'éducation, des affaires culturelles et des communications, *Délibérations*, juin-juillet 1977). One Anglophone pressure group, the Positive Action Committee, sarcastically commented on the bill: "The Anglophone collectivity has a place in Quebec on the condition that it is invisible and silent and progressively diminishes in number" (Alison d'Anglejan, "Language Planning in Quebec: An Historical Overview and Future Trends" in *Conflict and Language Planning in Quebec*, edited by Richard Y. Bourhis (Clevedon, England: Multilingual Matters Ltd., 1984), 29–52.

62. Only 9.5 percent of non-Francophones proposed to support the Parti Québécois in 1976; 22 percent intended to vote for the Union Nationale and its policy of "free choice"; 40 percent refused to answer, proposed to abstain, or did not know which party they would support (poll figures quoted in André Bernard, *Québec: élections 1976* (Montreal: Éditions Hurtubise-HMH, 1976), 49.

63. Anglophone reactions are analysed in Nadia Assimopoulous and Michel Laferrière, *Législation et perceptions ethniques: une étude du contenu de la presse anglaise de Montréal au vote de la loi 101* (Montreal: Office de la langue française, 1980).

64. These adaptations are examined in William D. Coleman, "From Bill 22 to Bill 101: The Politics of Language under the Parti Québécois," *Canadian Journal of Political Science* XIV, 3 (Sept. 1981), 459–485, and reprinted in this volume; also in William D. Coleman, "A Comparative Study of Language Policy in Quebec: A Political Economy Approach" in *The Politics of Canadian Public Policy*, edited by Michael M. Atkinson and Marsha A. Chandler (Toronto: University of Toronto Press, 1983), 21–42.

65. Claude Ryan, minister of education in the new Bourassa Liberal government (elected on 2 December 1985), stated that he would prefer to settle the problem of the estimated 1800 "illegals" on a case-by-case basis (*Le Devoir*, 28 et 29 janvier 1986). The government decided nevertheless on a general amnesty decried by critics because it rewarded those who disobeyed the law.

66. Gilles Rhéaume, president of two nationalist organizations, the Société Saint-Jean-Baptiste de Montréal and the Mouvement national des Québécois, declared that the courts had riddled Bill 101 with so many holes that it was beginning to look like a piece of Swiss cheese (*The Gazette*, 5 Jan. 1985).

67. In 1979, fewer than one of three Francophone Quebeckers thought that English should be allowed on public signs. A 1981 poll showed that two in three French-speaking Montrealers agreed with bilingualism on signs. By 1984, 80 percent of Francophone Quebeckers disagreed with the French unilingualism imposed by the sign stipulations in Bill 101 (Commissioner of Official Languages, *Annual Report 1984*, 37). 1985 polls conducted by the Centre de Recherches sur l'Opinion publique showed similar findings (*La Presse*, 20 janvier and 27 avril 1985).

68. The figure increased from 30 percent in 1976–77 to 57 percent in 1984–85 (Michel Paillé, "Conséquences des politiques linguistiques québécoises sur les effectifs scolaires selon la langue d'enseignement," *Le Devoir*, 29 mai 1985).

69. Numerous surveys have been conducted on this question. The Gendron Commission prepared a lengthy study of the question as it stood in the early 1970s. Sixty-four percent of Francophones declared that they worked almost solely in French (Commission d'enquête sur la situation de la langue française et sur les droits linguistiques au Québec, *Rapport*, Livre I: *La langue de travail* (Quebec, décembre 1972, 16–19). According to recent findings, 70 percent of Francophones now work only in French, and another 20 percent generally in French ("A Linguistic Scarecrow," editorial, *The Gazette*, 9 Jan. 1985).

70. André Raynauld and François Vaillancourt, *L'appartenance des entreprises: le cas du Québec en 1978* (Montreal: Office de la langue française, 1985).

71. One-half of Quebec's Anglophones (two-thirds of those under 30) are bilingual. The population of Anglo-Quebeckers, however, declined by 10 percent during the 1970s because of significant out-migration. Not surprisingly, research has shown that Anglophones who left tended to speak only English while Anglophones who remained tended to be bilingual (Statistics Canada, *Language in Canada*, quoted in *The Gazette* and *Le Devoir*, 26 Jan. 1985).

72. Commissioner of Official Languages, *Annual Report 1984*, 60. However, over half of all Francophone employees are in non-officer positions, including clerks, secretaries, and similar occupations.

73. Fifteen percent of Canadians class themselves as bilingual. Between 1971 and 1981, their number grew at double the rate of population increase. Only 7.6 percent of English Canadians are bilingual as

compared to 36.2 percent of French Canadians. Considering only the English-speaking provinces, 5.4 percent of the English speak French while 78.9 percent of the French know English. Quebec boasts by far the highest proportion of bilinguals: Statistics Canada, *Language in Canada* (Ottawa: Supply and Services Canada, Jan. 1985). French immersion programs in the English-speaking provinces have recently become extremely popular (Commissioner of Official Languages, *Annual Report 1984*, 25–29).

74. Sixty-nine percent of managers in Quebec, in the public and private sectors, are now French-speaking. French-speaking managers even have a slight majority in English-Canadian and in foreign firms established in the province (Arnaud Sales, *Décideurs et gestionnaires; étude sur la direction et l'encadrement des secteurs privé et public* (Quebec: Éditeur officiel, 1985), 177–202.

75. Language situations in which dominance is not based on demographic supremacy can easily produce social tensions. Such has been the case of Quebec. See Pierre E. Laporte, "Status Language Planning in Quebec: An Evaluation" in *Conflict and Language Planning in Quebec*, 57.

76. Polls conducted by the Conseil de la langue française, one of the organisms created by Bill 101, showed, in the opinion of the Conseil, that the young live "with the peacefulness of security brought about by the French language Charter." (Quoted in *The Gazette*, 22 April 1985.) The Conseil expressed shock when 40 percent of high school students queried affirmed that "living in French" was not necessary for their personal development! (*La situation linguistique actuelle* (Quebec, Conseil de la langue française, janvier 1985), 27.)

77. *La situation linguistique actuelle*, 18.

78. A study commissioned by the Conseil showed that Francophones spend about one-third of their television time watching English-language stations. Ibid., 12.

79. Jean-Pierre Proulx, "La question linguistique: la révolution informatique constitue le défi de l'heure," *Le Devoir*, 12 décembre 1985.

80. "Un constat de piètre qualité: l'apprentissage de la langue maternelle à l'école," *Le Soleil*, 17 janvier 1985; "L'apprentissage de la langue maternelle est en crise," *Le Devoir*, 16 janvier 1985.

81. Assemblée nationale du Québec, Commission parlementaire de la culture, *Le Québec à la croisée des chemins démographiques*, septembre 1985; Albert Juneau, "La défaite des berceaux," *Le Devoir*, 7 juin 1985; Jean-Claude Leclerc, "L'effondrement démographique: le réveil risque d'être tardif," *Le Devoir*, 8 novembre 1985; Georges Mathews, "La crise démographique au Québec," *Le Devoir*, 18 and 19 novembre 1985.

FROM BILL 22 TO BILL 101: THE POLITICS OF LANGUAGE UNDER THE PARTI QUÉBÉCOIS†

WILLIAM D. COLEMAN

Bill 101, the Charte de la langue française and flagship of the cultural policy of the Parti Québécois, was passed in the summer of 1977 evoking both joy and bitterness in Quebec. François-Albert Angers, the inheritor of the nationalist mantle of Groulx and Minville, described the event as follows: "Nous venons de vivre, avec le vote en troisième lecture de la loi 101, la Charte de la langue française au Québec, le plus grand moment de notre histoire depuis, pourrait-on dire, la fondation de Québec en 1608."[1] Such a statement, while seemingly extreme in its support of the law, was not uncharacteristic of the reactions to the new law in the nationalist societies, in the teachers' unions, and among PQ activists. When one compares these reactions to the bitterness, the anger and the dismay in the same circles that arose with the passage of the Bill 22, the Official Language Act of the Parti libéral du Québec (PLQ) just three years before, the differences could hardly be more striking. One would expect accordingly that the differences between the two laws would be immense and fundamental. Surprisingly, however, a careful examination of the two laws shows that the Charte of the PQ follows the legislative path that had been trod by the PLQ. The PQ can be said to have simply extended the path in question in order to penetrate further into society.

The differences between the two laws then become all the more important because they provide some additional insights for existing theories of the class basis and ideology of the nationalist movement in Quebec. They underline the middle class or *petite* bourgeois character of that movement and hence the comparative absence of strong employer support for it. The differences are also important because they illustrate the consequences of the opposed views on Quebec's future held by the PQ and the PLQ in the area of cultural policy. They also hint

†Canadian Journal of Political Science/Revue canadienne de science politique XIV, 3 (Sept. 1981): 459–85. The author wishes to thank Michel Bellavance, William Chandler, Jean LaPonce, Kenneth McRoberts, and Michael Stein for their comments on an earlier draft of this article.

at major cleavages between the two parties in their views of society and social policy, cleavages that show the PQ eager to pursue the train of reforms begun with the Quiet Revolution and the PLQ more hesitant and more conservative. In this way, a comparison of the respective language policies of the two parties may provide a window on the kinds of political debates we might expect in Quebec in the coming decade.

This article examines the differences between the language policies of Quebec's major political parties as they were presented in the mid-1970s. The comparison of the two laws will show that the important differences between them lie in their treatment of local public institutions and language use in the schools. A careful study of the development of the PQ policy involving a comparison between Bill 1, the first version of the PQ law, and Bill 101 will also demonstrate the fundamental similarity between the latter and Bill 22 in its treatment of the private sector of the economy. The contrast between the policy on language use in the private sector, on the one hand, and that in the schools and local public institutions, on the other, will be critical to our conclusions on the class basis and ideology of the nationalist movement.

The Concept of *"une société pluraliste"*

Political scientists have already studied to some degree the beliefs and states of affairs that combined to create strong pressure on politicians to develop a policy on the French language in Quebec.[2] These range from the prospective decline in demographic strength of French-speakers in Quebec's population to the emergence of a second "new middle class" oriented toward business and applied science.[3] That the leaders of the PLQ and PQ were responding to essentially the same pressures does not mean, however, that their policies would necessarily be similar. Different political actors may respond to the same set of conditions in various ways. Accordingly, to understand why there might be some common ground between the two parties' policies, it is advisable to look beyond these conditions to other factors.

In particular, it is essential to compare how the two parties tend to perceive the French-speaking society in Quebec. Both the PQ and the PLQ trace their roots to the Quiet Revolution and both tend to see themselves as carrying forth the torch lit during that period. Among other things in the dominant political circles in Quebec, the Quiet Revolution was characterized by a desire for economic *rattrapage*, that is, for the Francophone collectivity in Quebec to catch up economically with the rest of North America. This desire for *rattrapage* carried with it a basic acceptance of the advanced industrial society found in North America and a willingness to integrate French-Canadian society more fully into it. It was increasingly assumed that French-speaking Quebeckers shared important values and cultural norms with the rest of North America.

Within Quebec, among Francophone intellectuals and politicians, this assumption led many to redefine their own society as *pluraliste*. The concept of *pluralisme* was used to express the idea that the French-Canadian society in Quebec was heterogeneous, embracing individuals with diverse value systems and cultural orientations. This conception of the community stood in stark contrast to the traditional portrait of French Canada as homogeneous and even monolithic. The concept also carried the implication that the differences among individuals and groups *within* the French-speaking community were of the same order as those between that society and English-speaking North America. With traditional cultural barriers being lowered in magnitude, it was a logical step for those who defined the Francophone community as *pluraliste* to extend their perspective and see the whole population in Quebec forming a single *pluraliste* society. Acceptance of this latter perspective paved the way for policy-makers to lay the groundwork for the creation of a single set of institutions to minister to all of Quebec's cultural communities, Francophone and non-Francophone. The first push for such reforms came from the Royal Commission on Education, which called for a single bureaucracy to administer education in the province under the neutral wing of the state.

This new *pluraliste* conception of Quebec society has increasingly displaced an older view, which pointed to two societies coexisting in Quebec. Each of these had its own social, educational and cultural institutions that allowed it to live separately from the other. The first of these, English-speaking, managed the economy and provided skilled labour for several technologically advanced industries. The second, French-speaking and Catholic, ran the provincial government, provided the remainder of the labour force, and farmed the arable land.

Both the PLQ and the PQ accepted in principle this notion of *société pluraliste*; this acceptance gave their language policies a common philosophical base. Nevertheless, the differences between the two on the preferred relationship between Quebec and Canada was the first factor that led to important differences in the degree to which they were willing to apply such a notion and in the manner in which it was applied. The PLQ, while at times nationalistic, still saw Quebec as part of Canada and, accordingly, Quebec's English-speaking community as part of the majority group in Canada. When it came to defining a policy on language use in the new joint set of institutions created in the public sphere in the 1960s, the Liberals promoted "French priority."[4] French was to be the primary language of work or service in the institutions but room would be left for the use of English as long as it did not undercut the use of French. Further, when it came to deciding how far *pluralisme* would be implemented, and how much of the older dual structures would be replaced, the PLQ drew the line at local municipal, school and social service institutions. The PQ, on the other hand, viewed Quebec as an embryonic nation-state. It tended to downplay the ties between Quebec's Anglophone community and the rest of Canada and preferred to treat that community as a "national minority." Accordingly, the *péquistes* were predisposed to defining a unilingual policy for the new pluralist structures. The party was also less reluctant to push *pluralisme* and dissolution of dual structures right to the local level. Members felt that the nation's minorities should integrate themselves fully into institutions shared with the majority group.

If the difference in the constitutional positions of the two parties is the first factor creating a basis for policy differences, variation in the parties' support bases and in the backgrounds of their respective activists is the second. Studies have shown that the PLQ enjoys the overwhelming support of the non-Francophone communities and, within the Francophone community, of older voters, of those with management positions in the private sector, and of workers fearful of change.[5] Candidates and activists in the PLQ tend to be drawn proportionately more from the business community and from private sector professionals than in the PQ. On the other side, the PQ draws its support from the Francophone community only, especially from the young, and well-educated, the new middle class of journalists, teachers, academics, and *fonctionnaires*, and from workers desirous of change.[6]

The PQ was more likely, then, to perceive the English-dominated corporate establishment and the non-Francophone communities as "enemies" in Gusfield's sense of the term.[7] It distrusted them watching from afar and was predisposed to draft legislation that would coerce them into changing their language practices. The PLQ on the other hand was likely to view them as "deviants," to use a companion concept from Gusfield; that is, as acting somewhat unconsciously against the wishes of the majority. Its policy then would be more "assimilative" — more directed toward trying to *persuade* those involved to reform themselves.

Comparison of the Official Language Act of 1974 and the Charte de la langue française of 1977

The Charte de la langue française was the first major piece of legislation introduced by the Parti Québécois after its election to power in November 1976. The introduction of the legislation on 27 April 1977 by Dr. Camille Laurin, the minister of state for cultural development, was preceded by the publication of a White Paper that laid out the lines the legislation would follow.[8] Appropriately, the legislation was given the number Bill 1. After its introduction, the legislation was sent to the Permanent Parliamentary Committee on Education, Cultural Affairs and Communications, which proceeded to prepare for public hearings and submissions. The Committee began the hearings on 7 June 1977, and held its final session one month later. In its 21 sessions spanning 114 hours and 24 minutes, it heard 62 briefs out of a total of 270 submitted.[9] Bill 1 was then withdrawn by the government and reintroduced as Bill 101 in an attempt to speed up its passage in time for the coming school year. The latter bill contained a number of important changes and was amended further before being sanctioned as law on 26 August 1977.

The overall impression of the government's policy was heavily influenced by the White Paper and Bill 1. The public debate that began in early April and the televised committee hearings, in which Laurin dominated, alternatively defending the legislation, attacking its opponents, and courting the unconvinced, all centred on Bill 1. Bill 101 was not examined in committee and generated little debate in comparison; it was quickly dealt with in the summer months. Politically, this process had an important consequence. Quebec society became highly polarized over Bill 1 with the various nationalist groups on one side and the employer class and Anglophone organizations on the other. The nationalist societies whose support was central to the legislation thus felt bound to support the government despite the weakened formulation of Bill 101. Otherwise the legislation might have collapsed because the Anglophone community was sceptical about Bill 101 and has since viewed it as only a slight variation of Bill 1.

Bill 101 differed from Bill 1 in several key respects. These differences are particularly striking in the sections of the laws promoting the use of French in the private sector of the economy. Bill 101 appears much closer to Bill 22 here. In contrast, the sections of Bill 1 and Bill 101 treating language use in the public sector and language of instruction are very similar and quite distinct from the same sections in Bill 22. These points are demonstrated and their importance shown in the sections that follow.

Language Use in Public Institutions

The legislation affecting language use in public institutions is best examined in two parts, the first dealing with provincial-level bureaucracies (many of which were newly-formed in the 1960s), and the second with local institutions.[10] In the case of the former, the differences between the Charte and Bill 22 are not great.[11] Both sought to insure that these bureaucracies functioned primarily in French.

Both laws required that all agencies be designated in French only and both gave individual persons the right to communicate with and receive texts from the government in the language of their choice.[12] Both laws said that official documents and texts were to be in French, but Bill 22 allowed for an accompanying English version as well. Bill 101 had no such provision but added that in relations with entities outside Quebec, the government could presumably use any language, a position that was weaker than that of Bill 22 (Bill 101, article 15). Other similarities may be noted in the areas of contracts, of hiring policies, and of internal communications within the bureaucracy.

However, for local public institutions, Bill 101 departed from Bill 22 by having them conform to the essentially unilingual practices of the province-wide bureaucracies. Municipalities, school boards, local health and social service institutions were to draw up all official texts and documents in French. All external communications with the provincial government, other governments, and "moral persons" were to be in French. Promotions, hirings and transfers could only be arranged if the employee in question had an "appropriate" knowledge of French.[13] Internal communication was to take place in French in municipal institutions. School boards and health and social services agencies were allowed to communicate internally in French *and* "another language," if a majority of their clients were non-Francophone.[14] These practices were to be directly enforced through francization programs. All of these local institutions were to analyse how their practices diverged from the norm of the law and were to set up programs under the supervision of the Office de la langue française designed to remedy the deficiencies found (Bill 101, 129–131).

This approach to language use in local institutions differed from that found in Bill 22 where the architects of the law had treated these institutions separately from the provincial bureaucracies. Under the terms of the Liberal law, municipalities and school boards could draw up official texts and documents in both French and English where 10 percent of their clients were Anglophones (Bill 22, 9). Unlike Bill 101, Bill 22 grouped health and social service institutions with public utilities rather than with the municipalities and school boards (Bill 22, Annexe

B). They then could draw up documents in English as well as French with no restriction (Bill 22, 20). Where a majority of their clients were Anglophone, municipalities and school boards could use either French or English when communicating with other governments or moral persons and in internal communication (Bill 22, 13). Health and social service institutions were to communicate with the provincial government in French and to insure their services were available in French. No restrictions were placed on communications with moral persons or on internal communications. Finally, Bill 22 placed no conditions on the hiring, transfer, or promotion of employees in any of these local bodies, nor were francization programs required.

In conclusion, the Parti Québécois devised a policy that was based on the notion that Quebec embraced a single, predominantly French society. All the services that had been offered in the past in parallel institutions in the French and English communities — whether they be political, educational, or social, provincial or local — were now to be operated in French as one system everywhere in the province. This contrasted with the policy developed by the PLQ, which had "francized" the provincial administration but left the dualistic system of institutions at the local level relatively untouched. This commitment of the PLQ to some dualism in Quebec was symbolized by its implicit references to English in Bill 22. Bill 101 was more classically *pluraliste* using the term "langue autre que français" where its predecessor law had used "anglais."[15] Bill 101 left no barriers standing in the public sector to the creation of an integrated nation-state.

Language of Instruction

The question of the language to be used for the education of Quebec's youth has been highly controversial and bitter because it is here that the interest of the Francophone *petite* bourgeoisie and the employers are most in conflict.[16] The reforms begun with Bill 60 in 1964, reforms based on the concept of *pluralisme*, began to eliminate many of the structural and philosophical differences between the Catholic and Protestant education systems. With the transfer of control from the Catholic and Protestant committees of the Conseil de l'instruction publique to the state, a common curriculum and common path of development were gradually put in place. A concomitant dissociation between French-Canadian identity and Catholicism coupled with the drive to advance Quebec economically stimulated some Francophone parents to send their children to English-language schools. These children joined many new Canadians who had been streamed away from the French and Catholic system; together they increased enrolments in English-language schools. These trends were given legitimacy in 1969 when, in Bill 63, the Union Nationale government gave parents the right to choose the language in which their children were to be instructed. By 1973, 12.4 percent or 30,819 of those receiving instruction in English were Francophones.

For various reasons, these trends alarmed many members of the French-speaking *petite* bourgeoisie.[18] Accordingly, organizations based in this class gradually moved toward demanding a unilingual education system. This system, in their view, had to have a single language of instruction — French. The administration of the system down to the local level was also to be in French, as we have seen in the

TABLE 1

Distribution of Pre-Collegial School Population in Quebec by Language of Instruction 1969–1970 to 1977–1978 (in percentages)

Year	French	English
1969–70	84.4	15.6
1970–71	84.3	15.7
1971–72	84.3	15.7
1972–73	84.4	15.6
1973–74	84.0	16.0
1974–75	83.5	16.5
1975–76	83.3	16.7
1976–77	83.4	16.6
1977–78	83.7	16.3

SOURCE: Claude St-Germain, *La situation linguistique dans les écoles primaires et secondaires du Québec de 1971-72 à 1978-79* (Montreal: Conseil de la langue française, 1979), 19.

previous section. Instruction in the English language was to be a "privilege" granted on a temporary basis only to Anglophones born and raised in Quebec. In other words, in the view of these organizations, freedom of choice was to be a temporary option available only to these Quebec-based Anglophones. In promoting this position, the *petite* bourgeoisie came into direct conflict with two other groups. The representatives of the English-speaking *petite* bourgeoisie, particularly those working in the education system, wanted freedom of choice to be granted to all parents, while representatives from employer associations wanted the option to be available, at a minimum, to all those whose mother tongue was English.

Bill 22 attempted to bridge these disputants. In effect, it gave a free choice to all children who had a "sufficient knowledge" of either English or French but at the same time made provision for an upper limit on the number of students who could be instructed in English. The employer class was satisfied but the Anglophone educators, representatives of the smaller cultural communities, and the nationalist coalition were all intensely dissatisfied with this solution. The latter group was distressed because many new Canadians and Francophones still had a conditional right to English-language instruction. Figures on enrolment classified by language of instruction were not available on a systematic basis during Bill 22's short life span. Subsequent analysis, however, does confirm the suspicions of the nationalist coalition. Table 1 indicates that the percentage of Quebec's students below the CEGEP level taking instruction in English continued to increase in 1974–1975, the first year in which Bill 22 took effect, and in the two subsequent years. Among those who had neither French nor English as a mother tongue, 78.9 percent were receiving instruction in English in 1974–1975 and 79.5 percent in 1976–1977, the last year of operation of Bill 22.[19] Only among Francophones was there a visible move away from English-language instruction.[20]

Bills 1 and 101 sought much less to bridge the disputants and opted for the Francophone *petite* bourgeois position and sought to restrict freedom of choice as much as possible to Anglophones with historical roots in Quebec. They accomplished this by giving access to English-language instruction to four groups:

1. Children whose mother or father had received their primary schooling in Quebec in English.
2. Children whose father or mother lived in Quebec at the time of the promulgation of the law and who had received their primary instruction in English outside Quebec.
3. Children who in the previous school year had legally received instruction in English outside Quebec.
4. Younger brothers and sisters of the latter.

Like Bill 22, the bills commanded that graduation at the end of secondary school was to be contingent on knowledge of French, but unlike Bill 22 they had no provision designed to ensure that instruction in English as a second language was available and required. A regulation proclaimed at the same time as the Charte gave the option to those persons or their children staying in Quebec temporarily to apply for authorization to receive instruction in English. The authorization would last for three years with a possible renewal for an additional three years.[21] Finally, Bills 1 and 101 were more comprehensive than Bill 22 in that they applied to all private schools receiving subsidies from the province.

The reaction to these proposals was mixed. The nationalist societies, which were the organizers of the *petite* bourgeois-labour coalition, applauded the government's intentions but questioned its methods. Their primary worry was that a sizeable group of Francophones was granted the right to English-language instruction by the law. The Société Saint-Jean-Baptiste de Montréal noted that the bill "permet notamment aux francophones qui reçoivent présentement l'enseignement en anglais, ainsi qu'à leurs frères et soeurs cadets, de continuer à vivre en marge de la nation québécoise."[22] Hence the Société along with the Centrale de l'enseignement du Québec demanded that all Francophones receiving instruction in the English language be returned to the French system. The Mouvement Québec français suggested that the bill be rewritten to allow instruction in English only to children whose mother tongue was English and whose parents lived in Quebec when the law was proclaimed. All new arrivals to the province after the law would be directed to the French system.[23] The obvious consequence of this position would be the eventual disappearance of English-language schools, a consequence demanded by the Société Saint-Jean-Baptiste de Montréal.[24]

On the other side, the employer class was also unhappy. There was remarkable unity in this group with associations representing Francophones arguing no differently from their Anglophone counterparts. Several groups such as the Conseil du Patronat, the Chambre de Commerce du District de Montréal and the Centre des dirigeants d'entreprise suggested that freedom of choice should be extended to all children. All employers' associations argued that, at a minimum, Anglophones moving to Quebec from elsewhere in Canada should be able to educate their children in English. The groups representing new Canadians were especially upset because no provision was made for second language instruction in English, as had been the case under Bill 22.[25]

In the face of these pleas from both sides, the government remained relatively firm.[26] The education provisions of the Charte were implemented in an atmosphere that was more calm than had been the case with Bill 22. The bill was more clear and had managed to avoid the use of odious tests that were administered to ascertain the "sufficiency" of the knowledge of English under the previous system. Subsequently, the minister of education has shown flexibility in providing authorizations for English schooling for "temporary" residents.[27]

The Charte has apparently stopped the expansion of English-language schooling in Quebec. In its first year of operation, 1977–1978, the number of children with neither English nor French as a mother tongue enrolled in French-language schools jumped by 6.4 percentage points.[28] In 1977–1978, for the first time, the majority (51.7 percent) of parents whose mother tongue was neither English nor French with children entering kindergarten enrolled them in the French-language sector.[29] At the same time, these trends translated into a sharp decline in enrolment in the English system. For the first two years of the Bill's application, enrolment fell by 15.6 percentage points.[30]

Two political problems have been created, however, as a result of this rigorous application of unilingualism in the education system. First, a sustained decline in enrolment in English-language schools could have economic consequences. Large economic institutions could conceivably experience difficulty in recruiting for head offices in Quebec if restrictions on access to English-language instruction were too harsh, or if the quality of English-language schools were to decline. These very concerns were raised in the hearings of the parliamentary committee by such firms as Alcan, CIL,, Bell Canada, the Bank of Montreal and the Royal Bank of Canada. In their view, greater participation in the continental economy by Quebec enterprises required that Quebec have a range of enterprises from large, multinational, technologically-advanced firms to small local concerns. They argued that it would be increasingly difficult for the former to be viable in the province if a high-quality system of English-language education was not available. Second, the decline in enrolment in English-language instruction has been countered recently by a trend towards "bilingualization." English-language schools have been establishing classes where instruction is given in French. Thus, schools are becoming "bilingual" in the sense that they have instruction in English for those who can legally receive it and instruction in French for those who cannot under the Charte. Considerable concern has been voiced about this trend.[31] It augurs a situation where French-language and English-language schools might compete for immigrant children or where Francophones might be schooled in an English-language milieu.

Thus, the policies devised by the two parties in the field of education mirror those each developed in the public sector. The PQ designed a policy appropriate for a nation-state with an absolute linguistic majority where it sought to bring all citizens under a single French-language education system. The party allowed two exceptions to this policy: it gave Anglophones with some historical roots in Quebec and those living in the province on a temporary basis the "privilege" of choosing between instruction in either language. The PLQ, consistent with its vision of Quebec in Canada, placed no restrictions on the availability of English-language schools to English Canadians. Further, following from its view of a

TABLE 2

Responses to Bill 1: A Selected Summary

Virtually Unqualified Supporters

L'Association des enseignants du Sud-ouest du Québec
La Centrale de l'enseignement du Québec
Le Comité anglophone pour un Quebec unifie
La Confédération des syndicats nationaux
Le Conseil des Hommes d'affaires québécois
La Fédération des travailleurs du Québec
Les Fils du Québec
Le Mouvement national des Québécois
Le Mouvement Québec français
La Société Saint-Jean-Baptiste de Montréal
L'Union des producteurs agricoles

Virtually Unqualified Opponents

Ad Hoc Committee comprised of members of School Committees of the Richelieu Valley School System
McGill University
Provincial Association of Catholic Teachers
Protestant School Board of Greater Montreal

Qualified (Accept overall goals but are critical of numerous provisions)

Alcan
Bank of Montreal
Bell Canada
Canadian Industries Ltd.
Canadian Manufacturers Association (Quebec Division)
Le Centre des dirigeants d'entreprise
La Chambre de Commerce de la Province de Québec
La Chambre de Commerce du District de Montréal
Le Congrès national des Italo-Canadiens
Le Conseil du Patronat du Québec
Council for Canadian Unity
La Fédération des groups ethniques du Québec
Les Infirmiers et infirmières unis inc.
Montreal Board of Trade
Positive Action Committee
Provincial Association of Protestant Teachers
L'Ordre des ingenieurs du Québec
Royal Bank of Canada

Specialized but Limited Criticisms

Le Barreau du Québec
Le Comité des directeurs des centres de recherche industrielle
Grand Council of Crees
Les Indiens Naskapi de Schefferville
International Air Transport Association
Northern Quebec Inuit Association

SOURCE: Briefs submitted to the parliamentary committee studying Bill 1.

bilingual Canada, it tended to give anyone with a "sufficient knowledge" of English the choice of an English-language or a French-language education.

Economic Institutions

The realm of economic institutions, whether they be small family grocery stores or multinational corporations, differs fundamentally from the spheres discussed above. In those areas already mentioned, direct control over the orientation and conduct of the organizations involved was simultaneously in the hands of the Francophone majority and the provincial government. In economic institutions, ultimate control is private. Moreover, in Quebec, economic institutions were not only private as befits its capitalist economy, but also, in large part, were not controlled or managed by the Francophone majority. Francophones were progressively more underrepresented as one moved from the shop floor to the board rooms.

Both Bill 22 and Bill 101 were designed to introduce the use of French to all levels of the enterprise proportionate to the language's place in the province. Similarly, both the PLQ and the PQ wished to accomplish this goal without interfering unduly with the process of economic *rattrapage* and with economic growth. Nonetheless, it is evident that the pursuit of the first objective is potentially in conflict with the second. Within the PQ, two strategies for dealing with this contradiction have been present. The first position, expressed by a minority, holds that the realization of proportional use of French in the private sector is only possible if the state is no longer dependent on the private accumulation of capital, hence when the economy is no longer capitalist but socialist. This position appeared to gain some strength in the PQ in the early 1970s while the labour federations were radicalizing, and was reflected in the leftward turn that the program of the party took in 1973.[32] The second position, consistent with theories on the ideology of the new *petite* bourgeoisie outlined by Poulantzas, holds that the state must intervene directly in the marketplace both through public corporations and the use of strong regulations in order to "reform" capitalism.[33] Those holding this view proposed a Francophone-controlled public sector as the mechanism for progressive Francophone assertion. The PQ had little confidence that the private sector would pursue these objectives without coercion.

These two views are somewhat distinct from those held by the leadership of the Parti libéral in the 1970s. These leaders held that the proportional use of French had to be realized through persuasion and without direct intervention in the private sector. They believed that this was the only strategy that would not seriously weaken Quebec's position in the North American economy. We shall show that, once in power, the PQ moved toward this third position.

In short, to return to Gusfield, one would expect the PQ, being divorced from the corporate power-holders, to perceive those holders more as "enemies" than simple "deviants" needing reform. Consistent with this perception, one would predict further that the reforms of the PQ would be more coercive than "assimilative" or persuasive when directed at this group. Finally, if reasonable discussion were to take place between the PQ and the corporate sector, one might expect that the tendency toward coercion would be modified.

The discussions that took place between the PQ and the corporate sector during the sessions of the parliamentary committee studying Bill 1 are important for this very reason. The original approach to the francization of the private sector outlined in Bill 1 was developed without consulting the business community and was rather coercive in character. After the discussions that took place at the committee hearings, the approach to francization was changed in key places, thereby bringing it closer to that found in Bill 22. Hence, to begin this analysis, it is important to understand the character of Bill 1.

Bill 1 should be seen as a close approximation to the ideal language policy as it would have been drafted by the coalition of the Francophone *petite* bourgeoisie and organized labour first formed in order to oppose Bill 63 in 1969.[34] This position is plausible in light of several pieces of evidence. First, it is apparent from a reading of a selection of briefs submitted to the parliamentary committee studying Bill 1, that the unqualified supporters of the bill were drawn from this coalition of nationalist organizations of the *petite* bourgeoisie and the labour centrals. These groups generally lauded the legislation, making few concrete suggestions save in the area of education.[35] In contrast, the briefs that gave qualified support to the legislation were drawn from all wings, Francophone and Anglophone, of the employer class, along with representatives of cultural minorities and selected professions (see table 2). These groups presented briefs that supported the goals of the legislation but in a very detailed fashion reviewed and criticized the bill article by article.[36] The character of the specific criticisms did vary among these groups.

Second, particular aspects of the bill appeared to be responses to long-standing demands of this nationalist coalition. These aspects were in most cases symbolic and hence were relevant to the issue of status and to how particular groups were perceived. Thus, the bill was given the title of Charter to indicate its ascendancy over other laws.[37] Article 172 of the legislation gave the Charte pre-eminence over the Charter of Human Rights and Freedoms passed in 1975. This provision reflected the controversial position espoused by many nationalists that collective rights were superior to individual rights (this article was withdrawn from later versions of the law). Third, the bill was written in a fashion that emphasizes the *right* of Francophones to use their language, a style that differs from Bill 22 and to a lesser extent from Bill 101. Rights are defined in Bill 1 only for the use of French, thereby giving that language legal pre-eminence.

Finally, in several parts of Bill 1 (the preamble, articles 2, 6 and 112 respectively) the term "Québécois" is used in a sense that restricts it to French-speaking, possibly long-established, residents of the province. While these references were removed from Bill 101, they did signal the government's desire to give Francophones in Quebec rather than the French language a pre-eminent status. This action was particularly important to the traditional *petite* bourgeoisie — independent professionals, teachers, shopkeepers, farmers — who had a more exclusivist notion of French culture and probably saw this notion reinforced in the use of this term.

Bill 1, then, should be seen as an attempt to regulate the use of language based on the prescriptions of the Francophone nationalist *petite* bourgeoisie. It reflected the views of groups that were suspicious of the capitalist class in general and English-speaking capitalists in particular. These suspicions had been nurtured over a decade as a result of a series of struggles over language policy against the Anglophone middle class. The representatives of the Francophone middle classes had apparently concluded that co-operation with these opponents was not possible and that they would need to be forced to accept meaningful francization of the private sector.

Language Policy in the Private Sector

The PQ and PLQ developed policies that treated three aspects of language use in the private sector — the external image and communications of the enterprise, language on the shop floor, and language at the level of management. The external image and communications of the enterprise were further broken down into the firm name, the labelling of products, and notices and signs advertising products. Bill 22 sought to insure that for each of these components firms give priority to the French language but not to the exclusion of the use of English. For firm names and the labelling of products, Bill 101 followed this lead with minor changes. However, for notices and signs — communication tools more likely to be exclusive to Quebec than the other two — Bill 101 followed a policy of unilingualism consistent with its view of Quebec as an overwhelmingly Francophone nation-state in embryo. All such notices and signs were to be in French only.[38]

There were differences between Bill 22 and the Charte as well when it came to a policy on the use of French on the shop floor. These differences probably reflected the greater sensitivity of the PQ to the demands of organized labour. Bill 22 had required employers to draw up notices, directives, and the like, to employees in French with an English version allowed for Anglophone employees. It also had made a half-hearted attempt to make French the language of labour relations[39] (Bill 22, 25). That was all. In contrast, the Charte states (article 4): "Les travailleurs ont le droit d'exercer leurs activités en français." It then goes on to say that not only written communications from employers were to be in French, but also collective agreements and arbitration settlements of grievances as well (Bill 101, 41–44). Employers were forbidden to fire, lay off, or displace an employee because that employee spoke only French. Employers could be called upon to prove that a position required knowledge of another language and, barring that proof, could not demand knowledge of a language other than French for that position. Workers' associations were also required to use French in their communications with members, save in individual cases where the worker concerned had communicated in another language. The drafters of the Charte left very little to chance, reflecting a belief that the workplace would be "francized" only if employers were forced to do so. Unlike Bill 22, Bill 101 gave the right to work in French a firm legal basis and added the provisos needed to ensure that right could not be denied.

When one moves from the shop floor to supervisory and management positions, the question of language of work becomes more complex for two reasons. First, communications involved in carrying out tasks move away from the oral to the written and reading modes. Hence, the language of work is more dependent on a series of written documents, memoranda, and forms. Second, positions at this level have been largely filled by Anglophones, hence these same instruments of work were likely to be in English. To change this situation, it was not simply a matter of including two or three articles in a particular law but of initiating in most cases an expensive process of tranforming lexicons, documents and procedures over a period of time. The general approach used to set such a process in motion was virtually identical in Bills 22 and 1/101. Firms were asked to initiate contact with either the Régie de la langue française (Bill 22) or the Office de la langue française (Bills 1/101) after which they were given a provisional francization certificate. They were then to carry out a detailed analysis of the use of language in their operations for particular "organizational groups" in the firm. Upon completion of this analysis and after presenting it to the language bureau, the firm would be awarded a permanent francization certificate if it were merited or would be asked to set up a program leading to a state of affairs where such a certificate could be awarded. The philosophy behind the francization program itself and the modalities of the linguistic analysis were worked out jointly by the business sector and the Régie.[40] The Charte did not change this philosophy or these modalities. The forms used for the analysis are very similar in the two bills except for the additional considerations on labelling, signs, and the like, that characterized the Charte and were noted above. In both cases, as well, the costs are high. Allaire and Miller have estimated the annual costs of francization to Quebec firms to be $107,150,000.[41]

Nevertheless, the similarities in the method of francization for the two laws do not carry over to the application of the program to Quebec institutions. Where Bill 22 had relied upon a persuasive approach to francization, an approach desired by the employer group, the Charte used more direct coercion. In moving from persuasion to coercion, Bill 1 plays a particular role because it is the archetype of coercion and the treatment of employers as an "enemy," an archetype that is modified significantly in Bill 101. The legislation that finally emerged was more equitable, more true to pluralist assumptions, and more attuned to the specific demands of the employer class than Bill 22 had been.

The first difference between Bill 22 and Bill 1 relates to the modalities of francization in the private sector. In Bill 22, obtaining a francization certificate was optional, but desirable because it was a requirement for any firm that wished to receive premiums, subsidies, and so forth, from the government, or that wished to enter into any contract of purchase, service, public works or the like with the government (Bill 22, 18). Firms were thus given the option of undergoing the costs of francization and obtaining monies and contracts from the government or foregoing both. The result was that francization was not universal and hence a source of inequities in the marketplace. In contrast, Bill 1 made it compulsory for all firms employing fifty or more persons to obtain a francization certificate. It created stiff penalties and fines for those firms that failed to comply. Article 106 stated that firms not having such a certificate would not have the right to receive subsidies, premiums or even permits from the government. The latter could possibly include licences to operate a business, to use the facilities of Hydro-Québec and the like.[42]

Bill 1 also provided for a more rigorous monitoring of the francization process. It proposed the creation of a Commission de surveillance that had the power to investigate whether the law was being violated and to refer offending firms immediately to the attorney general for prosecution. Bill 22 had provided for a more informal and less bureaucratic monitoring process (Bill 22, 78–95). Offending parties were not referred to the courts but to the Régie. If the Régie could not persuade the firm in question to conform to the law, then it was to refer the matter to the cabinet.

Each of these provisions was criticized strongly by representatives from employer associations. The following statement on article 106 by the Canadian Jewish Congress was typical: "In a free and open society, persons and firms ought to have the right to do business with whom they wish and how they wish. Such intrusion by the state is a major departure from practices that have been followed in Quebec for generations."[43] The changes found in Bill 101 indicate that many of these criticisms were acted upon.

Article 106 was dropped altogether. The Commission de surveillance was required now to consult with a firm that was alleged to be breaking the law before any move to bring the firm to court. Provision was made for a Commission of Appeal to hear cases of firms which felt they had been unjustly treated under the terms of the law.[44] Bill 101 then went even further and allowed for the possibility that some firms could be exempted from the francization procedure. Bill 1, like Bill 22 before it, had already stated that francization programs were to take account of head office operations and of relationships firms had entered into outside the province. Bill 101 added that head offices, in lieu of participating in a francization program, could enter into a special agreement with the Office de la langue française. The definition of a head office contained in the regulation on this matter was not particularly restrictive in that it embraced individuals and operations involved in research and development as well as management.[45] In the end, then, the coercive aspects of Bill 1 were toned down and the process of francization was made more fair and more attuned to the North American context than even under Bill 22. The universal character of the law removed the market inequities possible under Bill 22 and the status of head offices and research facilities was clarified.

A second important difference between Bill 22 and Bill 1 related to the treatment of members of professions. Under the former, those occupations falling under Quebec's Code of Professions were required to designate their professional associations in French and to use French when communicating with the provincial government. Members of the professions were required to have a working knowledge of French in order to obtain a permit to practise in the province. Article 23 of the law, however, exempted professionals working exclusively for one employer and not having contact with the general public. This exemption was important because it meant that large corporations could bring professional staff to work in research facilities and head offices and have them work in English without penalty. Bill 1 followed in the steps of Bill 22 except for this exemption. This omission generated a strong protest from the banks, the Positive Action Committee, and the Canadian Jewish Congress. In Bill 101, the PQ restored the exemption.

A third difference between Bill 22 and Bill 1 in the area of francization related to the supervision of the language analysis and subsequent francization. Under the terms of Bill 22, the overseers of the program were the managers or owners of the enterprise. In Bill 1, this function was given over to a francization committee composed of at least six persons. One-third of the members of the committee were to be named by the workers in the firm. This provision was symbolic in that it gave workers increased status within the firm, but little additional power.[46] The committee was to serve as the firm's interlocutor on language with the Office de la langue française. The response from the employer sector, whether Francophone or Anglophone, was unanimously negative. The employers' representatives felt that the implementation of francization was the responsibility of management and hence that the government through such a provision was giving workers a share of management. The Positive Action Committee saw such committees as providing a new forum for conflict in relations with workers.[47] The employers clearly resisted any notion of sharing any management function with workers. Nonetheless, the committee concept was retained. At the same time a small amendment to the final version of Bill 101 weakened their role somewhat and reaffirmed the status of the employer. Under the terms of Bill 101, the committee, after its analysis was completed, was directed to report to the managers of the enterprise who would in turn communicate with the Office de la langue française (Bill 101, 149). The net effect was to give primary responsibility for francization back to management, which had been the practice under Bill 22.

Finally, there was an important difference between Bill 22 and Bill 1 in their respective statements of the objectives of the law. One of the stated objectives of Bill 22 was to increase "the Francophone presence in management" (Bill 22, 296). The companion objective in Bill 1 called for the "augmentation du nombre de Québécois à tous les niveaux de l'entreprise" (Bill 1, 112b). In this context, "Québécois" referred to members of the particular nationality traditionally called "*Canadiens français*." It thus shifted the emphasis in the bill from promoting the use of a particular language to promoting a particular group. This article of Bill 1 was strongly criticized by the employers' associations and others. Bill 101 returned implicitly to the spirit of Bill 22 because its corresponding article spoke of "l'augmentation . . . du nombre de personnes ayant une bonne connaissance de la langue française" (Bill 101, 141b).

In summary, then, the policies of the PQ for the private sector followed the lines set out in Bill 22 save in the areas of external advertising and the language of the shop where the use of French was promoted more strongly. The policy on the francization of management under the PQ converged in several important areas with that of the PLQ. We have argued that this convergence resulted from amendments to Bill 1 which contained the policy closest to the wishes of the Francophone middle classes. This shift in emphasis aroused little protest from the representatives of those classes.

This lack of protest may be seen as somewhat surprising given that the changes found in Bill 101 could be seen as setting aside two long-standing objectives of the nationalist movement — reversing outside control of the economy and implanting Francophones and the use of French at the pinnacles of economic power.

The key centres of decision making and power in the advanced industrial economy are the head offices from which the corporations are directed and centres where research and development-yielding technological innovation are carried on. Under the terms of the Charte, head offices and research centres are exempted from francization as a primary goal. Further, those professionals, whether in the financial, engineering, or scientific fields, who work solely from one firm away from the public (often the professionals of most value to the enterprise) are exempted from even having to know French. Hence the specific areas in the economy that are most important to economic growth and expansion are separated off by the language law from strong pressure to "francize." These areas pose little problem of legitimation in that they are out of the public eye. Moreover, the Charte drew this line with more rigour and less ambiguity than did Bill 22. In a sense, if the centres of economic power in Quebec are defined to be the head offices of large corporations and the private research institutes where technology is developed, then the law is saying that French is the language of operations in Quebec only to a point below these power centres. Beyond that point, the language used is left more or less up to the corporation itself. Similarly, if an objective of the law is to place graduates of Francophone universities in the private sector, then again the law is likely to be successful only at the level of middle management. The seeming acceptance of these more limited goals by nationalists provides a useful starting point for drawing the conclusions that result from this analysis.

Conclusion

Statements of immense satisfaction by nationalists, such as the one with which we began this article, are statements of approval for legislation that extended the scope of the concept of *pluralisme*. It is perhaps ironic that the acceptance of *pluralisme* is consistent with unilingualism. A *Québec pluraliste* is a Quebec of many communities with the Greek, Italian, and others considered to be equal in status to English. French, the language of 80 percent of the territory's residents, becomes the obvious *lingua franca* for these minority communities. It is either that, the logic goes, or the Tower of Babel. Hence the PQ's embrace of *pluralisme* led logically to the promotion of unilingualism in all institutions in the public sector, in the schools, and in the printed advertising of the business community. At the same time, for the PQ as well as the PLQ, the promotion of the use of French in the private sector was more circumspect; it did little to disturb the distribution of economic power in the province. By reflecting upon this disjunction between the policies in the public sector and those in the private sector, several conclusions follow.

Bourque and Frenette have argued that the PQ draws important support from what they call *les travailleurs de la langue* — teachers, journalists, academics, *fonctionnaires*, middle level officials in the co-operative sector and the labour centrals.[48] These are all individuals whose work is more in the realm of ideas than the production of goods. They have minimal links to the private sector. The intended application of unilingualism in Bill 101 would seem to correspond with the concerns of such a group. The public sector is more completely unilingual.

Public employees are no longer expected to communicate with local institutions in languages other than French. They are no longer to receive documents or texts in a "foreign" language. The linguistic integration of local institutions into the majority community is likely to create additional job opportunities for Francophones. The French language education system is assured, at a minimum, of keeping its existing proportion of the province's school children, thereby giving teachers added security. At the same time, these *travailleurs de la langue* have apparently little interest in pushing the French language hard in the private sector. The return to the spirit of Bill 22 found in Bill 101 produced no great protest, hardly a word of discontent. The nationalist movement appears in the light of these events somewhat oblivious to the goals of economic liberation evoked at the height of the Quiet Revolution. Its concerns are those of a middle class, a not unusual conclusion that has recently been forcefully argued by Niosi.[49]

This particular characterization of the nationalist movement and of the language policy of the PQ raises further questions related to a further theory about the party and its place in Quebec politics. In opposition to Niosi, Bourque and Frenette and Fournier have recently argued that the PQ seeks to promote the interests of a regional *bourgeoisie québécoise*.[50] This fraction of the bourgeoisie is said to have its base for capital accumulation mainly in Quebec and to be engaged in a struggle with English-Canadian capital for control of particular industries in the province. However, in reviewing our analysis of Bill 101 and particularly its similarity to Bill 22, it is hard to see where in the area of language policy this is the case. Both Bill 22 and Bill 101 are likely to have had the same effect — the provision of greater access to middle management positions in the private sector for Francophones. Such positions, however, would be in the established economic structures of the province and could be said at best to form the basis for a strengthened comprador French-speaking capitalist class. These are not individuals competing for control of the economy with English-Canadian capitalists but individuals being integrated into the institutions already controlled by English-Canadian and foreign capital. The legislation stopped quite consciously short of stimulating the expansion of a *bourgeoisie nationale*. In being structured this way, both Bill 22 and Bill 101 conformed to the wishes of such Francophone employer associations as the Chambre de Commerce du District de Montréal, the Chambre de Commerce de la Province de Québec, and the Centre de dirigeants d'entreprise. Each of these has continued to be adamantly opposed to the demands of the nationalist movement as articulated by the PQ.

One could perhaps go further and give a class interpretation of the more limited endorsement of *pluralisme* by the PLQ. One could point out that by exempting the local English-speaking institutions from the law, the Liberals are thereby facilitating the presence in Quebec of foreign capital. To rest the argument there, however, would be unsatisfactory because it would neglect a certain dynamic inherent in the concept of *pluralisme* itself. By extending the concept to embrace all public institutions in Quebec society, the PQ has gradually found itself talking about a multicultural Quebec. The party has come to recognize that a variety of cultural communities, not just the French and the English, make up Quebec and hence that the structures and institutions of that society must give some voice to these cultural particularities. A plural society requires plural institutions; institutions tailored to the culture of the *Canadiens français* must be revised so that all citizens of Quebec might feel at home. It is for this reason that Arnopoulos and Clift refer to Bill 101 as a Trojan Horse.[51] Its promulgation carried the seeds for fundamental changes in the institutions of the majority community.

The kinds of struggles likely to follow in the wake of the acceptance of a plural Quebec are already evident in the school system. A plural education system adequate to such a Quebec would be one where children from various cultural communities could come together and be educated in a fashion that treated the values of each equally. Such a system would stand in contrast to one where schools were more exclusivist, that is, were organized according to a value system emanating from the majority community and all were directed to conform to such a system. In 1974, a disparate group of parents sought to create a small elementary school, the École Notre Dame de Neiges, in the image of *pluralisme*.[52] They have been supported by the PQ in their quest. They have not yet realized their goal, however, because they have been successfully opposed by elements in the Francophone Catholic Church, including the Archbishop of Montreal. These latter individuals have campaigned vigorously against any school that is not rigorously Catholic and hence exclusive of competing value systems.

Our interpretation of Bill 22, however, indicates that the PLQ is less receptive to an integral application of *pluralisme*. The party supported the maintenance of the old dual system of structures at the local level. Such a policy, if maintained, could facilitate maintenance of more exclusivist structures for the French community at the local level whether these be schools, charities, museums or hospitals. These would be companions to parallel institutions controlled by the non-Francophone, especially the Anglophone, communities. If our interpretation of the PLQ philosophy is correct and if the party were to return to power, one would expect the party to refurbish the language autonomy of local institutions, to widen access to the English-language education system giving the privilege to English Canadians at a minimum, and finally to allow businesses at the local level to reflect the language of their communities in their external images. A de-emphasis on *pluralisme* — and this is an instructive irony of Quebec politics — would lead to a rebirth of language pluralism.

Notes

1. François-Albert Angers, "La montée vers un Québec maître de sa destinée," *L'Action nationale* 68 (1978), 28.

2. See, for example, Kenneth McRoberts and Dale Posgate, *Quebec: Social Change and Political Crisis* (Toronto: McClelland and Stewart, 1980) and William D. Coleman, "The Class Bases of Language Policy in Quebec, 1949–1975," *Studies in Political Economy* 3 (1980): 93–117.

3. Evidence for the emergence of this "second" new middle class is found in recent studies. The first MBAs were awarded in Quebec in 1966. Whereas between 1936 and 1955, nearly 68 percent of engineering degrees were awarded by Anglophone universities, in the last decade this figure has declined to 33.6 percent. Among those under 40 years of age, Francophones now obtain close to 80 percent of all engineering degrees. See Guy Girard, Jean-Claude Otis, and Normand Proulx, *Le Stock de Ressources humaines hautement qualifiées du Québec et la production des universités québécoises*, Étude No.2, La production des universités québécoises et la formation universitaire au Québec: 1975 (Montreal: Office de la langue française, 1978), 43–44.

4. The notion of "French priority" was first used in an unpublished White Paper on culture prepared in 1965 by Pierre Laporte who at that time was minister of cultural affairs in the Lesage government. For the subsequent history of the concept, see Coleman, "The Class Bases," 97–98.

5. See Richard Hamilton and Maurice Pinard, "The Bases of Parti Québécois Support in Recent Quebec Elections," *Canadian Journal of Political Science* 9 (1976), 16ff. and Vera Murray, *Le Parti québécois: de la fondation à la prise du pouvoir*, Cahiers du Québec (Montreal: Hurtubise HMH, 1976), 33–34.

6. Hamilton and Pinard, "The Bases," 16.

7. Joseph R. Gusfield, *Symbolic Crusade: Status Politics and the American Temperance Movement* (Urbana: University of Illinois Press, 1963). An "enemy" refers to an individual or group who challenges a particular norm directly. In contrast, a "deviant" is an individual or group who is perceived as deviating from a norm but not as rejecting that norm outright.

8. Dr. Camille Laurin, *La politique québécoise de la langue française* (Quebec: Éditeur officiel du Québec, 1977). It was released on 1 April 1977.

9. Those briefs presented publicly were chosen by the government. In a personal letter to the author, Pauline Veronneau of Dr. Laurin's office wrote that the government sought to choose those that were most representative. The order of presentation was decided upon by the minister, an order that usually counterbalanced a positive response with a critical one. No association refused to appear before the committee and no group protested about not being able to present its position publicly.

10. We are setting aside here the articles of the two laws dealing with the language to be used in the National Assembly and the provincial courts. Under section 133 of the BNA Act, these were made bilingual. The PLQ did not challenge this practice. The PQ, on the other hand, challenged it directly by seeking to make these same institutions unilingual. The PQ's policy was eventually overturned by the Supreme Court of Canada. The text of the court's decision was reprinted in *Le Devoir* under the byline "Le jugement sur la Charte de la langue française" on 14 December 1979. For a comment on the PQ's probable strategy in this matter see Michel Roy, "La langue de la justice," ibid.

11. References to the final versions of the two laws are Quebec, The Official Language Act, *Statutes of Quebec*, 1974, chap. 6; Quebec, La Charte de la langue française, *Lois du Québec*, 1977, chap. 5.

12. Both also required that the government communicate with moral persons in French (Bill 22, article 10; Bill 101, article 16).

13. The question of what was an "appropriate knowledge" was to be decided by the Office de la langue française and promulgated in a regulation.

14. This latter position on "internal communications" for school boards and social service agencies was a softening of the original provision in Bill 1. Article 21 of Bill 1 had stated that such institutions, whatever their clientele, were to communicate internally in French only.

15. In Bill 22, 17 of the 123 articles or 13.8 percent mentioned the English language at least once. In Bill 1, English is mentioned in 9 of the 177 articles or 5.1 percent, and in Bill 101, 13 of 232 or 5.6 percent of the cases. These practices removed a major objection of the Mouvement Québec français to Bill 22. It had seen the many references to the English language in Bill 22 as the creation of legal rights for that language in place of the unwritten "privileges" that already existed.

16. For this argument, see Coleman, "The Class Bases," 106–7.

17. These figures are calculated based on tables 2 and 8 in Claude St-Germain, *La situation linguistique dans les écoles primaires et secondaires du Québec de 1971–72 à 1978–79* (Montreal: Conseil de la langue française, 1979), 12, 27.

18. These reasons are outlined in Coleman, "The Class Bases," 107.

19. St-Germain, *La situation linguistique*, 24.

20. The percentage of Francophones receiving instruction in English dropped from 2.5 percent in 1974–75 to 2.2 percent in 1976–77 (ibid.).

21. Regulation respecting the language of instruction of persons staying in Quebec temporarily, O.C. 2851-77, 24 August 1977, *Gazette officielle du Québec*, 7 septembre 1977, 4615–16.

22. Brief to the parliamentary committee studying Bill 1, 23. (Hereafter, we shall refer to this body simply as "the parliamentary committee.")

23. Mouvement Québec français, brief to the parliamentary committee, 15ff. The argument about new arrivals was based on the notion that whatever their language, by definition, they could not be part of the Anglophone community in Quebec. The Fils du Québec wrote: "En effet, ces derniers [Anglophones from

other provinces], s'ils ont le plus souvent l'anglais comme langue, n'appartiennent pas pour autant à la communauté *culturelle* anglo-québécois qui se définit, non seulement par la lange anglaise, mais par un enracinement dans le territoire québécois" (brief to the parliamentary committee, 13).

24. Société Saint-Jean Baptiste de Montréal, brief to the parliamentary committee, 20.

25. The groups representing the various cultural minorities in Quebec hinged their support of the Charte on this issue. The Congrès national des Italo-Canadiens wrote: "Garantissez-nous un bon enseignement de l'anglais dans les écoles françaises, une bonne qualité de l'enseignement, une attitude accueillante tel que suggéré par le Rapport Parent et la Commission Gendron et nous vous garantissons une intégration harmonieuse avec la majorité francophone" (brief to the parliamentary committee, 15).

26. One small change was that, in the final version of Bill 101, a provision was added extending access to English language instruction to citizens moving to Quebec from other provinces if these same provinces had reached a reciprocal agreement with Quebec to provide French language schools in their territory (Bill 101, 86).

27. At least, this is what has been reported by several large companies in Quebec. See Michel Nadeau, "Des chefs d'entreprise projettent d'ouvrir à Montréal une École internationale trilinque," *Le Devoir*, 29 janvier 1980.

28. St-Germain, *La situation linguistique*, 24. In 1976–77, 20.5 percent received instruction in French; in 1977–78, the figure rose to 26.9 percent.

29. Ibid., 93.

30. Ibid., 38. Between 1977–78 and 1978–79, the decline in the French sector was only 2.9 percentage points, the smallest decline since the early 1970s.

31. Preliminary investigation indicates that the students in French-language classes in English schools tend to be from Quebec's smaller cultural communities. Recently, the Conseil de la langue française completed a preliminary study of this phenomenon. For a report on its findings, see Lise Bissonnette, "Les beaux principes d'hier," *Le Devoir*, 5 mars 1980. Also see Edith Bedard and Claude St-Germain, eds., *La cohabitation linguistique en milieu scolaire au Québec*, Conseil de la langue française, February 1980.

32. See Murray, *Le Parti québécois*, 44ff.

33. These ideas are derived from what Poulantzas calls the "power-fetishism" of the new *petite bourgeoisie*. This class sees the state as a neutral force that can arbitrate between social classes. Once "reformed," the state can be strengthened and made to serve the general interest. N. Poulantzas, *Classes in Contemporary Capitalism*, trans. by David Fernback (London: New Left Books, 1975), 289ff.

34. This coalition was institutionalized with the formation of the Front du Québec français in 1969. The FQF subsequently became the Mouvement Québec français and has been a major actor on the language stage since 1969. For a discussion of the origins of this coalition, see Coleman, "The Class Bases," 109.

35. A typical statement of this sort was made by the radical nationalist group, Les Fils du Québec: "La Charte de la langue française au Québec est la suprême affirmation du *Fait français* en Amérique, la victoire de la nation québécoise sur l'occupant anglophone, l'annulation de la défaite des plaines d'Abraham, et la MAGNA CARTA culturelle des Québécois" (brief presented to the parliamentary committee, 1).

36. The list of unqualified opponents of the bill is drawn mainly from the Anglophone school system, the institutions affected particularly strongly by the bill. The responses here were no more tempered than those of the supporters. The Protestant School Board of Greater Montreal wrote: "The fundamental premise of Bill One is that the existence of a healthy English-speaking minority is a menace; that this minority must be induced to immigrate or assimilate in the name of the survival of the majority; that English must be allowed as little public expression as possible, and the Anglophone community must be reduced in numbers" (brief presented to the parliamentary committee, 1).

37. The Mouvement Québec français and the Mouvement national des Québécois both suggested further that the law be given a kind of constitutional status indicating directly that it supersedes article 133 of the BNA Act.

38. There are now two exceptions to this basic rule. Bill 101 exempted businesses employing four persons or less and certain cultural activities of ethnic groups. Secondly, after considerable pressure from the Anglophone community in Quebec and from English Canadians prominent in the arts, new regulations were published in 1979 allowing all cultural and educational products to be advertised in French and another language (Règlement relatif à la langue du commerce et des affaires, A.C. 1847–79, *Gazette officielle du Québec*, 25 juillet 1979, 4990).

39. Article 25 of Bill 22 created no rights or obligations. It only made French the language of labour relations subject to conditions defined in the labour code. Consequently, neither collective agreements nor arbitration sentences were drawn up obligatorily in French. This interpretation of article 25 was given to the author by M Claude Séguin, Chef du Service juridique of the Office de la langue française in a personal letter.

40. For a brief description of the process involved, see Régie de la langue française, *Rapport annuel 1976*, Annexe 2.

41. Yvan Allaire and Roger Miller, *Canadian Business Response to the Legislation on Francization in the Workplace*, Accent Quebec series (Montreal: C.D. Howe Research Institute, 1980), 56.

42. This was not the government's intention it would appear. Permits were construed in a more limited sense. See the reply to the brief of the Canadian Manufacturers Association (Quebec Division) by Dr. Laurin, Assemblée nationale du Québec, Commission permanente de l'éducation, des affaires culturelles, et des communications. Auditions des mémoires sur le projet de loi no. 1: La Charte de la langue française au Québec, 20 June 1977.

43. Canadian Jewish Congress, brief to the parliamentary committee, 22.

44. For the modalities of this commission, see "Règlement régissant la Commission d'appel de francisation des entreprises," A.C. 465-79, 21 février 1979, *Gazette officielle*, 1915-16; and "Réglement fixant les modalités d'un appel interjeté auprès de la Commission d'appel de francisation des enterprises," A.C. 466-79, 21 février 1979, ibid., 1917-19.

45. For head offices, the criteria of the "ententes" were outlined in "Règlement pour préciser la porte de termes et expressions utilisés à l'article 144 de la Charte de la langue française et pour faciliter la mise en oeuvre de ladite Charte," A.C. 3645-78, 30 novembre 1978, *Gazette officielle* 1978, 7119-20. Head offices are defined in "Règlement de L'Office de la langue française relatif à la définition de siège sociale et à la reconnaissance des sièges sociaux pouvant faire l'objet d'ententes particulières avec l'Office," A.C. 3646-78, 30 novembre 1978, ibid., 7124-26.

46. This point was recognized by the Confédération des syndicats nationaux. See its brief to the parliamentary committee, 4.

47. Language of Work Group, Positive Action Committee, brief to the parliamentary committee, 38.

48. See Gilles Bourque and Anne Legaré, *Le Québec: La question nationale* (Paris: Maspéro, 1979), 208-15.

49. Jorge Niosi, "The New French Canadian Bourgeoisie," *Studies in Political Economy* 1 (1979): 113-61.

50. See in particular Bourque and Legaré, *Le Québec: La Question nationale*, 167-226; Pierre Fournier, "Les nouveaux paramètres de la bourgeoisie québécoise" in *Le capitalisme au Québec* (Montreal: Albert St-Martin, 1978), 135-82.

51. Sheila Arnopoulos and Dominique Clift, *The English Fact in Quebec* (Montreal: McGill-Queen's, 1980), epilogue.

52. For the pluralist viewpoint on this school, see Joceylne Durand, Guy Durand, Lucie Proulx and Jean-Pierre Proulx, *La Déconfessionalisation de l'École ou le cas de Notre-Dame-des-Neiges* (Montreal: Libre Expression, 1980).

SECTION 6

THE RISE OF THE PARTI QUÉBÉCOIS

Less than ten years after its founding convention in the fall of 1968, the Parti Québécois, under the leadership of René Lévesque, achieved power in a dramatic and surprising fashion in November 1976. Several months before its victory, Lévesque explained the PQ's *raison d'être* to the international community in the pages of *Foreign Affairs*. The road to power was a tumultuous and, at times, chaotic one. It all began in 1967 with Lévesque's decision to quit the Liberal Party, which he had served with such panache and effectiveness since 1960, because its leader and members refused to support his constitutional objective of sovereignty-association for Quebec. By the fall of 1968, Lévesque managed to create the Parti Québécois, a coalition of all the left-wing and right-wing independence movements that had cropped up in Quebec since the early 1960s. Only Lévesque's leadership skills and the shared goal of political independence kept the PQ functioning through noisy, bitter, and often highly divisive debates between moderate social democrats and radical socialists over the party's program and electoral strategy. While garnering twenty-four and thirty percent of the popular vote in the elections of 1970 and 1973, the PQ reaped only a handful of seats in the National Assembly prior to its remarkable victory in 1976.

The PQ did not achieve power on the issue of sovereignty-association. After the humiliating 1973 defeat, Claude Morin, the PQ strategist, managed to convince important elements in the party that the issue of political independence for Quebec should be left to a referendum once the party had achieved power. In fact, the Bourassa government, according to Raymond Hudon's "The 1976 Quebec Election," engineered its own defeat by mishandling in grand style a stagnating economy, the public and private sector union, partronage in high places, and the language question. The Liberal Party's inept labour policies drove radicalized union leaders into a formal alliance with the PQ, taking with them the votes of many Francophone workers. Secondly, Bill 22 forced many alienated Anglophones and immigrants to vote Union Nationale as a protest. Promising solid and effective government, the PQ attracted large numbers of Francophones throughout all regions of Quebec who had in previous elections voted Liberal. What remained unclear in the eyes of most PQ militants and supporters was whether or not the party would push beyond the liberal reforms of the Quiet Revolution and begin the process of organizing an independent Québécois society along social democratic lines.

FOR AN INDEPENDENT QUEBEC†

RENÉ LÉVESQUE

What does Quebec want? The question is an old cliché in Canadian political folklore. Again and again, during the more than 30 years since the end of World War II, it's been raised whenever Quebec's attitudes made it the odd man out in the permanent pull and tug of our federal-provincial relations. In fact, it's a question which could go back to the British conquest of an obscure French colony some 165 years before American Independence, and then run right through the stubborn survival of those 70,000 settlers and their descendants during the following two centuries.

By now, there are some six million of them in Canada, not counting the progeny of the many thousands who were forced by poverty, especially around the turn of the century, to migrate to the United States, and now constitute substantial "Franco" communities in practically all the New England states.

But Quebec remains the homeland. All along the valley of the St. Lawrence, from the Ottawa River down to the Gaspé peninsula and the great Gulf, in the ancient settlements which grew into the big cities of Montreal and Quebec, in hundreds of smaller towns and villages from the American border to the mining centers and power projects in the north, there are now some 4.8 million "Québécois." That's 81 percent of the population of the largest and second most populous of Canada's ten provinces.

What does this French Quebec want? Sometime during the next few years, the question may be answered. And there are growing possibilities that the answer could very well be — independence.

Launched in 1967–68, the Parti Québécois, whose platform is based on political sovereignty, now fills the role of Her Majesty's loyal Opposition in the National Assembly — as we nostalgically designate our provincial legislature. In its first

†Foreign Affairs 54, 4 (July 1976): 734–44.

electoral test in 1970, it already had had 24 percent of the votes. Then in 1973, a second general election saw it jump to 30 percent, and, although getting only six out of 110 seats, become what our British-type parliamentary system calls the Official Opposition, i.e., the government's main interlocutor and challenger.

The next election might come any time now: this year in the fall, just after the Montreal Olympics, or at the latest in the fall of 1977. Whenever it does, all available indicators, including an impressive series of public opinion polls, tell us that for the first time the outcome is totally uncertain. The present provincial government, a branch of that same Liberal Party which also holds power at the federal level under Pierre Elliott Trudeau, is obviously on the way out. It has been in power for six years, and ever since its second and Pyrrhic victory in 1973 (102 seats) it has been going steadily downhill. Apart from a host of social and economic troubles, some imported but many more of its own making, there is around it a pervasive smell of incompetence and corruption. The scandal-ridden atmosphere surrounding the Olympic construction sites, and the incredible billion-dollar deficit which is now forecast, are just the most visible aspects of a rather complete political and administrative disaster.

Looking for an alternative, the French voter is now leaning quite clearly toward the Parti Québécois. In that "national" majority, we are at least evenly matched with Premier Robert Bourassa's Liberals, and probably ahead. As for the Anglo-phone minority of over a million people, whose natural attachment to the status quo normally makes them the staunchest supporters of the reigning federalist party, they are confused as never before. Composed of a dwindling proportion of Anglo-Saxon descendants of eighteenth-century conquerors or American Loyalists, along with those of eighteenth-century Irish immigrants, and a steadily growing "ethnic" mosaic (Jewish, Italian, Greek, etc.), in the crunch most of this minority will probably end up, as usual, supporting the Liberals. But not with the traditional unanimity. Caught between the Charybdis of dissatisfaction and the Scylla of secessionism, many are looking for some kind of "third force." Others, especially among younger people, are ready to go along with the Parti Québécois, whose minority vote should be a little less marginal next time than last.

So, all in all, there is quite a serious possibility that an "independentist" govern-ment will soon be elected in Quebec. At first sight, this looks like a dramatically rapid development, this burgeoning and flowering over a very few years of a politic-al emancipation movement in a population which, until recently, was commonly referred to as quiet old Quebec. But in fact, its success would mean, very simply, the normal healthy end result of a long and laborious national evolution.

There was the definite outline of a nation in that small French colony which was taken over, in 1763, by the British Empire at its apogee. For over a century and a half, beginning just before the pilgrims landed in the Boston area, that curious mixture of peasants and adventurers had been writing a proud history all over the continent. From Hudson Bay to the Gulf of Mexico, and from Labrador to the Rockies, they had been the discoverers, the fur-traders, the fort-builders. Out of this far-ranging saga, historically brief though it was, and the tenacious roots which at the same time were being sunk into the St. Lawrence lowlands, there slowly developed an identity quite different from the original stock as well as from France of the *ancien régime*; just as different, in its way, as the American identity had become from its own British seeds. Thus, when the traumatic shock of the conquest happened, it had enough staying power to survive, tightly knit around its Catholic clergy and its country landowners.

Throughout the next hundred years, while English Canada was being built, slowly but surely, out of the leftovers of the American Revolution and as a rampart against America's recurrent attacks of Manifest Destiny, French Quebec managed to hang on — mostly because of its "revenge of the cradles." It was desperately poor, cut off from the decision-making centers both at home and in Great Britain, and deprived of any cultural nourishment from its former mother country. But its rural, frugal society remained incredibly prolific. So it grew impressively, at least in numbers. And it held on obstinately, according to its lights and as much as its humble means made it possible, to those two major ingredients of national identity — land and language. The hold on land was at best tenuous and, as in any colonial context, confined to the multitude of small farm holdings. Everything else—from the growth of major cities to the setting-up of manufacturing industries and then the rush of resource development — was the exclusive and undisputed field of action of "les Anglais," the growing minority of Anglo-Saxon and then assimilated immigrant groups who ran most of Quebec under the compact leadership of Montreal-based entrepreneurs, financiers and merchant kings.

As for the French elite, it remained mostly made up of doctors, lawyers, and priests — "essential services" for the bodies and souls of cheap labour, whose miraculous birthrate kept the supply continuously overabundant. And naturally, there were politicians, practically all of that typical colonial breed which is tolerated as long as it keeps natives happily excited about accessories and divided on essentials.

Needless to say, the educational system was made both to reflect this type of society and to keep it going nicely and quietly. There was a modest collection of church-run seminaries, where the main accent was on recruiting for the priesthood, and which, for over a century, led to just one underdeveloped university. For nine-tenths of the children, there was nothing but grammar school, if that. Read and write barely enough to sign your name, and then, without any time for "getting ideas," graduate to obedient respectful employment by any boss generous enough to offer a steady modest job.

Such was the culturally starved and economically inferior, but well-insulated and thus highly resistant, French Quebec which, 109 years ago, was led into the final mutation of British North America and its supreme defense against American expansionism: Confederation, of four eastern colonies as a beginning, but soon to run north of the border "from sea to sea." Into that impressive Dominion, originally as one of four and eventually one of ten provinces, Quebec was incorporated without trouble and generally without enthusiasm. From then on, it was to be a minority forever, and, with the help of dynamic federal immigration policy, a steadily diminishing one. In due time, it would probably merge and disappear into the mainstream, or at the most remain as a relatively insignificant and yet convenient ghetto: *la différence*.

As the building of Canada accelerated during the late nineteenth and early twentieth centuries, a tradition was established that Quebec was to get its measured share of the work, anytime there was enough to go around—and the same for rewards. And so, in a nutshell, it went until fairly recently. All told, it hasn't been such a bad deal, this status of "inner colony" in a country owned and managed by another national entity. Undoubtedly, French Quebec was (as it remains to this day) the least ill-treated of all colonies in the world. Under a highly centralized federal system, which is much closer to a unitary regime than American federalism, it was allowed its full panoply of provincial institutions: cabinet, legislature, courts, along with the quasi-permanent fun of great squabbles, usually leading to exciting election campaigns, about the defense or extension of its "state rights"! On three occasions during the last 80 years, one of "its own" has even been called upon — at times when there was felt a particular need to keep the natives quiet — to fill the most flattering of all offices, that of federal Prime Minister. Last but not least of the three, Mr. Trudeau, of whose "Canadian nationalism" it is naturally part and parcel, did as splendidly as was humanly possible for most of the last ten years in this big-chief-of-Quebec dimension of the job. But the law of diminishing returns, along with the inevitable way of all (including political) flesh, has been catching up with his so-called French Power in Ottawa. And no replacement seems to be in sight.

But this is getting ahead of our story. To understand the rise of Quebec's own new nationalism and its unprecedented drive toward self-government, we must go back at least as far as World War II. Not that the dream had completely vanished during the two long centuries of survival which have just been described—from an admittedly partisan, but, I honestly believe, no unfair viewpoint. In the 1830s, for instance, there even was an ill-advised and disastrous armed rebellion by a few hundred "Patriots," leading to bloody repression and lasting memories about what not to do. And it is rather significant, by the way, that it took until just now before the poor heroic victims of that abortive rebellion became truly rehabilitated in popular opinion.

Small and impotent though it was, and in spite of feeling that this condition would possibly last forever, French Quebec never quite forgot the potential nation it had once been, never quite gave up dreaming about some miracle which might bring back its chance in the future. In some distant, indescribable future. Now and then, there were stirrings: a writer here, a small political coterie there; a great upsurge of nationalist emotions, in the 1880s, around the Riel affair—the hanging by "les Anglais" of the French-speaking leader of the Prairie Métis; then in 1917, on the conscription issue, a bitter and frequently violent confrontation between the Empire-minded English and the "isolationist" French; faint stirrings again in the 1920s; stronger ones in the 1930s.

Then World War II, with a repeat, in 1944, of the total disagreement on conscription. But mostly, here as elsewhere, this most terrible of all wars was also a midwife for revolutionary change. Thankfully in less disruptive a manner than in other parts of the world, it did start a revolution in Quebec. Wartime service, both overseas and on the industrial home-front, dealt a mortal blow to the old order, gave an irresistible impetus to urbanization and started the breakup of the traditional rural-parish ideal, yanked women by the thousands into war-plant industry and as many men into battle-dress discovery of the great wide world. For a small cooped-up society, this was a more traumatic experience than for most others. And then when the postwar years brought the Roaring Fifties, unprecedented mobility, and television along with a consumer society, the revolution had to become permanent.

The beginning of the 1960s saw it baptized officially: the Quiet Revolution, with the adjective implying that "quaint old Quebec" couldn't have changed all that much. But it had. Its old set of values literally shattered, it was feeling collectively naked, like a lobster during its shedding season, looking frantically about for a new armor with which to face the modern world. The first and most obvious move was toward education. After so prolonged and scandalous a neglect of this most basic instrument of development, it was quickly realized that here was the first urgent bootstrap operation that had to be launched. It was done with a vengeance: from one of the lowest in the Western world, Quebec per capita investment in education rapidly became, and remains, one of the very highest. Not always well spent (but who is to throw the first stone?), with many mistakes along the way, and the job still far from complete, which it will never be anyway; but the essential results are there, and multiplying: human resources that are, at long last, getting required development along with a somewhat equal chance for all and a normal furious rise in general expectations. The same, naturally, is happening also in other fields, quite particularly in that of economics, the very first where such rising expectations were bound to strike against the wall of an entrenched colonial setup, with its now intolerable second-class status for the French majority, and the stifling remote control of nearly all major decisions either in Ottawa or in alien corporate offices.

Inevitably, there had to be a spillover into politics. More than half of our public revenue and most of the decisions that count were and are in outside hands, in a federal establishment which was basically instituted not by or for us, but by others and, always first and foremost, for their own purposes. With the highly centralized financial system that this establishment constitutionally lords over, this means, for example, that about 80 percent of Quebec savings and potential investment capital ends up in banks and insurance companies whose operations are none of our business. It also means, just for example once again, that immigration is also practically none of our business; and this could have, and is having, murderous effects on a minority people with a birthrate, changed like everything else in less than a generation, down from its former prodigious level to close to zero population growth.

Throughout the 1960s, these and other problems were interminably argued about and batted back and forth between federal politicians and bureaucrats ("What we have we hold, until we get more") and a succession of insistent but orthodox, no more than rock-the-boat, nationalists in Quebec. But while this dialogue of the deaf was going on and on, the idea of political independence reappeared as it had to. Not as a dream this time, but as a project, and very quickly as a serious one. This developed by leaps and bounds from easily ridiculed marginal groups to small semi-organized political factions, and finally to a full-fledged national party in 1967–68. These were the same two years during which, by pure coincidence, Mr. Trudeau was just as rapidly being elevated to the heights as a new federalist champion from Quebec.

But in spite of his best efforts and those of his party's branch-plant in provincial government, and through an unceasing barrage of money, vilification and rather repugnant fear-inducing propaganda, the voters have democratically brought the Parti Québécois ever closer to power. Which brings us right back to our starting point. . . .

Let us suppose it does happen, and Quebec peacefully elects such a government. What then?

The way we see it, it would have to go somewhat like this. There is a new Quebec government which is totally dedicated to political independence. But this same Quebec, for the time being, is still very much a component of federal Canada, with its quite legitimate body of elected representatives in Ottawa. This calls, first of all, for at least a try at negotiation. But fruitful talk between two equally legitimate and diametrically opposed levels of government, without any further pressure from the population — that would be a real first in Canadian political history! Obviously, there would have to be the referendum which the Parti Québécois proposes in order to get the decisive yes-or-no answer to the tired question: What does Quebec want? (This was precisely the procedure by which the only new province to join Confederation during our recent democratic past, Newfoundland, was consulted in 1948–49 about whether or not to opt in. So why not about opting out?) If the answer should be no, then there's nothing to do but wait for the momentum of change to keep on working until we all find out whether or not there is finally to be a nation here. If the answer is yes, out, then the pressure is on Ottawa, along with a rather dramatic surge of outside attention, and we all get a privileged opportunity to study the recently inked Helsinki Declaration and other noble documents about self-determination for all peoples.

Fully confident of the basic integrity of Canadian democracy, and just as conscious that any silliness would be very costly for both sides, we firmly believe that the matter would then be brought to a negotiated settlement. Especially since the Parti Québécois, far from aiming at any kind of mutual hostility or absurd Berlin Wall, will then repeat its standing offer of a new kind of association, as soon as it is agreed to get rid of our illusion of deep unshakeable national unity, when in fact here are two quite real and distinct entities in an obsolete and increasingly morbid majority/minority relationship. Our aim is simply full equality by the only means through which a smaller nation can reasonably expect to achieve it with a larger one: self-government. But we are definitely not unaware of the shock waves that such a break, after so long an illusion of eternity, is bound to send through the Canadian political fabric.

We do not accept the simplistic domino theory, where Quebec's departure is presented as the beginning of fatal dislocation, with "separatism" spreading in all directions like a galloping disease until the balkanized bits and pieces are swallowed up by the huge maw next door. In spite of the somewhat unsure character of its national identity and its excessive satellization by the American economic and cultural empire, Canada-without-Quebec has enough "difference" left, sufficient traditions and institutional originality, to withstand the extraction of its "foreign body" and find a way to go on from there. It might even turn out to be a heaven-sent opportunity to revamp the overcentralized and ridiculously bureaucratized federal system, that century-old sacred cow which, for the moment, nobody dares to touch seriously for fear of encouraging Quebec's subversive leanings!

Be that as it may, we know there would be a traumatic moment and a delicate transition during which things might go wrong between us for quite a while, or else, one would hope, start going right as never before. With this strange new-colored Quebec on the map between Ontario and the Maritime provinces, Canada must be kept from feeling incurably "Pakistanized," so we must address ourselves without delay to the problem of keeping a land bridge open with as much free flow of people and goods as is humanly possible; as much and more as there is, I would imagine, between Alaska and the main body of the United States over the western land bridge.

Such a scenario would call, as a decisive first step, for a customs union, as full-fledged as both countries consider to be mutually advantageous. We have, in fact, been proposing that ever since the Parti Québécois was founded, and naturally meeting with the most resonant silence in all orthodox federalist circles. But in the midst of that silence, not a single responsible politician, nor for that matter a single important businessman, has been heard to declare that it wouldn't happen if and when the time comes. For indisputably such a partnership, carefully negotiated on the basis of equality, is bound to be in the cards. Nothing prevents one envisaging it, for instance, going immediately, or at least very quickly, as far as the kind of monetary union which the European Common Market, with its original six and now nine members, has been fitfully aiming at for so many years. And building on this foundation, it would lead this new "northern tier" to a future immeasureably richer and more stimulating than the 109-year-old bind in which two nations more often than not feel and act like Churchill's two scorpions in the same battle.

What of Quebec's own national future, both internal and international, in this context of sovereignty-cum-interdependence?

The answers here, for reasons that are evident, have to be brief, even sketchy and essentially tentative. The perspective of nationhood, for people who haven't been there yet, is bound to be an uncertain horizon. The more so in a period of history like ours, when so much is changing so fast you get the feeling that maybe change itself is becoming the only law to be counted on. Who can pretend to know exactly what or where the country will be twenty-five or even just ten years from now?

One thing sure, is that Quebec will not end up, either soon or in any foreseeable future, as the anarchic caricature of a revolutionary banana republic which adverse propaganda has been having great sinister fun depicting in advance. Either-Ottawa-or is very simply inspired by prejudice, the origin of this nonsense mostly to be found in the tragic month of October 1970 and the great "crisis" which our political establishments, under the astutely calculating Mr. Trudeau, managed to make out of a couple of dozen young terrorists, whose ideology was a hopeless hodgepodge of anarcho-nationalism and kindergarten Marxism, which had no chance of having any kind of serious impact. What they *did* accomplish was two kidnappings and, most cynically welcome of all, one murder — highly unfortunate but then also particularly par for the course in the international climate at the time. What was not par at all, however, was the incredible abuse of power for which those events, relatively minor per se, were used as a pretext: the careful buildup of public hysteria, army trucks rolling in during the night, and then, for months on end, the application in Quebec, and solely in Quebec, of a federal War Measures Act for which no peacetime precedent exists in any democratic country. A great spectacle produced in order to terrorize the Québécois forever back into unquestioning submissiveness, and, outside, to feed the mill of scary propaganda about how dangerous this tame animal could nevertheless be!

In actual fact, French Quebec, with its normal share of troubles, disquiet, and, now, the same kind of social turmoil and search for new values that are rampant all over the Western world, remains at bottom a very solid, well-knit and nonviolent society. Even its new and demanding nationalism has about itself something less strident and essentially more self-confident than its current pan-Canadian counterpart. For Quebec has an assurance of identity, along with a relative lack of aggressiveness, which are the result of that one major factor of national durability lacking in the rest of Canada: a different language and the cultural fabric that goes with it.

Now how does the Parti Québécois see this society begin to find its way as an independent nation? What is the general outline of the political, social, and economic structure we hope to bring forth? Serious observers have been calling our program basically social-democratic, rather comparable to the Scandinavian models although certainly not a carbon copy since all people, through their own experiences, have to invent their own "mix."

The way we have been trying to rough it out democratically through half a dozen national party conventions, ours would call for a presidential regime, as much of an equal-opportunity social system as we could afford, and a decent measure, as quickly as possible but as carefully as indicated, of economic "repatriation." This last would begin to happen immediately, and normally without any great perturbation, through the very fact of sovereignty: with the gathering in of all of our public revenues and the full legislative control which any self-respecting national state has to implement over its main financial institutions, banks, insurance companies and the like. In the latter case, this would allow us to break the stranglehold in which the old British-inspired banking system of just a handful of "majors" has always kept the people's money and financial initiative. The dominant position in our repatriated financial circuit would be handed over to Quebec' co-operative institutions, which happen to be particularly well developed in that very field, and, being strongly organized on a regional basis, would afford our population a decent chance for better-balanced, responsible, democratic development. And that, by the way, is just one fundamental aspect of the kind of evolution toward a new economic democracy, from the lowest rung in the marketplace up to boardroom levels, which all advanced societies that are not already doing so had better start thinking about in the very near future.

As to non-resident enterprise, apart from the universal minimums concerning incorporations and due respect for Quebec taxes, language, and other classic national requirements, what we have been fashioning over the last few years is an outline of a policy which we think is both logical and promising. It would take the form of an "investment code," giving a clear-cut picture, by sectors, of what parts of our economic life (e.g., culturally oriented activities, basic steel and forest resources) we would insist on keeping under home ownership, what other parts we would like to see under mixed control (a very few selected but strategic cases) and, finally, the multitude of fields (tied to markets and to technological and/or capital necessities) where foreign interests would be allowed to stay or to enter provided they do not tend to own us along with their businesses.

In brief, Quebec's most privileged links, aside from its most essential relationship with the Canadian partner, would be first with the United States — where there is no imaginable reason to frown on such a tardy but natural and healthy development (especially during a Bicentennial year). Then Quebec would look to other Francophone or "Latin" countries as cultural respondents, and to France itself — who would certainly not be indifferent to the fact that this new nation would constitute the second most important French-speaking country in the world. In brief, such is the peaceful and, we confidently hope, fruitfully progressive state which may very well appear on the map of North America before the end of the decade.

THE 1976 QUEBEC ELECTION†

RAYMOND HUDON

Even four months after, it is still difficult to make original assessments of the outcome of what may come to be seen as the last "provincial" election in Quebec. By electing the Parti Québécois (PQ) on 15 November 1976, the Quebec people sent shock waves throughout Canada. The Quebec question has been reasserted in dramatic terms. People who considered the place of this province to be within the Canadian Confederation, and who did not really believe in the eventual election of a party clearly devoted to the separation of Quebec from the rest of Canada, have been forced to fundamentally reconsider their position.

As perceived from English Canada, the main effect of the election of a separatist party in Quebec has been to lead Canada to its most serious crisis since the beginning of Confederation. But while many people find it appropriate to develop scenarios outlining how to keep Quebec within Canada, only a few are thinking of how to negotiate a separation which is more likely to happen than it has ever been.

While this kind of preoccupation is undoubtedly relevant, it is more appropriate here to attempt an interpretation of the election before speculating on the future. After all, what is at issue is not only the future of Canada, but also the future of Quebec, regardless of whether or not it separates from Canada. I shall begin by describing briefly the context in which this election was called. Some elements of the campaign will then be discussed and analysed. Finally, recent developments in Quebec politics will be assessed in order to permit safer interpretations of the meaning of this election.

Premier Bourassa called this election only three years after the Quebec people had given the Liberals a very large majority (54.6 percent of votes, and 102 seats out of 110). Many factors account for this premature decision.

†*Queen's Quarterly* 84 (Spring 1977): 18–30. The author is grateful to Professor Hugh G. Thorburn for his comments on a first draft of this article, and for his stylistic assistance.

In the spring of 1976, public opinion surveys had already pointed out the sharp decline of support for the Liberals. In April, a poll prepared by the Centre de recherches sur l'opinion publique (CROP) showed the PQ with 41 percent of the popular support, leading the Liberals with 28 percent. The Liberals immediately replied by publishing the results of another survey, made by the Institut québécois de l'opinion publique (IQOP), showing that the PQ was trailing the Liberals 43 to 38 percent. In order to clarify the situation, *La Presse* ordered a Gallup Poll in May, which confirmed the large lead of the PQ (44 percent to 33 percent). It was asserted by some specialists that it was normal in mid-term for a government to lose support. But this disregarded the profound dissatisfaction of the electorate.

In fact, the Bourassa government was experiencing a series of problems of which a mere listing would suffice to show its uncomfortable position. It is clear that the Quebec government was not directly responsible for all its troubles. But every factor was working against the Liberals, in one way or another.

The party itself gave rise to discontent and protestation when, over the last few years, too many of its members, at one level or another, were found to be implicated in scandals and corrupt activities. As usual, such accusations were denied, but people began to doubt the quality of the government's administration. As long as a government is doing a good job in other areas, people do not usually care very much about these kinds of assertions. But the adverse effects of accusations of corruption and patronage increase spectacularly when combined with other factors. This was the case with the Bourassa government.

The economic situation was worsening: the rate of unemployment rose to its highest level since World War II. This factor worked against the Liberal government especially as it claimed to be the best one, under Bourassa's leadership, to cope with Quebec's economic difficulties.

Not only was the economy performing badly, but the public finances seemed to be in serious condition. In such a context, the exorbitant cost of the Olympic installations and of the James Bay hydro-electric development were perceived as serious. Almost everybody in Quebec agrees on the necessity of developing new sources of hydro-electric energy, but an increasing number of people were questioning the timing and the management of the James Bay project. For the Liberals on the other hand, it was hoped that the success of the Olympic Games, as an event, would benefit them electorally. But in spite of the success of the Games, people believed that the Bourassa government could have saved a lot of money by intervening earlier in the management of the total operation.

Other issues, too, had embarrassed the government in the last few years. Social tensions have been part of Quebec life for some time. As long as strikes are held against private employers, the government is not directly affected, but they may have some effect on the level of its popularity. However, when it is the government as employer which is so challenged, the situation is different. On the one hand, conservative people may find that governmental authority is not strong enough. On the other, radical people may consider the government to be a bad employer. In this regard, the year-long disputes, some lasting until the election day, saw employees and employers opposing each other in public and para-public institutions.

The Official Language Act, the well-known Bill 22, was also to create many problems for the Liberals. Anglophones in Quebec felt they had been betrayed by a party to which they had given stalwart support over decades. The dilemma was nevertheless not easy to cope with. The question for Anglophones was to decide how to express their discontent.

If Bill 22 created a peculiar climate among Anglophones, another linguistic issue was to develop feelings among Francophones. The dispute between the federal government and air traffic controllers and pilots posed once again the question of the status of French language in Canada. This dispute brought representatives of the Liberal and PQ parties with nationalist organizations and trade union activists over the campaign of Les Gens de l'air. In this dispute, some amazing statements were made. For instance, Guy Saint-Pierre, the minister of Industry and Commerce in the Bourassa government, confessed that he was revising, or at the least questioning, his position about federalism and, as a consequence, about the independence of Quebec.[1] A few days later, the President of the Quebec Liberal Party asserted that if the independence of Quebec were to be achieved, it would be done by the Liberal Party.[2] These unexpected statements were to be explained and clarified, but Premier Bourassa decided to call the election before this could be done. The priority concern then naturally became the winning of the election against "the separatist party."

Another "crisis" which occurred last summer was to create additional problems for a party which, until then, wanted to make clear its commitment to federalism. By reducing by 20 percent the production quotas of milk producers, the federal government gave roots to another form of discontent in Quebec's rural areas.

We shall see below the effects of some of these problems on the outcome of that election. However, we can already imagine that such a series of factors constituted sufficient ground for discontent. We can also see why Premier Bourassa, when calling the election, proposed two major themes: to put unions in their place, and to consider the future place of Quebec in Confederation. Other problems, however, were not to be disregarded by voters.

In fact, there were in Quebec "two" different electoral campaigns in October and November 1976. The outcome shows that the PQ benefited most from the political situation just described. However, at the level of the electorate, the reaction was expressed in two different ways. While Bill 22 and the necessity of stopping the PQ represented the most important issue for the Anglophones, the Francophones were more concerned about the bad economic situation and the weaknesses of Bourassa's leadership. This was apparent in the electoral choices: the PQ became the major party for the Francophones, and Anglophones continued to elect mainly Liberals, while switching for a significant part to the Union Nationale (UN), thereby electing a few UN candidates.

Despite many indications in this direction, a great majority of people still believed, until election night, that an election of a PQ government was unlikely. Some guessed that, with the help of scare tactics, Quebec people would make a "rational" choice once more. Many factors, however, should have led these people to predict the actual outcome. The premature call of the election constituted the first of a series of such indications. The decision of some prominent Ottawa "politicians" like Jean Marchand, Bryce Mackasay, Roland Comtois, and even André Raynauld, to involve themselves in this "provincial" campaign was another important element: they were coming to fight separatism. The disarray of the Liberals during the campaign represented another manifestation of their situation: some candidates were so nervous that, by the end of the campaign, they vigorously denounced their own leader, Bourassa. Finally, while pre-electoral opinion surveys quantified the respective position of parties among the voters, some still questioned the methodology and the accuracy of these surveys. Many people failed to note the correlation between the figures appearing in these last surveys and those prepared only six months before and referred to above.

A most interesting fact, demonstrated once again by the Quebec election, is that the level of voter dissatisfaction towards the government has increasingly become the safest indicator of the outcome of electoral contests.[3] The defeat of the UN government in 1970, the spectacular re-election of the Liberals in 1973, and the recent defeat of the Bourassa government can be accounted for in this way. The expression of this discontent took two different directions: a great many Anglophones switched from the Liberals to the UN, while Francophones enlarged their support for the PQ.

The decline in support for the Liberals was translated from the "national" level to the level of each riding in striking fashion. Indeed, the drop of 20 percent in their electoral support from 1973 to 1976 is clearly visible in almost every riding throughout Quebec. In fact, if we exclude "marginal" cases, we find out that they lost between 10 and 30 percent of their 1973 support in 96 ridings out of a total of 110. In five "marginal" ridings, the support for the Liberals dropped only by 10 percent or less. In three of these five ridings, however, their support was already below 40 percent in the previous election.[4] At the other end of the spectrum, there are nine other "marginal" ridings where the Liberals' proportion of votes dropped by 30 percent or more from 1973 to 1976. Save for the riding of Lotbinière where the UN leader, Rodrigue Biron, was a candidate, all the other ridings had non-Francophones comprising a goodly part of the electorate: Brôme-Missisquoi, Châteauguay, Jacques-Cartier, Marguerite-Bourgeois, Notre-Dame-de-Grâce, Orford, Pointe-Claire, and Robert Baldwin.

From the previous analysis, it is possible to assert that ethnic leavages significantly acount for the variations in voting behaviour in specific ridings.[5] This also provides a good part of the explanation of the PQ's "counter-performances," which are the fifteen ridings where this party increased its popular support by less than 5 percent.[6] Of these fifteen ridings, no fewer than eight are located in the West-Island of Montreal while two others, though located in the eastern part of the Montreal Island, are ridings where non-Francophones constitute a majority of the population. Two other so-called "counter-performances" were in two Montreal ridings where the PQ had already received more than 40 percent of the vote in the 1973 election. Finally, the three remaining ridings of this category show the influence of personal factors: they are Lotbinière, Gaspé, and Beauce-Sud where the Parti national populaire (PNP) elected its only candidate. Also, of the thirteen ridings where the PQ got less than 25 percent of votes, six are located in the West-Island of Montreal. Except for Pontiac-Témiscamingue, where a Liberal candidate was re-elected, these thirteen ridings elected a PNP candidate (Beauce-Sud) or a UN candidate. This flimsy ground was the basis for many people to say that there had been a rebirth of the UN. Such an assertion, however, must be explained.

The impression of the UN's rebirth was made in two ways. First, the Anglophones resolved their electoral dilemma in the following manner: fundamentally unhappy with the Liberals, many decided to vote for UN candidates. Second, the UN won eleven seats, although it had won none in 1973. To compare the UN's performance with its previous one is not really enlightening. We must remember that in the 1973 election, there was a clear polarization between the Liberals and the PQ. Many voters at the moment were concerned to stop the PQ: the UN lost out in this process. This must be taken into account in any evaluation of the UN's "rebirth." It is more appropriate, therefore, to compare the performance of the UN in the last election with that of 1970.

As a starting point, let us examine the twenty-seven ridings where the UN got 25 percent or more of the vote. The support for the UN decreased as compared to that of 1970 in nine of these ridings. In eight other ridings, the UN seemingly improved its position. However, when we consider altogether the support given in 1976 to both the UN and the Ralliement des Créditistes (RC) as compared to 1970, it can be seen that this support has once more dropped. It appears that the virtual disappearance of the RC[7] benefits the UN. More precisely, it is possible that the UN is getting back some votes it lost to the RC in 1970, but this is not enough to prevent a significant decline of their combined support. Finally, in the ten remaining ridings which have given a larger support to the UN, the eight most spectacular cases are ridings in which Anglophones are a majority or a significant part of the population. The last two ridings are Lotbinière and the peculiar case of Gaspé.

This statistical analysis, though limited, has shown: (a) the decline of the Liberals and the increasing support for the PQ were visible throughout Quebec; (b) these trends were disrupted almost solely by ethnic factors. In addition, it has permitted us to explain what has been called the rebirth of the UN.

If we continue to pass over the 1973 election as an exception, other significant trends appear about the evolution of parties' support in the longer term. Thus, the support for the UN is revealed as constantly declining since 1956. The same trend is also applicable to the Liberals since the 1962 election. On the other hand, the PQ has constantly improved its electoral position from the 1970 election through 1973 to 1976. Does this mean that electoral realignments are still going on in Quebec?[8]

This process appeared dramatically accelerated in the last election by the PQ's spectacular victory and the Liberals' sharp decline. It is important to recall that the polarization which occurred in 1973 only "artificially" benefited the Liberals. The impression of acceleration in the process was also amplified by the distortions created by the electoral law. It worked for the PQ in 1976 as it had worked for the Liberals in 1973.

Finally, it was hoped that scare tactics would prevent the election of a PQ government. But by promising a referendum on the question of separation, the PQ made these tactics less effective. In this regard, it may be asserted that the

Quebec people did not vote for separation. However, it has not refused to support a party openly committed to the idea of making Quebec a separate entity, independent from the rest of Canada. Does such a flirtation mean the beginning of the realization of the idea? To deal with such a question required a broader examination of recent political developments in Quebec.

The terms of the political debate in Quebec, as it appears through the strength of the support for various parties, have evolved significantly over the last twenty years. It is important to distinguish between politics relating to views of the general organization of a given society, and politics referring to the relationships between this society and the outside. Such a distinction cannot be firmly held in any appreciation of political developments in one society. Nevertheless, it is striking how politics relating to the internal organization of the Quebec society have too easily been amalgamated by some analysis with explanations of Quebec's relations with the outside. Indeed, most Quebec government policies were perceived in terms of nationalist aspirations.

The first point to make is that the nature of the political debate in Quebec has been completely changed in the last twenty years. In the late 1950s and early 1960s, the debate involved liberal values as against traditional values; the question in the last few years has concerned the desirability of replacing liberalism as the dominant ideology in Quebec. It is clear that the options promoted by various political parties do not represent accurately the new terms of the political debate in Quebec at the moment. In this respect, the PQ does not adequately represent the most radical alternative in Quebec politics, though it is, for the moment, to the left of any other major party.

Such a phenomenon is not new. Modifications at the level of superstructure come, at least most of the time, after changes have occurred at the level of economics and social relations. As elsewhere, this process of late adaptation of the superstructure must be related to the process of emergence of new dominant classes or strata, following transformations in the economic and social structures. Such a gap represents the major source of tension in almost every society. That was already visable in Quebec twenty years ago, although the questions under discussion were not the same as those debated in recent years.

For instance, until the 1950s, the dominant ideology promoted the preservation of the French community's traditional values: the faith and "the language as the guardian of the faith." The best way to ensure this aim was considered to be the preservation of the old social structure by keeping as many people as possible on the land and by providing community services around this core group of people. However, this dominant ideology could not prevent the industrialization, and more precisely the proletarianization, of a part of the Quebec people. The evolution of the Quebec social structure was irrevocably changing under pressures originating from the transformations in the Quebec economic structure. Thus, by the Second World War, it was obvious that "the ideology and old power structure in Quebec were becoming anachronistic in face of the demographic, economic, and social changes that Quebec went through between 1939 and 1945. Its irrationality was obvious."[9]

In this context, a new vision of Quebec society gradually took form. A group of intellectuals, especially some university social scientists, began to point to the necessity of modernizing the state apparatus in order to make it relate more closely to the actual economic structure. The Liberal Party was perceived as the instrument for such a reorientation through which the state became a much more important instrument in the organization of Quebec society.

The role of the state remained an instrumental one. It provided the private entrepreneurs with the necessary infrastructure: better roads; a modernized educational system (in which it replaced the Church as the principal agent of socialization); plus some complementary agencies such as research centres, etc. It also assumed the function of correcting the major contradictions created by the expansion of the capitalist mode of production, by implementing a large series of social policies. The state was sometimes used also as a possible competitor to private entrepreneurs, though this orientation remained tenuous. For the first time in the history of Quebec, the farmers were officially replaced by the capitalist entrepreneurs as the "idealized" class in the mind of the people. Although Quebec had been undergoing industrialization for some time, this change was legitimated only after an ideological struggle. Such was in essence the nature of the so-called "Quiet Revolution."

The surprising[10] election of a UN government in 1966 appeared, at first sight, as the end of the process of change in Quebec. Committed to the reinstatement of more traditional values, this party nevertheless met with failure because the actual economic and social structures no longer permitted such a move. This new government was forced to go with the process previously initiated by the Liberals. However, its unequivocal belief in the central role of private entrepreneurs in the implementation of that process clarified the rules of the game. Henceforth, the state would avoid competition with private entrepreneurs and would confine itself to a supplemental role. This paved the way for the election of the Bourassa government in 1970.

Although the Bourassa government is not responsible for the introduction of liberal ideology in Quebec, it is only with the return of the Liberals to power in 1970 that this ideology was fully implemented in the government policy. What was new with the Liberals as compared to the preceding government was that their basic commitments did not have to be compromised by any economic nationalism. The Bourassa government was rather unequivocally devoted to the functioning of a purely capitalist economy, while even apologizing for intervening either to assist the private sector of the economy or to correct some problems created by the way private entrepreneurs approached problems. In fact, creation of jobs became the final goal, de-emphasizing the development of a purely competitive and evenly developed economy.

The Liberal Party could have clarified its stand after the split that occurred in 1967: a good number of progressive (and nationalist) elements left the party and founded the Mouvement Souveraineté-Association (MSA). One year later, the merger of the MSA and the Ralliement national (RN) gave birth to the PQ, which was joined a few months later by a great number of militants from the Rassemblement pour l'indépendance nationale (RIN). Until 1972, the PQ did not represent a *radical* alternative to other parties: the solution was confined to discovering, through state intervention, how to make capitalism work in the interests of Quebec. But, as in the late 1950s, more progressive intellectuals and militants decided to involve themselves in the PQ's activities, in order to radicalize the party's platform. This was particularly visible in the national conventions of the party in 1973 and 1975. Perceived by these people as the instrument to throw out the Liberals, the PQ's program progressively became a typical moderate social-democratic one.

Such a modification will not long contain the more radical groups. The recent radicalization and the new militancy of the Quebec trade-union movement must be recalled.[11] This represents only one facet of militant organization in the "new" Quebec. Nevertheless, it is interesting to examine the stand adopted by workers' major organizations in the last Quebec election. Considering the class base of the PQ, how can one explain that the more a union is typically new petty bourgeois, such as the Centrale de l'enseignement du Québec (CEQ), the teachers' federation, the less enthusiastic is its support for the PQ? This phenomenon is still more interesting in that the CEQ is the federation which is the most "independentist" oriented. At the other end of the spectrum, the Fédération des travailleurs du Québec (FTQ) whose membership is heavily *working class* was the only federation openly supporting the PQ during the last electoral campaign.

Obviously, there is a structural factor: the members of the CEQ and of the Confédération des syndicats nationaux (CSN), whose many members are employed in public and para-public institutions, have to negotiate directly with the Quebec government as an employer. Consequently, they have to be cautious in their relationships with any government.[12] There is also a practical element: many members of the FTQ are organized workers who have experienced very tough fights against big enterprises, especially multinationals, in recent years. So, they may have conceived an election of a PQ government as an important step in improving their own position in relation to these employers. Finally, there is another very important political factor: since clarity in ideological orientations varies from the CEQ to the CSN to the FTQ (in that order), it seems that the more clearly defined the program and the more radical the critique, the more cautious the attitude vis-à-vis the PQ is (and the cooler the PQ's sympathies for the labour movement are).

While these facts account only for a part of the reality of Quebec politics, they show that the political realignment we have pointed to above is far from being a finished process. It then appears that the only factor which can postpone the appearance of new parties on the left of the PQ is the way "the national question" will be handled in the next few years.

As a party forming the government and clearly devoted to making Quebec an independent nation, the PQ supplies a "new" dimension in the evolution of the national question in Quebec. In fact, the most important contribution of the PQ in the evolution of Quebec nationalism is that it amalgamates the main national-ist trends which came to the surface in Quebec politics in the recent past.

Prior to the 1960s, almost every Quebec government was preoccupied with the cultural and linguistic problems raised by the situation of Francophones in the Canadian context. Most of these governments were primarily preoccupied with the survival (*la survivance*) of French communities — inside and outside Quebec. Greater autonomy in cultural and especially educational matters was repeatedly requested, but the commitment to French communities outside of Quebec prevented a really profound questioning of Canadian federalism.

In the course of the 1950s, a group of people, of whom one of the most prominent was Pierre Elliott Trudeau, vigorously contested this kind of approach to the destiny of the Quebec people. But while some members of this group switched to Ottawa in 1965, others had become involved in Quebec politics. From 1960 on, they began to implement their belief that the emancipation of Francophones in Quebec could be more appropriately ensured through economic development which would benefit Québécois more. The predominant character of this new nationalism noticeably modified the attitude of the Quebec government. The increased role given to the state in the process of modernization drove this government to ask for more power and larger fiscal resources from the federal government. These conditions incited the Quebec government to adopt a much more aggressive attitude in its negotiation with Ottawa. Though remaining a piecemeal tactical approach, this attitude nevertheless gave the impression that the Quebec government was only conditionally adhering to Canadian federalism.

A further step in the evolution of Quebec nationalism was initiated with the election of a UN government in 1966. Premier Johnson's slogan, *Egalité ou indépendance*, gave for a moment the impression that Canadian federalism was really being questioned. The predominant political trait of this new expression of Quebec nationalism provoked a reaction from English Canada: the Confederation of Tomorrow Conference followed by a series of federal-provincial constitutional conferences. Cultural and linguistic preoccupations were of course still behind this new orientation of the Quebec government vis-à-vis other "Canadian" governments. At the same time, within Quebec, the government adopted policies promoting economic nationalism, such as the campaign inviting people to purchase primarily Quebec products.

The results of these approaches were on both counts rather disappointing. Therefore, it was easy for the Liberals to maintain that, after all, the best tactic for Quebec was to try to get as much as possible from Canadian federalism. It was time to make federalism profitable for Quebec without embarking on "theoretical" discussions which, in the end, financially harmed Quebec. Once more, the adoption of such a stand had been made easier for the Liberals after the 1967 split.

Following its unconditional commitment to Canadian federalism, the Bourassa government began low-key piecemeal negotiations with the federal government. However, this was not to last for long. The position of the Quebec government at Victoria, in 1971, was a first indication that the Liberals' stand was not totally comfortable for a Quebec government. It also happened that the Bourassa government came, as other governments had already done, to emphasize the cultural problem in the Canadian context. "Cultural sovereignty" became its slogan, but many obstacles prevented the implication of this proposal.

The recent election of a PQ government has again put, more forcefully than ever before, the Quebec question. What is important in this recent development is that, for the first time, cultural, economic, and political elements already visible in previous forms of nationalism are brought together in an articulated program. It is also important to note, as the above review indicates, that successive Quebec governments have become increasingly severe in their questioning and criticisms of the Canadian federal arrangement. If one makes an exception of the last Liberal interlude, this trend manifests itself clearly. At first sight, the Bourassa period may appear as a pause in the evolution of Quebec nationalism, but this impression should be modified by taking into account the recent declarations, noted above, of Liberal representatives, particularly those of Guy Saint-Pierre and of some of his colleagues.

The appearance of the independence movement in the very first years of the "Quiet Revolution" in Quebec was considered a marginal phenomenon for a long time. Many people were troubled by the violent action of the Front de libération du Québec (FLQ),[13] but it was not believed that an independence party would reach power in a foreseeable future. This is now a fact.

Historians in the future will probably be able to measure accurately the importance of the October Crisis in the evolution of Quebec politics. The situation and the problems pointed out in the FLQ's manifesto did make sense for many Québécois at the moment. Some people, on the other hand, saw it as an opportunity to discredit the separatist movement in Quebec. We must not disregard the traumatizing effects of the application of the War Measures Act and military occupation on Quebec opinion at the end of 1970 and the beginning of 1971. It is possible to measure these effects in the short term,[14] but historical experiences of this sort may more likely have consequences in the longer term, although it is then more difficult to evaluate that precisely.[15]

What is going to happen in the next few years? Is Quebec really going to separate? At the two federal-provincial conferences held in December 1976, the PQ government reasserted its ultimate goal: to provide the Quebec nation with a homeland. It was obviously the only kind of statement we could expect from the new Quebec government. To deal more appropriately with the questions just put, other considerations should be faced. For instance, it would be relevant to outline the history of Quebec since the French Regime to understand better the meaning of the last Quebec election. In this respect, it appears clear that the recent election constitutes a very big step psychologically in the evolution of Quebec politics.

In any interpretation of Quebec politics, it must be recalled that the crisis in Quebec not only relates to the national question but also concerns the future organization of the society. In all that, it is evident that the national problem of Quebec is emphasized by its peculiar economic structure, which is dominated by "foreigners." It is nevertheless possible to imagine there will be a pause if ever independence appears likely in the very near future. But it will be only a pause. One may suspect that the PQ, perceived as a gathering of people sharing a specific political goal without necessarily agreeing on basic ideological points, will have problems of survival if ever the independence option meets with failure. Moreover, we may speculate that, if Quebec ever separates, the PQ will soon be revealed to have been a transitory party. But such speculations tend to disregard the influence of "external" forces. Among these factors, the next federal election appears crucial. The choice then made by both Québécois and other Canadians will be, in a manner of speaking, very determinant.

A full-scale assessment of the question of Quebec's independence would demand a kind of analysis completely different from that offered here. However, as long as we confine our analysis to the interpretation of the last Quebec election, we can say that this election represents the beginning of a new era in Quebec politics. Is the euphoria now visible in many Quebec milieux going to last for long? It is at least evident that social tensions will not come to an end simply because a new party is now in power. The most important question remains: are the many expectations raised by this election going to be satisfied by a PQ government?

Notes

1. See his interview in *La Presse*, 14 août 1976, A1.

2. See the interview in *Le Devoir*, 19 août 1976, 2.

3. For some developments on that and some other questions related to electoral studies, see my "Les études électorales au Québec: Les principales orientations et quelques débats," *Recherches sociographiques* 18 (1977).

4. The two other cases were the riding of Laurentides-Labelle, where the Liberals got a proportion of 41.7 percent of votes in 1973, and the riding of Charlevoix. As a matter of fact, this last riding was one of the only five ridings where the Liberal Party succeeded in keeping a proportion of more than 50 percent of the vote in the last election, the other four being ridings where a very important group of Anglophones can be found: D'arcy-McGee, Mont-Royal, Saint-Laurent, and Westmount.

5. For an analysis of the influence of the ethnic factor in the ridings of the Montreal metropolitan area, see Pierre Champagne, "Les caractéristiques cachées du dernier scrutin. Comment le facteur linguistique a influencé le résultat," in *Le Devoir*, 9 décembre 1976, 13, 19.

6. In fact, the PQ increased its support in every riding but Westmount where its proportion of votes dropped by one percent from 1973 to 1976.

7. In fact, the RC got more than 15 percent of the votes in only four ridings, of which three are specifically located in the Abitibi region. The other amazingly is Lotbinière: would this imply a kind of alliance against the UN's leader?

8. This is not surprising at all since we know that in 1966, 43.5 percent of the Quebec population already found desirable the emergence of a major party other than the UN and the Liberals: see Vincent Lemieux, Marcel Gilbert, and André Blais, *Une élection de réalignement: L'élection générale du 29 avril 1970 au Québec* (Montreal: Cahiers de Cité libre, Éditions du jour, 1970), 41.

9. Marcel Rioux, "The Development of Ideologies in Quebec" in *The Canadian Political Process: A Reader*, rev. ed., edited by Orest M. Kruhlak, Richard Schultz, and Sidney I. Polisbushaby (Toronto: Holt, Rinehart and Winston, 1973), 80.

10. In fact, the Union Nationale won a majority of seats, though only 41 percent of the votes, while the Liberals had the support of 47 percent.

11. A more in-depth analysis would require necessary distinctions between the degree of radicalization of workers' various organizations. Unfortunately, I cannot undertake such an analysis here. It is important to remember that our rough description would call for many nuances in a more lengthy analysis.

12. The experience of the early 1960s with the Liberals is still too fresh in memories to permit the repetition of such fallacious alliances with political authorities who are dependent more upon a structure than upon their program, unless this program aims to modify the structure fundamentally.

13. For a good analysis of the FLQ's actions and orientations, see Marc Laurendeau, *Les Québécois violents: Un ouvrage sur les causes et la rentabilité de la violence d'inspiration politique au Québec*, 2nd ed. (Sillery: Les Éditions du Boréal Express, 1974).

14. See Marcel Gilbert and Michel Bellavance, *L'opinion publique et la crise d'octobre* (Montreal: Éditions du jour, 1971).

15. It sometimes happens that history takes dramatic turns. To beat Bourassa in his own riding was possibly a sweet revenge for Gérald Godin, the PQ's candidate. As a matter of fact, Godin, a poet and publisher, who had become in the spring of 1976 the President of the Société Saint-Jean-Baptiste de Montréal, was, with his wife, singer Pauline Julien, one of some 450 people who were jailed in October 1970 in the course of the largest police operation ever made in Canada.

SECTION 7

THE FUTURE OF QUÉBÉCOIS NATIONALISM

The 1980s have proven to be difficult and challenging times for the Parti Québécois and the nationalist movement. Following the euphoria of the PQ victory in November 1976 there came the difficult and complex challenge of meeting the socio-economic and political aspirations of the various groups making up the coalition that had brought the party to power. Keeping the coalition together was the glue of nationalism. Since its formation in 1968, the PQ skillfully appropriated for itself the definition of Québécois nationalism. At the heart of that definition was the creation of a dynamic, social-democratic society that would not only improve the lives of individual Quebeckers but would, it was argued, considerably strengthen the collective foundations of the Francophone nation via the achievement of political independence for the province of Quebec. The achievement of an independent Québécois nation-state proved far more difficult than the PQ strategies had imagined.

The PQ hoped to accomplish this goal by gaining the respect of its citizens through the provision of solid, efficient government. Despite increasingly difficult economic conditions, the PQ expanded the services of the social-welfare state, provided added protection for unions on strike, and gave public and para-public employees handsome financial settlements. All of these efforts were in vain because the PQ lost its most crucial challenge, the 1980 referendum. While the PQ was returned to office in 1981 with increased popular support, it very quickly squandered its new mandate. The PQ suffered a devastating and humiliating defeat on the constitutional question and then, facing severe economic constraints brought on by its earlier generosity and a severe recession, was forced to adopt an authoritarian line with the public-sector unions. Has the decline and ultimate defeat of the PQ in 1985 also contributed, as some commentators have suggested, to an irreversible demise of nationalism in Quebec?

The referendum defeat in 1980, followed by the defeat of the PQ in 1984, symbolized the inability of the neo-nationalists to achieve the central goal of the Quiet Revolution, the merging of the Québécois nation with the Quebec state. Concerned observers are now asking themselves how and why events unfolded in this manner. Some suggest that the PQ undermined much of the basis for nationalism when it passed the Charter of the French Language giving priority to French as the language of work. Bill 101 consolidated Quebec's cultural sovereignty but undermined the need for political sovereignty because it opened more and better private sector jobs for highly educated, upwardly mobile Francophones. During the referendum campaign, the PQ was unable to convince many of its working-class supporters that political independence did not entail considerable economic risks. Others argue that the PQ further contributed to its demise with its shocking mishandling of the constitutional question as well as its undemocratic and unconstitutional attack on the public and para-public employees. The PQ had become a mean-spirited political party rather than a national movement. Nationalism suffered a decline because it was no longer deemed essential by the new middle class and because of its long association with the PQ, a party that had lost its *raison d'être* and was shortly to lose its leader and a provincial election.

Guy Rocher, a sociologist who has written extensively on the cultural evolution of Quebec society since 1945, provides some insights into the future of

Quebec society in his essay "A Half-Century of Cultural Evolution in Quebec." Unlike some doomsayers, he does not view the collapse of society as immanent. The cultural changes of the past fifty years, he argues, have been significant but not so dramatic as to undermine completely the ability of Francophone society to remain coherent and dynamic. The greatest challenge facing the society is whether or not it can integrate and eventually assimilate, on it own terms and for its own benefit, the American culture. He feels it is worth the effort.

In "Nationalism in Quebec in the 1980s," Jean-Louis Roy contends that the referendum constituted a defeat for one species of nationalism rather than nationalism in general. Roy outlines the various pressures forcing a redefinition of nationalism if the concept is to remain relevant. The political pressures include the defeat of the referendum, the exclusion of Quebec from the constitutional accord, the departure of Trudeau, and the victory of the federal Conservative Party. A new nationalism must take into account international economic and technological developments, must incorporate important aspects of the Canadian context, and finally, must adjust to internal factors such as the demographic crisis, the ambitions of the Francophone bourgeoisie, and the need for a renewal of Quebec's educational and cultural institutions.

A HALF-CENTURY OF CULTURAL EVOLUTION IN QUEBEC†

GUY ROCHER

Introduction

When I was a young sociology professor, in the early 1950s, my colleagues and I used to receive invitations from Canadian universities to explain why Quebec had not changed, why it hung on to its past and seemed to be rooted in the eighteenth century. However, since the late 1960s, we have been invited to talk about why Quebec has changed so rapidly, the ways in which it has evolved, and what it is likely to become in the short or long term.

This is a small and perhaps too personal an indication of the changes that Quebec has undergone during the past few years, but it is significant nonetheless. Anyone who had left Quebec in the 1930s and had come back today would discover a society profoundly changed, or at least one that gives the impression of having undergone profound changes. Of course, it could be an illusion; we will return to that later. At any rate, relations with other people, institutions, literature, and the general climate in Quebec lead us to believe in a definite evolution. The past fifty years have certainly not been characterized by stability, continuity, or a maintenance of the status quo. As well, if one consults the recent writings of the "professional observers" of society — political scientists, ethnologists, sociologists — the image of a Quebec that is moving, changing, and being transformed becomes even stronger, almost an obsession, or at the very least, commonplace.[1]

It would be wrong, however, to think that no change took place before the 1930s. Many developments had taken place at the end of the nineteenth and the

†"Un demi-siècle d'évolution culturelle au Québec," *University of Toronto Quarterly* 50, 1 (Fall 1980): 15–28. Translated by Barbara Krever.

beginning of the twentieth centuries, but these affected mostly the social organization and the structures of Quebec and hardly touched its mentality. The industrial revolution and urbanization took place in Quebec during these years. From the rural and artisanal society that it was until the mid-nineteenth century, Quebec became progressively more industrialized and urbanized, and the population began to cluster around certain large urban centres, first around both Quebec City and Montreal and ultimately mostly around Montreal. The decline of Quebec City's role as the second most important industrial centre is a major and unfortunate event in the structural and cultural development of Quebec.

Franco-Québécois reacted to this period of urbanization and industrialization *with a pre-industrial mentality*. Undoubtedly this is what struck the observers of the 1930s and 1940s: Quebec resembled a place where two large streams of water met without mingling. Elements of traditional and industrial society existed side by side without interpenetrating; in rural Quebec, large regions remained well-protected enclaves of purely traditional society.

Quebec was industrial in its production methods and yield, its division of labour, the development of its territory, and the urban concentration of its population; it was pre-industrial in its mentality, its ideology, its morality, and its ethos, so much so that one hesitated to call Quebec an industrial society. It was rather, according to the title of Everett C. Hughes' book written at this time, a society "in transition."[2]

This can be explained partly by the fact that Franco-Québécois were not responsible for the industrialization of Quebec. It was carried out under the auspices of foreign, or at least English-Canadian, capital and by means of a qualified labour force of which French Canadians constituted only the lower levels. Any profit that French Canadians gained was not as partners or shareholders, but only as subordinates. A harsh light is shed on the situation when one studies the linguistic dividing line in companies, which was at the level of the foreman in most important enterprises until around the 1950s: the foreman was generally bilingual, so as to be able to speak French to his employees and English to the office staff and to superiors in the company. It is only recently that the linguistic dividing line for Francophones has begun to be raised from one echelon to another to the top or head-office level, where it is now.[3]

Within North American industrial society, Francophone Quebec had retained the appearance of a sort of homogeneous cultural reserve characterized by the predominance of the Catholic Church, the alliance between the state and the Church, a government that could be called "clericocratic" (so much so that Quebec was referred to in English as "the priest-ridden province"), an educational system still marked by the influence of the eighteenth century, a moral code directly inspired by the Catholic religion, and a family lifestyle that sociologists called "traditionalist."

As for culture in the stricter, less anthropological, sense, literary and artistic production was very uneven. Apart from certain breakthroughs that were remarkable precisely because they were isolated cases, on the part of a few poets (such as Émile Nelligan, Saint-Denys Garneau) or painters (such as Borduas), the greatest share of literary and artistic production was inspired by a rhetoric and aesthetic that did not belong to this century.

Culture, both in anthropological and in the more restricted sense, has undergone a radical and dramatic evolution in the last few decades. This does not exclude the fact that certain structural changes have also taken place over the same years. There has been a rapid and unexpected decline in the birth rate, resulting in a decrease in population unprecedented in Quebec's history; there is also the process of state-building, which entailed an increase in public bureaucracy, and an ever-increasing intervention in sectors that had previously been controlled by the church or by private enterprise. However, these structural transformations were themselves the product of cultural evolution, of the change in the mentality, mind, and soul of Franco-Québécois.[4]

My task will be to describe a few of the profound cultural changes that have taken place in contemporary Quebec and to look at a few explanatory factors. I will end with a few judgments on the present and the future.

A Culture in the Process of Modernization

One of the most visible traits that characterizes the recent evolution of Québécois culture is the flourishing of that culture. For almost two hundred years, it was polarized between two linguistic and cultural communities, the French and the English. It remained so almost until the Second World War. The Francophone community was particularly homogeneous due to its religion, historic roots, customs, mentality, and lifestyle. The English-speaking community in Quebec, while less unified, still had a distinct style: it had its traditions, its leadership, its own universe that made it different from other English-speaking communities in other parts of Canada.

Two things happened. First of all, the homogeneity of the Francophone community broke down. There was no longer the same religious unanimity, and consequently a diversity of personal rules of moral conduct came to replace the former unity. Tradition and the past lost their position of privilege. Also, in the economic sector, new professions and diverse interest groups sprang up. New elites appeared that were representative of new social groups.[5] "Unanimity is no more," was the way Gérard Pelletier summed it up in a resounding article that appeared in the magazine *Cité libre* in the late 1950s.

Secondly, the Anglophone community became diversified as well, less from the inside than from the addition of new elements. Immigration over the last thirty years has added to its number. The old Anglophone stock was supplemented by Allophones from Greece, Italy, Germany, and from Latin countries or regions such as Spain, Portugal, and South America. The majority of immigrants — especially those who arrived in Quebec after the Second World War — chose to live in the Anglophone community: they adopted English as their language and sent their children to English-speaking schools, whether Protestant or Catholic.[6] This is one of the most powerful causes of Quebec neo-nationalism, of the separatist or sovereign ideology, and of the recent language legislation (Bill 101). But a true "assimilation" of these Allophones into the Anglophone community of British origin never came about: the Allophones adopted the English language and elements of Anglophone culture without being entirely accepted or integrated into the original Anglophone community. As a result, what we usually call the "Anglophone community" in Quebec has become a very complex reality, made up of disparate elements of diverse origins and cultures.

Quebec, then, became a pluralistic society from the cultural point of view. Value and identity conflicts became more and more intense; this is a new reality with which Quebec must learn to live.[7]

A second characteristic, which is not without a link to the first, is the recent secularization that can be observed in the Québécois mentality, especially in the Francophone community. If the Catholic Church has withdrawn from public power and turned inward upon itself, abandoning to the state the many functions that it used to serve in teaching, health, and social assistance, it is because it now has only limited aid and support from the population of Quebec. Québécois no longer turn to the church first; they no longer expect services and instruction from it. Recruitment of clergy has almost run dry, both for men and women, and consequently religious communities and clergy are no longer able to fill the functions they had previously. For a growing number of Québécois, a greater dissociation than before has taken place between religion and morality, with the latter no longer necessarily obeying the commands of the former. Even couples who have remained attached to the Catholic Church, and who have taken the sacraments faithfully, have resorted to the use of contraceptives in family planning without feeling a contradiction to their religious allegiance.

Another important trait of contemporary Quebec: it has been much more open to the world than before. Quebec, Francophones as well as Anglophones, were always great travellers. Long ago, many of them were *coureurs des bois*, explorers, navigators, etc. As well, many Québécois families had members, male and female, who were missionaries in China, Africa, South America, or in the Canadian North. Many of the accounts related in the missionaries' sermons made up a frequently repeated and lively folklore of exotic stories.

Today, Québécois themselves travel for their own pleasure. Almost all young Québécois have travelled outside of Quebec; many have stayed for quite long periods in various countries in Africa, Asia, South America, as well as in Europe or in the United States. Of course, their experiences abroad are more or less superficial, depending on the individual case, and the resulting influence on the rest of their lives is not always substantial. But, for the majority of young Québécois, Quebec is no longer the centre of the world or the only measure of things; they have experienced culture shock elsewhere and will be marked by it forever. . . .

The last trait that deserves to be emphasized is the diversification and proliferation of art forms on the part of artists, performers, writers, poets, Franco-Québécois *chansonniers*. In spite of the fact that it happened rather late, Quebec is nonetheless in the process of making itself more and more well-known, especially in the Francophone world, for its poetry, novels, theatre, and music. Without exaggerating the quality of the literary and artistic work it has produced, one can at least maintain that it is enjoying a period of rebirth, that it is making its comeback in the contemporary world of literature and the arts.

One word can perhaps sum up this cultural evolution of the past few years: modernization. It is an ambiguous term, one that sociologists tended to overuse for some time and that they now hesitate to use. The evolutionary connotation that it seems to carry is objectionable. It remains nonetheless that, if we exclude any value judgment as to whether modernization is good or bad, fortunate or harmful, we can recognize a society's leap into the twentieth century. This is what happened in Quebec, especially to its Francophone community.

A Few Explanatory Factors

It is very probable that the gap between an industrial society and the pre-industrial mentality was becoming more and more unbearable in Quebec, and, by the 1940s, one could predict that Quebec could not survive much longer under such circumstances. There was a sort of schizophrenia involved in living inside a mental universe that was dissociated from everyday reality.

The Second World War contributed greatly to the evolution toward a more modern mentality. There is a definite reason why historians date historic periods in relation to certain wars. Throughout human history, wars have had considerable influence on people's lives, mentalities, beliefs, ideologies. Quebec did not escape from the immense shakeup of the Second World War. Many women went to work in wartime industries, while a great number of young men in the army and in military campaigns were going through unanticipated experiences. At the end of such a disturbing period, Quebec could never be the same. Perhaps it was due to these events in particular that Quebec became more open to the outside world, as was mentioned earlier.

Another factor is the educational revolution that took place at this time. This is not to say that this revolution is only a recent one. During the 1930s, there was a great debate, which I believe was a sign of things to come, surrounding the introduction of sciences into the traditional classical curriculum, which had been based mainly on arts and philosophy and which had neglected math and the precise sciences. The curriculum had remained true to the intellectual universe of classicism, or at least this was the defence for what it had become. In the 1950s, those who supported the teaching of science triumphed. The classical curriculum was substantially modified.[8]

However, it was in the 1950s and even more in the 1960s that major reform was undertaken. Reform in the 1930s only applied to classical education; the changes in the 1960s would transform the whole system.

While still remaining distinct from each other, the Protestant and Catholic sectors were unified under one authority, with identical standards and rules. But it was especially the Catholic sector that underwent profound changes, with regard to its structures, programs, and mentality. This transformation was characterized in particular by the abandonment of the classical curriculum, such as it was, by the unification of the whole of the system (which had up until then been made up of parts more or less independent of each other), by democratizing access to secondary, college, and higher education, by creating a broader range of programs, and by reasserting the value of public education, which for a long time had been neglected for private education. For those who were educated in the Quebec system thirty or forty years ago, today's system is unrecognizable. That is what very often causes confusion and anguish for parents who no longer feel capable of following their child in an educational system that has almost nothing in common with the one they knew.[9]

Are these changes in education a reflection of cultural evolution or an agent of this transformation? The educational revolution, especially in the 1960s, was probably both. It was both prompted by and an indication of a new mentality and it helped to accentuate the new aspects of this mentality.

Finally, this evolution in Quebec can probably not be explained without reference to the changes in mentality that took place in the whole of contemporary Western civilization. It is possible that, for reasons not yet analysed, Quebec, and especially the Francophone community in Quebec, has been more sensitive than other societies to the great cultural transformations that Western civilization has seen in the last few decades. At any rate, some sectors of Québécois society have enthusiastically welcomed cultural innovation, whether in the area of morals, literary or artistic creation, political ideologies, or counterculture. This can be observed, for example, in young poets, feminist movements, in the formation of certain "communes," and in various religious movements alike.

Progress or Regression?

In the face of this evolution, one can wonder whether the new conditions that are predominant in Quebec are more or less favourable than before for the cultural development of individuals, groups, and for the whole of society. Are the changes that we just mentioned unfortunate disturbances that created havoc in a universe that was until then orderly and relatively functional? Or is it a question of a cultural and spiritual renewal apt to come soon to fruition?

First of all, it is true that for some years now Quebec has experienced a renewal of political conscience. When they left the Catholic Church, Québécois turned to political power, which required them to take on roles and responsibilities that they had up until then refused. At the same time, the question of national identity, an old problem, latent in the French-Canadian conscience for more than 150 years, re-emerged in many different ways — Québécois neo-nationalism, FLQ revolutionary and other secret movements, periods of terrorism and violence, and the emergence of the Parti Québécois. Many English-Canadians tend to interpret these phenomena more negatively than positively. However, all these stirrings of political thought and criticism made up a favourable atmosphere for cultural development in Quebec, an important source of inspiration for many artists in their novels, poems, plays, songs. There are not often great nationalistic moments in the life of a people; such moments are often marked by violence and by a certain romanticism that touches every human being.

Bill 101, the recent legislation on language in Quebec, can be seen in the same light. The legislation also suffers from a bad reputation in English-Canadian circles, where they have tried to paint it as repressive and even tyrannical legislation. The English-language press, especially in Quebec but also in other provinces, lashed out against this bill. People too easily forget to consider the bill as an important gesture of self-affirmation on the part of the Franco-Québécois community. There were not only economic reasons that led the government of

Quebec to enact this law, whose obvious aim was to re-establish a certain balance of power between Quebec's two linguistic communities in the areas of employment and the economy; there was also the pressure of a nationalistic ideology that found support in pride in the language, in its purity and quality as well as in the use to which it was put. This bill was an attempt to express the new-found respect for the French language, both as a vehicle for expressing thought and as a symbol of cultural identity. It is understandable that the caricature that Canada's English-speaking community too often made of it was particularly irritating for a good number of Franco-Québécois. Lack of understanding of the current evolution of contemporary Quebec was only too obvious in this situation and was quite shocking.

It is obvious that relations between the Franco-Québécois community and other linguistic communities in Quebec have not improved. One can even say that they are more tense than they have ever been.[10] The "two solitudes" that Hugh MacLennan described symbolically in his novel still exist; one could say that they have been replaced by several solitudes, with the increase of new ethnic communities (Greek, Italian, Portuguese, Spanish, etc.). There are still very few cultural exchanges between Francophone, Anglophones, and Allophones in Quebec. One group is unaware of the activities of another, even when there is not a climate of mistrust and misunderstanding between them. It is probably the Anglophone sector that has made the most progress in the area of cultural exchange. A growing number of Anglo-Québécois have made great efforts to gain a better knowledge of the language and culture of their Francophone compatriots, probably at the time of the latter's political and cultural awakening. For their part, the Francophones are still too obsessed with themselves and too involved with their cultural and political renewal to have the time and inclination to understand other cultural groups in Quebec. The great possibilities for reciprocal enrichment characteristic of such a co-habitational situation as we have in Quebec have not yet been explored. And for now, it is probable that the political climate will remain a negative factor, such that one cannot expect a rapid change in this situation.

Another factor is that both the Francophone and Anglophone communities are deeply marked by the American influence, and this influence is becoming stronger. It is easy to assume that the Francophone community is protected from American influences by its language. There is, of course, a certain barrier, but it is insufficient, considering the powerful pressure represented by American civilization at our doorstep. The influence of that civilization leaves its mark on the entire world, far beyond geographical limits and language barriers.

For both Anglophones and Francophones in Quebec, as well as for the whole of Canada, the proximity of the American colossus surely represents the greatest challenge to the future. Will we be able to develop a culture of our own, with its own originality, without being a simple copy of U.S. culture? Personally, I believe it is purely utopian to think that either Canadian or Québécois culture can be totally and entirely independent of American culture. But I also think that it is possible for a collectivity such as ours not to give in passively to this influence, but rather to assimilate U.S. culture, to integrate it with our past and with what we have already acquired of it, and to turn all this into a new product that would have a certain originality. In order to do this, it will be necessary to know how to communicate with the most lively intellectual circles in the United States (which we do infrequently in Canada and even less in Quebec), those that harbour inner feelings of dissent about U.S. civilization. American influences flood our homes and our lives, especially through the mass media and through the consumer habits we share with our neighbours to the south.[11] But we have not yet been able to seek out that which is intellectually and spiritually exciting in the U.S., that which is non-conformist and goes against the well-established order.

In Quebec, protest movements, whether by youths, the left, or within the Catholic church, have almost no contact, strangely enough, with their American counterparts. They believe it preferable to take their inspiration from European movements, whether French, German, or British. However, they have much more in common with American than European movements. This is a strange paradox. And if we do not solve this ambiguity, we will never be able to assimilate American culture (assimilate in the strong sense of the term, i.e., to make it our own by adapting it to ourselves and transforming it to fit our substance): we will only be under its influence and ultimately be its victims.

There is an encouraging phenomenon that can be observed in Quebec over the last few years: the development of cultural forces in regions other than Montreal and Quebec City. There has been first an economic, and increasingly, a cultural focus in regional development. For example, people are beginning to object to the fact that, all too often, radio and television carry exclusively Montreal-based programs, and that programming on the whole is too much influenced by Montreal. We are seeing small, more or less militant groups beginning to take charge of regional cultural development. This is happening, for example, to community radio and television, to Radio-Québec, to a certain regional press, to regional and local educational institutions.[12]

There is evidence here more of frustrated aspirations than of gratification. The regions, especially the peripheral ones, still only have limited financial and human resources for taking charge of and supporting cultural institutions of good quality. Moreover, a long-lived habit of passivity makes it difficult and sometimes problematical for the population to participate in new regional enterprises that are sometimes daring and sometimes even suicidal. It is always a minority, and always the same one, that finds itself participating in all the business activities in a region. Often, because of this, the clientele, which is not yet ready to take part in a regional enterprise, is dissatisfied as are those who support a regionalist ideology of participation.

In spite of these difficulties and limits in regional cultural development, I believe that there is hope for the future. Regions outside Montreal and Quebec City harbour cultural wealth that is rooted in the past and that is kept up in a more authentic way than in the major centres. This is one of the sources of original cultural development from which we could profit in developing a North American, non-U.S., culture.

Let us end by coming back to a remark made at the beginning of this article: was there perhaps a tendency to exaggerate the actual changes that Quebec underwent during the last two decades? There was a time, especially in the 1960s, when we built up the changes into an ideology. Evolution was good, status quo bad; virtue resided in change, and stopping meant stagnation. The effect was that we wanted to see change everywhere, and we probably saw more than there was.

At present, we are witnessing, in Quebec as well as almost everywhere in the world, a return to conservative positions that are more reassuring, more orderly, and apparently wiser. Changes that came about in the 1950s and 1960s have come to a standstill. Important sectors of the population, even of youth, are questioning the changes that came about, for example, in the school system or in the intervention of the state in cultural matters, and are hoping, strangely enough, to revert to the way things were. This new and rather unexpected situation forces us to take a look at the ground covered, to wonder what has really changed and whether we were so afraid of witnessing change that we overestimated the extent of the cultural evolution.

These doubts, applying both to the extent of changes that were brought about and to their appropriateness, create a climate of perplexity that is hardly favourable to an intense cultural life and activity. We are living rather in an atmosphere of inhibition, of discomfort, of timidity, which does not encourage innovation, inventiveness, or imagination. After being marked by the "new wave" of youth in the 1960s, our era has just entered a phase that seems dominated by a feeling of old age. If we believe in demographic findings, and if we attribute a certain importance to them, we will have to wait several years before we emerge into more enlightening times!

Conclusion

Must we end on this pessimistic note or may we add a few words of optimism? It seems to me that a mixture of the two is appropriate. Some conditions that are favourable to the cultural development of Quebec and others that are not rub shoulders, thus making an analysis of the present situation difficult and any prediction of the future uncertain.

But it is perhaps precisely because of this tension of uncertainty, debate, value conflicts, and ebb and flow of past and future ideologies that a new cultural development could flourish. Great periods of cultural creation were not all associated with times of peace, calm, collective euphoria, and confidence in the future— far from it! But we must make certain that the forces that inhibit the free and creative spirit will not be dominant enough to stifle positive motivations and inclinations.

How to succeed? Merely the will of individuals and groups is not enough. Success depends on accidents of history, on games of chance, on the imponderables of great historic tendencies. Individuals are not in complete control of history; the future is revealed only partially, and often falsely, to them. But the will to realize something, in spite of the trials of the times in which we live, leads us all to try to leave our mark.

Notes

1. The list of works mentioned here could be long, as there has been extensive material written on Quebec in the last few years. We limit ourselves to mentioning some of them while keeping in mind that the list if far from exhaustive. The first works quoted are in English, the order being chronological: Hugh Bingham Myer, ed., *The Quebec Revolution* (Montreal: Harvest House, 1964); Ramsay Cook, *Canada and the French-Canadian Question* (Toronto: Macmillan, 1966; reprinted by Copp Clark Pitman, 1986); Edward M. Corbet, *Quebec Confronts Canada* (Baltimore: Johns Hopkins University Press, 1967); Marcel Rioux, *La Question du Québec* (Paris: Segher, 1969); Fernand Dumont, *La Vigile du Québec* (Montreal: Hurtubise HMH, 1971); Marcel Rioux and Yves Martin, ed., *La Société canadienne française* (Montreal: Hurtubise HMH, 1971), first published in English: *French-Canadian Society* (Toronto: McClelland and Stewart, 1964); Jean-Luc Migué, ed., *Le Québec d'aujourd'hui. Regards d'universitaires* (Montreal: Hurtubise HMH, 1971); Claude Ryan, ed., *Le Québec qui se fait* (Montreal: Hurtubise HMH, 1973); Gabriel Gagnon and Luc Martin, ed., *Québec 1960–1980. La crise du développement* (Montreal: Hurtubise HMH, 1973); Marcel Rioux, *Les Québécois* (Paris: Seuil, 1974); Denis Monière, *Le Développement des idéologies au Québec, des origines à nos jours* (Montreal: Québec Amérique, 1977); Edouard Cloutier and Daniel Latouche, ed., *Le Système politique québécois* (Montreal: Hurtubise HMH, 1979).

2. Everett C. Hughes, *French Canada in Transition* (Chicago: University of Chicago Press, 1941). For the history of industrialization in Quebec, see for example, Albert Faucher's article "Le Caracterè continental de l'industrialisation au Québec," *Recherches sociographiques* 6, 3 (1965): 219–36.

3. Everett C. Hughes' study reveals a great deal about the situation in the 1930s. The split in the early 1970s is well described by Serge Carlos, *L'Utilisation du français dans le monde du travail au Québec*, Study E3, carried out on behalf of the Commission of Inquiry on the Position of the French Language and on Language Rights in Quebec (Quebec, July 1973).

4. See the two articles by Gary Caldwell and B. Dan Czarnocki, "Un rattrapage raté. Le Changement social dans le Québec d'après-guerre, 1950–1974: Une comparison Québec/Ontario," *Recherches sociographiques* 18, 1 (1977): 9–58; et "Un rattrapage raté II. La Variation à court terme," *Recherches sociographiques* 18, 3 (1977): 366–96. The two authors discuss particularly what they call the "disjunctive" model that I suggested for an analysis of the evolution of Quebec since the Second World War. However, they reproach me for having minimized the structural changes that took place during this period and for having concentrated on cultural changes. It is a question of emphasis: without denying certain structural changes, I believe that they were enveloped and even carried along by the great cultural transformations that Quebec has undergone in the last three decades.

5. Guy Rocher, "Multiplication des élites et changement social au Canada français," *Revue de l'Institut de sociologie* 1 (1968): 79–94.

6. See, for example, Richard J. Joy, *Languages in Conflict* (Ottawa, 1967), particularly chapter 9, "Immigration: 95% English-speaking."

7. This evolution and the present situation are thoroughly described and analysed in the government of Quebec's White Paper, *La Politique québécoise du développement culturel* (Quebec: Éditeur officiel, 1978), vol. 1, chap. 3.

8. Nicole Gagnon, "L'Idéologie humaniste dans la revue *L'Enseignement secondaire*," *Recherches sociographiques* 4, 2 (1963): 167–200, reproduced in *École et société au Québec*, edited by Pierre W. Bélanger and Guy Rocher, 2nd ed. (Montreal: Hurtubise HMH, 1975), 1: 59–89.

9. Much has been written on this reform. One could consult, in particular, the *Rapport de la Commission d'Enquête sur l'enseignement au Québec* (Quebec, 1963–66), 5 volumes. The reform is also put in perspective in *Rapport Parent, dix ans après* (Montreal: Bellarmin, 1975) and in numerous articles in various issues of the magazine *Prospectives*.

10. Rainer Knopff, "Language and Culture in the Canadian Debate: The Battle of the White Papers," *Canadian Review of Studies in Nationalism/Revue canadienne des études sur le nationalisme* 6, 1 (1979): 66–82. The author analyses certain ambiguities in the linguistic policies of the Lévesque and Trudeau governments, but his analysis is ambiguous as well. This in itself shows the difficulty of the subject. It also seems that the Liberal Party of Quebec, under the direction of Claude Ryan, is not ready to clear up these same ambiguities.

11. Gilbert Maistre, "L'Influence de la radio et de la television americaines au Canada," *Recherches sociographiques* 12, 1 (1971): 51–75.

12. In this regard, the Radio-Québec Bill, as it was recently amended, constitutes a very important step forward. It establishes regional committees with important responsibilities for programming and production of programs; at the same time, it modifies the board of directors by having half of it made up of presidents of the regional committees. Thus, there is a chance that Radio-Québec could, two or three years from now, become a public television body where part of the programming would be planned and carried out in the regions. This would be the culmination of a long evolution, as much in the regions as in the central offices of Radio-Québec and in the Government of Quebec.

NATIONALISM IN QUEBEC IN THE 1980s: AFTER FAILURE, THE CHALLENGE OF RELEVANCE†

JEAN-LOUIS ROY

Disarray, backing down from commitments, disbelief, anger: these were some of the consequences of the failure of a certain expression of nationalism in Quebec at the beginning of the 1980s. Five years later, some people have not yet accepted the way in which a society that rejects the protection of an ideology expresses its freedom.

Others celebrated the outcome of the referendum. In their opinion, this outcome rested on the prospect of a more generous, more promising alternative. It expressed, in particular, fidelity to another expression of nationalism deeply rooted in the history of Quebec.

These diverging evaluations illustrate the complexity of nationalism in Quebec. There is no such thing as *one* expression of nationalism in Quebec, univocal and all-pervasive. There are, instead, *various* expressions of nationalism in Quebec.

This pluralism is not a recent phenomenon. It has always been at the very heart of our history. What is new, is the decision, taken at the end of the 1960s, by a segment of the political class to break with a tradition that incorporated the more radical currents of nationalism into the mainstream where they exercised only a marginal influence.

The foundation of the Parti Québécois put an end to this century-old tradition. Suddenly, the most strident national aspirations moved to the foreground and became the centre of all political debates. They became, within a few short years, universal prism and attraction pole. They led to a new interpretation of history that became even more relevant after the Parti Québécois came to power in 1976. They fed a new strategy that was bound to fail, since it could not stand up to the test of history.

---

†"Le nationalisme québécois dans les années 80," *Le Devoir*, 1 juin 1985. From the text of a speech given by the former publisher of *Le Devoir* to a meeting of the Canadian Historical Association, 28 May 1985. Translated by Henri Malebranche.

We have not properly sized up the scope of the changes that this break wrought. Besides, the very people who claimed responsibility for this new strategy tried to tone down its importance. They proclaimed, at every opportunity, continuity with Quebec's past and an affiliation with the Quiet Revolution. I, for one, reject this alleged continuity and this affiliation.

The fundamental objective of the PQ went completely beyond those pursued by successive governments in Quebec between 1960 and 1976, even if the governments of Lesage, Johnson, and Bourassa bent the course of events. The fundamental objective of the PQ evinced a complete change of nature, the pursuit of autonomy within confederation having given way to the will to gain sovereignty with economic association with Canada. This radical objective thus drastically changed the political expression of nationalism.

The single most important occurrence of the early 1980s was to force Quebeckers to choose between these two schools of nationalism, between these irreconcilable expressions, and to push the struggle between them to the extreme. It says a lot about the importance of nationalism in the 1980s to acknowledge its presence at the head of our commitments and desires to master the course of our history. However, from focus and pole of attraction, nationalism became a divisive and polarizing factor that led to the weakening of Quebec.

A Nationalism in Transition

Both the referendum campaign and its outcome illustrated the rejection by the majority of a certain school of Québécois nationalism. But it would be grossly mistaken to conclude that nationalism is dead and to write, as some people did, elegant obituaries.

From a historical perspective, the first phase of the PQ adventure represents a rather limited episode. Québécois nationalism was not born with René Lévesque's uprising. Québécois nationalism was not the child of the PQ. It corresponds to wider and more permanent realities.

Without claiming an absolute singularity — which would give an absurdly Albanian vision to our destiny — the Francophones in Quebec are still bound to a certain conception of their destiny that makes up Quebec's special character within the Canadian fabric and on the North American continent. They are bound to feel and react in a similar manner whenever certain topics are brought up that relate to their history, their territory, and their continued survival as Francophones. They know that this special character must be incorporated within the framework of Canadian and Quebec policies and they will keep on struggling to maintain this special character.

The failure of the PQ's strategy and policy, and its eventual rejection by the electorate, do not mean that no one has stood up, or will not rise in the future, to defend the interests of Quebec and secure a political status that takes its very special character into consideration.

Besides, the PQ itself has been forced to revise its analysis of the aspirations of the people of Quebec and its interpretation of history. The words of René Lévesque summarize better than any long-winded commentary the motive of this revision. "Along the road," he wrote on 20 November 1984,

We did not succeed, and less and less so with the passing of time, to draw a lesson from what was happening to us. . . . However, for some time already, I, like others, have been forced to start "thinking better of it." And to realize that it could not go on like that any longer.

Even if they are still far apart, Quebec's political parties seem to be headed for a kind of rapprochement on their views, which yesterday were still contradictory, on how to perceive and defend Quebec's interests. Of course, this rapprochement will not lead to a complete agreement. The recent introduction of a "projet d'accord constitutionnel" by the Lévesque government and the Liberal program "Maîtriser l'avenir," outline very clearly the room in which the political parties of Quebec will manoeuvre over the next few years.

The various schools of Québécois nationalism must redefine how they perceive themselves and the future, unless they dismiss the referendum defeat, the patriation of the constitution, Trudeau's departure, and the election of a Conservative government as unimportant.

These are the first motives, political ones, that bring me to talk about a nationalism in transition.

The Need for a New Synthesis

But there are other, possibly more compelling motives resulting essentially from new international realities, conditions in Canada, and major changes that have permeated Quebec society.

Nationalism, in its broadest sense, is nothing more than a synthesis of the aspirations, the needs, and the interests that are either dormant or at work in a given society, some of which are more permanent in character while others are a response to certain events. Any other definition would be a misrepresentation. Citizens who cannot relate to this definition will say so if given the chance. In any event, they will pull away if the synthesis cannot be verified by facts and the experience of their daily lives.

Quebec in the 1980s is called upon to look for a new coherence, to remake the image it has of itself. This necessity is already at work in our society. It is not a matter of liking or disliking what we are becoming. What matters is to understand this process, to measure its full impact and, while keeping a certain critical distance, not to deny it. It matters more than ever to make it fully ours and, if necessary, to build counterweights to it.

Nationalism is not a category in itself. It is bound to change also. Its permanence is indissociable from its relevance. Hence, its relation to the currents that transform society and alter it at the same time.

I would like to end by identifying some of the changes confronting us, changes that nationalism will have to assimilate lest it condemn itself to insignificance, marginality, and the severe censure of events.

International Factors

It is more than ever impossible to think of Quebec all by itself. Some decisive international factors have thrown a monetary order, which is a thing of the past, out of gear, intensified international competition among new and old industrial-ized countries and also called for massive technological adjustments and major changes in attitudes and ways of thinking.

Considering its main characteristics, our nationalism was fashioned by and large during that bygone period of real and constant economic growth. This rhythm is now broken and along with it a certain way of visualizing and plan-ning changes.

Even without having to alter its nature, nationalism simply cannot disregard these realities.

A number of other international factors press heavily on the concerns of our fellow citizens. Nationalism ought to take them into consideration also. What we are talking about here is the impossibility of defining, exclusively from within, the whole range of concerns and priorities. Issues such as nuclear energy, the environment, new technological challenges, the tremendous cultural diversity we have begun to experience and that is yet to come, give a wider dimension to the already complex "cohabitation" process.

The Canadian Factor

The nationalism that has been predominant among us over the last years had managed, until a few months ago, to ignore the Canadian context. So many works of all kinds, from inaugural speeches to reports of commissions of inquiry took their inspiration in a vision, a geography, an economy of a truncated world from which Canada was absent. In theory, this magic trick removed a lot of constraints. It made it possible to plan without those tiresome irritants and both-ersome juxtapositions that are the lot of all nations in the world. This way of seeing things has died a natural death.

A responsible Quebec nationalism must constantly keep in mind the ties that bind us to our immediate neighbours, to deem as essential Quebec's capacity for initiative within a whole that we wish might have been different but whose very existence we cannot deny. Historically and constitutively, the Canadian factor rests in the very heart of Quebec and the Quebec factor rests in the very heart of Canada.

A Society in Transformation

In many respects, Quebec society is very different from what it was fifteen or even ten years ago. Hence, the need to revise our teaching and representations.

"Le déclin du Québec est-il inévitable?" The subtitle of Georges Mathews's book [*Le choc démographique* (Boréal Express, 1984)], which deals with the demo-graphic crisis, aptly summarizes the enormous challenge confronting Quebec society on account of its demographic condition. In 1950, Quebec still had the highest birth rate in the Western world. Within thirty years, following an unprece-dented drop of 62 percent, it had fallen to next to last.

If the current trend were to continue, the decline in Quebec's demographic importance would become quite pronounced by the year 2006. All regions in Canada would, by then, register a substantial population increase: 12.4 percent in the Maritimes, 19.3 percent in Ontario, 32.5 percent in the West. Quebec's population would have increased by only 7.7 percent.

The change in the birth rate presents us with disturbing problems concerning social organization and civilization. It is certain that Quebec will have to resort to massive immigration simply to maintain its population at the present level. It is reckoned that the annual number of immigrants would have to treble just to ensure the replacement of the generations. Is this a practicable solution? And what would be the consequences on Quebec's ethnic composition, on the so-called national aspirations of the Quebeckers?

There is on this situation food for thought for the various expression of nationalism in Quebec, even some arguments in favour of a specific Quebec policy on this issue, given Canada's indifference in the matter. Quebec's sense of belonging will be diversified. The concept of otherness will become central. The major challenges that the Francophone majority would have to face on account of this unexplored path, which they will have to follow to ensure their very renewal, are still unknown and unclear.

And while we are on the topic of decline, the reduction, inevitable in this case, of the role of the state will present the various schools of Québécois nationalism with a formidable challenge. As far as symbols and realities are concerned, it is the action of the state that has most effectively set the parameters of the nationalist debate in Quebec over the last quarter century. Without falling into the currently fashionable notion that wants the state to be the cause of all nightmares, one has to recognize that the prevailing trend in all industrialized societies, aimed at stopping the growth of the public sector and cutting its size, is also at work in Quebec.

Quebec would have to think up its own way to stop the growth of the state with prudence and vigilance insofar as the development functions of the state are to a considerable degree directed towards maintaining this distinct society that we constitute.

Quebec nationalism will have to incorporate in its quest this reversal in the political realities.

The rapid emergence of a class of Francophone entrepreneurs in Quebec and the emphasis on private initiative are further new elements in the national and social fabric of the province. For some, it is a change that portends the decline of nationalism. Quite frankly, there is nothing to prove the accuracy of such a thesis.

I, for one, believe that the die has not yet been cast. This emergence and this emphasis are both too recent for us to grasp their full signification. Admittedly, we have here a new alliance and power bloc, a new force that will demand to play a role in charting and shaping Quebec's future. If we do not stint them on this role, these new entrepreneurs could well be in a position to converge their business logic with the interests of Quebec, and this they could achieve better than we think, although through means that are not always obvious. And they will do so all the more convincingly insofar as they are truly partners and their needs and concerns will have been incorporated into those of the society at large.

Lastly, the expressions of nationalism cannot remain indifferent to two essential priorities for a nation such as ours. By this we mean the defence of the internal territory — education and culture. I will not say anything more about education . . . other than to remark that our statistical progress is not worth much unless it is also accompanied by intellectual progress. In spite of all the claims set forth in political speeches, Quebec is still distressingly underequipped in education; its population remains undereducated in the areas that are truly of importance.

The immense field of culture now lies fallow in Quebec just when the input coming from a panoply of sources is increasing dramatically in this area. Only a substantial investment in culture and an increase in the number of places where freedom and relevance of creation blossom will give meaning to an otherwise indefensible claim to a specificity rich enough to be worth preserving.

The time has come to mesh nationalism with functional politics, those famous elements of a debate that to date remains unsolved.

The intellectuals are once again required to make their contribution. It is their responsibility to present the realities in an order that does justice to their importance. Immunized, on account of their calling, against preconceived ideas and old-fashioned clichés, it is their responsibility to protect the internal borders of culture and development, to bring the evidence, and to try, with the only means and motivations at their disposal, to do justice to what has been and what is. It is their duty to keep manicheism, this voracious and blind predator, at bay, to guard against the attractions of exercising power, a development that, as a rule, leaves them isolated, seared by political defeats that ruin them.

The political failure of a certain expression of nationalism at the beginning of the 1980s is beyond question. But is this failure, in the end, any less portentous than our demographic decline, the fact that we are lagging behind in education, our cultural poverty, our social lack of discipline, the marginalization of one million of our fellow Quebeckers who are unemployed and on welfare?

That nationalism exists in our province is self-evident. It is the question of its relevance that has become central.

How can we, in the second half of the 1980s, make it relevant, incorporate into Quebec's project those potential and emerging worlds we just evoked: new population, check of the public sector, Francophone presence in the private sector of the economy, reforms from within of a stagnant and bureaucratized educational system, devotion to freedom of creation?

To this already impressive list one should add the alienation of our younger citizens who did not find in nationalism and in politics, which were the dominant topics in our province during the last years, and in the institutions available to them an environment attractive and stimulating enough to give them the desire to contribute to Quebec's enrichment. This break constitutes no doubt one of the most pressing concerns for Quebec's nationalists, unless they wish to dismiss the only relief there really is.

These are, among others, the constraints, the failures, and the challenges confronting nationalism in Quebec in the 1980s. A force dreadfully battered by unparalleled divisions in our history, except maybe for those that occurred during the first period of the union government. A force broken by a crushing defeat that in the end affected the whole of Quebec.

Some people have tolled the knell of nationalism. They are certainly unaware of its foundation and of the need for it. But its relevance should not be taken for granted as long as the Franco-Québécois are confronted with such numerous and enormous challenges.

More than the referendum defeat, what might prove decisive in the end is our inability to set in motion the process of changes that, from within as well as from without, press for a reversal of analyses, attitudes, and commitments. This inability might well condemn Quebec to be pushed irremediably to one side.

FURTHER READING

Duplessis and His Critics

While somewhat dated, the standard work on the politics of the Duplessis era remains H.F. Quinn's *The Union Nationale*, rev. ed. (Toronto: University of Toronto Press, 1979). Duplessis has been the subject of two sympathetic biographies, Conrad Black's *Duplessis* (Toronto: McClelland and Stewart, 1979) and Robert Rumilly's *Maurice Duplessis et son temps*, 2 vols. (Montreal: Fides, 1973). Somewhat more impressionistic accounts are provided by Leslie Roberts, *The Chief: A Political Biography of Maurice Duplessis* (Toronto, 1963) and Pierre Laporte, *The Truce Face of Duplessis* (Montreal, 1960). Cursory but revealing attempts to provide a critical analysis are made by Richard Desrosiers in "Duplessis et l'idéologie dominante," *Revue d'historie de l'Amérique française* (hereafter *RHAF*) XXV, 3 (décembre 1971): 385–8, and René Durocher in "Le long règne de Duplessis: un essai d'interpretation," *RHAF* XXV, 3 (décembre 1971): 392–6. For an extensive critique of the economic policies of the Duplessis government from a Marxist perspective, readers should consult Gérard Boismenu's *Le duplessisme: politique economique et rapports de force, 1944–1960* (Montreal: Les Presses de l'Université de Montréal, 1981).

For an extensive discussion of the neo-nationalist and *Cité libre* critics of the Duplessis regime, see Michael D. Behiels, *Prelude to Quebec's Quiet Revolution* (Montreal and Kingston: McGill-Queen's University Press, 1985). Jean-Louis Roy, in *La marche des Québécois: le temps de ruptures (1945–1960)* (Montreal: Leméac, 1976), undermines the myth that this was the era of "la grande noirceur" by revealing the growing demands for modernization emerging from the unions, the co-operative movements, business organizations, the municipalities, teachers' associations, and the scientific community. A very enlightened and highly readable first-hand account of the struggle against clerical and political authoritarianism by one of the leading *Citélibristes* can be found in Gérard Pelletier's *Years of Impatience, 1950–1960* (Toronto: Methuen, 1985).

The Quiet Revolution: Origins and Impact

The most comprehensive description of the major development of the Quiet revolution to date can be found in Dale Thomson's *Jean Lesage and the Quiet Revolution* (Toronto: Macmillan, 1984). Two early but still useful accounts of the Quiet Revolution are those of Richard Jones, *Community in Crisis* (Toronto: McClelland and Stewart, 1972), and E.M. Corbett, *Quebec Confronts Canada* (Baltimore: Johns Hopkins University Press, 1967). A reprint of the Quebec Liberal Party's 1960 platform, which comprised a shrewd mixture of liberal and nationalist goals, can be found in Jean-Louis Roy, *Les Programmes électoraux du Québec II* (Montreal: Leméac, 1976).

For an analysis of the ideological, social, and economic forces underlying the Quiet Revolution, the reader must turn to *Quebec: Social Change and Political Crisis,* rev. ed. (Toronto: McClelland and Stewart, 1980) by Kenneth McRoberts and Dale Posgate, as well as *The Independence Movement in Quebec, 1945–1980* (Toronto: University of Toronto Press, 1984) by William D. Coleman. Coleman, relying on the studies of Dorval Brunelle (*La désillusion tranquille* (Montreal: Hurtubise HMH, 1978)) and Gilles Bourque and Anne Legaré (*Le Québec: La question nationale* (Paris: Maspéro, 1979)), rejects the new middle-class thesis. The new middle class was not the catalyst but rather the product of the Quiet Revolution. Colemen argues that the postwar transition to monopoly capitalism accelerated the cultural and social integration of Francophone society into the North American mainstream. A coalition of classes, comprising a threatened Francophone bourgeosie, organized labour, and elements of the traditional middle class, responded to the emergence of monopoly capitalism by developing an interventionist, secular, Francophone-controlled Quebec state capable of supporting the creation of a Francophone bourgeoisie and thereby overcoming the economic inferiority of French Canadians. When the coalition broke down in the mid-1960s, the resulting confusion created the social and ideological conditions for the emergence of the independence movement led by the Parti Québécois.

Journalists and participants also offer valuable insights into various facets of the era. *René: A Canadian in Search of a Country* (Toronto: McClelland and Stewart, 1976) by Peter Desbarats describes the pivotal role played by René Lévesque in the Lesage government and the consolidation of the independence movement in the PQ. Blair Fraser, a very perceptive analyst of Quebec affairs, revealed in "Quebec's New Power Elite," *Macleans*, 21 August 1965, the emergence of a brilliant and ambitious group of Quebec mandarins responsible for developing and implementing the reform program of the Quiet Revolution. Lesage's deputy minister of family and social welfare, Roger Marier, demonstrates in his "Les objectifs sociaux du Québec," *Canadian Public Administration* 12, 2 (1969): 181–97, that the gap between Francophone expectations in the area of social policy and the government's ability to deliver was wider than in any other province. In his view, only a more autonomous Quebec government could fulfil the social needs of its citizens. Roland Parenteau in "L'expérience de la planification au Québec (1960–1969)," *Actualités économiques* XLV, 4 (1970): 679–96, outlines some of the trials and tribulations of trying to apply the tenets of state planning to Quebec's regional economic problems. James I. Gow, "Modernisation et administration publique" in *La Modernization politique du Québec*, edited by Edmond Orban (Montreal: Boréal Express, 1976), 157–85, describes the successes and the setbacks associated with the bureaucratization and centralization of the state administrative structures between 1960 and 1975. Quebec's state builders encountered far more problems than anyone had anticipated, namely the Bourassa government's decision to resort to more traditional methods of administering the affairs of government.

Organized Labour in Transition

The best general survey histories of organized labour in Quebec can be found in *Histoire du mouvement au Québec. 150 ans de luttes* (Montreal: CSN & CEQ, 1984) as well as in a forthcoming survey by Jacques Rouillard, a labour historian at the Université de Montréal. *Working People* (Ottawa: Deneau & Greenberg, 1980) by Desmond Morton and Terry Copp is helpful in placing Quebec development in the Canadian labour context.

The ideological and organizational evolution of Quebec's two major labour centrals is outlined in Louis-Marie Tremblay's *Le syndicalisme québécois. Idéologies de la CSN et de la FTQ (1940-1970)* (Montreal: PUM, 1972); Bernard Sollasse's "Les idéologies de la Fédération des travailleurs du Quebec et de la Confédération des syndicats nationaux, 1960-1978," in Fernard Dumon et al., *Idéologies au Canada français 1940-1976* (Montreal: PUL, 1981), II: 219-94; S.H. Barnes' "The Evolution of Christian Trade Unions in Quebec," in *Readings in Canadian Labour Economics*, edited by A.E. Kovacs (Toronto, 1961), 58-74; and Fraser Isbester's "Quebec Labour in Perspective, 1949-1969, "in *Canadian Labour in Transition*, edited by Richard U. Miller and Fraser Isbester (Scarborough, Ont.: Prentice-Hall, 1971), 240-66.

The *Asbestos Strike* (Toronto: James Lewis and Samuel, 1974), edited and introduced by Pierre Elliott Trudeau, provides valuable insights into the complex relationship between the Catholic labour movement, the Catholic Church, the state, and big business after the war. The contributors viewed the 1949 Asbestos strike as the long overdue emancipation of Quebec's working class from the outmoded clerical and petty-bourgeois ideologies that had held it in line for nearly a a century. Hélène David also analyses this same relationship in her "La grève et le bon Dieu. La grève de l'amiante au Québec," *Sociologie et société* 1, 2 (novembre 1969): 249-76, and concludes that the state and big business emerged the winners at the expense of the Church. The most thorough analysis of the Front general strike of 1972 and its background is provided in *Les travailleurs contre l'État bourgeois* (Montreal: L'Aurore, 1975) by Diane Ethier, Jean-Marc Piotte, and Jean Reynolds.

The best entry to the history of women in the labour movement can be found in the excellent general survey *L'histoire des femmes au Québec depuis quatre siècles* by Micheline Dumont et al. (Montreal: Quinze, 1982). Francine Barry in her *Le Travail de la femme au Québec: l'évolution de 1940-1970* (Montreal: Presses de l'Université du Québec, 1977) provides insights into the working conditions of women in this period of transition and affirmation of rights. Marise Thivierge's "La syndicalisation des institutrices catholiques, 1900-1959," in *Maitresses de maison, maitresses d'école. Femmes, famille et éducation dans l'histoire du Québec*, edited by Nadia Fahmy-Eid et Micheline Dumont (Montreal: Boréal Express, 1983), 171-89, is an excellent rebuttal to those who contend that there were significant reforms underway in the field of education prior to 1960. Duplessis' 1946 law to ensure the progress of education and other legislative measures effectively terminated all efforts of the teachers, rural and urban, to organize collectively and to negotiate for better wages and working conditions.

In the 1970s, all three union centrals published position papers on women's issues: FTQ, *Travailleuses et syndiquées* (1974), CSN, *La Lutte des femmes, combat de tous les travailleurs* (1976), and CEQ, *Le Droit au travail pour les femmes* (1979). The most complete guide to all the literature pertaining to women in the work force and in the labour movement can be found in *La recherche sur les femmes au Québec: bilan et bibliographie* (Montreal: Institut québécois de recherche sur la culture, 1982) by Denise Lemieux and Lucie Mercier.

Quebec versus Ottawa: The Struggle for Equality

Quebec's constitutional battles with Ottawa between 1960 and 1976 have been fully documented by Richard Arès s.j. in his *Nos grandes options politiques et constitutionnelles* (Montreal: Bellarmin, 1967), and Jean-Louis Roy, *La choix d'un pays: le débat constitutionnel Québec-Canada, 1960–76* (Montreal: Leméac, 1978). A firsthand account by one of the central Québécois participants is related in *Quebec vs. Ottawa* (Toronto: University of Toronto Press, 1976) by Claude Morin. A number of political scientists have tried to provide a running analysis of the various clashes. One can profitably consult two studies by Edward McWhinney, *Quebec and the Constitution, 1960–1978* (Toronto: University of Toronto Press, 1979) and *Canada and the Constitution* (Toronto: University of Toronto Press, 1982), and Donald Smiley's *Canada in Question: Federalism in the Eighties*, 3rd ed. (Toronto: McGraw-Hill Ryerson, 1980). The fallout from the Quebec referendum and the patriation of the BNA Act is dealt with in *And No One Cheered. Federalism, Democracy and the Constitution Act*, edited by Keith Banting and Richard Simeon (Toronto: Methuen, 1983).

Important primary sources to be consulted include The Tremblay Report, edited by David Kwavnick (Toronto: McClelland and Stewart, 1973); the *Report of the Royal Commission on Bilingualism and Biculturalism*, 5 vols. (Ottawa: Queen's Printer, 1965–70), especially the introduction to volume one; the Quebec Liberal Party's *A New Canadian Federation* (Montreal, n.d.), and the Parti Québécois, *Quebec-Canada: A New Deal* (Quebec, 1979). One can also usefully consult Pierre Elliott Trudeau's four speeches on the "Referendum Campaign" as well as those of René Lévesque and Claude Ryan.

The Politics of Language

The best overview of Quebec's language policies, as well as copies of Bills 85, 63, 22, and pertinent excerpts from the Gendron and Bilingualism and Biculturalism Commissions, can be found in John R. Mallea, ed., *Quebec's Language Policies: Background and Response* (Quebec: Les Presses de l'Université Laval, 1977). A range of excellent studies can be found in Richard Y. Bourhis, ed., *Conflict and Language Planning in Quebec* (Clevedon, England: Multilingual Matters Ltd., 1984), and John R. Mallea and Jonathan R. Young, eds., *Cultural Diversity and Canadian Education* (Toronto: Carleton Library, 1983). For a solid analysis of the Gendron Commission Report and the forces that contributed to its recommendations and subsequent government action see Robert J. MacDonald, "Education, Language Rights and Cultural Survival in Quebec, A Review Essay," *Journal of Educational Thought* 9, 1 (April 1975): 49–64.

The issue of language policy and its formulation is a highly complex subject and has provoked economists, sociologists, and political scientists into advancing a wide range of theories based on a wide range of methodologies and assumptions. Albert Breton, an economist critical of nationalism, attempts to demonstrate in his "Nationalism and Language Policies," *Canadian Journal of Economics* II (Nov. 1978): 656–68, that the language policies pursued by the church and the state are responsible for the fact that the "average incomes of Francophones in Quebec are lower than those of other language groups." Another economist, François Vaillancourt in his study, "La Charte de la Langue Française du Québec: un essai d'analyse," *Canadian Public Policy* 4, 3 (1978): 284–308, concludes that the potential economic and cultural benefits for Francophones from the Charter will outweigh the costs. On the other hand, the political economy approach of William Coleman in his studies, "The Class Bases of Language Policy in Quebec, 1949–1983" in *Quebec. State and Society*, edited by Alain G. Gagnon (Toronto: Methuen, 1984), 388–409, and "A Comparative Study of Language Policy in Quebec: A Political Economy Approach" in *The Politics of Canadian Public Policy*, edited by M.M. Atkinson and M.A. Chandler (Toronto: University of Toronto Press, 1983), 21–42, brings into serious question the effectiveness of the Charter in enhancing the use of the French language in the middle and upper echelons of the corporate sector of Quebec's economy. The nationalists failed to understand clearly the implications of the changes made to the original Charter, Bill 1.

A very important dimension of Quebec's language debate involves Ottawa's decision to support the concept of official bilingualism beginning in 1969. Two studies, one by Kenneth McRoberts, "Bill 22 and Language Policy in Canada," *Queen's Quarterly* 83 (Fall 1976): 464–77, and a second by Hubert Guidon, "The Modernization of Quebec and the Legitimacy of the Canadian State," *Canadian Review of Sociology and Anthropology* 15, 2 (1978): 227–45, demonstrate the clash between two fundamentally different approaches adopted by the federal and Quebec governments. Ottawa, influenced by the Report on Bilingualism and Biculturalism, based its legislative approach on a concept of linguistic rights for individuals belonging to Canada's two founding societies no matter where they lived in the country. Quebec, concerned with the collective rights of Francophones, based its language policy on the "territorial" principle. The Bourassa government in Bill 22 gave the French language pre-eminent status in Quebec's public institutions and, to a lesser degree, in the private sector. Only the "territorial" approach, according to McRoberts and Guidon, reflects the demographic and linguistic reality of modern Canada and therefore constitutes the best chance of meeting the needs of Quebec's Francophone majority while keeping the country united.

The Rise of the Parti Québécois

Since its inception, the Parti Québécois has attracted constant attention from social scientists and journalists. The best general study on the rise of the PQ remains *Quebec, Social Change and Political Crisis* (Toronto: McClelland and Stewart, 1980) by Kenneth McRoberts and Dale Posgate. John Saywell has written a cursory but revealing monograph entitled *The Rise of the Parti Québécois, 1967–1976* (Toronto: University of Toronto Press, 1977). Much of the early focus has been on the leader. Both Peter Desbarats' *René: A Canadian in Search of a Country* (Toronto: McClelland and Stewart, 1976) and Jean Provencher's *René Lévesque: Portrait of a Québécois* (Agincourt, Ont.: Gage, 1975) offer some quite revealing insights into the strengths and weaknesses of their subject.

The PQ's ideology and program have been thoroughly analysed by Very Murray in *Le parti québécois: de la fondation à la prise du pouvoir* (Montreal: Hurtubise-HMH, 1976) and in Richard Jones, "L'idéologie du Parti Québécois," in Fernand Dumont et al., *Idéologies au Canada français 1940–1976* (Quebec: Les Presses de l'Université Laval, 1981), III: 235–63). A comprehensive analysis of the PQ's electoral progress to power between 1970 and 1976 can be found in the many studies of Maurice Pinard and Richard Hamilton, two of which are "The Parti Québécois Comes to Power: An Analysis of the 1976 Quebec Election," *Canadian Journal of Political Science* XI, 4 (Dec. 1978): 739–75, and "The Quebec Independence Movement," in *National Separatism*, edited by H.C. Williams (Vancouver: UBC Press, 1982), 203–33, and the collection of essays by André Bernard, *Québec: Élections 1976* (Montreal: Hurtubise-HMH, 1976).

The arrival of the PQ on the political scene in the late 1960s initiated among Quebec's Marxist intellectuals an intense debate about the class basis of the Quiet Revolution, and, in particular, the Parti Québécois. Dorval Brunelle maintained in his *La Désillusion tranquille* (Montreal: Hurtubise HMH, 1978) that a French-Canadian bourgeoisie, supported momentarily by the unions and the traditional petty-bourgeosie, was the major catalyst in the creation of an interventionist modern state in Quebec. This Francophone bourgeoisie was soon displaced by a Francophone state bourgeoisie working closely with the Anglophone-Canadian and American bourgeoisies. Pierre Fournier's *The Quebec Establishment: The Ruling Class and the State*, rev. ed. (Montreal: Black Rose Books, 1978) demonstrates in considerable detail the close ties between the Bourassa government and the Quebec-based bourgeoisie located in the co-operative movement, the crown corporations, and the private sector. According to Fournier, the same dynamic continued when the Parti Québécois gained power in 1976. In *Canadian Capitalism: A Study of Power in the Canadian Business Establishment* (Toronto: Lorimer, 1981), Jorge Niosi refutes this approach. He outlines the origins and development of a modern Francophone bourgeoisie that, he argues, is staunchly federalist and, therefore, the class most capable of thwarting the new middle class's drive for sovereignty-association, represented by the Parti Québécois. Several essays, some proposing other variations on this theme, can be found in Alain G. Gagnon, ed., *Quebec: State and Society* (Toronto: Methuen, 1984).

The PQ was no sooner in power when many of these Marxist academics began to prefer some highly critical assessments of its performance based on their perceptions of the class basis, either bourgeois or new middle class, of the party. Three collection of articles include J.F. Léonard, ed., *La chance au coureur* (Montreal: Nouvelle-Optique, 1978); Pauline Vaillancourt, ed., *Quebec and the Parti Québécois* (San Francisco: A Synthesis Publication, 1978); and Pierre Fournier, ed., *Capitalisme et politique au Québec* (Montreal: Éditions coopératives Saint-Martin, 1981). Jacques Dofny, "The PQ Government: Year One," *Our Generation* XII, 2 (Fall 1977): 25–34, offers a somewhat more sympathetic treatment. A very judicious and enlightening account of the PQ's trials and tribulations since coming to power is offered by Graham Fraser, *René Lévesque and the Parti Québécois in Power* (Toronto: Macmillan, 1985). Lysiane Gagnon's *Chroniques politiques* (Montreal: Boréal Express, 1985) is full of perceptive insights about how the exercising of power, the loss of the referendum, and the humiliating defeat on the constitutional issue, undermined both the independence movement and its political vehicle, the Parti Québécois.

The Future of Québécois Nationalism

By far the best analysis of the trials and tribulations of the PQ in power is *PQ: René Lévesque and the Parti Québécois in Power* (Toronto: Macmillan, 1985) by the prominent political journalist Graham Fraser. Pierre Fournier's "The Future of Quebec Nationalism," in *And No One Cheered: Federalism, Democracy, and the Constitution Act*, edited by Keith Banting and Richard Simeon (Toronto: Methuen, 1983), 154–73, predicted a resurgence of nationalism in Quebec if the necessary compromises that would allow Quebec to sign the constitutional accord were not forthcoming from Ottawa and the provinces. The fact that this has not happened brings one to question Fournier's thesis about the regional nature and aspirations of the Quebec bourgeoisie.

Ramsay Cook, in a revealing essay entitled "Has the Quiet Revolution Finally Ended?" *Queen's Quarterly* 90, 2 (Summer 1983): 330–42, suggests that the PQ undermined its slim chance of winning the referendum by implementing Bill 101, which consolidated Quebec's cultural sovereignty and made a high-risk political sovereignty less necessary. One of the first journalists to sense fully a significant shift in values taking place in Quebec during the late 1970s was Dominique Clift. In his *Quebec Nationalism in Crisis* (Montreal and Kingston: McGill-Queen's University Press, 1982), Clift explains how increasing numbers of middle-class Francophones were shifting their allegiance from the conservative, collective values of the national state to the values of individualism and liberalism. The end result, he maintained, was going to be a decline in the role of nationalism in Quebec society at all levels. Two philosophers, Michel Morin and Claude Bertrand, reached similar conclusions from a different perspective in their *Le territoire imaginaire de la culture* (Montreal: Hurtubise HMH, 1979). This perceived decline has provoked considerable apprehension in some quarters. An anthropologist, Marc-Adélard Tremblay, argues with considerable vigour but with little concrete evidence in his *L'indentité québécois en péril* (Sainte-Foy: Les Éditions Saint-Yves Inc., 1983) that rapid technological and institutional changes coupled with the PQ's failure to resolve the "National Question" have engendered a serious identity crisis in Quebec. For an English version, see his "The Identity of Francophone Quebeckers: Theoretical Perspectives and Trends," *Transactions of the Royal Society of Canada*, 4th series, XXII (1984): 3–18.

An honest attempt has been made to secure permission for all material used, and, if there are errors or omissions, these are wholly unintentional and the Publisher will be grateful to learn of them.

Richard Jones, *Duplessis and the Union Nationale*, Canadian Historical Association booklet no. 35. Reprinted by permission of the Canadian Historical Association.

Michael D. Behiels, "Quebec: Social Transformation and Ideological Renewal, 1940–1976," Reprinted by permission of the author.

Marc Renaud, "Quebec. New Middle Class in Search of Social Hegemony," *International Review of Community Development*, new series 39/40 (1978). Reprinted by permission of the journal.

Kenneth McRoberts, "The Sources of Neo-Nationalism in Quebec," *Ethnic and Racial Studies*, 7, 1 (Jan. 1984). Reprinted by permission of Routledge and Kegan Paul.

Jacques Rouillard, "Major Changes in the Confédération des travailleurs catholiques du Canada, 1940–1960," translated from "Mutations de la Confédération des travailleurs catholiques du Canada, 1940–1960," *Révue d'histoire de l'Amérique française* 34, 3 (1980) with the permission of the author and journal.

Carla Lipsig-Mummé, "The Web of Dependence: Quebec Unions in Politics Before 1976," *Studies in Political Economy* 3 (1980). Reprinted by permission of the journal.

Mona-Josée Gagnon, "Women in the Trade-Union Movement in Quebec," translated from "Les femmes dans le mouvement syndical québécois," *Sociologie et société* VI, 1 (1974), with the permission of the author.

Gérard Bergeron, "The Québécois State Under Canadian Federalism," translated from "L'État du Québec sous le fédéralisme canadien," in *L'État du Québec en devenir*, edited by Gérard Bergeron and Réjean Pelletier (Montreal: Boréal Express, 1980); Claude Morin, "Quebec and Canadian Federalism," translated from "L'expérience québécoise du fédéralisme canadien," *La Modernization politique du Québec*, edited by Edmond Orban (Montreal: Boréal Express, 1976). Translations printed with the permission of the authors and publisher.

Gil Rémillard, "Under What Conditions Could Quebec Sign the Constitution Act of 1982?" translated from "À quelles conditions le Québec peut-il signer La Loi constitutionnelle de 1982?" *Le Devoir* 26–28 février 1985; Jean-Louis Roy, "Nationalism in Quebec in the 1980s," translated from "Le nationalisme québécois dans les années 80," *Le Devoir* 1 juin 1985. Translations printed with the permission of *Le Devoir*.

Richard Jones, "Politics and the Reinforcement of the French Language in the Province of Quebec, 1960–1986." Printed by permission of the author.

William D. Coleman, "From Bill 22 to Bill 101: The Politics of Language Under the Parti Québécois, "*Canadian Journal of Political Science* XIV, 3 (Sept. 1981). Reprinted by permission of the author and the Canadian Political Science Association.

René Lévesque, "For An Independent Quebec," *Foreign Affairs* 54, 4 (July 1976). Reprinted by permission of *Foreign Affairs*, July 1976. Copyright, 1976, by the Council on Foreign Relations, Inc.

Raymond Hudon, "The 1976 Quebec Election," *Queen's Quarterly* 84 (Spring 1977). Reprinted by permission of the author.

Guy Rocher, "A Half-Century of Cultural Evolution in Quebec," translated from "Un demi-siècle d'évolution culturelle au Québec," *University of Toronto Quarterly* 50, 1 (Fall 1980). Translated and printed by permission of the author and University of Toronto Press.